Programming with Qt

Programming with Qt

Matthias Kalle Dalheimer

O'REILLY®

Beijing · Cambridge · Farnham · Köln · Paris · Sebastopol · Taipei · Tokyo

Programming with Qt
by Matthias Kalle Dalheimer

Copyright © 1999 O'Reilly Verlag GmbH & Co. KG.
Printed in the United States of America
Published by O'Reilly Verlag GmbH & Co. KG,
Balthasarstr. 81, D-50670 Köln, Germany
Email: bookquestions@oreilly.com

Editor: Elke Hansel

Contributing Editor: Paula Fergusson

Printing History:
> April 1999: First Edition
> July 1999: Minor Corrections

ISBN: 1-56592-588-2   [7/99]

Table of Contents

Preface . . . . *xvii*

1: Introduction *1*

   Why GUI Toolkits? 1

   Why Portability? 3

   Why Qt? 3

   Implementing Cross-Plattform GUI Libraries 4

   Acquiring Qt 6

   Compiling and installing Qt 7

   C++ as used by Qt 9

   Getting Help 11

2: First Steps in Qt Programming *13*

   Hello World! 13

   Using the Qt Reference Documentation 16

   Adding an Exit Button 19

   Introduction to Signals and Slots 21

   Event handling and simple drawings with QPainter 29

3: Learning More About Qt *37*

   Adding Menus 37

   Adding a Scrolled View 47

   Adding a Context Menu 55

   File-I/O 63

4: A Guided Tour Through the Simple Widgets *75*

  General Widget Parameters 77
  Widget Styles 77
  Buttons 79
  Selection Widgets 81
  Widgets for Bounded Range Input 85
  Scroll bars 87
  Menu-related Widgets 89
  Arrangers 91
  Text Entry Fields 94
  Labels 95
  Widgets for the "Office Look" 98
  Progress bars 104
  Scrolled Views 105
  List Views 106
  Widgets for Tabular Material 111

5: A Guided Tour Through the Qt Dialogs *113*

  Predefined Dialogs 113
  Building Blocks for Your Own Dialogs 118

6: Using Layout Managers *125*

  Layout Manager Basics 125
  Laying Out Widgets in Rows and Columns 127
  Nested Layout Managers 130
  Grid Layout 132

7: Some Thoughts on GUI Design *137*

8: Container Classes *143*

  Available Container Classes 143
  Choosing a Container Class 145
  Working with Container Classes 145
  Caching Data 147
  Iterators 148
  Stacks and Queues 149

9: Graphics *151*

    Animations 151

    Printing 153

    Managing Colors 157

    Basic QPainter: Drawing Figures 161

    Advanced QPainter: Two-dimensional Transformations and
View Transformations 163

    Double Buffering and Other Nifty Techniques 168

    Loading and Saving Custom Image Formats 173

    Setting a Cursor 177

10: Text Processing *179*

    Validating User Input 179

    Working with Regular Expressions 184

11: Working with Files and Directories *189*

    Reading a Text File 189

    Traversing a directory 191

    File Information 193

12: Inter-Application Communication *197*

    Using the clipboard 197

    Drag and Drop 202

13: Working with Date and Time Values *209*

14: Writing Your Own Widgets *211*

    Implementing a Coordinate Selector 213

    Implementing a Browse Box 222

15: Focus Handling *237*

16: Advanced Event Handling *241*

    Event Filters 241

    Sending Synthetic Events 243

17: *Advanced Signals and Slots* *245*

Signals and Slots Revisited 245
Connecting Several Buttons to One Slot 248

18: *Debugging* *251*

19: *Portability* *253*

Why Portability Is Desirable 253
How to Write Portable Programs 254
Danger Ahead: When Even Qt Is Not Portable 256
Building Projects Portably with tmake 257

20: *Using GUI Builders* *263*

QtArchitect 264
QtEZ 266
EBuilder 268

21: *Qt Network Programming* *271*

22: *Interfacing Qt with Other Languages and Libraries* *279*

OpenGL Programming with Qt 279
Writing Netscape Plugins 283
Integrating Xt Widgets 291
Interfacing Qt with Perl 293

23: *Using the Visual C++ IDE for Qt Programs* *301*

Importing an Existing Makefile 301
Creating Your Own Project from Scratch 302
Using tmake to Create a Project File 303

24: *Sample Qt Projects* *305*

The KDE Project 305
OrthoVista 306

25: *A First Look at Qt 2.0* *309*

Unicode Support and Improved QString 309
Improved Layout Management 310

Internationalization Support 310
Themability 311
New or Improved Widgets 311
Debugging Help 311
Preventing Namespace Pollution 312
Miscellaneous Changes 313
The Future of Qt 313

Appendix: Answers to Exercises **315**

Bibliography **337**

Index **339**

List of Figures

Figure 2-1:   Screenshot of the first Qt program   16
Figure 2-2:   The start page of the Qt reference documentation   17
Figure 2-3:   The reference documentation for QLabel   18
Figure 2-4:   Output of the Button Program   20
Figure 2-5:   A slider and a number display   27
Figure 2-6:   Output from Example 2-4   33
Figure 3-1:   Output of Example 3-1   42
Figure 3-2:   Output of Example 3-2   54
Figure 4-1:   Push-button in Windows style   79
Figure 4-2:   Push-button in Motif style   79
Figure 4-3:   Check-boxes in Windows style   80
Figure 4-4:   Check-boxes in Motif style   80
Figure 4-5:   Radio buttons in Windows style   80
Figure 4-6:   Radio buttons in Motif style   80
Figure 4-7:   A listbox in Windows style   82
Figure 4-8:   A listbox in Motif style   82
Figure 4-9:   A combo box in old Motif style   83
Figure 4-10: A read-only combo box in Window style   83
Figure 4-11: A read-only combo box in new Motif style   83
Figure 4-12: A read-write combo box in Windows style   83
Figure 4-13: A read-write combo box in new Motif style   83
Figure 4-14: A slider in Windows style   85
Figure 4-15: A slider in Motif style   85
Figure 4-16: Spin boxes in Windows style   86
Figure 4-17: Spin boxes in Motif style   86
Figure 4-18: A scroll bar in Windows style   87
Figure 4-19: A scroll bar in Motif style   87
Figure 4-20: A pop-up menu in Windows style   89
Figure 4-21: A pop-up menu in Motif style   89
Figure 4-22: A menu bar in Windows style   90
Figure 4-23: A menu bar in Motif style   90

Figure 4-24: A group box in Windows style 92
Figure 4-25: A group box in Motif style 92
Figure 4-26: A splitter arranging two labels in Windows style 92
Figure 4-27: A splitter arranging two labels in Motif style 92
Figure 4-28: A single-line text-entry field in Windows style 94
Figure 4-29: A single-line text-entry field in Motif style 94
Figure 4-30: A multi-line text-entry field in Windows style 94
Figure 4-31: A multi-line text-entry field in Motif style 94
Figure 4-32: A label in Windows or Motif style (both are the same here) 95
Figure 4-33: A LCD number widget in Windows and Motif style
            (both are the same here) 97
Figure 4-34: Tool bars in Windows style 99
Figure 4-35: Tool bars in Motif style 99
Figure 4-36: Tool bars with big pixmaps in Windows style 99
Figure 4-37: Tool bars with big pixmaps in Motif style 99
Figure 4-38: A status bar in Windows style 100
Figure 4-39: A status bar in Motif style 100
Figure 4-40: A What's This window 103
Figure 4-41: A progress bar in Windows style 104
Figure 4-42: A progress bar in Motif style 104
Figure 4-43: QListView in Windows style 106
Figure 4-44: QListView in Motif style 107
Figure 4-45: A simple table view in Windows style 111
Figure 4-46: A simple table view in Motif style 111
Figure 5-1: A file dialog in Windows style 114
Figure 5-2: A file dialog in Motif style 114
Figure 5-3: A message box in Windows style 115
Figure 5-4: A message box in Motif style 115
Figure 5-5: A progress dialog in Windows style 117
Figure 5-6: A progress dialog in Motif style 117
Figure 5-7: A tab dialog in Windows style 121
Figure 5-8: A tab dialog in Motif style 121
Figure 6-1: A simple layout of buttons in a dialog 127
Figure 6-2: Different stretch factors for the buttons 129
Figure 6-3: Nested layouts 130
Figure 6-4: Using a grid layout 133
Figure 9-1: The print dialog provided by Qt on Unix systems 154
Figure 14-1: The coordinate selector 213
Figure 14-2: A browse box 222
Figure 20-1: Building a dialog with QtArchitect 265
Figure 20-2: Editing pixmaps with QtArchitect 265
Figure 20-3: Editing menus with QtEZ 267
Figure 20-4: Editing dialogs with QtEZ 267
Figure 20-5: The tree view window of EBuilder 269
Figure 20-6: The mask for creating a new dialog in EBuilder 269

Figure 22-1: A Sierpinski gasket with the Qt OpenGL extension 283
Figure 24-1: A KDE Desktop 306
Figure 24-2: OrthoVista, an Application for Aerial Mapping and Photography
             Written With Qt 307
Figure 25-1: QDeveloper at work 312

List of Tables

Table 10-1: Meta characters in Qt regular expressions 185
Table 10-2: Escape sequences in Qt regular expressions 185
Table 19-1: Qt Methods That Behave Differently on Windows and Unix 256
Table 19-2: tmake Options 260

Preface

A Productive Weekend...

A few months ago someone e-mailed me on a Friday. He wanted to start a small project, but did not really have the resources for it. He outlined the requirements, and asked how long it would take me.

The next Monday, he phoned me to ask if I thought the project was feasible, and how much time I would need. I was able to say that I already had a working prototype. I had hacked it together in a few hours the day before—and because I had used Qt, I had still found enough time to play with my son. Needless to say, I got the contract.

Does this sound too good to be true? Well, I must admit, I lied a bit. It was raining cats and dogs that Sunday, and we had to play inside. But the rest is true.

The class library Qt makes it easy to write applications that are visually attractive, fast, and ready to run on both Windows and Unix in a very short time. Had I used Motif, gtk, or another toolkit for this task, I might not have managed it in such a short time. If I had to port my program to Windows, the number of choices would have been even smaller.

Until now, there has not been much Qt documentation for beginners. The package itself includes a tutorial, but leaves out a lot. There are other example programs, but often you have to search through several to find what you are looking for, and sometimes you don't find it at all. Some people think it's hard to get started with Qt, but after they have overcome the initial hurdles, they see that Qt helps them in a lot of ways when writing their applications. That's why I decided to write this book. It will teach you how to program with Qt from the start, and it will help you make more sense of the documentation that comes with Qt.

What You Should Know

Qt, written and distributed by the Norwegian company Troll Tech, is a C++ class library, and this book requires some C++ knowledge. However, you don't have to be a C++ expert to start programming with Qt. We have included a short overview of C++ language features that are used in Qt programs.

Qt is mostly about GUI programming (although it can also help you write a web server). Accordingly, it helps to know a bit about how GUI programs are written. If you already know what an event loop is and how GUI programs are usually structured, this will make things easier for you at the beginning. But I have tried to keep this book as self-contained as possible, though, so if you have never written a GUI program before, now would be a good time to start. Qt makes GUI programming much easier, easier even than with most (if not all) other toolkits.

I assume that you know how to use a text editor to enter program source code, and that you know how to start your compiler and linker to generate an executable program. Unless there is something Qt-specific about these operations, I won't talk about these topics. All programs in this book were tested with Linux 2.0.33 and the G++ compiler and MS-Windows NT 4.0 and the Microsoft Visual C++ compiler. If you use another version of Unix or Windows 95, you should have no problems. If you use a Macintosh or OS/2[1], however, you are out of luck. Qt has not been ported to these platforms, and as far as I know such a port is not planned, either.

Organization of This Book

This book is organized to make finding the information you need as easy as possible. If you have not programmed with Qt, you should read Chapters 1, 2 and 3 first to grasp the basic concepts. The following chapters and sections are relatively independent, and you should be able to jump around and read whatever you are interested in. If your application contains any custom graphics, you will probably want to read Chapter 9. Reading Chapter 4 and Chapter 5 is a very good idea, because you can make better use of Qt's features if you know what is available. To help you set up your own tour through the book, the following list of chapters includes short descriptions of their contents. Of course, if you simply decide to read through the whole book, I would be more than glad!

Chapter 1, *Introduction*

> introduces you to basic Qt concepts. It gives you some information about why people use GUI toolkits in the first place, and explains what is special about Qt. You will learn how and where you can get Qt, whether you have to pay for it or not, and where to go if you are stuck with a Qt-related problem.

---

1 You should be able to run Qt programs with XFree86 for OS/2, but I have never tried this.

Chapter 2, *First Steps in Qt Programming*
is a Qt programming primer. We start with a simple "Hello World" example, learn about signals and slots, and finish the chapter by creating a small painting program that lets you scribble on a virtual canvas in various colors.

Chapter 3, *Learning More About Qt*
continues the Qt tutorial. We develop the painting application into something more useful. By the end of this chapter, you will know about using files, programming menus, and other features of Qt.

Chapter 4, *A Guided Tour Through The Simple Widgets*
is a presentation of all simple widgets available in Qt. This chapter can help you pick the right widget for any given task. If an appropriate widget is not listed, you'll know that you have to develop your own. You will also find explanations of the most useful methods, code examples, and usability hints for using existing widgets.

Chapter 5, *A Guided Tour Through The Qt Dialogs*
continues the tour through the available GUI elements in Qt, and shows which dialogs are available. It also shows you how to program your own dialogs and tab dialogs.

Chapter 6, *Using Layout Managers*
explains how widgets are automatically laid out within their parent window so that their positions are computed at runtime according to their needs. This is a complicated topic, so I provide several examples to make it easier to understand.

Chapter 7, *Some Thoughts on GUI Design*
provides you with some hints about writing applications that users will like. This includes guidelines about when to use which widget.

Chapter 8, *Container Classes*
explains how to use classes for building up lists, arrays, and dictionaries, and how to traverse all elements in a container.

Chapter 9, *Graphics*
is about creating custom graphics, including animations, printing, colors, and two-dimensional transformations.

Chapter 10, *Text Processing*
has sections on working with regular expressions and on checking input into text-entry fields. The classes explained here can often reduce the length of your code and ease your programming efforts.

Chapter 11, *Working with Files and Directories*
explains how to access files and directories and maintain portability using the classes that Qt provides. These classes can shield your code from the native APIs.

Chapter 12, *Inter-Application Communication*
tells you how Qt applications can exchange data with each other, or with other applications. It describes the clipboard and drag and drop.

Chapter 13, *Working with Date and Time Values*
provides information about working with date and time values, including how to use a stop watch.

Chapter 14, *Writing Your Own Widgets*
explains how to write your own widgets.

Chapter 15, *Focus Handling*
explains how to control the way Qt passes the keyboard focus to widgets. This is not crucial for getting an application up and running, but it is important if you don't want your users to hate you.

Chapter 16, *Advanced Event Handling*
contains information about advanced event handling such as filtering the events that go to a widget, and sending synthetic events.

Chapter 17, *Advanced Signals and Slots*
builds on the introduction to signals and slots in the tutorial, and informs you about advanced usage of signals and slots.

Chapter 18, *Debugging*
offers hints about Qt that can make debugging easier.

Chapter 19, *Portability*
explains how you can best achieve portability for your Qt programs.

Chapter 20, *Using GUI Builders*
introduces you to some GUI-builders that can save you the work of programming each dialog in an application by hand.

Chapter 21, *Qt Network Programming*
gives an example of using Qt for non-GUI tasks by presenting a little HTTP server program created with this toolkit.

Chapter 22, *Interfacing Qt with Other Languages and Libraries*
explains how to interface Qt with other languages and libraries. Its sections include using Qt with Perl, integrating Qt and Xt widgets, using OpenGL in Qt programs, and writing Netscape plug-ins with Qt.

Chapter 23, *Using the Visual C++ IDE for Qt Programs*
provides hints about how to use the Visual C++ IDE (Visual Studio) from Microsoft for writing Qt programs.

Chapter 24, *Sample Qt Projects*
presents two sample Qt projects: a freeware project and a commercial application that should give you an idea of what other people have accomplished with Qt.

Chapter 25, *A first look at Qt 2.0*
contains information about the new features in Qt 2.0.

Appendix A, *Answers to Exercises*
provides complete, commented answers to all exercises in the tutorial.

Qt programming Online

The web site for this book is *http://www.oreilly.com/catalog/prowqt/*. You can download the examples from this book at that location. As typos or errors are reported, you can also find an errata list at this web site.

Conventions Used in This Book

The following typographic conventions appear in this book:

Italic
> is used for file names and command names. It is also used to highlight comments in command examples, and to define terms the first time they appear.

`Constant Width`
> is used in examples and in regular text to show operators, variables, and the output from commands or programs.

`Constant Bold`
> is used in examples to show the user's actual input at the terminal.

`Constant Italic`
> is used in examples to show variables for which a context-specific substitution should be made. The variable `filename`, for example, would be replaced by an actual filename.

Footnotes
> are used to attach parenthetical notes which you *should not* read on your first perusal of this book. Often, the material in the footnote will be advanced information that might only confuse you until you have thoroughly mastered the basics.

Request for Comments

Please help us improve future editions of this book by reporting any errors, inaccuracies, bugs, misleading or confusing statements, and plain old typos that you find anywhere in the book. Email your bug reports and comments to us at *bookquestions@oreilly.com*. (Before sending a bug report, you may want to check for an errata list at *http://www.oreilly.com/catalog/prowqt/* to see if the bug already has been submitted.)

Also let us know what we can do to make this book more useful to you. We take your comments seriously, and will try to incorporate your suggestions into future editions.

Acknowledgements

A book like this is always a major undertaking. Without the help of many other people, this book would never have become a reality at all.

When it comes to technical content, I owe much to the tremendous guys at Troll Tech: Haavard Nord, Eirik Eng, Eirik Aavitsland, Paul Olav Tvete, Arnt Gulbrandsen, Warwick Allison, and Matthias Ettrich. They have provided me with an unimaginable amount of support, and never tired of reading through the various drafts I have produced. Haavard Nord deserves special mention, because this book was his idea in the first place, and he helped convince the people at O'Reilly that it would be A Good Thing.

Several other people helped improve the quality of this book by reading drafts, correcting errors and making suggestions, among these are Ashley Winters, author of Perl-Qt; Stefan Taferner and Uwe Thiem from the KDE team; and Safuat Hamdy from the University of Hamburg.

As always, my colleagues at O'Reilly Germany were very helpful. Elke Hansel, the editor of this book, got the ball rolling and managed the production process. She also handled the relations with our American colleagues. Since this is our first American-German coproduction—written and produced in Germany, copyedited in Cambridge, Massachusetts—I can imagine that a lot of organizational work was done behind the scenes. Add to this the technical proof-readers in Des Moines, Washington; Norway, Germany, Austria, and Namibia, you can see that this book is truly an international effort.

Of our American colleagues, I have to give special credit to Paula Ferguson. Her expertise and experience with books about GUI programming helped give this book a better structure. If you find this book to be well-organized, this is Paula's work as much as it is mine.

When an author hands over the final draft of a book to the editor, only part of the work has been done. Lots of people are involved in correcting spelling mistakes, copy-editing, layout, printing, binding and lots of important jobs before the book finally hits the stores. As an author, you often don't even get to know the names of these production people, but I'd like them to know anyway that I appreciate their work very much. When an author with German as a native language writes a book in English, there is probably more copy-editing to do than usual.

Also, a huge "thank you" goes to the KDE developers, especially the leader and founder of the KDE project, Matthias Ettrich. Without this project, I would probably never have delved so deeply into Qt coding. Teaching KDE and Qt programming at various workshops has given me a lot of insight into where people have problems with Qt programming, and I have tried to incorporate all these into this book.

There were numerous other people out there in Netland who helped a lot, either by asking the right questions or by giving the right answers. For example, Valient Gough of Stellacore provided helpful insight into using Qt for a large graphics-intensive commercial application.

For some reason, authors always list their family last in these acknowledgment sections. I don't know why this is so, but who am I to break with tradition? So here I go: I cannot really say that my son Jan Lennart, who will be two years old by the time this book arrives on the shelves, has helped me in writing the book. However, he sure has taught me that some things are way more important than programming, books, or even computers. Pouring water from one bucket to another for hours, setting up wooden miniature railways, and inventing new ways to get to the cookie jar are among these. This has not stopped me from teaching my son, who also liked to sit on my lap while I was typing away, how to use XEmacs. He even knows how to get into modes I had never heard of! Finally, a huge thank you to my wife Tanja, who was supportive as ever, and accepted that there were evenings when I had to write instead of going to the cinema with her. Family support is probably the most underestimated "tool" that any author has!

1

Introduction

Qt is a C++ class library and GUI toolkit for Unix and X11 systems. In this chapter, we will introduce GUI programming in general and Qt programming in particular. We tell you why you need a GUI toolkit, and why Qt is a good choice for such a toolkit. You can check the "C++ as Used by Qt" section to make sure you know enough about C++. This chapter also tells you where you can turn to if you have any problems with Qt.

Why GUI Toolkits?

GUI toolkits are not well-known in the MS-Windows or Macintosh world, but they are ubiquitous on Unix. This is because the Windows GUI programming API and Macintosh programming tools already contain high-level features like buttons, scroll bars and functions for manipulating colors, fonts, and other visual flourishes. On Unix systems, things are different. The preeminent windowing system on Unix, the X Window System is very flexible, but it does not offer the programmer much help. About the only thing you get are functions to draw primitive graphics like lines and rectangles, set the foreground and background color, and have user interactions and other events reported back to you. All of this is network-transparent, which is a very good thing, but these limited graphical features are nevertheless difficult to program. There is nothing for creating buttons or scroll bars, let alone more complex items like dialog boxes, toolbars, or tab pages.

Of course, nobody wants to code an entire application this way, not even the toughest of hard-core Unix programmers. This is why several toolkits have been invented to facilitate GUI programming tasks for Unix. There are many toolkits to choose from. Probably the most well-known of them is Motif, because many major Unix vendors have adopted it as their native GUI toolkit. The modern Common Desktop Environment (CDE) which now ships with Unix-based operating systems like Solaris and HP-UX, is based on Motif. Motif is not only a GUI toolkit, but is also a specification for a certain look-and-feel. Motif is fairly standard, having been developed by an organization supported by many vendors: the Open Software Foundation, now The Open Group. Why shouldn't you use it?

According to many programmers, using Motif is notoriously difficult, error-prone, and not very much fun. This is because it's based on the Xt Intrinsics, an old framework for GUI toolkits that ships with every implementation of the X Window System. The Intrinsics try to emulate object-orientation in C. They succeed to a certain extent, but programming with this style feels a bit awkward, and sacrifices niceties like type safety. Also, Motif programs are much longer than Qt programs that accomplish the same thing.

But Motif is a standard, especially in the look-and-feel department. It would be nice if you could have the same look, but with an easier programming API. Well, that's exactly what Qt provides—although that's not all it can do.

We have talked for some time about Unix, so it's time to make the Windows people feel at home, too. The Windows-API contains functions that can create GUI elements, manipulate colors, and so on. This is undoubtedly easier than programming the X Window System directly, but it's still too cumbersome to get some real work done. The Windows tools like Microsoft Foundation Classes (MFC) are really at the same state as those for Unix: High-level functions are available, but they are not easy enough to use to facilitate the creation of sophisticated user interfaces. Programmers still have to spend too much time creating the user interface, instead of concentrating on their application's core. This is where application frameworks come in, and Qt is such an application framework.

A framework is a little bit more than a toolkit or a GUI-programming API. It is a complete programming system, that hides the boring, error-prone low-level details from the application programmer. For example, we would expect a framework to automatically distribute user interactions, such as key presses or mouse-clicks, to whatever function or procedure we have defined to handle these interactions. The programming language C++ is well-suited for GUI programming, which is why most frameworks use it. There are frameworks for Smalltalk, Objective-C and other languages as well, but we won't talk about them here.

Our framework should allow us to define objects that represent one user-interface element, such as a button or a menu, and to handle all user interactions with these elements. We want to be able to define relationships between elements in terms of parent-child relations and geometrical relations. We also want to have all the boring initialization and termination stuff set up for us automatically.

With a good framework to tackle these details, you should be able to concentrate on your application's functionality as much as possible. Your toolkit should help you as much as possible in creating the user interface.

Why Portability?

You might have asked yourself why portability is such an important goal. If you develop software for a living, probably the most important reason for portability is that you increase your possible target market. Why should you leave out the millions of Unix users just because you are a Windows programmer? And can you afford not to try to sell your programs for Windows just because you prefer Unix? Toolkits make it feasible to develop a program once and recompile it to run on other platforms. Mind you, it is still not easy, and there are pitfalls to watch out for. But without such a toolkit, multi-platform programming is feasible only for the largest companies.

Even if you don't develop your software for the open market, your custom software clients may require you to write programs in a portable fashion, so that they can sell or use them on additional platforms.

Even if you develop free software, you should still consider the fact that portable software often means better software. There might be hidden bugs in your program that a version for another platform uncovers easily. Also, following standards makes it easier for other people to read and maintain your code. In addition, you can get more users if you write software that can be compiled on more than one platform, making the development of free software more satisfactory.

Why Qt?

On Unix systems, Qt is the best option: It's portable, it's fast, and it's rather easy to use. Also, if you write free software for Unix-like operating systems like Linux, FreeBSD or Solaris, programming with Qt is free. In other words, you don't have to pay any license fees. We will talk more about this in the "Acquiring Qt" section.

If you are a Windows programmer, you have undoubtedly heard about MFC, the Microsoft Foundation Classes. These are shipped with most Windows compilers nowadays, and they fulfill all the requirements that we informally stated earlier. They are rather complete in terms of supported user-interface elements, and you can buy a lot of third-party add-ons.

If MFC contains everything you need, why should you try another library, one that's completely unknown to most Windows programmers? There's one big answer: portability. When you use Qt, you can write your programs once on Windows, then recompile them to run on a lot of Unix variants, too. In addition, a lot of programmers who have used both MFC and Qt consider programming with Qt to be easier. After you have overcome the initial hurdles, you will find that programming with Qt is "the way it should be"—it just feels natural. There's another reason, too, one that will appeal to most programmers: Programs written with Qt tend to be very fast. This is because the programmers who wrote Qt spent a lot of time optimizing it.

Of course, there are other products that allow portable programming for Unix and MS Windows. These include commercial libraries like Zinc, and free libraries like wxWindows. I have evaluated most of them for my projects, and I have almost always found Qt to be the best option. Of course, you should judge their merits for yourself. Try several alternatives, write sample applications, and see which toolkit is the best for you.

Of course, Qt has its share of bugs, and we will mention these as we go along. Fortunately, Qt has rather short release cycles, so chances are that you can download or purchase a new and improved version in a few weeks or months. In the meantime, Qt developers can often help you with workarounds.

Implementing Cross-Platform GUI Libraries

GUI toolkits[1] that allow cross-platform programming can follow one of several strategies, according to how the native toolkit API is used. For Windows, this native toolkit API is, of course, the Win32 API. For the purposes of this discussion, we will assume that Motif is the "native" toolkit API on Unix systems, even though no one toolkit on Unix is truly native. Motif comes closest, because it is most common.

API layering

Many cross-platform toolkits use *API Layering*. This means that they provide their own API on top of the native API. There is one implementation of this toolkit for every native API that it supports. One such toolkit is wxWindows. The wxWindows methods map to Win32 API calls on Windows, and to either Motif or Xt API calls on Unix.

The advantages of API Layering are that the toolkit is relatively easy to program, and that the look-and-feel is 100% compatible with the native look-and-feel. The disadvantages should not be ignored, however: Programs written with toolkits that use API Layering are usually slower than those that use the native APIs directly, because each call has to be routed through an additional layer. Native toolkits can differ significantly in their structure, which can lead to awkward control flow in the portable toolkit. In addition, those toolkits typically provide the lowest common denominator of functionality, offering only those functions that are available in all toolkits used. Finally, it is difficult to inherit widgets and specialize them, because widgets are drawn by the native toolkit and not by the relatively thin C++ wrapper.

API emulation

Some other portable toolkits emulate the API of one system on all other systems. These include products like MainWin by Mainsoft or Wind/U by Bristol Technology which provide the Win32 API on Unix systems. Obviously, no additional software is needed for the emulated platform, because the native API of this platform is used. The API emulation is only needed for other platforms.

---

1   If you are interested in how many platform-independent GUI toolkits exist, see the PIGUI FAQ at *http://www.zeta.org.au/˜rosko/pigui.htm.*

While this might sound like a good idea, it often isn't. Platforms are too different for making API emulation very practical. Also, programs on platforms that are not emulated are faster than those on the emulated platform, again because of the additional layer. The towering of layers can be even more frightful: It is not uncommon to have an MFC layer on top of the Win32 layer on top of a Motif layer on top of an Xt layer on top of the Xlib layer... you get the idea. A further disadvantage is that all base toolkits have some features that are undocumented, but are used or exploited nevertheless, and all will have a few hidden bugs. API-emulating toolkits are very unlikely to also emulate bugs and undocumented features, so programs created with them may turn out to be unstable.

GUI emulation

The so-called GUI-emulating toolkits include Qt and other toolkits. GUI-emulating tool-kits don't use any native-toolkit calls at all. Instead, they use the drawing or graphics primitives of the respective platforms. Each and every widget is drawn inside the emu-lating toolkit.

Again, this procedure has advantages and disadvantages. The advantages are obvious: Since no additional layers except the most primitive ones are used, Qt and other GUI emulators are faster than other cross-platform toolkits. Also, since all drawing is done inside the toolkit, it is easy to display an application in Motif style on MS-Windows, or in Windows-style on Unix. With GUI emulation, it is also very easy to inherit any widget, and to redefine its behaviour.

This technique also has some disadvantages. First of all, the emulation might not always be 100% exact, resulting in little differences in the look-and-feel between programs written with the native calls and programs written with Qt. Usually, these differences are so small that users hardly notice them. The second disadvantage might have more impact. For every new widget that is introduced to a platform from the manufacturer of the native toolkit, code has to be written that draws this widget in all possible states including normal, active, and disabled. This is a lot of work, so that it can take quite a lot of time until some widgets are supported in the cross-platform toolkit, and some might never be supported. This applies not only to the makers of the toolkit, but also to users who want to add widgets of their own. If they want to do a complete emulation, they have to write drawing code for all supported platforms. However, the same caveat also applies to users of API-layering and API-emulating toolkits.

In sum, despite its disadvantages, the GUI-emulation technique is the most powerful. Users care much more about the GUI's responsiveness than about the fact that it does or does not use the latest UI gimmicks. There's no denying the fact that GUI-emulating toolkits *are* faster.

Acquiring Qt

As of this writing, there are no resellers for Qt. The only way you can acquire a commercial license for Qt is to order it directly from the manufacturer, Troll Tech. Troll Tech accepts credit cards and fax orders, and you can find pricing information and an order form at *http://www.troll.no/purchase/*. When ordering, you can decide whether you want to get Qt delivered via normal mail on floppy disks or on CD, or you would prefer to download it from the vendor's FTP server.

If you only develop open-source software on Unix, you don't need the commercial edition. Simply download the source code of Qt from the FTP server at *ftp://ftp.troll.no/qt/ source*. You will have to compile the source code yourself, as explained in the next section. If you are running Linux, you can also find precompiled binaries on Troll Tech's FTP site. If you are unsure of which file to get, go to *http://www.troll.no/dl/* to be guided to the file you need.

If you are running one of the increasingly popular free Unix-like operating systems, such as Linux or FreeBSD, chances are that your distribution already contains a version of Qt. It might not always be the latest version, however. It is quite common for quality distributions nowadays to carry Qt.

Red Hat's position towards Qt

There has been some disagreement in the free software community about whether it is a good thing to use Qt for free software development, especially since the very popular free desktop for Unix and Linux systems, KDE (see the "The KDE Project" section), uses Qt. In spite of KDE's popularity, Red Hat, a well-known Linux distributor, does not ship Qt or KDE with its Linux distribution. Their opinion is that since Qt is not free according to their own definition of "free", people should not use Qt to write free software. Their's is also one of the very few Linux distributions that does not contain Qt, even though their distribution used to contain commercial software and their official German version still contains both Qt and KDE.

There have been a lot of flame wars on Usenet about the usage of Qt for free software. Since most of the arguments presented there are based on wrong or incomplete information anyway, I won't comment on them here, but just want to state my opinion on this subject. Note that if you develop commercial software or software for Windows in general, you will probably be wondering what this is all about. Rest assured: You don't need to know it.

- If you develop free software for Unix systems, you can use Qt for free and do not have to pay any license fees.

- Nobody who uses Qt simply by using a program written with it has to pay any license fees. There is no such thing as a runtime license fee.

- In my opinion, good commercial software is better than bad free software, which is why I would rather use a very good commercial toolkit like Qt (especially if the developers let me use it for free) than an inferior free toolkit.

- Since developers of free software are not paid for their work, they are driven only by their own motivation. This motivation is undoubtedly higher if they have high-quality tools that let them achieve the desired results as soon and as painlessly as possible. The same applies to GUI toolkits, and Qt is such a high-quality tool.

- I have the firm opinion that one of the most important things about freedom is the freedom of choice. I want to be able to choose between different word processors and different GUI toolkits, and not be hindered in doing so by an unnecessary barrier like the non-inclusion of a very good toolkit in a distribution (that otherwise includes a lot of GUI toolkits, including those that are definitely inferior to Qt). It might well be the case that for some particular project of yours, Qt might not be the best choice. But without evaluating it, you will never know what you are missing.

Compiling and Installing Qt

Installing Qt on Unix systems

Whether you have bought Qt on disk or downloaded the commercial or free version, you will end up with a tar file.[2] Unpack this file by issuing the command:

```
zcat qt-1.42.tgz | tar xvf -
```

If you have the GNU version of tar on your system, you can also use the command:

```
tar xvzf qt-1.42.tgz
```

Qt will be unpacked in a directory called *qt-1.42*. Of course, you can save yourself some work if you unpack the archive where you want to have it, which might be */usr/local*. You should now read the file *INSTALL* in this directory to see if there are any special directions for your system.

In most cases, building the Qt library is straightforward. The process has two steps. The first configures Qt for your system, and the second builds the Qt library and examples.

A note about version numbers: When you read this book, there could already be a newer version of Qt. In this case, the version numbers in the filenames will of course change, but the general process will most probably not.

Start by simply executing the command

```
make
```

Qt will respond with the following list of targets, i.e., platforms that Qt can be built for:

```
aix-g++-shared          hpux-g++-static          osf1-cxx-shared
aix-g++-shared-debug    hpux-g++-static-debug    osf1-cxx-shared-debug
aix-g++-static          irix-64-shared           osf1-cxx-static
```

---

2 For platforms like Linux, precompiled binaries in various package formats may be available. Please see your operating system documentation for information about how to install these.

```
aix-g++-static-debug        irix-64-shared-debug       osf1-cxx-static-debug
aix-xlc-shared              irix-64-static             osf1-g++-shared
aix-xlc-shared-debug        irix-64-static-debug       osf1-g++-shared-debug
aix-xlc-static              irix-dcc-shared            osf1-g++-static
aix-xlc-static-debug        irix-dcc-shared-debug      osf1-g++-static-debug
dgux-g++-shared             irix-dcc-static            sco-g++-shared
dgux-g++-shared-debug       irix-dcc-static-debug      sco-g++-shared-debug
dgux-g++-static             irix-g++-shared            sco-g++-static
dgux-g++-static-debug       irix-g++-shared-debug      sco-g++-static-debug
freebsd-g++-shared          irix-g++-static            solaris-cc-shared
freebsd-g++-shared-debug    irix-g++-static-debug      solaris-cc-shared-debug
freebsd-g++-static          irix-n32-shared            solaris-cc-static
freebsd-g++-static-debug    irix-n32-shared-debug      solaris-cc-static-debug
gnu-g++-shared              irix-n32-static            solaris-g++-shared
gnu-g++-shared-debug        irix-n32-static-debug      solaris-g++-shared-debug
gnu-g++-static              linux-g++-shared           solaris-g++-static
gnu-g++-static-debug        linux-g++-shared-debug     solaris-g++-static-debug
hpux-acc-shared             linux-g++-static           sunos-g++-shared
hpux-acc-shared-debug       linux-g++-static-debug     sunos-g++-shared-debug
hpux-acc-static             netbsd-g++-shared          sunos-g++-static
hpux-acc-static-debug       netbsd-g++-shared-debug    sunos-g++-static-debug
hpux-cc-shared              netbsd-g++-static          ultrix-g++-static
hpux-cc-shared-debug        netbsd-g++-static-debug    ultrix-g++-static-debug
hpux-cc-static              openbsd-g++-shared         unixware-g++-shared
hpux-cc-static-debug        openbsd-g++-shared-debug   unixware-g++-shared-debug
hpux-g++-shared             openbsd-g++-static         unixware-g++-static
hpux-g++-shared-debug       openbsd-g++-static-debug   unixware-g++-static-debug
```

Almost all of these target names consist of three parts, separated by dashes. The first part is the operating system. You should not have any problem finding out what applies to you here. The second part names the compiler to use. Note that for some operating systems, only one compiler is available. The third part of the target name determines whether Qt should be built as a shared or a static library. Shared libraries are supported for most platforms. If they are supported for your platform and compiler, you should build a shared library. You will save a lot of disk space.

For example, if you are running Linux, use the GNU compiler g++, and want to build a shared library, your next step would be issuing the command:

```
make linux-g++-shared
```

Obviously, if you have another system, you have to use your target here instead of `linux-g++-shared`.

You will see some messages that makefiles are created. When you get back to the shell prompt, simply type

```
make
```

Now go get yourself some tea, or even a full lunch—Qt is not small and all the example programs have to be built, too. Note that if you plan to debug Qt itself, because you want to see how it works internally or you suspect a bug in Qt, you will have to choose a target that ends in debug so that debugging symbols will be included in the library.

When the compiler is done, you are almost ready to use Qt. There is no real "install" step. You should set the environment variable `QTDIR` to the name of your Qt directory, add `$QTDIR/bin` to your `PATH`, and add `$QTDIR/lib` to the environment variable that tells your dynamic loader where to look for shared libraries. On Linux and Solaris systems, this is `LD_LIBRARY_PATH`. For other systems, please consult your system documentation.

On some systems, you can also add the directory that contains the library to a system configuration file, such as *etc/ld.so.conf* on Linux systems.

Finally, when compiling Qt programs, don't forget to tell your compiler about the include files with `-I$QTDIR/include`, and to inform your linker about the library with `-L$QTDIR/lib -lqt`

Compiling and installing Qt on Windows 95/98 and Windows NT

Compiling and installing Qt on Windows is very easy, if you use the Visual C++ compiler. All you have to do is unpack the Qt zip file with a program like *pkunzip* or *winzip*, and then set the environment variable `QTDIR` to the directory where you have unpacked Qt. Next, change to the *src* directory and simply type

```
nmake
```

After some time, Qt will be built and ready to use. You might want to add the directory *qt/include* to the environment variable that your compiler uses for locating header files, and add *qt/lib* to the environment variable that your compiler uses for locating libraries.

C++ as Used by Qt

If you are unsure whether your C++ knowledge is expansive enough for programming with Qt, this section can help. It gives you a short rundown of the part of C++ that Qt and Qt programs use, so you will know if you are lacking some C++ skills.

If you want to read about some of the language features mentioned here, we recommend *C++: The Core Language* by Gregory Satir and Doug Brown, published by O'Reilly & Associates. This book restricts itself to the most important parts of the language, and covers almost everything mentioned here.

Objects and classes

Of course, Qt uses classes—it *is* a class library. You should know what member functions are, how to call them, and so on. Also, you need to know how to write your own classes, and how to derive a new class from an existing one. You do not need to be an experienced designer of class hierarchies, though. We will provide enough information here on building up your hierarchies for GUI programming.

Access methods

Qt uses a lot of access methods, which are methods that get and set values of private class variables. Set methods usually start with "set...", while get methods have no prefix (not even "get"). This is fairly basic stuff, there's no sophistication involved here.

Polymorphism and virtual functions

Qt uses virtual functions to notify your objects about low-level events, so you should be comfortable with these. Unlike other toolkits and class libraries, Qt uses the innovative signal/slot mechanism rather than virtual functions as the central means of communication between objects. This is specific to Qt, so it is covered later in this book.

Inheritance

Of course, Qt uses inheritance, but for the most part, it relies on single inheritance. Multiple inheritance is rarely used—in fact, it is used so rarely that you might never get to see it. And if you have never understood what this "virtual inheritance" means, rest assured: Qt does not use this at all.

Operator overloading

Qt overloads some operators, but usually these "just work". For example, you can pass a QString object to a function that expects a `const char*`, because an operator jumps in to convert your QString object to a character pointer.

Templates

Qt uses templates for its collection classes. You cannot compile Qt with a compiler that does not understand templates, or one that has a broken implementation of templates. The usage of templates is not yet compulsory in your own code, but it probably will be in future versions of Qt, if you want to use the collection classes. Even if you want to use Qt's collection classes (see Chapter 8, *Container Classes*), you can use an alternative, macro-based API if you feel uncomfortable with templates. On the other hand, we strongly advise you to try them, because they offer some advantages, such as type safety, that macros do not. Still, macros might be the better choice if your compiler tends to generate huge code for template instantiations.

The datatype `bool`

Naturally, Qt uses the new data type `bool` quite often. Unfortunately, some old compilers don't support it, and consequently don't know the keywords `true` and `false`, either. In these cases, you can use the replacement macros `TRUE` and `FALSE` that are provided by Qt. In this book, we use `true` and `false`, but if you have one of those outdated compilers, you can always replace `true` with `TRUE` and `false` with `FALSE`.

Other features

Qt does not use namespaces, run-time type identification (RTTI), new-style casts, and other features that have been added to C++ lately.

Getting Help

You may run into problems that you cannot solve with the Qt reference documentation or this book. There are several places where you can ask for help:

- If you have a professional license for Qt, you are entitled to technical support via e-mail. You will receive the e-mail address with your copy of Qt. Usually you will get answers very quickly, but if your questions are difficult, please be patient.

- You can subscribe to the Qt Interest mailing list, where Qt users exchange ideas and help each other. The Qt developers monitor this mailing list as well, and often jump in if nobody else knows an answer. Please keep in mind that the other developers on this list are not there just to help you. Most of them are very supportive, but nobody is required to answer your questions. To subscribe, send an e-mail message with the text `subscribe` *`insert your e-mail address here`* in the subject to *qt-interest-request@troll.no*. After you have subscribed, you can post to the list by sending e-mail to *qt-interest@troll.no*.

- The KDE (K Desktop Environment, see the "The KDE Project" section) mailing list is populated with some very experienced Qt developers, too, so you can ask for help here, if you are writing a KDE application. Remember that all KDE programmers do their work voluntarily, so please be polite and do not demand quick answers! To subscribe to the main KDE list, send an e-mail message to *kde-request@kde.org* that contains the text `subscribe` *`insert your e-mail address here`* in the subject and has an empty body.

2

First Steps in Qt Programming

The time has come to start getting our hands dirty with some real code. Of course, our first program will be the traditional "Hello world" exercise. We'll then gradually build from there to create a small but complete paint program. The topics in this chapter are important building blocks for almost every Qt programming task, so make sure you understand them.

Hello World!

This program, which will create a little window with "Hello World" in it, is very simple, but it contains code that you will see again and again in Qt programs. The code is in Example 2-1.[1]

Example 2-1: Hello World in Qt

```
 1  #include <qapplication.h>
 2  #include <qlabel.h>
 3
 4  int main( int argc, char* argv[] )
 5  {
 6    QApplication myapp( argc, argv );
 7
 8    QLabel* mylabel = new QLabel( "Hello world" );
 9    mylabel->resize( 80, 30 );
10
11    myapp.setMainWidget( mylabel );
12    mylabel->show();
13    return myapp.exec();
14  }
```

---

1 In industry-quality programs, you should check the return value of every memory allocation. We omit these checks in the example programs to avoid hiding the actual purpose.

Let's go through this code line by line. The first two lines include Qt header files. For most cases, there is a one-to-one relationship between Qt classes and Qt header files. The header file names are almost always the same as the class names, with all letters in lowercase and the conventional *.h* appended to each name. In some rare cases, several classes are grouped together in one header file. For example, you can find both the class declarations of `QListView` and `QListViewItem` in *qlistview.h*.[2] When in doubt, check the documentation.

In this example, *qapplication.h* is for the class `QApplication`, and *qlabel.h* is for `QLabel`.

Line 6 is the next crucial line. Here, an object of class `QApplication` is created. Every Qt application must have exactly one object of class `QApplication`. This object is responsible for all event handling, and it holds everything together. It also provides some useful methods that we'll talk about later.

You probably have noticed that the command-line parameters that our application receives from the runtime library are passed to the constructor of the `QApplication` object. This is done because `QApplication` accepts some special command-line arguments, which it handles and afterwards removes from the command-line variables. Your application never sees these special command-line arguments. Among these are `-style`, which tells Qt which widget style to use by default on Unix systems; and `-nograb`, which tells Qt never to grab the mouse or the keyboard to facilitate debugging. If your application interprets its own command-line parameters, make sure to interpret them after having passed the command line to `QApplication`.

In line 8, we create an object of class `QLabel`. This class provides a simple label UI element that can be used for labeling other UI elements. Labels contain text or images; we'll use some text here for simplicity. Note that we pass the text to be shown in the constructor. We could have chosen to set it afterwards, instead.

The label is called a widget. Unix programmers might be familiar with the term "widget", which is a contraction of window and gadget, but Windows programmers might never have heard it used in a programming context. If you have some experience with Windows programming, you know the concept, though: The same things are called "controls" in Windows programming lingo. Almost everything that you see in a user interface written with Qt is a widget. A button is a widget, a scroll bar is a widget, and a complete dialog box is a widget, too. Widgets may also have subwidgets, as in the case of the dialog that contains buttons, text-entry fields, and the like. Technically, a widget is an object of a class that is derived from `QWidget`. Qt contains many predefined widgets, and you can also define your own.

---

2 In earlier releases of Qt, the names of the header files were shorter and harder to guess. For example, instead of *qapplication.h*, you had to use *qapp.h*. The old names are still available to ensure backward compatibility.

WARNING In Qt, every widget should be constructed on the heap, because they will be automatically deleted when their parent is deleted. Creating widgets on the stack (i.e., not with new) is a common mistake for Qt beginners and can lead to very hard-to-find bugs. This behavior of Qt is advantageous, because you often do not need to hold pointers to widgets if all you will do with them in the future is delete them. This can make your code much simpler. You don't have to understand this fully for now, as long as you remember to always construct your widgets on the heap (i.e., with new).

In line 9, we resize the label widget. That means that we tell the widget to get another width and height. We use a width of 80 pixels and a height of 30 pixels here, because that is just big enough to display the "Hello World" text.

Line 11 is very important, too, though you may not understand it yet. In this line, we tell the QApplication object that the label is its main widget. The *main widget* is the widget that makes the application exit when it is closed. If we did not define a main widget, we could close the window with the usual close button, but the program would still exist invisibly. This wastes resources, so remember to set a main widget.

The next thing to do is show your widgets. In line 12, there's only one widget, the label. Every widget can be either shown or hidden, and widgets that are not children of some other shown widget are hidden by default. If we did not show the label widget here, the program would run, but we would not see anything.

Finally, we start event processing. This is done by calling the method QApplication::exec(). The application object pools all needed events from the underlying window system and dispatches them to the widgets where they belong. Since widgets know how to draw themselves, there is nothing left to do. Even if we obscure our program window with another window, then pull it back to the front so that it needs repainting, the application object and the widget will take care of that themselves—no application code is needed. This is one of the differences between a toolkit where you usually have to dispatch the events yourself and an application framework that does all that for you.

Now it's time to compile and run our program. If you are using Windows and the Microsoft Visual C++ compiler, the following command line should work for you, if you have installed Qt in c:\qt:

```
cl -Ic:\qt\include helloworld.cpp c:\qt\lib\qt.lib \
    user32.lib gdi32.lib comdlg32.lib ole32.lib uuid32.lib wsock32.lib
```

If you use another compiler, please see your compiler documentation for details about invoking the compiler and linker. Chapter 23 explains how to use the Visual C++ IDE for Qt programs.

On Unix systems, a command-line like the following one should suffice, if you set the environment variable QTDIR as described in the "Compiling and Installing Qt" section (assuming that you have saved the code in a file called *helloworld.cpp*):

```
c++ -I$QTDIR/include -L$QTDIR/lib -lqt -o helloworld helloworld.cpp
```

The command for calling the C++ compiler might be different on your system. Starting with c++ usually works on all systems that use the GNU C++ Compiler. On AIX use xlC; on Solaris you can try CC.

When you are done with compiling and linking, you can start your program. You should see a little window greeting you with "Hello World". Congratulations! You have just compiled and run your first Qt program. Figure 2-1 shows how it will look like.

Figure 2-1: Screenshot of the first Qt program

Before we whip up some more interesting UI elements, we'll first talk about how you find your way in the Qt reference documentation.

Exercises

Exercises probably wouldn't make much sense to you at this point. Just make sure that you can compile a Qt application like the one presented in this section on your system, and get your web browser ready for the next section.

Using the Qt Reference Documentation

Qt comes with documentation in HTML format, and it is simply excellent. That's the main reason you won't find a reference section in this book. It's not very difficult to find your way around the documentation, but it pays to take some time to get acquainted with it. It will help you work faster.

To read the documentation, fire up your web browser. Since Qt does not use any special HTML tricks, nor does it rely on Java™ or JavaScript, you can use any web browser. Netscape Navigator, Internet Explorer, or Opera is fine, for example. If you have several browsers to choose from, use the one you already know best, and if you still don't know which browser to use, pick one with good bookmark support. If you are serious about portable programming, it might be a good idea to use a web browser that is available on Windows as well as on Unix, such as Netscape Communicator or Mosaic.

Point your browser to the file *index.html* in the *html* directory of your Qt installation. You will see something similar to the page in Figure 2-2.

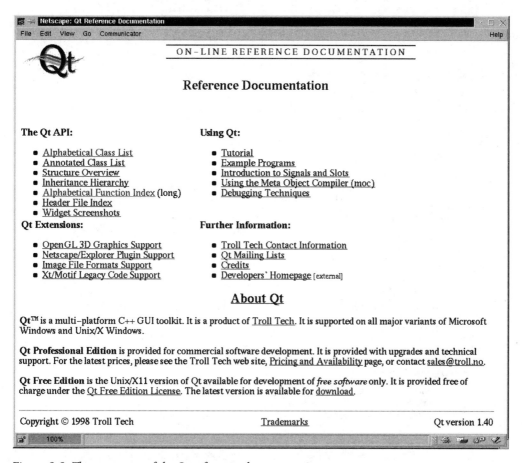

Figure 2-2: The start page of the Qt reference documentation

To get an impression of how Qt's class tree is organized, choose the item Annotated Class List. If you click on this link, you will be presented with a list of all public Qt classes with a one-line description of what each one does. After you have worked with Qt for some time, you will probably have mastered this information, allowing you to simply choose Alphabetical class list. This list does not contain annotations and shows more classes on a single screenful, but for now we will stick with the *annotated class list*.

Let's read a bit about one of the two classes that we know already, QLabel. Click on the word QLabel (the classes are sorted alphabetically) and you will see a screen like the one shown in Figure 2-3.

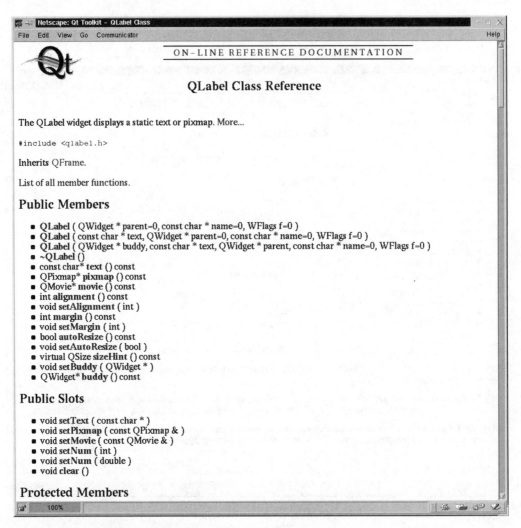

Figure 2-3: The reference documentation for QLabel

The first thing you see is a repetition of the one-line description of the class. The name of the header file and the name or names of the base class or base classes follow. The link to the "list of all member functions" is important, in case you are unsure about which methods this class inherits from its ancestors. But the main thing to look for in every class description is the list of its public member functions. These form the first large block. It may suffice to look at this block to find the method you need, because the names are usually rather self-explanatory. If you need more information about a method, just click on its name to be led to its long description. Since the complete documentation is interlinked, you can also click on the names of other Qt classes that might appear as parameter types, and thus jump to their descriptions.

After the list of public and protected members, you will find the detailed description of the class. Here you often find complete examples about how to use this class, which you can copy into your sources.

Let's jump back one more time to the start page of the documentation. In the section "Tutorial and other documentation", you will find more interesting stuff about Qt, but most of these things are of little use to the beginner. Come back after you have read the first two chapters of this book.

If you like printed documentation better than hyperlinked online help, you don't have to print all 500 pages of documentation from your web browser. Troll Tech, the maker of Qt, provides PostScript files that contain all of the documentation in several page sizes. These files can be downloaded from its web server at *http://www.troll.no/dl/qtps-doc-dl.html*.

Exercises

1. Read about the other class you already know, `QApplication`, in the reference documentation.

2. Using the Qt reference documentation, find out which class `QFrame` is derived from, and which classes are derived from it. For example, check to see if you can set the frame style of an object of class `QLabel`. (Hint: Use the class overview.)

Adding an Exit Button

In this section, we will extend our little "Hello World" program with a push-button. A push-button is a common interface element on every platform: You just click on it, and something happens. In Qt, push-buttons are represented by the class `QPushButton`, which is a subclass of `QButton`, which itself is a subclass of `QWidget`, the base class for all Qt UI elements. Besides showing how to create a push-button, which is really not very different from the label we created two sections ago, this example gives you a first impression of how to react to user interaction in Qt. The first task will be very simple: When the user presses the button (which will ingeniously be labeled "Quit"), the whole program will terminate.

Before we start explaining, you should look at the program in Example 2-2 and its output in Figure 2-4.

Example 2-2: Adding a push-button to Hello World

```
1 #include <qapplication.h>
2 #include <qlabel.h>
3 #include <qpushbutton.h>
4
5 int main( int argc, char* argv[] )
6 {
7   QApplication myapp( argc, argv );
```

Example 2-2: Adding a push-button to Hello World (continued)

```
 8
 9    QWidget* mywidget = new QWidget();
10    mywidget->setGeometry( 400, 300, 120, 90 );
11
12    QLabel* mylabel = new QLabel( "Hello world", mywidget );
13    mylabel->setGeometry( 10, 10, 80, 30 );
14
15    QPushButton* myquitbutton = new QPushButton( "Quit", mywidget );
16    myquitbutton->setGeometry( 10, 50, 100, 30 );
17    QObject::connect( myquitbutton, SIGNAL(clicked()), &myapp, SLOT(quit()) );
18
19    myapp.setMainWidget( mywidget );
20    mywidget->show();
21    return myapp.exec();
22 }
```

Figure 2-4: Output of the Button Program

We had to change some things here to accommodate more than one widget. Since we now have two, we have to create an additional widget to serve as a container for the label and the push-button. This additional widget is represented by the variable `mywidget`. It is an object of the class `QWidget`, meaning that it has no special widget properties, but knows about all the general things that widgets can do, like resizing and moving.

In the constructors for the `QLabel` object and the `QPushButton` object in lines 12 and 15, we pass the address of `mywidget` as the second argument. This is important, because it makes `mywidget` the parent of the label and the push-button widget. Much of GUI programming is getting the parent-child relationships between the widgets right. If a parent is not shown, its children aren't either. In our little program, the parent widget `mywidget` mainly serves to group the other two widgets together and to provide a main widget for the application (remember, it's important to set a main widget).

Another difference you probably have noticed is that we set the positions with the method `setGeometry()` in this example. This method is defined in `QWidget`, and is therefore available for both the push-button and the label. The four parameters are horizontal position, vertical position, width, and height, all expressed in pixels. The horizontal and vertical positions are always relative to the parent widget. In the case of `mywidget`, there is no parent widget; the positions are therefore relative to the whole screen.

Line 17 probably looks like complete magic to you. We'll talk about these things in detail in the "Introduction to Signals and Slots" section, but whenever a push-button is clicked, it emits a *signal*, in this case a `clicked()` signal. This signal means "To whom it may concern: Somebody clicked me. Do whatever you want with this information." Other parts of the program can then *connect* to the widget in order to be notified whenever the user clicks the push-button. To connect to a signal you have to provide a *slot*, which is then connected to the signal. You can do whatever is needed to handle the button-click in this slot. In this case, we use a predefined slot from the `QApplication` class. This slot, `quit()`, simply terminates the whole application.

The signal-and-slot mechanism is the single most important thing to know when programming with Qt. That's why the next section explores it further.

Exercises

1. Add another push-button, which should sit above the "Hello world" label to the program shown in Example 2-2. This button should be labeled "Click me", and should also terminate the application when clicked. Note: You will have to adjust the button and label positions.

2. Change the program you wrote for the last exercise so that one of the buttons terminates the application when it is pressed (i.e., so that the mouse button does not have to be released). Hint: Use the signal `pressed()`.

Introduction to Signals and Slots

As explained in the last section, signals and slots are the most important topic in Qt programming. To make it easier to understand how signals and slots work, we'll take a short look at how other GUI toolkits link events, such as the user pressing a button, to program code. We will see why there are disadvantages with these methods, which will give us a better understanding of why the developers of Qt chose the signal-and-slot mechanism. If you already know about other GUI toolkits or libraries like MFC or Motif, you can skip the next section.

The problem of callback functions

The underlying window system reports user interactions with so-called "events". These are usually very primitive, and just say "the user pressed the left mouse button while the mouse was at position 100, 200" or "the user pressed the k key". Of course, it would be possible to determine from the mouse position which widget the mouse was over when the user pressed the button and then react accordingly, but this would be a very boring, cumbersome and error-prone task—a task that we rightfully expect the toolkit to take over for us.

Accordingly, the toolkit determines which widget the mouse was over—in other words, which widget should be informed about the mouse click. The next question is how and where the programmer should put the code to be executed in reaction to the mouse-click. GUI toolkits differ most fundamentally in how they answer this question.

Motif uses *callbacks*[3]. These are C functions that must accept certain arguments, and are "registered" with a widget. Every Motif widget knows about certain callback types for which callback functions may be registered. For example, the push-button knows about callbacks when the mouse is pressed, released and clicked. The disadvantage of this method is the missing type-safety. If you register a function with an incorrect signature, so that it accepts the wrong types of parameters, your application is likely to crash. The compiler cannot guard you from this.

There is no connection between the widget and the callback, which is just any other standalone function that happens to be registered as a callback function. In addition, when it comes to object-oriented programming with C++, callbacks are even more awkward. Because of the implicitly passed `this` pointer, you can only use static methods as callbacks.

A free C++ GUI toolkit for Unix and Windows systems, wxWindows, relies exclusively on virtual methods. Whenever you want to be informed about a user event on a widget, you have to derive your own class from that widget's class and override a certain virtual method there. Usually, a widget class has several virtual functions to override, just like a Motif widget knows about several callback types. You override only those for which you want to define a reaction. This has the advantage of being a clean C++-like solution, but it does not scale well to large user interfaces. You find yourself deriving new classes all the time, just because you wanted to react to a button-click. Also, a common wish when programming GUI programs is to separate the user interface from the core application functionality, which is not possible when you have to program application functionality in virtual methods of GUI classes. Of course, you can simply call functions or methods from other classes there, but it is still not very nice.

The MFC (Microsoft Foundation Classes), which are now bundled with most C++ compilers on the MS-Windows platform, use yet another way. They use macros to link C++ methods to events from the window system (called "messages" in Windows lingo). This avoids problems with virtual functions, and means less overhead in the executable code. Virtual functions always involve a *vtable*, a jump table for all the virtual functions of a class, and another pointer indirection when calling them. But other problems are introduced here. First, the message maps that these macros form together are hard to read, and hard to write. This might not be a severe problem for most MFC programmers, since the IDE usually provides "smart" dialogs or wizards to help create them. On the other hand, many programmers believe that a toolkit should be usable on its own, without support from a certain type of IDE. In addition, one of the design goals of C++

---

3   The term "callback" is sometimes used for these functions in other toolkits as well, even though these functions might have another official name in that toolkit's lingo. Whenever you hear "callback", think "function that is called in reaction to some user interaction on a widget".

was to remove the need for the preprocessor. The message maps are not type-safe in any way, since macros can never be type-safe. This is no problem if your IDE ensures that you cannot get the types wrong, but it would be much better if the compiler had a chance to do it.

A new approach

To overcome some of the difficulties mentioned in the last section, the developers of Qt invented the signal-and-slot mechanism. While it has some disadvantages of its own, its many advantages have led to the adoption of this general principle in other GUI toolkits as well.

The idea is that a widget sends out (*emits*) a signal[4] that something has happened without knowing who will use it. This is not unlike the old telephone switchboards, where incoming lines were connected to outgoing lines via patch cables. Neither the incoming nor the outgoing lines needed to know anything about the other lines; they didn't even need to know whether they would be used.

On the other side is the program code, which should be executed whenever a signal is emitted. This program code can connect to any signal that has an appropriate type (we'll see in a minute what that means). The only thing this code (or rather its programmer) has to know is which signals are available and what their types are, just like you have to know which incoming and outgoing lines are available in order to use them on a switchboard. To bring the signal and your code together, you have to *connect* them— just like plugging a patch cable into the two outlets in question. Your code must fulfill one technical condition: It must be declared a *slot*. We'll see in a minute what that means.

We now have signals that are emitted by widgets (not only by widgets, by the way, but that is the most common use) and slot code that should be called whenever a certain signal is emitted. The widget that emits the signal does not know who has connected to it.[5] In fact, in most programs, many signals will never be connected to any slot. On the other hand, when you write a slot, you do not have to know beforehand which signals you will connect to it. Some dark and mysterious part of the Qt library, nebulously called the "Qt kernel" and manifested in the class `QObject`, takes care of the connections, and passes signals on to slots when this is desired.

As you can see, there is a strict separation between the different parts. The reason this strict separation is desirable is that it lends itself to component-based programming. In this programming paradigm, you write components that fulfill a defined role. The components are defined via their external interface. In Qt components, this mainly consists of the signals they emit and the slots they provide. Components can then be exchanged between applications.

---

4 Note that Qt signals have nothing to do with Unix signals, even though both are notification mechanisms.

5 It can ask for this information by reimplementing `QObject::connectNotify()`, but this is generally not a good idea, because it makes for tighter coupling of the components.

Component-based programming has been around for quite a long time, but has only really come to the attention of a wider public with the advent of *JavaBeans*™. The main point about components is, *components should not need to know what they will be used for.*

Signals and slots in Qt

It's time that we take a closer look at how the signal-and-slot mechanism is embedded in C++, a language that makes no special provisions for component-based programming apart from its abstraction mechanisms.

Qt defines some new keywords, which are translated by the preprocessor into syntactically correct C++. In addition, a special kind of additional preprocessor is needed that extracts information about signals and slots from class definitions, then generates some glue code. While this might not be an optimal solution, it is not as inconvenient as it sounds, and it enables a very efficient implementation.

Let's start with some general requirements. Signals and slots are only available within a C++ class—you cannot make a standalone function a slot. This is not a real restriction, because standalone functions should be used very sparingly in C++ anyway. Next, every class that wants to define at least a single signal or slot must be derived from the class QObject. Since you will find yourself deriving classes from QWidget or even more specialized classes most of the time, you usually don't have to worry about this, because QWidget is derived from QObject. Finally, every definition of a class that wants to declare at least a single signal or slot must contain the macro Q_OBJECT somewhere. Remember not to put a semicolon after the Q_OBJECT macro, because some compilers will choke on this.

To put this together, here is a general skeleton for a class that uses signals and/or slots:

```
class MyClass : public QObject
{
Q_OBJECT
  ...
signals:
  // Your signals go here, e.g.
     void somethingDone();
...
public slots:
  // Your public slots go here, e.g.
     void slotDoSomething();

private slots:
  // Your private slots go here, e.g.
     void slotDoSomethingInternal();

  // You can of course have more declarations.
};
```

Signals are declared by using the keyword `signals:` just like an access specifier in your class declaration. Apart from that, you declare them just like any member function. You never have to implement signals directly, you just declare them, and Qt takes care of the rest.

When your component wants to send out a signal, it uses the keyword `emit`.[6] This could look like the following (provided that `void highlighted(int)` has been declared as a signal in the class declaration):

```
emit highlighted( 5 );
```

Slots are declared and implemented just like any other C++ method. In fact, they are methods that can just as well be called the conventional way. The only thing you have to take care of is adding the keyword `slots` to the access specifier for the methods, as shown in the previous example.

Of course, you can also define protected slots, and making them virtual is no problem. The only thing you can't do with them is make them static.

Slots can have any parameters, but to be connected to a certain signal, they must use the same parameter types as the signal. If you want to connect your slot later to a signal that has one `int` parameter, your slot should have one `int` parameter, too.[7] It's a good idea to use generic (possibly built-in) types for the parameters of your slots. This way, chances are higher that you can reuse your component. If you use `int` as a parameter type, everyone can connect to your slot because every program knows about `int`. On the other hand, if you use `MySpecialAndSomehowRestrictedIntegerType` as a parameter type, only those programs that know about this type can reuse your component.

Another thing to think about when determining the types of the arguments of signals and slots: Most of the time, it is not advisable to pass full objects around; this can be very slow. You should instead use references or pointers. There are, however, quite a lot of classes in Qt that are implicitly shared, which means that copying them and passing them around is not much slower than using pointers or references. Among these classes is the class `QColor`, which is why we pass full objects of this class around in the examples in this and the next chapter.

You can name your slot any way you want, but some programmers have adopted the convention to have the term `slot` in the slot name. If you don't mind typing the extra four letters, this could be a good idea. On the other hand, the predefined Qt slots don't adhere to this convention. Decide for yourself.

To use signals and slots in your code, you must be able to bring them together. This is done with the method `QObject::connect()`, which connects one signal to one slot. It comes in many overloaded variants, but for the first part of this book, we will use only

---

6   Note that `emit` is absolutely Qt-specific; it is not some strange and unknown feature of your C++ compiler. The preprocessor makes sure that `emit` resolves to valid C++ code.

7   It is also possible for a slot to discard parameters. For example, a signal with an `int` parameter can be connected to a slot with no arguments.

the static variant with four parameters. This one can be used everywhere in a program, even in standalone functions. We would even go so far as to recommend always using this version, since you don't have to remember which parameter to leave out in which position.

This method needs to know four things: the object that sends out the signal, the signal that it should connect the slot to, the object that will receive the signal, and the slot that will be connected to the signal. The signal and the slot are just typed in with their names and parameter types, and wrapped with SIGNAL() and SLOT(), respectively. A common mistake in this place is to specify values instead of types, as in writing SIG-NAL(3) instead of SIGNAL(int). Also, Qt does not allow default arguments.

To make this less abstract, here is an example:

```
QObject::connect( mymenu, SIGNAL( activated( int ) ),
                  mycodeobject, SLOT( slotDoMenuFunction( int ) ) );
```

You don't need to understand the exact parameters now, this is just to give you an impression of what a connect() call looks like.

You can connect any number of slots to a signal, and you can connect any number of signals to a slot. The order in which the slots are called is not guaranteed. Therefore, you cannot rely on the fact that the slots will be called in the order in which you have connected them to the signals. There are some plans to define an order for the calls of the slots, but so far, you should not rely on any order.

Another example for signals and slots

The following example is more complex. Since you do not yet know how to write your own widgets, we won't emit user-defined signals here. We'll just connect a predefined signal with a predefined slot.

Our example consists of a QSlider, a longish widget with a knob for choosing a numerical value within a range, and a QLCDNumber, a nice little widget that displays a number, as seven-segment LCD displays do. Naturally, the number display should reflect the setting of the slider. You can find the code in Example 2-3. Figure 2-5 shows what the output should look like.

Example 2-3: Connecting a slider and a LCD number

```
 1 #include <qapplication.h>
 2 #include <qslider.h>
 3 #include <qlcdnumber.h>
 4
 5 int main( int argc, char* argv[] )
 6 {
 7   QApplication myapp( argc, argv );
 8
 9   QWidget* mywidget = new QWidget();
10   mywidget->setGeometry( 400, 300, 170, 110 );
```

Example 2-3: Connecting a slider and a LCD number (continued)

```
11
12
13    QSlider* myslider = new QSlider( 0,                      // minimum value
14                                       9,                      // maximum value
15                                       1,                      // step
16                                       1,                      // initial value
17                                       QSlider::Horizontal, // orientation
18                                       mywidget           // parent
19                                     );
20    myslider->setGeometry( 10, 10, 150, 30 );
21
22    QLCDNumber* mylcdnum = new QLCDNumber( 1,        // number of digits
23                                            mywidget // parent
24                                          );
25    mylcdnum->setGeometry( 60, 50, 50, 50 );
26    mylcdnum->display( 1 ); // display initial value
27
28    // connect slider and number display
29    QObject::connect( myslider, SIGNAL( sliderMoved( int ) ),
30                      mylcdnum, SLOT( display( int ) ) );
31
32    myapp.setMainWidget( mywidget );
33    mywidget->show();
34    return myapp.exec();
35 }
```

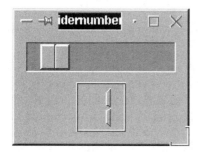

Figure 2-5: A slider and a number display

In lines 13 through 19, a QSlider widget is created. We pass several parameters in the constructor that determine which values can be chosen, how the slider looks, etc. In lines 22 through 24, we create a QLCDNumber widget and make it display one digit only. The crucial lines in this program are 29 and 30. We connect the slider's signal sliderMoved(), which is emitted whenever the user moves the slider knob, to the display's display() slot. Now the position of the slider knob is automatically reflected by the number display—without a single line of application code (apart from the connect() call, of course).

Note how we call the `display()` slot manually in line 26 in order to display an initial value in the number display. We can do this, since a slot is just another ordinary method of a class.

Also note how the parameters of the signal and the slot match: both have one parameter of type `int`. This is a case in which a value is passed from the signal to the slot. Compare this with the `clicked()` signal in Example 2-2, where the emission of the signal was the information itself. Here, we get two bits of information: that the slider was moved, and its new value. This value is passed to the slot just as any other actual parameter would be.

Running moc

Whenever you define a class of your own that uses signals and/or slots, it is not enough to simply compile it. You must also run *moc*, the *Meta-Object Compiler* supplied with Qt, on the file the class declaration is in. Running *moc* outputs glue code that is needed for the signal/slot mechanism to work. You have two possibilities to add this glue code to your application:

- Include the code generated by *moc* in one of your source files—usually the source file that implements the class declaration *moc* was run on—with a simple `#include` statement. This is a very easy solution, but including program code via the preprocessor is considered bad style and does not scale well to large programs. For small examples, this does the job, though.

  To do so, run *moc* on the file containing the class declaration:

  ```
  moc -o moc_file.cpp myfile.h
  ```

  and then compile *myfile.cpp* the usual way. It will then include the *moc*-generated code.

- Compile the code generated by *moc* separately and link it to your application. This is the preferred style. You can simply define rules in your makefiles to do so and there are programs available that generate these rules automatically. We'll talk about these in the "Building Projects Portably with tmake" section in Chapter 19, *Portability*. To follow this method, call *moc* as shown, then compile both the normal source file and the *moc*-generated file. Finally, link the two resulting object files together.

If you fail to either include `Q_OBJECT` in your class or link the *moc*-generated code to your application, the compiler or the linker will tell you. It's not always easy to find out what you have done wrong, however, especially if you are not yet accustomed to using *moc*. For example, here is a typical linker output, you might see if you forget to link the *moc*-generated file, from *g++* on a Unix system:

```
/tmp/cca183071.o: In function `qstrlen(char const *)':
/usr/local/qt/include/qevent.h:113: undefined reference to `MyClass::QPaintDevice
virtual table'
/tmp/cca183071.o: In function `qstrlen(char const *)':
/usr/local/qt/include/qstring.h:72: undefined reference to `MyClass virtual table'
/tmp/cca183071.o: In function `main':
```

```
/home/kalle/oreilly/buecher/qt/examples/test.cpp:68: undefined reference to
`MyClass::~MyClass(void)'
/home/kalle/oreilly/buecher/qt/examples/test.cpp:68: undefined reference to
`MyClass::~MyClass(void)'
collect2: ld returned 1 exit status
```

Here is the same message from Visual C++:

```
test.obj : error LNK2001: unresolved external symbol "protected: virtual void
__thiscall MyClass::initMetaObject(void)" (?initMetaObject@MyClass@@MAEXXZ)
test.obj : error LNK2001: unresolved external symbol "public: virtual char const *
__thiscall MyClass::className(void)const " (?className@MyClass@@UBEPBDXZ)
test.obj : error LNK2001: unresolved external symbol "private: static class
QMetaObject * MyClass::metaObj" (?metaObj@MyClass@@0PAVQMetaObject@@A)
test.exe : fatal error LNK1120: 3 unresolved external links
NMAKE : fatal error U1077: 'D:\PROGRAMME\DEVSTUDIO\VC\BIN\link.exe' : return code
'0x19'
Stop.
```

If you forget to include the `Q_OBJECT` macro, *moc* itself will give you the following error message:

```
Error: The declaration of the class "MyClass" contains slots and/or signals
       but no Q_OBJECT macro!
```

In addition, there will be compiler error messages.

Exercises

1. Change Example 2-3 so that the number is updated only when the user releases the slider knob. (Hint: Check the documentation of `QSlider` for other signals it emits.)

2. Add two push-buttons to Example 2-3 to increment and decrement the slider value by one.

Event Handling and Simple Drawings with QPainter

Now that you know how to create widgets and how to use signals and slots, we can target our initial goal: writing a small paint program. In this section, we will learn how to use the class `QPainter`, which encapsulates Qt's fast drawing routines. At the end of this section, we will have a small program for scribbling your own drawings in a predefined color. You will also learn a bit about handling low-level events.

Even though it looks quite common at first, `QPainter` is one of Qt's strengths. It is a class that bundles many highly optimizing routines for drawing graphical objects, such as lines, circles, and Bezier curves. In addition, it supports different coordinate systems and geometrical transformations including rotating, scaling, and shearing. It also supports the use of these operations with widgets, pixmaps, metafiles, and printers alike.

Since we want to use the mouse for drawing, we have to learn how to react to mouse events that are not related to special widgets like push-buttons. We will have to be notified that the mouse has been pressed, released, or dragged in the plain void. You might suspect that we are in for more signals and slots now, but that is not the case. The developers of Qt have chosen another mechanism to report low-level events: virtual methods.

As you may recall from the last chapter, toolkits like wxWindows rely exclusively on virtual methods for event reporting. We have already explained why this is a bad idea: You always have to derive your own classes just to get notified about a button-click.

This criticism applies only to widgets that work out of the box, though: A push-button does everything itself. When the user clicks on it, it changes its appearance accordingly and notifies the application program via a signal. When it is obscured by some other window and later unhidden again, it automatically redisplays itself without help from the application or the window system.

This situation is different in roll-your-own widgets. You have to derive your widget from QWidget anyway to handle the redisplay, and if you already have derived your own class, it does not matter much if you override some virtual methods for low-level events like mouse movements and key-presses.

Some Qt programming beginners are confused as to why Qt has two ways to report user interaction to the application: signals and virtual methods. They are not sure in which case Qt uses which method. To use an analogy from language, look at low-level events like mouse movements and key-presses as pure syntax: There is no meaning associated with them. On the other hand, pressing and releasing the mouse button over a push-button has semantics: Obviously the user wanted to click that button. These higher-level events are reported with signals, while low-level events like simple mouse movements are reported with virtual methods. We will call the former "semantic events" or "high-level events," and the latter "syntactic events" or "low-level events".

Let's plunge right into the code for the first iteration of our painting application. You can find it in Example 2-4 along with the output in Figure 2-6.

Example 2-4: qtscribble1.cpp: A first try at a painting program

```
 1 #include <qapplication.h>
 2 #include <qpainter.h>
 3 #include <qpixmap.h>
 4 #include <qwidget.h>
 5
 6 /**
 7  * A class that lets the user draw with the mouse. The
 8  * window knows how to redraw itself.
 9  */
10 class ScribbleWindow : public QWidget
11 {
12 public:
13    ScribbleWindow();
```

Example 2-4: qtscribble1.cpp: A first try at a painting program (continued)

```
14
15 protected:
16    virtual void mousePressEvent( QMouseEvent* );
17    virtual void mouseMoveEvent( QMouseEvent* );
18    virtual void paintEvent( QPaintEvent* );
19    virtual void resizeEvent( QResizeEvent* );
20
21 private:
22    QPoint _last;
23
24    QPixmap _buffer;
25 };
26
27 /** The constructor. Rather simple for now. */
28 ScribbleWindow::ScribbleWindow()
29 {
30    // don't blank the window before repainting
31    setBackgroundMode( NoBackground );
32 }
33
34
35 /**
36   * This virtual method is called whenever the user presses the
37   * mouse over the window. It just records the position of the mouse
38   * at the time of the click.
39   */
40 void ScribbleWindow::mousePressEvent( QMouseEvent* event )
41 {
42    _last = event->pos(); // retrieve the coordinates from the event
43 }
44
45
46 /**
47   * This virtual method is called whenever the user moves the mouse
48   * while the mouse button is pressed. If we had called
49   * setMouseTracking( true ) before, this method would also be called
50   * when the mouse was moved without any button pressed. We know that
51   * we haven't, and thus don't have to check whether any buttons are
52   * pressed.
53   */
54 void ScribbleWindow::mouseMoveEvent( QMouseEvent* event )
55 {
56    // create a QPainter object for drawing onto the window
57    QPainter windowpainter;
58    // and another QPainter object for drawing into an off-screen pixmap
59    QPainter bufferpainter;
60
61    // start painting
62    windowpainter.begin( this );     // this painter paints onto the window
63    bufferpainter.begin( &_buffer ); // and this one paints in the buffer
```

Example 2-4: qtscribble1.cpp: A first try at a painting program (continued)

```
64
65      // draw a line in both the window and the buffer
66      windowpainter.drawLine( _last, event->pos() );
67      bufferpainter.drawLine( _last, event->pos() );
68
69      // done with painting
70      windowpainter.end();
71      bufferpainter.end();
72
73      // remember the current mouse position
74      _last = event->pos();
75  }
76
77
78
79  /**
80    * This virtual method is called whenever the widget needs
81    * painting, for example, when it has been obscured and then revealed again.
82    */
83  void ScribbleWindow::paintEvent( QPaintEvent* event )
84  {
85      // copy the image from the buffer pixmap to the window
86      bitBlt( this, 0, 0, &_buffer );
87  }
88
89
90  /**
91    * This virtual method gets called whenever the window is resized. We
92    * use it to make sure that the off-screen buffer is always the same
93    * size as the window.
94    * In order to retain the original scribbling, it is first copied
95    * to a temporary buffer. After the main buffer has been resized and
96    * filled with white, the image is copied from the temporary buffer to
97    * the main buffer.
98    */
99  void ScribbleWindow::resizeEvent( QResizeEvent* event )
100 {
101     QPixmap save( _buffer );
102     _buffer.resize( event->size() );
103     _buffer.fill( white );
104     bitBlt( &_buffer, 0, 0, &save );
105 }
106
107
108 int main( int argc, char* argv[] )
109 {
110     QApplication myapp( argc, argv );
111
112     ScribbleWindow* mywidget = new ScribbleWindow();
113     mywidget->setGeometry( 50, 50, 400, 400 );
```

Example 2-4: qtscribble1.cpp: A first try at a painting program (continued)

```
114
115    myapp.setMainWidget( mywidget );
116    mywidget->show();
117    return myapp.exec();
118 }
```

Figure 2-6: Output from Example 2-4

In this example, we define a class called `ScribbleWindow` that is derived from `QWidget`. We override four virtual methods: `paintEvent()`, `mousePressEvent()`, `mouseMoveEvent()`, and `resizeEvent()`. The constructor only calls `setBackground-Mode( NoBackground )` to reduce flickering when the window is repainted.

In `mousePressEvent()`, we record that the mouse has been pressed at this position. When we receive notification that the mouse has been moved, we draw a line from this point to the new mouse position. This gives us a smooth, contiguous line instead of just a lot of scattered points.

`mouseMoveEvent()` is one of the most interesting methods in this example. Here it is again:

```
void ScribbleWindow::mouseMoveEvent( QMouseEvent* event )
{
    // create a QPainter object for drawing onto the window
    QPainter windowpainter;
    // and another QPainter object for drawing into an off-screen pixmap
    QPainter bufferpainter;
```

```
    // start painting
    windowpainter.begin( this );     // this painter paints onto the window
    bufferpainter.begin( &_buffer ); // and this one in the buffer

    // draw a line in both the window and the buffer
    windowpainter.drawLine( _last, event->pos() );
    bufferpainter.drawLine( _last, event->pos() );

    // done with painting
    windowpainter.end();
    bufferpainter.end();

    // remember the current mouse position
    _last = event->pos();
}
```

To explain why almost all the code here comes in two pairs, we have to talk about paint events.

Every widget should be able to paint itself. The window system usually does not help the widget to remember its contents when it becomes obscured.[8] Therefore, the widget has to remember whatever has been painted into it so that it can repaint itself whenever the window system sends it a paint event. There are several ways for a widget to remember its contents:

- It can use another off-screen buffer that is the same size as the widget that contains a copy of the widget contents. This off-screen buffer holds pixels just as the widget does, but it does not show them on-screen. Qt provides the class `QPixmap` for these off-screen buffers, which is like the `QWidget` derived from `QPaintDevice`, and can be used for drawing just like `QWidget` can. This is a simple technique, but it is only suitable for small programs. Another amount of memory proportional to the size of the widget is needed to store the buffer.

- The widget can represent its contents non-graphically. For example, in our program, we only work with lines between two points. We could maintain a list of the lines that the user has drawn, and restore the widget contents by reading this list and redrawing the lines. This method is mainly used in object-oriented drawing programs, such as CAD programs, because these programs have to save the drawn objects anyway.

- The third possibility is saving the drawings in a non-graphical way. Instead of drawing into a `QWidget` or a `QPixmap` object, we can draw into a `QPicture` object that records the drawing actions, such as "drawing a line from (10,10) to (20,20)", rather than the pixels.

Back to `ScribbleWindow::mouseMoveEvent()`. Since we want to paint in two different QPaintDevices—the window and the pixmap that is serving as an off-screen buffer—we need two `QPainter` objects. You may draw things with a `QPainter` object

---

8   Some X servers for the X Window System on Unix platforms have a backing store that does this, but you cannot expect your user to have the necessary hardware to utilize it.

only after you have "opened" it for painting, and you must "close" it afterwards. That's what the methods `QPainter::begin()` and `QPainter::end()` are for. `QPainter::begin()` expects a pointer to a `QPaintDevice` (e.g. a `QWidget` or a `QPixmap`) object on which the `QPainter` will draw.[9] We draw our line in both the window and the buffer and finally record the new mouse position as a starting point for the next line.

If we had used the second of the three techniques mentioned earlier, we would not have any drawing operations here. Instead, we would just record what to draw later and make all the drawing operations in `paintEvent()`.

Let's move on to `ScribbleWindow::paintEvent()`, which is repeated here:

```
void ScribbleWindow::paintEvent( QPaintEvent* event )
{
  // copy the image from the buffer pixmap to the window
  bitBlt( this, 0, 0, &_buffer );
}
```

This method is called whenever the window needs refreshing. Since we have an exact copy of the image that the window should show in our buffer, we simply copy this into the window. For this, we use the function `bitBlt()` whenever rectangular areas of pixels should be copied from one place to another. This function supports different raster-operations, which allow logical operations between the pixel source and the destination. See the Qt documentation on `QPaintDevice` for more information.

Since we repaint the whole window anyway by copying the whole buffer over, it is absolutely not necessary that Qt clears the window before calling `paintEvent()`. To turn off this default behavior, we have called `setBackgroundMode( NoBackground )` in the constructor of our class. This tells Qt never to clear the window when repainting is necessary. (For more about this technique, see the "Double Buffering and Other Nifty Techniques" section in chapter 9.)

Finally, we have to look at the method `ScribbleWindow::resizeEvent()`:

```
void ScribbleWindow::resizeEvent( QResizeEvent* event )
{
  QPixmap save( _buffer );
  _buffer.resize( event->size() );
  _buffer.fill( white );
  bitBlt( &_buffer, 0, 0, &save );
}
```

In this method, we make sure that the off-screen buffer is always the same size as the window itself. This is important, because the buffer must be able to contain all the pixels drawn into the window. If you never resize the window yourself, this method will only be called once when `ScribbleWindow::setGeometry()` is called from within `main()`. However, if you do resize the window, this method is called each time you do so.

---

9   If you just create the `QPainter` object for a few drawing operations on a single window and then throw it away, you can just pass the `QPaintDevice` object to draw on in the constructor of `QPainter`. In this case, you do not need the calls to `begin()` and `end()`.

There is an additional twist here: If you resize a pixmap object to a size that is larger than the previous one, the additional pixels have an undefined value. Therefore, we fill the whole pixmap with white. Unfortunately, this also destroys the scribblings made so far, and since the user will not expect his scribblings to disappear just because he resized the window, we have to think of a solution. In this case, we chose the easiest one: The old state of the buffer pixmap is simply copied over to a new pixmap `save` as a temporary buffer. After the buffer pixmap `_buffer` has been cleared, we simply copy over the saved data from the temporary buffer with `bitBlt()`. If your buffer is already large, you might not want to do this. In this case, you could fill only the new parts of `_buffer`, but this requires more code.

Exercises

1. Extend the program in Example 2-4 so that it draws thicker lines when you draw with the right mouse button. You can find out how to differentiate between mouse buttons in the documentation of `QMouseEvent`.

2. Extend the program in Example 2-4 so that you can change line colors with key-presses. You have to implement `ScribbleWindow::keyPressEvent( QKey-Event* )` to be notified about key presses in the scribble window. You can use the method `QPainter::setPen()` to choose another drawing color. You can pass it either a `QColor` object that you have created yourself or you can pass just one of the predefined color objects: `black`, `white`, `darkGray`, `gray`, `lightGray`, `red`, `green`, `blue`, `cyan`, `magenta`, `yellow`, `darkRed`, `darkGreen`, `darkBlue`, `dark-Cyan`, `darkMagenta`, `darkYellow`. You do not need to provide access to all the colors—pick three or four that you like best.

3. Extend the program in Example 2-4 so that double-clicking the mouse in the window exits the program. You can be notified about double-clicks by overriding `QWidget::mouseDoubleClickEvent()` in the class `ScribbleWindow`. Closing the application can be done by calling `qApp->quit()`.

Learning More About Qt

By now, you know the basics of programming with Qt, but we have only begun. In this chapter, we continue to work on our painting program by adding some features like menus and file access. Stay tuned!

Adding Menus

In this section, you will learn how to work with menus. Qt menus mainly consist of two classes: QMenuBar and QPopupMenu. Both are derived from a common base class, QMenuData. Because of this, working with menu bars and pop-up menus is very similar. A menu bar serves as a container for its menus which are just objects of type QPopupMenu. These menus can have other submenus, again objects of type QPopupMenu. In addition, you can also pop up pop-up menus directly, for example when the user presses the right mouse button.

For our painting program, we will define three menus for now: a File menu that will currently only contain a Quit entry, a Color menu that will allow the user to choose the painting color, and a Help menu that will only contain an About entry. We'll add more items to these menus later.

Again, we first present you with the complete code and tell you how it works afterwards. The code is in Example 3-1, its output in Figure 3-1.

Example 3-1: qtscribble2.cpp: Adding a menu bar to our painting application

```
1 #include <qapplication.h>
2 #include <qmenubar.h>
3 #include <qmessagebox.h>
4 #include <qpainter.h>
5 #include <qpixmap.h>
6 #include <qpopupmenu.h>
7 #include <qwidget.h>
```

Example 3-1: qtscribble2.cpp: Adding a menu bar to our painting application (continued)

```
 8
 9 enum MenuIDs{
10     COLOR_MENU_ID_BLACK,
11     COLOR_MENU_ID_RED,
12     COLOR_MENU_ID_BLUE,
13     COLOR_MENU_ID_GREEN,
14     COLOR_MENU_ID_YELLOW };
15
16 /**
17  * A class that lets the user draw with the mouse. The
18  * window knows how to redraw itself.
19  */
20 class ScribbleWindow : public QWidget
21 {
22   Q_OBJECT  // necessary because ScribbleWindow contains slots
23
24 public:
25   ScribbleWindow();
26   ~ScribbleWindow();
27
28 protected:
29   virtual void mousePressEvent( QMouseEvent* );
30   virtual void mouseMoveEvent( QMouseEvent* );
31   virtual void paintEvent( QPaintEvent* );
32   virtual void resizeEvent( QResizeEvent* );
33
34 private slots:
35   void slotAbout();
36   void slotAboutQt();
37   void slotColorMenu( int );
38
39 private:
40   QPoint _last;
41   QColor _currentcolor;
42
43   QPixmap _buffer;
44   QMenuBar* _menubar;
45   QPopupMenu* _filemenu;
46   QPopupMenu* _colormenu;
47   QPopupMenu* _helpmenu;
48 };
49
50 #include "qtscribble2.moc"
51
52 /** The constructor. Initializes the member variables and the menu
53  * system.
54  */
55 ScribbleWindow::ScribbleWindow()
56 {
57   _currentcolor = black;
```

Example 3-1: qtscribble2.cpp: Adding a menu bar to our painting application (continued)

```
58
59    // don't blank the window before repainting
60    setBackgroundMode( NoBackground );
61
62    /* The next lines build the menu bar. We first create the menus
63     * one by one, then add them to the menu bar. */
64    _filemenu = new QPopupMenu; // create a file menu
65    _filemenu->insertItem( "&Quit", qApp, SLOT( quit() ) );
66
67    _colormenu = new QPopupMenu; // create a color menu
68    _colormenu->insertItem( "B&lack", COLOR_MENU_ID_BLACK );
69    _colormenu->insertItem( "&Red", COLOR_MENU_ID_RED );
70    _colormenu->insertItem( "&Blue", COLOR_MENU_ID_BLUE );
71    _colormenu->insertItem( "&Green", COLOR_MENU_ID_GREEN );
72    _colormenu->insertItem( "&Yellow", COLOR_MENU_ID_YELLOW );
73    QObject::connect( _colormenu, SIGNAL( activated( int ) ),
74                      this, SLOT( slotColorMenu( int ) ) );
75
76    _helpmenu = new QPopupMenu; // create a help menu
77    _helpmenu->insertItem( "&About QtScribble", this, SLOT( slotAbout() ) );
78    _helpmenu->insertItem( "About &Qt", this, SLOT( slotAboutQt() ) );
79
80    _menubar = new QMenuBar( this ); // create a menu bar
81    _menubar->insertItem( "&File", _filemenu );
82    _menubar->insertItem( "&Color", _colormenu );
83    _menubar->insertSeparator();
84    _menubar->insertItem( "&Help", _helpmenu );
85  }
86
87
88  /**
89   * The destructor. Does nothing for now.
90   */
91  ScribbleWindow::~ScribbleWindow()
92  {
93  }
94
95
96  /**
97   * This virtual method is called whenever the user presses the
98   * mouse over the window. It just records the position of the mouse
99   * at the time of the click.
100  */
101 void ScribbleWindow::mousePressEvent( QMouseEvent* event )
102 {
103   _last = event->pos(); // retrieve the coordinates from the event
104 }
105
106
107 /**
```

Example 3-1: qtscribble2.cpp: Adding a menu bar to our painting application (continued)

```
108    * This virtual method is called whenever the user moves the mouse
109    * while the mouse button is pressed (this is also known as
110    * "dragging"). If we had called setMouseTracking( true ) before,
111    * this method would also be called when the mouse was moved without
112    * any button pressed. We know that we haven't, and thus don't have
113    * to check whether any buttons are pressed.
114    */
115   void ScribbleWindow::mouseMoveEvent( QMouseEvent* event )
116   {
117      // create a QPainter object for drawing onto the window
118      QPainter windowpainter;
119      // and another QPainter object for drawing into an off-screen pixmap
120      QPainter bufferpainter;
121
122      // start painting
123      windowpainter.begin( this );     // this painter paints onto the window
124      bufferpainter.begin( &_buffer ); // and this one in the buffer
125
126      // set a standard pen with the currently selected color
127      windowpainter.setPen( _currentcolor );
128      bufferpainter.setPen( _currentcolor );
129
130      // draw a line in both the window and the buffer
131      windowpainter.drawLine( _last, event->pos() );
132      bufferpainter.drawLine( _last, event->pos() );
133
134      // done with painting
135      windowpainter.end();
136      bufferpainter.end();
137
138      // remember the current mouse position
139      _last = event->pos();
140   }
141
142
143
144   /**
145      * This virtual method is called whenever the widget needs
146      * painting, such as when it has been obscured and then revealed again.
147      */
148   void ScribbleWindow::paintEvent( QPaintEvent* event )
149   {
150      // copy the image from the buffer pixmap to the window
151      bitBlt( this, 0, 0, &_buffer );
152   }
153
154
155   /**
156      * This virtual method is called whenever the window is resized. We
157      * use it to make sure that the off-screen buffer is always the same
```

Example 3-1: qtscribble2.cpp: Adding a menu bar to our painting application (continued)

```
158    * size as the window.
159    * In order to retain the original drawing, it is first copied
160    * to a temporary buffer. After the main buffer has been resized and
161    * filled with white, the image is copied from the temporary buffer to
162    * the main buffer.
163    */
164   void ScribbleWindow::resizeEvent( QResizeEvent* event )
165   {
166     QPixmap save( _buffer );
167     _buffer.resize( event->size() );
168     _buffer.fill( white );
169     bitBlt( &_buffer, 0, 0, &save );
170   }
171
172
173   void ScribbleWindow::slotAbout()
174   {
175     QMessageBox::information( this, "About QtScribble 2",
176                               "This is the QtScribble 2 application\n"
177                               "Copyright 1998 by Matthias Kalle Dalheimer\n"
178                               );
179   }
180
181
182   void ScribbleWindow::slotAboutQt()
183   {
184     QMessageBox::aboutQt( this, "About Qt" );
185   }
186
187
188   void ScribbleWindow::slotColorMenu( int item )
189   {
190     switch( item )
191       {
192       case COLOR_MENU_ID_BLACK:
193         _currentcolor = black;
194         break;
195       case COLOR_MENU_ID_RED:
196         _currentcolor = darkRed;
197         break;
198       case COLOR_MENU_ID_BLUE:
199         _currentcolor = darkBlue;
200         break;
201       case COLOR_MENU_ID_GREEN:
202         _currentcolor = darkGreen;
203         break;
204       case COLOR_MENU_ID_YELLOW:
205         _currentcolor = yellow;
206         break;
207       }
```

Example 3-1: qtscribble2.cpp: Adding a menu bar to our painting application (continued)

```
208 }
209
210
211 int main( int argc, char* argv[] )
212 {
213   QApplication myapp( argc, argv );
214
215   ScribbleWindow* mywidget = new ScribbleWindow();
216   mywidget->setGeometry( 50, 50, 400, 400 );
217
218   myapp.setMainWidget( mywidget );
219   mywidget->show();
220   return myapp.exec();
221 }
```

Figure 3-1: Output of Example 3-1

The first thing to note is the inclusion of the macro Q_OBJECT in the class declaration of ScribbleWindow. It is needed, because this class uses the signal-and-slot mechanism. It does so by providing three slots: slotAbout(), slotAboutQt() and slotColor-Menu().

The constructor is much larger now, because we create our menu system here:

```
ScribbleWindow::ScribbleWindow()
{
  // initialize member variables
  _currentcolor = black;

  // don't blank the window before repainting
  setBackgroundMode( NoBackground );

  /* The next lines build up the menu bar. We first create the menus
   * one by one and add them afterwards to the menu bar. */
  _filemenu = new QPopupMenu; // create a file menu
  _filemenu->insertItem( "&Quit", qApp, SLOT( quit() ) );

  _colormenu = new QPopupMenu; // create a color menu
  _colormenu->insertItem( "B&lack", COLOR_MENU_ID_BLACK );
  _colormenu->insertItem( "&Red", COLOR_MENU_ID_RED );
  _colormenu->insertItem( "&Blue", COLOR_MENU_ID_BLUE );
  _colormenu->insertItem( "&Green", COLOR_MENU_ID_GREEN );
  _colormenu->insertItem( "&Yellow", COLOR_MENU_ID_YELLOW );
  QObject::connect( _colormenu, SIGNAL( activated( int ) ),
                    this, SLOT( slotColorMenu( int ) ) );

  _helpmenu = new QPopupMenu; // create a help menu
  _helpmenu->insertItem( "&About QtScribble", this, SLOT( slotAbout() ) );
  _helpmenu->insertItem( "About &Qt", this, SLOT( slotAboutQt() ) );

  _menubar = new QMenuBar( this ); // create a menu bar
  _menubar->insertItem( "&File", _filemenu );
  _menubar->insertItem( "&Color", _colormenu );
  _menubar->insertSeparator();
  _menubar->insertItem( "&Help", _helpmenu );
}
```

First, we create each menu by creating objects of class `QPopupMenu` and adding menu entries with `insertItem()`. Then, we create an object of class `QMenuBar`, and insert the menus into this menu bar. You could also use the class `QMainWindow`, which can automatically provide an empty menu bar and arrange it in the application window, together with any tool bars and status bars that you might have. For now, we will insert our menu bar by hand.

There are nine different overloaded versions of `QMenuData::insertItem()`, most of which have default arguments. The version you have to use depends on two things: whether you want to insert a string, a pixmap, or both in the menu, and how you want to be notified when a certain menu entry is chosen. You can either name a slot for a certain menu entry, or you can just assign ID numbers to the entries and connect to a signal for the whole menu. The ID of the selected entry will then be passed to your slot. We will use it there to determine which menu entry has been selected.

The global variable qApp is declared and defined in *qapplication.h*, and is guaranteed to hold a pointer to the only object of the class QApplication. You can always use this to refer to your application object.

In our example, we use only text as entries (using pixmaps will be one of the exercises), but we use both methods of notification. For example, look at the entries in the Help menu. After the text for the entry, there are parameters for the object that contains the slot, and the name of the slot itself. Whenever the menu entry in question is selected, the named slot will be invoked. The parameters of this form are like the "second half" of a call to QObject::connect(). In fact, there is also a method QMenu-Data::connectItem(), which you can use to connect a slot to a menu entry after it has been inserted.

The second method is used for the Color menu. The menu entries are inserted along with an ID number, and the whole menu is connected via its activated(int) signal to the slot slotColorMenu(). As you would expect, the parameter of the signal contains the ID number of the menu entry that was selected. If you peek ahead to the slot slot-ColorMenu(), you will find a switch statement that chooses a color based on this ID. If you want to be really clever, you could create an array of colors that uses the menu ID as an index, thus saving this switch statement. This would not necessarily lead to code that is easier to read and understand, however.

It's not always easy to decide whether you should use one slot method for each entry in a menu or one slot method for the whole menu. A guideline could be that whenever the menu entries denote parameters of the same function—as in the case of the color menu (where the entries could be considered color parameters of the function "change-Color")—you should use only one slot. On the other hand, if the entries denote completely different functions, such as "search and replace" and "paste" in an Edit menu, it's probably better to use different methods.

You might have wondered why there are ampersand characters in the text for the menu entries. These denote shortcuts; you can use the letter after the ampersand character to manage the menu via the keyboard. For example, when the File menu is popped up, you can move to the Blue entry by pressing the b key.

In this version of the painting application, we have also defined a destructor, but for now it is not yet needed. We leave it blank.

The next changes are in the method ScribbleWindow::mouseMoveEvent():

```
void ScribbleWindow::mouseMoveEvent( QMouseEvent* event )
{
    // create a QPainter object for drawing onto the window
    QPainter windowpainter;
    // and another QPainter object for drawing into an off-screen pixmap
    QPainter bufferpainter;

    // start painting
    windowpainter.begin( this );     // this painter paints onto the window
    bufferpainter.begin( &_buffer ); // and this one in the buffer
```

```
    // set a standard pen with the currently selected color
    windowpainter.setPen( _currentcolor );
    bufferpainter.setPen( _currentcolor );

    // draw a line in both the window and the buffer
    windowpainter.drawLine( _last, event->pos() );
    bufferpainter.drawLine( _last, event->pos() );

    // done with painting
    windowpainter.end();
    bufferpainter.end();

    // remember the current mouse position
    _last = event->pos();
}
```

We assign the `color` that has been selected via the `color` menu to the two `QPainter` objects in use here.

Even though there are no changes to `ScribbleWindow::resizeEvent()`, we would like to draw your attention to something you might not have thought about yet. The menu bar is a child of the scribble window, and thus occupies some of its space in which the user cannot draw. This is no problem, since the user can resize the window when more space is needed. In a real application, however, we would have to take this into account. What would be needed here is called "geometry management": the black art of arranging the widgets that form a GUI so that each widget gets the space and position it needs, and the window still looks okay when it is resized. You can't see it, but we already have a bit of geometry management going on here: the menu bar automatially resizes itself so that it always has the same width as its parent.

In the method `slotAbout()`, you make the acquaintance of another class, `QMessageBox`, which is used to communicate important information to the user:

```
    void ScribbleWindow::slotAbout()
    {
      QMessageBox::information( this, "About QtScribble 2",
                               "This is the QtScribble 2 application\n"
                               "Copyright 1998 by Matthias Kalle Dalheimer\n"
                               );
    }
```

You probably won't have any problems recognizing a message box when you see one. Although you can put together a `QMessageBox` all on your own by adding child widgets, it is mostly used by its comfortable static methods `information()`, `warning()`, `error()` and `fatal()`. You pass at least the parent widget, the title string, and the text of the message. You can also pass the text that should appear on up to three buttons. In `ScribbleWindow::slotAboutQt()`, we use another static method of `QMessageBox`, `aboutQt()`, which shows a dialog with information about Qt. You can add this to your help menu.

The method `ScribbleWindow::slotColorMenu()` serves as the slot for a whole menu:

```
void ScribbleWindow::slotColorMenu( int item )
{
  switch( item )
    {
    case COLOR_MENU_ID_BLACK:
      _currentcolor = black;
      break;
    case COLOR_MENU_ID_RED:
      _currentcolor = darkRed;
      break;
    case COLOR_MENU_ID_BLUE:
      _currentcolor = darkBlue;
      break;
    case COLOR_MENU_ID_GREEN:
      _currentcolor = darkGreen;
      break;
    case COLOR_MENU_ID_YELLOW:
      _currentcolor = yellow;
      break;
    }
}
```

The parameter passed is the ID number of the menu entry selected. It is a good idea to use symbolic constants, both when you insert the entries into the menu and when you react to menu selections. This way, your program won't get out of sync if you add new menu entries in between.

You now know what is going on in the code, but you might not yet know how exactly to compile it. Since we are using slots here, we have to use *moc*. You have probably already seen the line

```
#include "qtscribble2.moc"
```

This includes the code generated by *moc*. This file can be generated by issuing

```
moc -o qtscribble.moc qtscribble2.cpp
```

on the command line. You might want to add such a line to your makefiles or to your build environment. I would like to emphasize that I still consider it a better style to compile the *moc*-generated file separately and link the resulting object file to your application. Alas, this works only when you have the class declaration in a separate header file, which is not really suitable for toy programs found in books like this one. This is why I will continue this style of including the *moc*-generated files. Keep in mind, though, that the other style is preferable and scales better to larger projects.

You now know how to create a menu bar for your application. This lets you provide many functions to your users, since menus are still the best way to organize large amounts of functionality. In the next section, we'll expand our painting application further by adding scroll bars.

Exercises

1.   Replace the text entries in the `color` menu in Example 3-1 by pixmaps. To do this, you will have to create a `QPixmap` object for every entry, give it a suitable size, and fill it with the respective color. Here is a code snippet that you might use:

```
redpixmap = new QPixmap( 20, 20 );
redpixmap.fill( red );
```

2.   Change the code from the previous exercise again so that the `color` menu shows colored pixmaps and text together.

3.   Add another menu called `Pen width` which lets the user select pen thicknesses (for example 1, 2, and 4; pen width 3 looks nasty). You can set a pen thickness in a `QPainter` object with the following code:

```
painter.setPen( QPen( color, width ) );
```

With variables in place, this might read:

```
painter.setPen( QPen( red, 2 ) );
```

This creates a pen with the specified characteristics and assigns it to the `QPainter` object.

Adding a Scrolled View

The drawing area in a painting application should not be constrained by the size of the application window. With horizontal and vertical scroll bars, you can let the user draw into an area that is much bigger than the application window. Since version 1.40, Qt provides the class `QScrollView`. This class allows you to easily add scroll bars to your programs. You simply specify the widget you want to make scrollable, and `QScroll-View` does the rest for you. You can specify whether the scroll bars should be always visible, always off (in this case, you will have to provide another means of scrolling, such as with the keyboard), or automatic. Automatic scroll bars are only visible when the visible area of the scrolled widget is smaller than the widget itself; in other words, when there is something to scroll.

The code in Example 3-2 whose output can be found in Figure 3-2 shows how to add a `QScrollView` to our painting application.

Example 3-2: qtscribble3.cpp: Painting application with scroll bars

```
1  #include <qapplication.h>
2  #include <qmenubar.h>
3  #include <qmessagebox.h>
4  #include <qpainter.h>
5  #include <qpixmap.h>
6  #include <qpopupmenu.h>
7  #include <qscrollview.h>
```

Example 3-2: qtscribble3.cpp: Painting application with scroll bars (continued)

```
 8 #include <qwidget.h>
 9
10 enum MenuIDs{
11     COLOR_MENU_ID_BLACK,
12     COLOR_MENU_ID_RED,
13     COLOR_MENU_ID_BLUE,
14     COLOR_MENU_ID_GREEN,
15     COLOR_MENU_ID_YELLOW };
16
17 /**
18  * A class that lets the user draw scribbles with the mouse. The
19  * window knows how to redraw itself.
20  */
21 class ScribbleArea : public QWidget
22 {
23   Q_OBJECT  // necessary because ScribbleArea contains a slot
24
25 public:
26   ScribbleArea();
27   ~ScribbleArea();
28
29 public slots:
30   void setColor( QColor );
31
32 protected:
33   virtual void mousePressEvent( QMouseEvent* );
34   virtual void mouseMoveEvent( QMouseEvent* );
35   virtual void paintEvent( QPaintEvent* );
36   virtual void resizeEvent( QResizeEvent* );
37
38 private:
39   QPoint _last;
40   QColor _currentcolor;
41
42   QPixmap _buffer;
43 };
44
45
46 class ScribbleWindow : public QWidget
47 {
48   Q_OBJECT
49
50 public:
51   ScribbleWindow();
52   ~ScribbleWindow();
53
54 private slots:
55   void slotAbout();
56   void slotAboutQt();
57   void slotColorMenu( int );
58
```

Example 3-2: qtscribble3.cpp: Painting application with scroll bars (continued)

```
59  signals:
60     void colorChanged( QColor );
61
62  protected:
63     virtual void resizeEvent( QResizeEvent* );
64
65  private:
66     QMenuBar* _menubar;
67     QPopupMenu* _filemenu;
68     QPopupMenu* _colormenu;
69     QPopupMenu* _helpmenu;
70     QScrollView* _scrollview;
71     ScribbleArea* _scribblearea;
72  };
73
74
75  #include "qtscribble3.moc"
76
77  /**
78   * The constructor. Initializes the member variables.
79   */
80  ScribbleArea::ScribbleArea()
81  {
82    // initialize member variables
83    _currentcolor = black;
84
85    // don't blank the window before repainting
86    setBackgroundMode( NoBackground );
87  }
88
89
90  /**
91   * The destructor. Does nothing in this version.
92   */
93  ScribbleArea::~ScribbleArea()
94  {
95  }
96
97
98  /**
99   * This slot sets the current color for the scribble area. It will be
100  * connected with the colorChanged( QColor ) signal from the
101  * ScribbleWindow.
102  */
103 void ScribbleArea::setColor( QColor new_color )
104 {
105   _currentcolor = new_color;
106 }
107
108
109 /**
```

Example 3-2: qtscribble3.cpp: Painting application with scroll bars (continued)

```
110    * This virtual method is called whenever the user presses the
111    * mouse over the window. It records the position of the mouse
112    * at the time of the click.
113    */
114 void ScribbleArea::mousePressEvent( QMouseEvent* event )
115 {
116    _last = event->pos(); // retrieve the coordinates from the event
117 }
118
119
120 /**
121    * This virtual method is called whenever the user moves the mouse
122    * while the mouse button is pressed. If we had called
123    * setMouseTracking( true ) before, this method would also be called
124    * when the mouse was moved without any button pressed. We know that
125    * we haven't, and thus don't have to check whether any buttons are
126    * pressed.
127    */
128 void ScribbleArea::mouseMoveEvent( QMouseEvent* event )
129 {
130    // create a QPainter object for drawing onto the window
131    QPainter windowpainter;
132    // and another QPainter object for drawing into an off-screen pixmap
133    QPainter bufferpainter;
134
135    // start painting
136    windowpainter.begin( this );     // this painter paints onto the window
137    bufferpainter.begin( &_buffer ); // and this one in the buffer
138
139    // set a standard pen with the currently selected color
140    windowpainter.setPen( _currentcolor );
141    bufferpainter.setPen( _currentcolor );
142
143    // draw a line in both the window and the buffer
144    windowpainter.drawLine( _last, event->pos() );
145    bufferpainter.drawLine( _last, event->pos() );
146
147    // done with painting
148    windowpainter.end();
149    bufferpainter.end();
150
151    // remember the current mouse position
152    _last = event->pos();
153 }
154
155
156
157 /**
158    * This virtual method is called whenever the widget needs
159    * painting, such as when it has been obscured and then revealed again.
```

Example 3-2: qtscribble3.cpp: Painting application with scroll bars (continued)

```
160   */
161   void ScribbleArea::paintEvent( QPaintEvent* event )
162   {
163     // copy the image from the buffer pixmap to the window
164     bitBlt( this, 0, 0, &_buffer );
165   }
166
167
168   /**
169    * This virtual method is called whenever the window is resized. We
170    * use it to make sure the off-screen buffer is always the same
171    * size as the window.
172    * To retain the original drawing, it is first copied
173    * to a temporary buffer. After the main buffer has been resized and
174    * filled with white, the image is copied from the temporary buffer to
175    * the main buffer.
176    */
177   void ScribbleArea::resizeEvent( QResizeEvent* event )
178   {
179     QPixmap save( _buffer );
180     _buffer.resize( event->size() );
181     _buffer.fill( white );
182     bitBlt( &_buffer, 0, 0, &save );
183   }
184
185
186   ScribbleWindow::ScribbleWindow()
187   {
188     /* The next few lines build the menu bar. We first create the menus
189      * one by one, then add them to the menu bar. */
190     _filemenu = new QPopupMenu; // create a file menu
191     _filemenu->insertItem( "&Quit", qApp, SLOT( quit() ) );
192
193     _colormenu = new QPopupMenu; // create a color menu
194     _colormenu->insertItem( "B&lack", COLOR_MENU_ID_BLACK );
195     _colormenu->insertItem( "&Red", COLOR_MENU_ID_RED );
196     _colormenu->insertItem( "&Blue", COLOR_MENU_ID_BLUE );
197     _colormenu->insertItem( "&Green", COLOR_MENU_ID_GREEN );
198     _colormenu->insertItem( "&Yellow", COLOR_MENU_ID_YELLOW );
199     QObject::connect( _colormenu, SIGNAL( activated( int ) ),
200                       this, SLOT( slotColorMenu( int ) ) );
201
202     _helpmenu = new QPopupMenu; // create a help menu
203     _helpmenu->insertItem( "&About QtScribble", this, SLOT( slotAbout() ) );
204     _helpmenu->insertItem( "About &Qt", this, SLOT( slotAboutQt() ) );
205
206     _menubar = new QMenuBar( this ); // create a menu bar
207     _menubar->insertItem( "&File", _filemenu );
208     _menubar->insertItem( "&Color", _colormenu );
209     _menubar->insertSeparator();
```

Example 3-2: qtscribble3.cpp: Painting application with scroll bars (continued)

```
210    _menubar->insertItem( "&Help", _helpmenu );
211
212    /* We create a QScrollView and a ScribbleArea. The ScribbleArea will
213     * be managed by the scroll view.*/
214    _scrollview = new QScrollView( this );
215    _scrollview->setGeometry( 0, _menubar->height(),
216                              width(), height() - _menubar->height() );
217    _scribblearea = new ScribbleArea();
218    _scribblearea->setGeometry( 0, 0, 1000, 1000 );
219    _scrollview->addChild( _scribblearea );
220    QObject::connect( this, SIGNAL( colorChanged( QColor ) ),
221                      _scribblearea, SLOT( setColor( QColor ) ) );
222 }
223
224
225 ScribbleWindow::~ScribbleWindow()
226 {
227 }
228
229
230 void ScribbleWindow::resizeEvent( QResizeEvent* event )
231 {
232   /* When the whole window is resized, we have to rearrange the geometry
233    * in the ScribbleWindow as well. Note that the ScribbleArea does not need
234    * to be changed. */
235   _scrollview->setGeometry( 0, _menubar->height(),
236                             width(), height() - _menubar->height() );
237 }
238
239
240 void ScribbleWindow::slotAbout()
241 {
242   QMessageBox::information( this, "About QtScribble 3",
243                            "This is the QtScribble 3 application\n"
244                            "Copyright 1998 by Matthias Kalle Dalheimer\n"
245                            );
246 }
247
248
249 void ScribbleWindow::slotAboutQt()
250 {
251   QMessageBox::aboutQt( this, "About Qt" );
252 }
253
254
255 void ScribbleWindow::slotColorMenu( int item )
256 {
257   switch( item )
258     {
259     case COLOR_MENU_ID_BLACK:
```

Example 3-2: qtscribble3.cpp: Painting application with scroll bars (continued)

```
260          emit colorChanged( black );
261             break;
262      case COLOR_MENU_ID_RED:
263          emit colorChanged( darkRed );
264             break;
265      case COLOR_MENU_ID_BLUE:
266          emit colorChanged( darkBlue );
267             break;
268      case COLOR_MENU_ID_GREEN:
269          emit colorChanged( darkGreen );
270             break;
271      case COLOR_MENU_ID_YELLOW:
272          emit colorChanged( yellow );
273             break;
274        }
275 }
276
277
278
279 int main( int argc, char* argv[] )
280 {
281   QApplication myapp( argc, argv );
282
283   ScribbleWindow* mywidget = new ScribbleWindow();
284   mywidget->setGeometry( 50, 50, 400, 400 );
285
286   myapp.setMainWidget( mywidget );
287   mywidget->show();
288   return myapp.exec();
289 }
```

The first thing we do in this code is fix a fundamental design flaw we made in Example 3-1. Making the menu a child of the widget in which the user draws was a bad idea as we already have seen. Until now, the only problem was that the menu bar obscured a part of the drawing area, making it unavailable for drawing. With the new scrolled view, we have an additional problem: If the menu bar is still a child of the drawing area, which is the widget we want to scroll, the menu bar would scroll along with the rest! Clearly, this is unacceptable.

We fix this by renaming ScribbleWindow to ScribbleArea, and then introducing a new ScribbleWindow class. This class serves as a common parent for the menu bar and the drawing area. ScribbleArea retains most of its methods, since the drawing code is still valid. ScribbleWindow has two children, the menu bar and the QScroll-View object, which itself manages the ScribbleArea.

We don't have to do much with the QScrollView object to use it. It has quite an impressive interface, but for the simple application we are writing here, simply creating it and assigning the widget to be scrolled with addChild() is enough (line 219).

Figure 3-2: Output of Example 3-2

One other major change to Example 3-1 is made here: the menu system. Since the new ScribbleWindow is now the parent of the menu bar, the menu system is created and destroyed here, and it seems only reasonable to have the slots for the menus here, too. For slotAbout() and slotAboutQt(), this is no problem at all, but slotColor-Menu() requires more thought.

The only thing slotColorMenu() does is set the variable _currentcolor. It does not make sense for ScribbleWindow to have this variable as a member, however, because it does not need to know about colors. Instead, this variable has been moved to ScribbleArea. Of course, it would have been possible to leave it where it is, making it available for the method ScribbleArea::mouseMoveEvent(), but this would not have been a good design.

Still, we would like to leave slotColorMenu() in ScribbleWindow, because that is where all the menu code is. The solution here is a technique called "signal forwarding". slotColorMenu() now emits the signal colorChanged(QColor) which is connected to the slot setColor(QColor) in the ScribbleArea object.

This way, the selection of the color is separated from its usage. Now we could replace ScribbleArea with something else and still keep the color menu. The new widget would not even have to name the slot setColor(QColor); only the call to QObject::connect() would have to be changed accordingly.

When you use pointers to types that are not built-in, as we are doing here, you have to ensure that the object the pointer references stays valid and is not destroyed, because the receiver could still be using it. We are taking the safe road here by making a copy of the color object in `setColor( QColor )`, so `ScribbleWindow` could even delete it. Of course, we are currently only working with predefined colors, which are never deleted during the runtime of the application anyway.

You now know how to create scrolled views of your widget. There is no limit as to which widgets you could make scrollable. `QScrollView` is rather flexible, so you should read through its documentation to learn more about how it can be used.

Exercises

1. Make the drawing area scrollable with the cursor keys. For this, you will have to override the method `keyPressEvent()` in `ScribbleWindow` and call `QScroll-View::scrollBy()`.

2. Experiment with `QScrollView::setHScrollBarMode()` and `QScrollView::setVScrollBarMode()`. You can pass one of the values `Auto`, `AlwaysOn` and `AlwaysOff` to these methods. What are the dire consequences when you use `AlwaysOff`?

Adding a Context Menu

Our next improvement to the paint application will be a pop-up menu. A pop-up menu is a menu that pops up in response to a mouse click, usually with the right button, rather than being pulled down from a menu bar. Of course, many things could be added to such a pop-up menu, but for now we will content ourselves with one menu entry: `Clear`, which wipes the entire drawing off the screen.

Like the other menus in a menu bar, pop-up menus are objects of type `QPopupMenu`. The only difference is that you do not attach them to a `QMenuBar` object by calling `insertItem()`. Instead, you create a `QPopupMenu`, and show it afterwards by calling either `exec()` or `popup()`. The former performs a blocking pop-up of a pop-up menu, which means that the method call returns only when the menu has been popped down again either by selecting a menu entry or by clicking somewhere else. In contrast, `popup()` pops up the menu in a non-blocking fashion; the method call returns immediately.

No matter how you pop up the menu, you can always be notified by connecting to the normal signals `activated( int )` and `highlighted( int )`. In addition, when you pop up the menu in a blocked way via `exec()`, this method returns the item number of the item selected. It returns `-1` if no item has been selected, because the menu has been popped down by clicking somewhere else.

As you might already have guessed from the last two paragraphs, you need not be concerned with popping down pop-up menus. Qt does this automatically for you.

Normally, you will want to pop up a menu in response to a mouse-click at the position where the mouse was clicked. QPopupMenu makes it very easy to do this because both exec() and popup() accept a QPoint as the first parameter that indicates the *global* coordinates of the pop-up menu. Since you can get the global mouse coordinates by simply calling QCursor::pos(), all you have to do in response to a mouse-click is call:

```
mypopupmenu->exec( QCursor::pos() );
```

If you would rather have your pop-up menu aligned with some other widget, you must first translate that widget's coordinates to global coordinates with the method QWidget::mapToGlobal(). Assuming that you want to pop up a menu so that its upper left corner lies 10 points down and 10 points right from the upper left corner of the widget pointed to by mywidget, you would call:

```
mypopupmenu->exec( mywidget->mapToGlobal( QPoint( 10, 10 ) ) );
```

Example 3-3 shows what you need to do to add a pop-up menu. There is no screenshot for this program—you wouldn't see much difference.

Example 3-3: qtscribble4.cpp: Adding a pop-up menu to the paint program

```
 1  #include <qapplication.h>
 2  #include <qmenubar.h>
 3  #include <qmessagebox.h>
 4  #include <qpainter.h>
 5  #include <qpixmap.h>
 6  #include <qpopupmenu.h>
 7  #include <qscrollview.h>
 8  #include <qwidget.h>
 9
10  enum MenuIDs{
11      COLOR_MENU_ID_BLACK,
12      COLOR_MENU_ID_RED,
13      COLOR_MENU_ID_BLUE,
14      COLOR_MENU_ID_GREEN,
15      COLOR_MENU_ID_YELLOW };
16
17  /**
18   * A class that lets the user draw with the mouse. The
19   * window knows how to redraw itself.
20   */
21  class ScribbleArea : public QWidget
22  {
23    Q_OBJECT  // necessary because ScribbleArea contains a slot
24
25  public:
26    ScribbleArea();
27    ~ScribbleArea();
28
29  public slots:
30    void setColor( QColor );
31
```

Example 3-3: qtscribble4.cpp: Adding a pop-up menu to the paint program (continued)

```cpp
32 protected:
33   virtual void mousePressEvent( QMouseEvent* );
34   virtual void mouseMoveEvent( QMouseEvent* );
35   virtual void paintEvent( QPaintEvent* );
36   virtual void resizeEvent( QResizeEvent* );
37
38 private slots:
39   void slotClearArea();
40
41 private:
42   QPoint _last;
43   QColor _currentcolor;
44
45   QPixmap _buffer;
46   QPopupMenu* _popupmenu;
47 };
48
49
50 class ScribbleWindow : public QWidget
51 {
52   Q_OBJECT
53
54 public:
55   ScribbleWindow();
56   ~ScribbleWindow();
57
58 private slots:
59   void slotAbout();
60   void slotAboutQt();
61   void slotColorMenu( int );
62
63 signals:
64   void colorChanged( QColor );
65
66 protected:
67   virtual void resizeEvent( QResizeEvent* );
68
69 private:
70   QMenuBar* _menubar;
71   QPopupMenu* _filemenu;
72   QPopupMenu* _colormenu;
73   QPopupMenu* _helpmenu;
74   QScrollView* _scrollview;
75   ScribbleArea* _scribblearea;
76 };
77
78
79 #include "qtscribble4.moc"
80
81 /**
```

Example 3-3: qtscribble4.cpp: Adding a pop-up menu to the paint program (continued)

```
 82    * The constructor. Initializes the member variables, and creates a
 83    * pop-up menu that will pop up when the right mouse button is
 84    * clicked.
 85    */
 86   ScribbleArea::ScribbleArea()
 87   {
 88     // initialize member variables
 89     _currentcolor = black;
 90
 91     // don't blank the window before repainting
 92     setBackgroundMode( NoBackground );
 93
 94     // create a pop-up menu
 95     _popupmenu = new QPopupMenu();
 96     _popupmenu->insertItem( "&Clear", this, SLOT( slotClearArea() ) );
 97   }
 98
 99
100   /**
101    * The destructor. Deletes the pop-up menu.
102    */
103   ScribbleArea::~ScribbleArea()
104   {
105     delete _popupmenu;
106   }
107
108
109   /**
110    * This slot sets the current color for the drawing area. It will be
111    * connected with the colorChanged( QColor ) signal from the
112    * ScribbleWindow.
113    */
114   void ScribbleArea::setColor( QColor new_color )
115   {
116     _currentcolor = new_color;
117   }
118
119
120   /**
121    * This slot clears the drawing area by filling the off-screen buffer with
122    * white and copying it over to the window.
123    */
124   void ScribbleArea::slotClearArea()
125   {
126     // fill the off-screen buffer with plain white
127     _buffer.fill( white );
128
129     // and copy it over to the window
130     bitBlt( this, 0, 0, &_buffer );
131   }
```

Example 3-3: qtscribble4.cpp: Adding a pop-up menu to the paint program (continued)

```
132
133
134  /**
135   * This virtual method is called whenever the user presses the
136   * mouse over the window. When the right mouse button is pressed, it
137   * pops up a previously constructed pop-up menu. Otherwise, it just
138   * records the position of the mouse at the time of the click.
139   */
140  void ScribbleArea::mousePressEvent( QMouseEvent* event )
141  {
142    if( event->button() == RightButton )
143      _popupmenu->exec( QCursor::pos() );
144    else
145      {
146        _last = event->pos(); // retrieve the coordinates from the event
147      }
148  }
149
150
151  /**
152   * This virtual method is called whenever the user moves the mouse
153   * while the mouse button is pressed. If we had called
154   * setMouseTracking( true ) before, this method would also be called
155   * when the mouse was moved without any button pressed. We know that
156   * we haven't, and thus don't have to check whether any buttons are
157   * pressed.
158   */
159  void ScribbleArea::mouseMoveEvent( QMouseEvent* event )
160  {
161    // create a QPainter object for drawing onto the window
162    QPainter windowpainter;
163    // and another QPainter object for drawing into an off-screen pixmap
164    QPainter bufferpainter;
165
166    // start painting
167    windowpainter.begin( this );    // this painter paints onto the window
168    bufferpainter.begin( &_buffer ); // and this one in the buffer
169
170    // set a standard pen with the currently selected color
171    windowpainter.setPen( _currentcolor );
172    bufferpainter.setPen( _currentcolor );
173
174    // draw a line in both the window and the buffer
175    windowpainter.drawLine( _last, event->pos() );
176    bufferpainter.drawLine( _last, event->pos() );
177
178    // done with painting
179    windowpainter.end();
180    bufferpainter.end();
181
```

Example 3-3: qtscribble4.cpp: Adding a pop-up menu to the paint program (continued)

```
182    // remember the current mouse position
183    _last = event->pos();
184  }
185
186
187
188  /**
189   * This virtual method is called whenever the widget needs
190   * painting, such as when it has been obscured and then revealed again.
191   */
192  void ScribbleArea::paintEvent( QPaintEvent* event )
193  {
194    // copy the image from the buffer pixmap to the window
195    bitBlt( this, 0, 0, &_buffer );
196  }
197
198
199  /**
200   * This virtual method is called whenever the window is resized. We
201   * use it to make sure that the off-screen buffer is always the same
202   * size as the window.
203   * To retain the original drawing, it is first copied
204   * to a temporary buffer. After the main buffer has been resized and
205   * filled with white, the image is copied from the temporary buffer to
206   * the main buffer.
207   */
208  void ScribbleArea::resizeEvent( QResizeEvent* event )
209  {
210    QPixmap save( _buffer );
211    _buffer.resize( event->size() );
212    _buffer.fill( white );
213    bitBlt( &_buffer, 0, 0, &save );
214  }
215
216
217  ScribbleWindow::ScribbleWindow()
218  {
219    /* The next few lines build up the menu bar. We first create the menus
220     * one by one, then add them to the menu bar. */
221    _filemenu = new QPopupMenu; // create a file menu
222    _filemenu->insertItem( "&Quit", qApp, SLOT( quit() ) );
223
224    _colormenu = new QPopupMenu; // create a color menu
225    _colormenu->insertItem( "B&lack", COLOR_MENU_ID_BLACK );
226    _colormenu->insertItem( "&Red", COLOR_MENU_ID_RED );
227    _colormenu->insertItem( "&Blue", COLOR_MENU_ID_BLUE );
228    _colormenu->insertItem( "&Green", COLOR_MENU_ID_GREEN );
229    _colormenu->insertItem( "&Yellow", COLOR_MENU_ID_YELLOW );
230    QObject::connect( _colormenu, SIGNAL( activated( int ) ),
231                      this, SLOT( slotColorMenu( int ) ) );
```

Example 3-3: qtscribble4.cpp: Adding a pop-up menu to the paint program (continued)

```
232
233    _helpmenu = new QPopupMenu; // create a help menu
234    _helpmenu->insertItem( "&About QtScribble", this, SLOT( slotAbout() ) );
235    _helpmenu->insertItem( "About &Qt", this, SLOT( slotAboutQt() ) );
236
237    _menubar = new QMenuBar( this ); // create a menu bar
238    _menubar->insertItem( "&File", _filemenu );
239    _menubar->insertItem( "&Color", _colormenu );
240    _menubar->insertSeparator();
241    _menubar->insertItem( "&Help", _helpmenu );
242
243    /* We create a QScrollView and a ScribbleArea. The ScribbleArea will
244     * be managed by the scroll view.*/
245    _scrollview = new QScrollView( this );
246    _scrollview->setGeometry( 0, _menubar->height(),
247                              width(), height() - _menubar->height() );
248    _scribblearea = new ScribbleArea();
249    _scribblearea->setGeometry( 0, 0, 1000, 1000 );
250    _scrollview->addChild( _scribblearea );
251    QObject::connect( this, SIGNAL( colorChanged( QColor ) ),
252                      _scribblearea, SLOT( setColor( QColor ) ) );
253 }
254
255
256 ScribbleWindow::~ScribbleWindow()
257 {
258 }
259
260
261 void ScribbleWindow::resizeEvent( QResizeEvent* event )
262 {
263    /* When the whole window is resized, we have to rearrange the geometry
264     * in the ScribbleWindow as well. Note that the ScribbleArea does not need
265     * to be changed. */
266    _scrollview->setGeometry( 0, _menubar->height(),
267                              width(), height() - _menubar->height() );
268 }
269
270
271 void ScribbleWindow::slotAbout()
272 {
273    QMessageBox::information( this, "About QtScribble 4",
274                             "This is the QtScribble 4 application\n"
275                             "(C) 1998 by Matthias Kalle Dalheimer\n"
276                             );
277 }
278
279
280 void ScribbleWindow::slotAboutQt()
281 {
```

Example 3-3: qtscribble4.cpp: Adding a pop-up menu to the paint program (continued)

```
282    QMessageBox::aboutQt( this, "About Qt" );
283  }
284
285
286  void ScribbleWindow::slotColorMenu( int item )
287  {
288    switch( item )
289      {
290      case COLOR_MENU_ID_BLACK:
291          emit colorChanged( black );
292          break;
293      case COLOR_MENU_ID_RED:
294          emit colorChanged( darkRed );
295          break;
296      case COLOR_MENU_ID_BLUE:
297          emit colorChanged( darkBlue );
298          break;
299      case COLOR_MENU_ID_GREEN:
300          emit colorChanged( darkGreen );
301          break;
302      case COLOR_MENU_ID_YELLOW:
303          emit colorChanged( yellow );
304          break;
305      }
306  }
307
308
309
310  int main( int argc, char* argv[] )
311  {
312    QApplication myapp( argc, argv );
313
314    ScribbleWindow* mywidget = new ScribbleWindow();
315    mywidget->setGeometry( 50, 50, 400, 400 );
316
317    myapp.setMainWidget( mywidget );
318    mywidget->show();
319    return myapp.exec();
320  }
```

Note how little is needed to achieve this additional functionality. The class
ScribbleArea gets a new slot, slotClearArea(), which implements the new functionality. Also, popupmenu is added as a member. We do this because we can create the
pop-up menu when the scribble area is made, rather than creating and destroying it
every time it should be popped up. ScribbleWindow is not touched.

The pop-up menu is created in the constructor of ScribbleArea, and destroyed again
in the destructor. There is nothing special here, except the fact that the pop-up menu
has to be destroyed explicitly. Since it is not a child of the ScribbleArea object, it will
not be deleted automatically.

The new slot `slotClearArea()` is fairly obvious as well. The scribble area is cleared by filling the off-screen buffer with plain white, then copying that over to the window.

`ScribbleArea::mousePressEvent()` is the core of the new functionality:

```
void ScribbleArea::mousePressEvent( QMouseEvent* event )
{
  if( event->button() == RightButton )
    _popupmenu->exec( QCursor::pos() );
  else
    {
      _last = event->pos(); // retrieve the coordinates from the event
    }
}
```

Until now, we have simply noted the coordinates. Now we will check which button has been pressed. If it was the right button, we pop up the menu by calling `QPopup-Menu::exec()`. Otherwise, we record the coordinates as before.

Adding pop-up menus to your application is very easy. In fact, it is so easy that every application should have pop-up menus that are popped up when the right mouse button is clicked. The contents of these menus should be relative to the current state of the application and the mouse position. Adaptive menus like these are called "context menus". Users are so accustomed to context menus today that applications without them are often not accepted.

Exercise

Change the structure of the pop-up menu in Example 3-3 so that the popped up menu has two submenus. One submenu, `Edit`, should contain the `Clear` menu item from Example 3-3, another submenu, `Color`, should contain the entries from the `Color` menu in the menu bar.

File-I/O

In this section, we will explore some issues related to input and output of data to and from files. Our goal will be to load and save the drawings to a file that can be specified in a file selection dialog.

There are several issues involved here. The first is the file-selection dialog. Fortunately, Qt provides the class `QFileDialog`, so you don't have to roll your own. Actually, the methods `getOpenFileName()` and `getSaveFileName()` will do almost all of the work for you.

The next item is the file format. There are several options to explore here. The first is simply saving the data from the off-screen buffer. This is easy, because it is an object of type `QPixmap`, and `QPixmap` provides a method `save()` for storing the data in one of several supported file formats.

Another option is to record all the drawings in a `QPicture` object instead of a `QPixmap`. We mentioned this before as an option for managing off-screen data. Like `QPixmap`, `QPicture` has a `save()` method. `QPicture` uses a file format of its own, which is portable across all platforms that Qt supports, but cannot be read by any non-Qt application. The difference between the `QPixmap` variant and the `QPicture` variant is mainly one of storing pixel data or storing vector-based graphics data. The goals of your application will determine what the best option is. For our application, it does not really matter, but given that we use a rather large virtual drawing area, a vector-based file format would probably be more space-efficient. On the other hand, saving with `QPixmap` means using a well-known file format, so you are able to check the results of the save operation with tools like *MS-Paint* on Windows or *pixmap* on Unix systems. Therefore, we have decided to use `QPixmap` for the save operations here.

Now that we have made our basic decisions, we can start to implement the load and save operations. Example 3-4 contains the program.

Example 3-4: qtscribble5.cpp: Load and Save Operations

```
 1  #include <qapplication.h>
 2  #include <qfiledialog.h>
 3  #include <qmenubar.h>
 4  #include <qmessagebox.h>
 5  #include <qpainter.h>
 6  #include <qpixmap.h>
 7  #include <qpopupmenu.h>
 8  #include <qscrollview.h>
 9  #include <qwidget.h>
10
11  enum MenuIDs{
12      COLOR_MENU_ID_BLACK,
13      COLOR_MENU_ID_RED,
14      COLOR_MENU_ID_BLUE,
15      COLOR_MENU_ID_GREEN,
16      COLOR_MENU_ID_YELLOW };
17
18  /**
19    * A class that lets the user draw with the mouse. The
20    * window knows how to redraw itself.
21    */
22  class ScribbleArea : public QWidget
23  {
24    Q_OBJECT  // necessary because ScribbleArea contains a slot
25
26  public:
27    ScribbleArea();
28    ~ScribbleArea();
29
30  public slots:
31    void setColor( QColor );
32    void slotLoad( const char* );
33    void slotSave( const char* );
```

Example 3-4: qtscribble5.cpp: Load and Save Operations (continued)

```
34
35 protected:
36    virtual void mousePressEvent( QMouseEvent* );
37    virtual void mouseMoveEvent( QMouseEvent* );
38    virtual void paintEvent( QPaintEvent* );
39    virtual void resizeEvent( QResizeEvent* );
40
41 private slots:
42    void slotClearArea();
43
44 private:
45    QPoint _last;
46    QColor _currentcolor;
47
48    QPixmap _buffer;
49    QPopupMenu* _popupmenu;
50 };
51
52
53 class ScribbleWindow : public QWidget
54 {
55    Q_OBJECT
56
57 public:
58    ScribbleWindow();
59    ~ScribbleWindow();
60
61 private slots:
62    void slotAbout();
63    void slotAboutQt();
64    void slotColorMenu( int );
65    void slotLoad();
66    void slotSave();
67
68 signals:
69    void colorChanged( QColor );
70    void load( const char* );
71    void save( const char* );
72
73 protected:
74    virtual void resizeEvent( QResizeEvent* );
75
76 private:
77    QMenuBar* _menubar;
78    QPopupMenu* _filemenu;
79    QPopupMenu* _colormenu;
80    QPopupMenu* _helpmenu;
81    QScrollView* _scrollview;
82    ScribbleArea* _scribblearea;
83 };
```

Example 3-4: qtscribble5.cpp: Load and Save Operations (continued)

```
84
85
86  #include "qtscribble5.moc"
87
88  /**
89   * The constructor. Initializes the member variables and creates a
90   * pop-up menu that will pop up when the right mouse button is
91   * clicked.
92   */
93  ScribbleArea::ScribbleArea()
94  {
95    // initialize member variables
96    _currentcolor = black;
97
98    // don't blank the window before repainting
99    setBackgroundMode( NoBackground );
100
101   // create a pop-up menu
102   _popupmenu = new QPopupMenu();
103   _popupmenu->insertItem( "&Clear", this, SLOT( slotClearArea() ) );
104 }
105
106
107 /**
108  * The destructor. Deletes the pop-up menu.
109  */
110 ScribbleArea::~ScribbleArea()
111 {
112   delete _popupmenu;
113 }
114
115
116 /**
117  * This slot sets the current color for the drawing area. It will be
118  * connected with the colorChanged( QColor ) signal from the
119  * ScribbleWindow.
120  */
121 void ScribbleArea::setColor( QColor new_color )
122 {
123   _currentcolor = new_color;
124 }
125
126
127 /**
128  * This slot clears the drawing area by filling the off-screen buffer with
129  * white, and then copying it over to the window.
130  */
131 void ScribbleArea::slotClearArea()
132 {
133   // fill the off-screen buffer with plain white
```

Example 3-4: qtscribble5.cpp: Load and Save Operations (continued)

```
134    _buffer.fill( white );
135
136    // and copy it over to the window
137    bitBlt( this, 0, 0, &_buffer );
138  }
139
140
141  /**
142   * This method does the actual loading. It relies on QPixmap (and the
143   * underlying I/O machinery) to determine the filetype.
144   */
145  void ScribbleArea::slotLoad( const char* filename )
146  {
147    if( !_buffer.load( filename ) )
148      QMessageBox::warning( 0, "Load error", "Could not load file" );
149
150    repaint(); // refresh the window
151  }
152
153
154  /**
155   * This method does the actual saving. We hard-code the file type as
156   * BMP. Unix users might want to replace this with something like XPM.
157   */
158  void ScribbleArea::slotSave( const char* filename )
159  {
160    if( !_buffer.save( filename, "BMP" ) )
161      QMessageBox::warning( 0, "Save error", "Could not save file" );
162  }
163
164
165  /**
166   * This virtual method is called whenever the user presses the
167   * mouse over the window. When the right mouse button is pressed, it
168   * pops up a previously constructed pop-up menu. Otherwise, it just
169   * records the position of the mouse at the time of the click.
170   */
171  void ScribbleArea::mousePressEvent( QMouseEvent* event )
172  {
173    if( event->button() == RightButton )
174      _popupmenu->exec( QCursor::pos() );
175    else
176      {
177        _last = event->pos(); // retrieve the coordinates from the event
178      }
179  }
180
181
182  /**
183   * This virtual method is called whenever the user moves the mouse
```

Example 3-4: qtscribble5.cpp: Load and Save Operations (continued)

```
184    * while the mouse button is pressed. If we had called
185    * setMouseTracking( true ) before, this method would also be called
186    * when the mouse was moved without any button pressed. We know that
187    * we haven't, and thus don't have to check whether any buttons are
188    * pressed.
189    */
190 void ScribbleArea::mouseMoveEvent( QMouseEvent* event )
191 {
192    // create a QPainter object for drawing onto the window
193    QPainter windowpainter;
194    // and another QPainter object for drawing into an off-screen pixmap
195    QPainter bufferpainter;
196
197    // start painting
198    windowpainter.begin( this );     // this painter paints onto the window
199    bufferpainter.begin( &_buffer ); // and this one in the buffer
200
201    // set a standard pen with the currently selected color
202    windowpainter.setPen( _currentcolor );
203    bufferpainter.setPen( _currentcolor );
204
205    // draw a line in both the window and the buffer
206    windowpainter.drawLine( _last, event->pos() );
207    bufferpainter.drawLine( _last, event->pos() );
208
209    // done with painting
210    windowpainter.end();
211    bufferpainter.end();
212
213    // remember the current mouse position
214    _last = event->pos();
215 }
216
217
218
219 /**
220    * This virtual method is called whenever the widget needs
221    * painting, such as when it has been obscured and then revealed again.
222    */
223 void ScribbleArea::paintEvent( QPaintEvent* event )
224 {
225    // copy the image from the buffer pixmap to the window
226    bitBlt( this, 0, 0, &_buffer );
227 }
228
229
230 /**
231    * This virtual method is called whenever the window is resized. We
232    * use it to make sure that the off-screen buffer is always the same
233    * size as the window.
```

Example 3-4: qtscribble5.cpp: Load and Save Operations (continued)

```
234    * To retain the original drawing, it is first copied to a temporary
235    * buffer. After the main buffer has been resized and filled with
236    * white, the image is copied from the temporary buffer to the main
237    * buffer.
238    */
239   void ScribbleArea::resizeEvent( QResizeEvent* event )
240   {
241     QPixmap save( _buffer );
242     _buffer.resize( event->size() );
243     _buffer.fill( white );
244     bitBlt( &_buffer, 0, 0, &save );
245   }
246
247
248   ScribbleWindow::ScribbleWindow()
249   {
250     /* The next few lines build the menu bar. We first create the menus
251      * one by one and add them afterwards to the menu bar. */
252     _filemenu = new QPopupMenu; // create a file menu
253     _filemenu->insertItem( "&Load", this, SLOT( slotLoad() ) );
254     _filemenu->insertItem( "&Save", this, SLOT( slotSave() ) );
255     _filemenu->insertSeparator();
256     _filemenu->insertItem( "&Quit", qApp, SLOT( quit() ) );
257
258     _colormenu = new QPopupMenu; // create a color menu
259     _colormenu->insertItem( "B&lack", COLOR_MENU_ID_BLACK );
260     _colormenu->insertItem( "&Red", COLOR_MENU_ID_RED );
261     _colormenu->insertItem( "&Blue", COLOR_MENU_ID_BLUE );
262     _colormenu->insertItem( "&Green", COLOR_MENU_ID_GREEN );
263     _colormenu->insertItem( "&Yellow", COLOR_MENU_ID_YELLOW );
264     QObject::connect( _colormenu, SIGNAL( activated( int ) ),
265                       this, SLOT( slotColorMenu( int ) ) );
266
267     _helpmenu = new QPopupMenu; // create a help menu
268     _helpmenu->insertItem( "&About QtScribble", this, SLOT( slotAbout() ) );
269     _helpmenu->insertItem( "About &Qt", this, SLOT( slotAboutQt() ) );
270
271     _menubar = new QMenuBar( this ); // create a menu bar
272     _menubar->insertItem( "&File", _filemenu );
273     _menubar->insertItem( "&Color", _colormenu );
274     _menubar->insertSeparator();
275     _menubar->insertItem( "&Help", _helpmenu );
276
277     /* We create a QScrollView and a ScribbleArea. The ScribbleArea will
278      * be managed by the scroll view.*/
279     _scrollview = new QScrollView( this );
280     _scrollview->setGeometry( 0, _menubar->height(),
281                               width(), height() - _menubar->height() );
282     _scribblearea = new ScribbleArea();
283     _scribblearea->setGeometry( 0, 0, 1000, 1000 );
```

Example 3-4: qtscribble5.cpp: Load and Save Operations (continued)

```
284    _scrollview->addChild( _scribblearea );
285    QObject::connect( this, SIGNAL( colorChanged( QColor ) ),
286                      _scribblearea, SLOT( setColor( QColor ) ) );
287    QObject::connect( this, SIGNAL( save( const char* ) ),
288                      _scribblearea, SLOT( slotSave( const char* ) ) );
289    QObject::connect( this, SIGNAL( load( const char* ) ),
290                      _scribblearea, SLOT( slotLoad( const char* ) ) );
291  }
292
293
294  ScribbleWindow::~ScribbleWindow()
295  {
296  }
297
298
299  void ScribbleWindow::resizeEvent( QResizeEvent* event )
300  {
301    /* When the whole window is resized, we have to rearrange the geometry
302     * in the ScribbleWindow as well. Note that the ScribbleArea does not need
303     * to be changed. */
304    _scrollview->setGeometry( 0, _menubar->height(),
305                              width(), height() - _menubar->height() );
306  }
307
308
309  void ScribbleWindow::slotAbout()
310  {
311    QMessageBox::information( this, "About QtScribble 5",
312                             "This is the Scribble 5 application\n"
313                             "(C) 1998 by Matthias Kalle Dalheimer\n"
314                             );
315  }
316
317
318  void ScribbleWindow::slotAboutQt()
319  {
320    QMessageBox::aboutQt( this, "About Qt" );
321  }
322
323
324  void ScribbleWindow::slotColorMenu( int item )
325  {
326    switch( item )
327      {
328      case COLOR_MENU_ID_BLACK:
329          emit colorChanged( black );
330          break;
331      case COLOR_MENU_ID_RED:
332          emit colorChanged( darkRed );
333          break;
```

Example 3-4: qtscribble5.cpp: Load and Save Operations (continued)

```
334      case COLOR_MENU_ID_BLUE:
335          emit colorChanged( darkBlue );
336          break;
337      case COLOR_MENU_ID_GREEN:
338          emit colorChanged( darkGreen );
339          break;
340      case COLOR_MENU_ID_YELLOW:
341          emit colorChanged( yellow );
342          break;
343      }
344 }
345
346
347 /**
348  * This is the slot for the menu item File/Load. It opens a
349  * QFileDialog to ask the user for a filename, then emits a save()
350  * signal with the filename as a parameter.
351  */
352 void ScribbleWindow::slotLoad()
353 {
354     /* Open a file dialog for loading. The default directory is the
355      * current directory, the filter *.bmp.
356      */
357     QString filename = QFileDialog::getOpenFileName( ".", "*.bmp", this );
358     if( !filename.isEmpty() )
359         emit load( filename );
360 }
361
362
363 /**
364  * This is the save equivalent to slotLoad(). Again, we just ask for a
365  * filename and emit a signal.
366  */
367 void ScribbleWindow::slotSave()
368 {
369     /* Open a file dialog for saving. The default directory is the
370      * current directory, the filter *.bmp.
371      */
372     QString filename = QFileDialog::getSaveFileName( ".", "*.bmp", this );
373     if( !filename.isEmpty() )
374         emit save( filename );
375 }
376
377
378 int main( int argc, char* argv[] )
379 {
380     QApplication myapp( argc, argv );
381
382     ScribbleWindow* mywidget = new ScribbleWindow();
383     mywidget->setGeometry( 50, 50, 400, 400 );
```

Example 3-4: qtscribble5.cpp: Load and Save Operations (continued)

```
384
385    myapp.setMainWidget( mywidget );
386    mywidget->show();
387    return myapp.exec();
388 }
```

To understand the new code, you first have to realize that we are using the *signal forwarding* technique again. The load and save slots are located in `ScribbleWindow` because that's where the menus are. But only the `ScribbleArea` can know how to save and load the data because it holds the off-screen buffer that we save from or load to. `ScribbleWindow::slotLoad()` and `ScribbleWindow::slotSave()` show a file selection dialog by calling `QFileDialog::getOpenFileName()` and `QFileDialog::getSaveFileName()`, respectively. Each method accepts the directory that the dialog should show first (the current directory, in our case), a filename filter (here `*.bmp`), and the parent widget as parameters. It then returns the selected filename. If the user did not select a filename but closed the dialog with `Cancel` instead, the returned string is empty. We check for this condition, and emit a `load()` or `save()` signal with the filename as a parameter.

At the other end sit the slots `ScribbleArea::slotLoad()` and `ScribbleArea::slotSave()`. They do the actual work which is very simple here: The methods only call `QPixmap::load()` and `QPixmap::save()`. When one of these methods returns `false`[1], it means that an error has occurred. In this case, we show a warning with `QMessageBox`.

`QPixmap::load()` has the interesting feature of being able to determine the file format automatically. When it can recognize the file format used by the file in question, it invokes the appropriate loading routine. Of course, you have to pass the desired file format to `QPixmap::save()`, since this method cannot guess the file format that you want to use.[2] This is about all there is to simple loading and saving. You are now at the end of this tutorial, and we hope, you learned the basics of programming with Qt. Again, we like to encourage you to explore the features of the classes mentioned here. In most cases, we have just scratched the surface of what they can do.

Exercises

1. Experiment with other file formats. Try to load GIF or XPM files, for example.

2. Expand Example 3-4 to show the name of the currently loaded file in the titlebar of the application. You can set the text in the titlebar by calling `QWidget::setCaption()` at the top level widget, in our case the `ScribbleWindow` widget. The text

---

1 A general remark for those outdated compilers that still don't support `bool`, `true` and `false`: Qt also defines TRUE and FALSE, which can be used instead on those compilers. An even better solution would be to switch compilers.

2 You could argue that it could guess the format from the filename extension, but that would probably not be a very good idea.

should be QtScribble: *filename* when a file has been loaded and QtScribble: unnamed when no file has been loaded yet.

3.   Expand Example 3-4 so that it records whether the current scribble is dirty or not— in other words whether there is unsaved data. When a user quits the program a new image should be loaded, and the program should display a warning if there is still unsaved data and offer the user a chance to save the current drawing first.

You will have to define a flag dirty that is true when there is unsaved data, and false otherwise. Any drawings with the mouse should change this flag to true, saving the current scribble to a file and loading a new one should set it back to false. At startup, it should be false, too, of course.

4

A Guided Tour Through the Simple Widgets

Qt is a rich library, and as a beginner, you could easily find yourself reinventing the wheel when there is already a Qt class that meets your needs. This is why we have decided to include this chapter and the next, in which we present widgets that are already available and their most useful methods. We will also provide some guidelines about when to use a certain widget.

This widget tour has two parts. This chapter presents so-called "simple" widgets, such as push-buttons and labels. The next chapter contains the predefined dialogs that Qt provides for common tasks like opening files, as well as the building blocks for defining your own dialogs.

For your convenience, the following table contains all widgets that ship with version 1.4x of Qt. They are listed in alphabetical order, each with a short description and a reference to the section of this book where they are explained further.

Widget	Description	Section
QButtonGroup	Organizes QButton widgets in a group	*Group boxes*
QCheckBox	Check-box with a label, either a text or a pixmap	*Buttons*
QComboBox	Combined button and pop-up list	*Combo boxes*
QFrame	The base class of widgets that have an (optional) frame	*Frames*
QGroupBox	Group box frame with a title	*Group boxes*
QHeader	List view header	*Widgets for Tabular Material*
QLabel	Displays a static text, a pixmap or an animation	*Simple labels*
QLCDNumber	Displays a number with LCD-like digits	*QLCDNumber*

Widget	Description	Section
QLineEdit	Simple line editor for inputting text	*the "Text Entry Fields" section*
QListBox	Single-column list of items that can be scrolled	*List boxes*
QListView	Implements a list/tree view	*List Views*
QMainWindow	Typical application window with a menu bar, some tool bars and a status bar	*The main window*
QMenuBar	Horizontal menu bar	*Menu-related Widgets*
QMultiLineEdit	Simple editor for inputting text	*Text Entry Fields*
QPopupMenu	Pop-up menu widget	*Menu-related Widgets*
QProgressBar	Horizontal progress bar	*Progress bars*
QPushButton	Push-button with a text or pixmap label	*Buttons*
QRadioButton	Radio button with a label, either text or a pixmap	*Buttons*
QScrollBar	Vertical or horizontal scroll bar	*Scroll bars*
QScrollView	Provides a view of contents, as well as scroll bars to move through the view	*Scrolled Views*
QSlider	Vertical or horizontal slider	*Sliders*
QSpinBox	Spin box widget, sometimes called up-down widget, little arrows widget or spin button	*Spin boxes*
QSplitter	A splitter widget for distributing the space between two widgets	*Splitters*
QStatusBar	Horizontal bar suitable for presenting status messages	*Status bars*
QToolBar	Simple tool bar	*Tool bars*
QToolButton	Push-button whose appearance has been tailored for use in a QToolBar	*Tool bars*
QToolTip	Provides tiny information windows about other widgets	*Tool tips and "What's This" windows*
QWhatsThis	Provides information windows about other widgets that are larger than those created by QToolTip	*Tool tips and "What's This" windows*
QWidgetStack	Shows one of its children at a time	*Widget stacks*

General Widget Parameters

All of the widgets in this chapter serve as building blocks for your application; most of them are commonly found in dialogs. Of course, these widgets have all the general properties of Qt widgets. You can, for example, set their fonts and colors. See the reference documentation for `QWidget` for these methods. The method `setEnabled()`, which accepts a `bool` parameter for influencing whether a widget is available for user interaction, is very important. Enabling and disabling widgets depending on the situation is very important for creating good user interfaces. All too often, you see programs where you can choose some settings, and are then told "Sorry, this choice is not possible." Worse, you may be offered choices that have absolutely no effect. This wastes the user's time. Remember this when you design your application—your users will thank you for it.[1]

Other settings that apply to all widgets are the font, which is set with `setFont()`, and the palette for drawing, which is set with `setPalette()`.

Also note the uniformity of the constructors of widgets in Qt. Most widgets have a constructor with three parameters: a `QWidget*` that specifies the parent, a name (see Chapter 18 to find out how this is used), and *widget flags*, which only apply to top-level widgets and are rarely needed even for those. Since all three parameters usually default to 0, you can create a top-level widget without passing any parameters to the constructor. You can create any other widget simply by passing the parent.

Some widgets also provide additional overloaded constructors. These provide parameters for setting additional initial properties. For example, you can pass the label for the push-button as a parameter to the constructor of the class `QPushButton`. If there are additional parameters, these usually come before the standard ones.

Widget Styles

Qt uses GUI emulation, so it can use widgets with a Windows style in Unix, and widgets with a Motif style in Windows. You could even mix widgets with different styles in your application, but this is not recommended, because it leads to very awkward-looking user interfaces.

There are several ways to set the style of widgets:

* You can set the style for an individual widget by calling `setStyle()` on the widget object and passing either `WindowsStyle` or `MotifStyle`. As noted before, this is not recommended.

---

1   OK, ungrateful as most users are, they probably won't thank you personally—but at least they won't curse you.

- You can set the default for all widgets by calling the static method `QApplica-`
  `tion::setStyle()`. You should do this before any widget has been created, or
  repaint all the widgets afterwards. This repainting can be done with the following
  code:

```
// newstyle is either WindowsStyle or MotifStyle

// set the default
QApplication::setStyle( newstyle );

// get a list of all top-level widgets of the application
QWidgetList* widgetlist = QApplication::topLevelWidgets();
// create an iterator over the list
QWidgetListIt widgetlist_it( *widgetlist );

// do the following for each top-level widget
while( widgetlist_it.current() ) {
  // take one widget from the list
  QWidget* widget = widgetlist_it.current();
  // advance iterator to next element
  ++widgetlist_it;

  // apply the new style to this widget
  widget->setStyle( newstyle );
  // get a list of all descendants of this widget that are widgets
  // themselves
  QObjectList* objectlist = widget->queryList( "QWidget", 0, 0, true );
  // create an iterator over this list
  QObjectListIt objectlist_it( *objectlist );

  // apply the new style to all descendant widgets
  while ( objectlist_it.current() ) {
    ++objectlist_it; // advance iterator to next element
    QWidget *child = (QWidget *)( objectlist_it.current() );
    child->setStyle( newstyle );
  }
  delete objectlist;
}

delete widgetlist;
```

  You might be surprised about the two `delete` calls here because there is no `new`
  call to be seen. Qt has allocated these objects itself.

- The last possibility (and often the most advisable) is only available on Unix systems: You can set the widget style on the command line. Of course, this only
  works if none of the other two methods has been used. You can call any Qt program with one of the command-line switches `-style=windows` or `-style=motif`.

Buttons

Buttons are probably the most common GUI element. You can group them according to how they are used: push-buttons yield some kind of action such as closing a dialog or invoking a program-specific function. On the other hand, radio buttons and check boxes, which together could be named *option buttons*, are used to select options and not to invoke actions. With push-buttons, this is usually not possible, because something happens right away when they are pushed.[2] There is also a visual difference: push buttons appear "pressed in" only while clicked, while option buttons stay like that when they are checked.

Push-buttons

Push-buttons are represented by the class QPushButton (see Figures 4-1 and 4-2) in Qt. These yield some kind of action, such as closing a dialog or invoking a program-specific function. They can be labeled with either text or pixmaps, using the method set-Text() or setPixmap(). A text string can also be passed in the constructor. You usually connect a slot to the signal clicked(), which is emitted when the mouse is pressed and released again over the button.

The signals pressed() and released() are also available, but you should be careful with these, since you are almost certainly on your way to designing a difficult-to-understand, non-standard GUI if you use them. There is also a signal called toggled(), which is only emitted in a special mode of a QPushButton object (we will talk about this later).

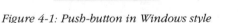
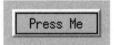

Figure 4-1: Push-button in Windows style   *Figure 4-2: Push-button in Motif style*

A push-button that resides in a dialog can become the *default push-button*. This is the push-button that is "clicked" when the user presses the Enter key. Of course, there can only be one default button in a dialog. You make a push-button the default button by calling setDefault() on it. A related method is setAutoDefault(), which makes a button an auto-default button. Unlike the default button, there can be more than one auto-default button. An auto-default button becomes the new default button when it gets the keyboard focus, and it loses this property again when the keyboard focus moves to some other widget.

It is very good practice to always have a default button to facilitate using your dialog with the keyboard only.

---

2 Of course, when clicking a push-button invokes a dialog, closing with Cancel effectively undoes the action. The user interface has changed, however, at least temporarily.

Radio buttons and check-boxes

Option buttons are represented in Qt by the classes QCheckBox (see Figures 4-3 and 4-4) and QRadioButton (see Figures 4-5 and 4-6). These differ mainly in how the choices for the user are restricted. Check-boxes are used for "many of many" choices; any number of check-boxes in a group, including none, can be checked. Radio buttons are for "one of many" choices, so exactly one radio button in a group can be checked. Both styles of buttons have special appearances that reflect their choice model, for example on MS-Windows check-boxes are square and radio buttons are circular. On Windows, your users would be completely confused if you used square buttons that have radio button behaviour.

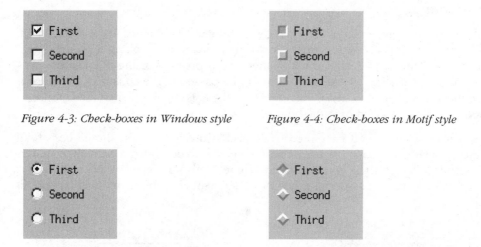

Figure 4-3: Check-boxes in Windows style   *Figure 4-4: Check-boxes in Motif style*

Figure 4-5: Radio buttons in Windows style   *Figure 4-6: Radio buttons in Motif style*

As a programmer, you need to know whether radio buttons and check-boxes are checked. You find this out with the methods QCheckBox::isChecked() and QRadioButton::isChecked(), respectively. When you want to set or unset an option button programmatically (for example to set a default value), you use QCheckBox::setChecked() or QRadioButton::setChecked(). These methods accept a bool parameter that indicates whether the button should be set or unset.

Like push-buttons, option buttons can have text or a pixmap as a label. Unlike push-buttons, these are not shown in the button itself, but close to it. Clicking on the text has the same effect as clicking on the button.

Normally, you will just check for the values of the option buttons in a dialog when the dialog has been closed with OK. Sometimes, however, you may want to react immediately to user interaction. This could be the case when setting or unsetting an option button influences the availability of other buttons. In this case, you can use the signals clicked(), released(), pressed(), and toggled(), just as you do with push-buttons.

To achieve "one of many behavior" with radio buttons, you have to do slightly more work than simply creating them. Your application must know which buttons form a group because there could be two or more groups of radio buttons, each with exactly one button checked.

You can group your radio buttons by means of a QButtonGroup object. This should also be used to visually identify your buttons as a group, but for now we will just talk about enforcing radio-button behavior. You have two options for using QButtonGroup. You can make your radio buttons children of a QButtonGroup object, which is already enough for enforcing radio button behaviour:

```
QButtonGroup* bgroup = new QButtonGroup( "Heading", parent );
QRadioButton* radio1 = new QRadioButton( "Choice1", bgroup );
QRadioButton* radio2 = new QRadioButton( "Choice2", bgroup );
QRadioButton* radio3 = new QRadioButton( "Choice3", bgroup );
```

The other possibility is inserting the radio buttons into a button group by calling QButtonGroup::insert():

```
QButtonGroup* bgroup = new QButtonGroup( "Heading", parent );
QRadioButton* radio1 = new QRadioButton( "Choice1", parent );
bgroup->insert( radio1 );
QRadioButton* radio2 = new QRadioButton( "Choice2", parent );
bgroup->insert( radio2 );
QRadioButton* radio3 = new QRadioButton( "Choice3", parent );
bgroup->insert( radio3 );
```

Sometimes you want a button that looks like a push-button, but acts like an option button. An example would be a dialog in a word processor, which lets you choose the alignment (flush left, flush right, centered, or blocked) of a paragraph. The four choices could be depicted by icons, and it would be graphically more attractive (and more obvious to the user) if the icons themselves could be clicked.

To achieve this, use QPushButton objects and make them toggle buttons with setToggleButton(true). You can then also connect the signal toggled() to your slot.

Selection Widgets

This section discusses widgets that let the user choose one (or several) items from a given selection. This includes combo boxes and list boxes, which are mainly used for selecting text items, but can also present graphical data to the user.

List boxes

List boxes are represented by the class QListBox (see Figures 4-7 and 4-8) in Qt. List boxes are a common concept in user interfaces; they let the user select one or more entries from a list of items. If there are more items than can fit into the screen space allocated for the list box, the user can use scroll bars to look through the items.

Figure 4-7: A listbox in Windows style   *Figure 4-8: A listbox in Motif style*

There are three techiques for inserting items into the list box. The most general is the method `QListBox::insertItem()`, which exists in three variants for inserting strings, pixmaps, or items of type `QListBoxItem`. The latter can be used to define items apart from text and pixmaps, but it is most commonly used to define items that can show text and a pixmap at the same time. If you want to insert several strings in a row and already have them in a `QStrList` (see Chapter 8), you can use `insertStrList()`. Finally, there is `inSort()`, which maintains a sorted order of the entries in the list box.

After inserting entries, you need to be informed about the entries that have been selected. If the list box allows selection of only one entry at a time (the default, see next paragraph on how to change this), you can simply ask for the currently selected item with `QListBox::currentItem()`. This yields a position number, which you can pass to `QListBox::text()` or `QListBox::pixmap()` to retrieve the text or pixmap at that position.

If you have switched your list box to multi-selection mode by calling `QListBox::set-MultiSelection( true )`, things are a little more difficult. You can loop over all the entries, asking each of them if it is selected, as in the following code:

```
for( int i = 0; i < listbox->count(); i++ )
{
    if( listbox->isSelected( i )
        // item i (whose text is listbox->text( i ) or whose
        // pixmap is listbox->pixmap( i )) is selected
}
```

Of course, you can also be notified at the time an item is selected. When an item has been highlighted with a single mouse-click, the signals `highlighted( int )` and `highlighted( const char* )` are emitted. When an item is selected by doubleclicking it or by pressing the Enter key, the signals `selected( int )` and `selected( const char* )` are emitted. Variants with an `int` parameter pass the position number, while the variants with the `const char*` parameter pass the text of the item.

In multi-selection list boxes, the signal `selectionChanged()` can be useful. When several items are selected in a row by dragging the mouse over them, `selection-Changed()` is emitted only once.

`QListBox` contains many methods for customizing its operation. Please refer to the reference documentation for more details.

Combo boxes

A combo box can be an alternative to a list box. Its main advantage is the lower amount of screen real-estate that it occupies. When not in use, a combo box shows only the currently selected item with a downward arrow. When the user clicks on the combo box, a list of items pops down, from which the user can choose one. After the user has chosen an item by clicking on it, the combo box folds together again and shows the new selection.

Combo boxes are represented by the class QComboBox (see Figures 4-9, 4-10, 4-11, 4-12 and 4-13) in Qt. They can contain text and pixmaps, but no user-defined item types like list boxes. You can have read-only and read-write combo boxes. Read-write combo boxes allow users to insert new items at runtime. These combo boxes have a text-entry field that displays the currently selected item and can also be used for entering new text. Whether the user is allowed to do so, and where in the list new items will be inserted, is governed by an "insertion policy". This is set with QComboBox::setInsertionPolicy(). See the reference documentation for the available policies.

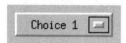

Figure 4-9: A combo box in old Motif style

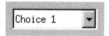

Figure 4-10: A read-write combo box in Windows style

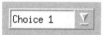

Figure 4-11: A read-write combo box in new Motif style

Figure 4-12: A read-only combo box in Windows style

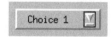

Figure 4-13: A read-only combo box in new Motif style

A caveat: If you use read-write combo boxes, you cannot have pixmaps as items since it is not possible to edit the pixmaps in a text-entry field. When you try to insert a pixmap into a read-write combo box as an item, nothing will happen.

If you are using Motif style, you can choose between old-style combo boxes (read-only) and new-style combo boxes. The old ones look like those found in Motif 1.x programs, the new ones like those in Motif 2.x programs. Windows has only one style of combo boxes. The constructor determines whether an old-style or a new-style combo box is created. If you create your combo boxes with

```
QComboBox* combo = new QComboBox( parent );
```

you will get an old-style combo box. If the first parameter is a Boolean value, a new-style combo box is created. This Boolean value determines whether or not the combo box will be read-write:

```
QComboBox* combo1 = new QComboBox( true, parent ); // read-write
QComboBox* combo2 = new QComboBox( false, parent ); // read-only
```

The interface for inserting items into combo boxes is much like the insertion interface for list boxes: You can either insert your text or pixmap items with `insertItem()`, or you can insert whole string lists in the form of `QStrList` objects with `insertStrList()`.

As with list boxes, you can ask the combo box for the currently selected item with `QComboBox::currentItem()`. You can also be notified when an item has been highlighted (the mouse is over the item but still pressed) or selected (the mouse has been released over an item) with the signals `highlighted()` and `activated()`. These come in an `int`- and a `const char*`-version, as with `QListBox`.

When you use read-write combo boxes, you may want to check user input for validity before accepting it as a new item in the combo box. This can be done with *validators* which are represented in Qt by the class `QValidator`. We will talk about this class in the "Validating User Input" section in Chapter 10, *Text Processing*.

Again like list boxes, combo boxes have a lot of methods with which you can customize their appearance and behaviour. You should at least skim the reference documentation to see what is in store for you.

There sometimes is confusion about whether to use a list box or a combo box. Choosing the wrong one for a given situation can lead to an awkward user interface. Here are some guidelines, but remember, there is no absolute truth. Use your own judgement.

- When you need non-standard items (items that are neither text or a pixmap), you have to use a list box—but there are better choices. If the only thing you want to do is combine a text and a pixmap, such as when you want to offer the user a selection of countries and want to add their flags to the items, you can always use pixmaps and draw the text into the pixmaps.

- When you want to allow the user to add new items at runtime, you have to use a read-write combo box.

- When screen real-estate is scarce and dialogs are already crowded, use a combo box. On the other hand, think about whether your dialog is really well-designed. Dialogs with too many options are incomprehensible to casual users. Consider splitting up the dialog.

- When you want to permit the user to choose more than one item, you must use a list box.

- When you have just a few items to choose from, use neither a combo box nor a list box, but a group of radio buttons or check boxes.

Widgets for Bounded Range Input

The slider and spin box widgets allow you to choose a numerical value from a given set. With a slider, the minimum and maximum values are fixed. This is usually not the case with a spin box.

Sliders

While it is not always obvious whether you should use a list box or a combo box, it is almost always obvious when you should use a slider. In Qt, sliders are represented by the class `QSlider` (see Figures 4-14 and 4-15). A slider is a longish widget with a knob that you can drag to choose a numeric value from a predefined range. The position of the knob is proportional to the value with respect to the range. Early versions of Qt did not have a slider, which is why some programmers still use a scroll bar to achieve the same effect. Don't do this: your users will become confused.

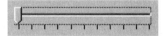

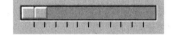

Figure 4-14: A slider in Windows style   *Figure 4-15: A slider in Motif style*

Sliders have a number of parameters. The minimum value and the maximum value define the range from which the value can be selected, the step width determines how much the knob moves when you click in the slider trough instead of dragging the knob, and the initial value determines the initial position of the knob. Finally, the orientation says whether the slider should be arranged horizontally or vertically. Since these values usually don't change over the lifetime of a slider, they should be set in the constructor:

```
QSlider* slider = new QSlider( 0 /* min */, 200 /* max */,
                               5 /* step */, 100 /* initial */,
                               QSlider::Horizontal /* orientation */,
                               parent, "name" );
```

This creates a slider with which you can choose an integer between 0 and 200. Clicking in the trough decrements or increments the slider value by 5, the initial value is 100, and the slider is positioned horizontally.

`QSlider` inherits from `QRangeControl`, which gives methods like `setRange()`, `setSteps()` and `setValue()` to change these parameters. `QSlider` itself adds `setOrientation()`. Remember that changing this visual parameter after the slider has been shown can be very irritating to the user.

If the slider is long, it can be useful to provide visual clues as to where a certain value might be on the slider "scale". These clues are tickmarks, which you can add to a slider by calling `setTickmarks()`. You can choose whether you want the tickmarks to be above, below, left, right, or on both sides of slider, or whether you want none at all. There is no general rule about when to use tickmarks, but we suggest you use them only when the slider is longer than 200 pixels or so to avoid visual overload.

To retrieve the slider's set value, either you can call `QSlider::value()`, or you can be notified when the slider value changes. The signal `sliderMoved( int )` is emitted whenever the knob is moved so much that a new value has been chosen; the parameter contains the new value. If you want to be notified only when the user is done selecting a value (i.e., the user has released the knob), connect to the signal `valueChanged( int )`. When you have set `setTracking( true )`, `valueChanged( int )` behaves just like `sliderMoved( int )`. If you are interested in knowing when the user has pressed or released the knob, you can also connect to the signals `sliderPressed()` or `sliderReleased()`, but you will rarely need to do so.

It's interesting and useful to connect a `QSlider` object to a `QLCDNumber` object. You will learn about `QLCDNumber` later in this chapter, but for now you only need to know that it shows a value with a predefined number of digits in the form of the well-known seven-segment LCD displays. Such a display can be used to represent the value chosen with the slider:

```
QSlider slider = new QSlider( 0, 9, 1, 1, QSlider::Horizontal, parent );
slider->setGeometry( ... );
QLCDNumber number = new QLCDNumber ( 1, parent );
number->setGeometry( ... );
QObject::connect( slider, SIGNAL( sliderMoved( int ) ),
                  number, SLOT( display( int ) ) );
```

This combination is so useful that you will probably see more combinations of sliders with `QLCDNumber` objects than single sliders. For a full example, see the section "Another example for signals and slots" on pp 26-29.

Spin boxes

Spin boxes (see Figures 4-16 and 4-17), implemented by the class `QSpinBox`, consist of a text-entry field and two arrow buttons, one for incrementing and one for decrementing the numerical value in the text field. This is a convenient combination for entering integer values because the UI element can be operated easily with the mouse. But if this becomes cumbersome (for example, the value desired is far away from the current value), the keyboard can be used as well.

Figure 4-16: Spin boxes in Windows style   *Figure 4-17: Spin boxes in Motif style*

Note that without any extra precautions, this is not a foolproof method for inputting integer numbers in a given range, because the user can enter any text whatsoever into the widget. You can use the methods described in the "Validating User Input" section to make sure that the users enter only integer numbers in the desired range.

The most obvious methods are `setValue()` and `value()` for setting and retrieving the current value, but there are more. You can change the display in various ways. For example, you can set a prefix and a suffix that are displayed in front of and behind the value in question, respectively. This is done with `setPrefix()` and `setSuffix()`. A related method that also influences the display, but not the value itself, is `setSpecial-ValueText()`. Say that you want to let the user choose a font size, but you also want to provide some kind of "default value", which could mean "take the font from the previous paragraph". You can have a value like 0 that is an impossible value for the font size as a marker for the font, but it would be difficult to explain this to the user. This is where `setSpecialValueText()` comes in. With this method, you set text that is shown instead of the actual value when the smallest possible value has been chosen. In our example, this could be `<default>`.

Two more methods to change the value programmatically are `stepUp()` and `step-Down()`, which simulate clicking the up arrow and the down arrow buttons, respectively.

Normally, when the user clicks on one of the arrow buttons and the minimum or maximum value that is set together with `setRange()` is reached, the value does not change any more. But if you have called `setWrapping( true )`, the values wrap around and start at the maximum or minimum value again.

Last, there are two signals, both with the name `valueChanged()`. One has an integer parameter, the other a `const char*` parameter. By connecting to these signals, your program can be informed whenever the value of the spin box changes. By choosing the right signal, you can either get just the numerical value or the whole string in the input field, including the prefix and suffix, if any.

Scroll bars

Like buttons, scroll bars are intuitively understood by most users. You can either use them directly by creating objects of type `QScrollBar` (see Figures 4-18 and 4-19), or use them by means of `QScrollView`. Usually you'll do the latter, because it is much more convenient and relieves you from doing all the geometry management related to scroll bars that are attached to an application window.

Figure 4-18: A scroll bar in Windows style   *Figure 4-19: A scroll bar in Motif style*

Like sliders, scroll bars have a minimum value, a maximum value, a current value, and an orientation. There is a "line step size", which is the amount the scroll-bar knob moves when you click on one of the buttons at the end of the scroll bar. The "page step size" is the amount the knob moves when you click in the trough of the scroll bar.

It is most convenient to set these values when creating the scroll bar:

```
QScrollBar* scrollbar = new QScrollBar( 0, /* minimum value */
                              500, /* maximum value */
                              1, /* line step value */
                              10, /* page step value */
                              0, /* initial value */
                              QScrollBar::Vertical, /* orientation */
                              parent );
```

but you can also set these with `setRange()`, `setSteps()`, `setValue()`, and `setOri-entation()`. The latter accepts the values `QScrollBar::Vertical` and `QScroll-Bar::Horizontal`.

To use the scroll bar, you must know when it is operated by the user, no matter whether the user does this via the knob, by clicking on the arrows, or by clicking in the trough. Your application can be notified of any changes by a plethora of signals. The most important of these are `sliderMoved( int )` and `valueChanged( int )`. With these signals, the parameter contains the new scroll-bar value. The `sliderMoved( int )` signal is emitted whenever the value changes, no matter whether the user has dragged the knob or clicked on some part of the slider. The `valueChanged( int )` signal is emitted only when the user clicks on the scroll bar, or drags the slider and releases the knob again, unless `setTracking( bool )` has been called before. In this case, `valueChanged( int )` behaves just like `sliderMoved( int )`.

There are four other signals, `nextPage()`, `nextLine()`, `prevPage()`, and `prevLine()`, which are emitted when the slider value changes by a line step or a page step. The last two remaining signals, `sliderPressed()` and `sliderReleased()`, are probably less useful. They are emitted when the user has started or quit operating the knob. You could use these when you have to prepare your application window for being scrolled.

The most common use for scroll bars is moving the view that an application window provides on the application data. There is usually a horizontal scroll bar below the application window, and a vertical scroll bar to the right of the application window. Sometimes the scroll bars are only shown on demand—for example, only when the representation of the application data is larger than the visible area. You could arrange this yourself, but it is much easier to use the class `QScrollView`.

You have already seen the basic use of `QScrollView` in the "Adding a Scrolled View" section, so you know that the widgets to be scrolled can be set with `addChild()` and that the scroll bars can be made on-demand or not by calling `setHScrollBarMode()` and `setVScrollBarMode()`.

`QScrollView` supports the notion of a "corner widget". This can be any widget, is set with `setCornerWidget()`, and appears in the lower right corner between the horizontal and vertical scroll bars. Some applications use this to add a button here that can change the presentation mode of the application data. Any other purpose is probably inappropriate, because your users will assume that the corner widget is somehow related to the scroll bars.

Another interesting method is `ensureVisible()`, which exists in two overloaded variants. Both make sure that a certain coordinate of the window is within the visible part. The first two parameters are the coordinates of a point in the scrolled widget that is guaranteed to be at least 50 pixels away from each margin after the call. If this is not possible because either the width or the height of the visible area is smaller than 100 pixels, the point will be located at the center. You can override the default of 50 pixels by passing a third and fourth parameter that contain a minimum distance from the left, right, top, and bottom margins. Again, if this requirement cannot be fulfilled, the point will be centered. For example, `ensureVisible()` is useful in a word processor that contains a "Goto Page" function. You only have to compute where in the view widget this page starts, and pass these parameters to `ensureVisible()`. The two `ensureVisible()` methods are slots, but there are currently no signals that would have the required signature to be able to be connected to these slots.

The `center()` method is very similar to `ensureVisible()`. It has the same parameters, except for the fact that the optional third and fourth parameters are of type `double` instead of type `int`. Of course, these methods ensure that the given point will be located at the center of the visible area after the call. The optional third and fourth parameter indicate a deviation from the center that can be accepted. A value of `1.0` signifies that no deviation from the center is accepted in the given direction, `0.0` signifies that it is tolerable that the point is exactly at the margin of the visible area in that direction. If you pass a tolerance smaller than `1.0`, the visible area is moved as little as possible to fulfill the constraint. Deviation values must lie within the range `0.0 - 1.0`.

Menu-related Widgets

To program menus, Qt provides the three classes `QPopupMenu` (see Figures 4-20 and 4-21), `QMenuBar` (see Figures 4-22 and 4-23) and `QMenuData`. A warning ahead: the menu system is one of the least flexible parts in Qt. For example, it is not possible to use the same menu object both as a pop-up menu that pops up when you press the right mouse button, and as a menu that is pulled down from a menu bar, even though they are technically the same.

Figure 4-20: A pop-up menu in Windows style   *Figure 4-21: A pop-up menu in Motif style*

Figure 4-22: A menu bar in Windows style   *Figure 4-23: A menu bar in Motif style*

You have already seen the basic usage of menus—pull-down menus and pop-up menus alike—in the "Adding Menus" section, so we will focus on some special uses here.

It is very easy to provide accelerators in menus. Accelerators are key combinations that can be used to directly access a function bound to a menu item without first popping up the menu. They should not be confused with underlined letters in menu entries, which can be used to jump to the entries when the menu is already open.

Set an accelerator for a menu item by calling `QMenuData::setAccel()`, which accepts a key code and a numeric identifier. The identifier is the value returned by `QMenu-Data::insertItem()` when you insert the menu entry. The keycode is an expression like `CTRL + Key_O` or `SHIFT + ALT + Key_P`. See the header file *qkeycode.h* for a complete list of keycodes. Qt automatically generates a string like "Ctrl-O", which is appended to the menu-item label. It would be better if you could override this, because in non-English-speaking countries this text might not be the correct choice.[3] If this is a problem for you, your only option is to add this string yourself and use `QAccel` for the accelerators instead of `QMenuData::setAccel()`.

Until now, you have mostly seen first-level menus, which pop up in response to a user event like a mouse-click, or pop up from a menu bar. But you don't have to learn anything new to add second-level menus, which pop up from another pop-up menu. Simply add the second-level menu with `insertItem()` to the first-level menu.

Qt does not directly support dynamic menus, that change their contents as the application changes, but it is easy to implement them. Connect to the signal `highlighted ( int )` of the parent menu. For a first-level menu, this would be the menu bar; for a higher-level menu, it would be the menu of the next lower level. In this slot, you check the ID passed: When it is the ID of a menu item that has a dynamically changed submenu, you change the menu with `QMenuData::removeItem()`, `QMenuData::updateItem()`, `QMenuData::setItemEnabled()` or whatever you like. The only problem is that you cannot get the `QPopupMenu` object to the ID, so you have to keep a table that maps IDs to `QPopupMenu` objects somewhere.

Apart from bringing up pop-up menus synchronously with `exec()` as described in the "Adding Menus" section, you can also pop them up asynchronously. This makes it possible to continue background processing while the menu is popped up, but since the menu has to grab the mouse, the next mouse click will lead to closing the menu, no matter where it occurs. If you use asynchronous menus, you won't be able to check the selected menu item via the return code, only via the signal `activated( int )`.

---

3   For example, in German-speaking countries, the correct text would be "Strg-O".

Arrangers

Qt contains five classes that are mainly meant for arranging other widgets: QFrame, QGroupBox, and QButtonBox draw a frame around their contents; while QSplitter lets the user change the relative position of two widgets to each other. QWidgetStack arranges widgets on top of each other so that only one of the widgets is visible at any time. With one exception (see the next section), QFrame is only useful as a base class for your own widgets. It serves as a base class for several Qt widgets, as well. On the other hand, you will rarely derive classes from QGroupBox or QButtonGroup; these are mainly for consumption as is, just like QSplitter and QWidgetStack.

Frames

QFrame draws a frame and then calls drawContents(). You should reimplement this method in the classes that you derive from it, the default implementation does nothing. The most useful method of QFrame is setFrameStyle(), which accepts a large number of flags. These come in two groups: frame shapes and shadow styles. You can pick one flag from each of these groups and join them with bitwise-or. The frame shapes group contains flags like Box, for a simple box; or WinPanel, for Windows 95-like panels. The shadow styles group contains the three flags Plain, Raised, and Sunken.

It is hard to imagine how a frame shape and shadow style will look when combined. The Qt reference documentation contains an image that shows all possible combination. You simply have to pick one!

If you want to customize your frames further, you can also use the methods QFrame::setLineWidth() and QFrame::setMidLineWidth(), but this leads to nonstandard interfaces.

You can also make the contents of the frame keep a certain distance from the frame itself by calling setMargin() and passing the distance as an integer value. This margin is then subtracted from the contents rectangle reported by contentsRect(), and that should be respected in your implementation of drawContents().

There is one case where using a QFrame object alone is useful: QFrame objects make fine separator lines. The object must be enabled to have a line shape, but since this is the default in the constructor, you usually don't have to worry about this requirement.

Group boxes

While QFrame is a building block for your widgets, QGroupBox (see Figures 4-24 and 4-25) and QButtonGroup can be used as is. They simply draw a frame that can visually group widgets that are logically related, such as a group of mutually exclusive radio buttons. Both widgets work the same way, although QButtonGroup has some additional facilities for working with buttons.

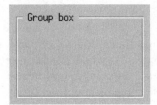

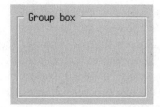

Figure 4-24: A group box in Windows style   *Figure 4-25: A group box in Motif style*

It is almost always a good idea to add a description to widgets that are grouped together by a `QGroupBox` or `QButtonGroup` object. This can be done by calling `QGroup-Box::setTitle()`, which adds a label to the upper frame line. You can also pass this title as the first argument in the constructor. While most group boxes have their title on the left side of the upper frame, you can also change this setting by calling `QGroup-Box::setAlignment` with the parameter `AlignCenter` or `AlignRight`.

The main use of `QButtonGroup` is to enforce radio button behavior, so that only one button in a group can be checked at a time. You can either make your radio buttons children of a `QButtonGroup` object, or insert them manually with `QButton-Group::insert()`. Inserting a radio button into a button group automatically makes it exclusive. If you want to have the same behavior for non-radio buttons, you have to call `QButtonGroup::setExclusive( true )` explicitly.

Another useful application of `QButtonGroup` is connecting one slot to the signals of several buttons. See the "Connecting Several Buttons to One Slot" section to learn how to do this.

Splitters

Splitters manifest themselves as small knobs (see Figures 4-26 and 4-27) that can be used to distribute the available space between two widgets. In Qt, this is implemented by the class `QSplitter`, which also contains the machinery for resizing the widgets. Example 4-1 contains a very simple program for using `QSplitter`.

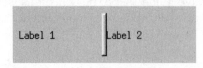

Figure 4-26: A splitter arranging two   *Figure 4-27: A splitter arranging*
labels in Windows style   *two labels in Motif style*

Example 4-1: Using `QSplitter` to divide the space between two widgets

```
1 #include <qsplitter.h>
2 #include <qapplication.h>
3 #include <qlabel.h>
```

Example 4-1: Using `QSplitter` *to divide the space between two widgets (continued)*

```
 4
 5  int main( int argc, char* argv[] )
 6  {
 7    QApplication a( argc, argv );
 8
 9    QSplitter* splitter = new QSplitter();
10    a.setMainWidget( splitter );
11
12    QLabel* label1 = new QLabel( "Label 1", splitter );
13    QLabel* label2 = new QLabel( "Label 2", splitter );
14
15    splitter->show();
16
17    return a.exec();
18  }
```

Two label widgets are created as children of the splitter, and are thus automatically registered as being arranged by the splitter. Of course, a vertical arrangement is also possible. This can be achieved by passing `QSplitter::Vertical` either as an additional first parameter to the `QSplitter` constructor, or to `setOrientation()`.

When you compile and run the program in Example 4-1, you will find it possible to make one widget almost completely disappear. You may want a certain amount of space to be available for each widget. This is easily done by calling `setMinimumSize()` at the widget as usual:

```
label1->setMinimumSize( label1->sizeHint() );
```

This ensures that `label1` will always be large enough to display its contents.

`QSplitter` respects this and `setMaximumSize()`. Also, you can determine whether a widget should also be resized when the whole splitter is resized by calling `setResize-Mode()`, then passing the pointer to the widget in question as the first and either `Stretch` or `KeepSize` as the second parameter.

Normally, `QSplitter` resizes the widgets it arranges at the end of a resizing operation, when the user stops dragging the knob. If you call `setOpaqueSize( true )` on the `QSplitter` object, the widgets get all the resize events. This is useful for providing the user with immediate feedback, but can slow down the resizing operation if the resized widgets are large, complex, or slow to redraw.

Widget stacks

The last of the widgets that arrange other widgets is `QWidgetStack`. Unlike the other widgets, this one has no visual appearance. It simply shows one of its children at a time, as specified by the user. This is useful when you have several widgets but want to make only one at a time visible.

QWidgetStack is easy to use. After creating an object of this class, create the widgets that you want to be arranged by the widget stack with the widget stack as parent, then add these to the widget stack with addWidget(). This method expects a pointer to the widget in question and an integer ID. The widget should be a child of the QWidget-Stack object. If this is not the case, it will be made into one. You can also remove widgets from the widget stack again by calling removeWidget().

To show a certain widget on the stack, call raiseWidget(). You can either pass it a pointer to the widget that you want to make visible, or the integer ID that you passed to addWidget().

Text Entry Fields

Text entry is so basic that every toolkit provides some way to do it. In Qt, it's done via the two widgets QLineEdit (see Figures 4-28 and 4-29) and QMultiLineEdit (see Figures 4-30 and 4-31) for single-line and multi-line text entry fields, respectively. Their use is very simple. In most cases, it suffices to create the widget and set its geometry. You can pre-set text with setText() and retrieve the entered text with text(). You can restrict the maximum number of characters entered in QLineEdit objects, and decide whether the characters entered should be shown, not shown or replaced by asterisks. The latter two options are useful mainly for entering passwords. QMultiLineEdit does not have these options.

Figure 4-28: A single-line text-entry field in Windows style

Figure 4-29: A single-line text-entry field in Motif style

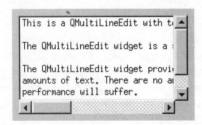

Figure 4-30: A multi-line text-entry field in Windows style

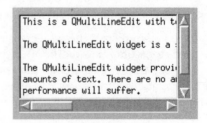

Figure 4-31: A multi-line text-entry field in Motif style

QMultiLineEdit also lets you insert text programmatically with QMultiLine-Edit::insertAt() and QMultiLineEdit::insertLine(), and then remove it again with QMultiLineEdit::removeLine(). In addition, you can use this widget as a simple text viewer by calling QMultiLineEdit::setReadOnly(true).

`QMultiLineEdit`, but not `QLineEdit`, can work with the system clipboard. Simply use the methods `cut()`, `copyText()`, and `paste()`. You do not need to create a `QClip-board` object for this. See Example 12-2 for an example.

Both widgets report state changes via the signals `returnPressed()` and `text-Changed()`. The `textChanged` signal is emitted whenever the text in the text-entry field changes. It has a `const char*` parameter with `QLineEdit` that contains the new contents. Retrieving the text from a `QMultiLineEdit` is an expensive operation, which should not be done often. Note that if you want to connect to `textChanged()` to validate the input, you should use a `QValidator` object instead (see the "Validating User Input" section).

Labels

Labels are widgets that display information. The user cannot interact with them. In Qt, there are two classes provided for this: `QLabel` can display text, a pixmap, or animation, while `QLCDNumber` shows a numerical value with a predefined number of digits.

Simple labels

`QLabel` (Figure 4-32) is probably the simplest widget in all of Qt. It can display a piece of text, a pixmap, or an animation which you set via `QLabel::setText()`, `QLabel::setPixmap()`, or `QLabel::setMovie()`. If you want to set text, you can also pass it as the first argument in the constructor.

Figure 4-32: A label in Windows or Motif style (both are the same here)

When the contents do not fit in the label, you can set the alignment, by indicating where in the space for the label the contents should be located. This is done by calling `setAlignment()`, which accepts several flags including `AlignLeft` and `AlignV-Center`. See the reference documentation for `QLabel` for the full details.

The `setAlignment()` method also knows about two flags that are not directly related to alignment: `ExpandTabs` tells the label to expand tab characters to spaces, and `Word-Break` tells it to automatically break the lines at the border of the label. Of course, these two flags only make sense with labels that show text. They have no effect when the label shows a pixmap or an animation.

It is interesting, that `QLabel` inherits from `QFrame`, and thus can have various frame styles (see the following section about `QFrame` below).

An other interesting QLabel feature is the ability to assignment "buddies". You already know that most widgets that are intrinsically labeled, such as buttons, can have an ampersand in their label. This is output as an underscore below the next letter after the ampersand. This letter serves as a shortcut key for this widget. Labels can have shortcut keys, too, but they would not make much sense without the buddy mechanism, because labels don't provide any means of user interaction. Instead, when you set a buddy widget with QLabel::setBuddy(), keyboard focus is transferred to the buddy widget whenever the shortcut key of the label is pressed. The usual applications of this feature are labeled text-entry fields or labeled combo boxes:

```
QLabel* label = new QLabel( "labeltext", parent );
label->setGeometry( ... );
label->setAlignment( AlignRight | AlignVCenter );
QLineEdit* edit = new QLineEdit( parent );
edit->setGeometry( ... ); // position right to the label
label->setBuddy( edit );
```

It's often overlooked that labels are the easiest way to show some graphics. For example, Example 4-2 shows a complete graphics viewer that already supports several formats. Note that in this example, debug() is used for a diagnostic message. This is very useful for messages that you only want to see during development. In Unix, these messages go to standard error; in Windows, they go to the debugger. Where they are shown depends on your IDE. In Visual C++, they are shown in the "Debug" window that is by default located in one of the tabs at the bottom of the screen.

Example 4-2: pixview.cpp: A simple graphics viewer with QLabel

```
 1 #include <qapplication.h>
 2 #include <qlabel.h>
 3 #include <qpixmap.h>
 4
 5 int main( int argc, char* argv[] )
 6 {
 7   QApplication myapp( argc, argv );
 8
 9   if( argc != 2 )
10     {
11       debug( "Usage: pixview filename\n" );
12     }
13
14   QPixmap mypixmap;
15   mypixmap.load( argv[1] );
16
17   QLabel* mylabel = new QLabel();
18   mylabel->resize( mypixmap.size() );
19   mylabel->setPixmap( mypixmap );
20
21   myapp.setMainWidget( mylabel );
22   mylabel->show();
23   return myapp.exec();
24 }
```

There is one situation where using a `QLabel` object is not the best choice for displaying static text: If you want to let the user copy text from the label to the clipboard, you should use a `QLineEdit` set to read-only mode instead. For multi-line labels, a read-only `QMultiLineEdit` can give you more flexibility at the cost of higher memory requirements.

QLCDNumber

`QLCDNumber` (see Figure 4-33) is a nice little widget for displaying numeric information. It can display numbers with a fixed but arbitrary number of digits in decimal, octal, hexadecimal and binary representation, can add a decimal point, and can even display a restricted number of strings. It uses a so-called "seven segment display", which should be well-known to everyone who has ever seen a digital clock.

Figure 4-33: A LCD number widget in Windows and Motif style (both are the same here)

`QLCDNumber` is commonly used in connection with a `QSlider` object. (See the "Selection Widgets" section for details.)

You create, size, and show a `QLCDNumber` like any other widget. You can either pass the number of digits as the first argument to the constructor or set it afterwards with `QLCDNumber::setNumDigits()`. The number or text to be shown is set with `display()`, to which you can pass either an `int`, a `double`, or a `const char*` parameter. The reference documentation for `QLCDNumber` contains the letters that can be displayed. All others are replaced by spaces.

When you display a numeric value, you can determine the base in which it will be displayed. This can either be chosen by calling `setMode()` with `BIN`, `DEC`, `HEX`, or `OCT` as parameter, or you can use `setBinMode()`, `setDecMode()`, `setHexMode()`, `setOctMode()`, or `setDecMode()`, respectively. Decimal representation is the default.

You can influence the appearance of the displayed data in two ways. You can choose a style for the segments by calling `setSegmentStyle()` with one of the parameters `Outline`, `Filled`, or `Flat`. In addition, you can determine whether a possible decimal point will be shown in a position of its own, or between two positions, by calling `setSmallDecimalPoint()` and passing either `true` or `false`. Note that `QLCDNumber` does not support background pixmaps.

Often you'll want to know whether a given number will fit into the available digits. This can be determined by calling `QLCDNumber::checkOverflow()`, to which you can pass either a `double` or an `int` parameter. It will return a `bool` that is true if the number cannot be displayed within the available digits.

If this is not an option for you because the value is set in a slot called by a signal from somewhere else, you can at least take action afterwards by connecting to the signal `overflow()` that is emitted whenever a number or a string that does not fit into the available digits is passed to `display()`.

Widgets for the "Office Look"

The Microsoft Office suite has set an interface standard that most Windows applications follow today. On top of the application window is a menu bar, below which you can find tool bars—rows of buttons that provide quick access to frequently-used functionality. Buttons in tool bars are usually labeled with images rather than text. Because of their small size, these images are not always easy to recognize. Tool tips have been invented to remedy this problem. A tool tip is a short phrase that is shown in a small window over a button when the user places the mouse over the button. Most programs have only one tool bar, but it is not uncommon to have three or even more of them. Below the tool bar is the main application area. In a spreadsheet application, this would be the spreadsheet that you are working on. At the bottom margin, a status bar is often found that contains information about the current state of the application.

This section explains the widgets that Qt provides for creating standard application windows. For more extensive examples, see the directory *examples/application* in your Qt distribution.

The main window

In Qt 1.40, a new widget called `QMainWindow` was introduced. This widget organizes a menu bar, any number of tool bars, a status bar, and a *central widget*, and manages their geometry.

`QMainWindow` is very easy to use. If you add children of the classes `QMenuBar`, `QTool-Bar`, or `QStatusBar`, `QMainWindow` automatically detects and uses them for their respective purposes. In addition, you can have `QMainWindow` create a menu bar or status bar on-demand by calling `menuBar()` or `statusBar()`, respectively. These methods either return a previously created menu bar or status bar, or create a new one.

Tool bars are added by hand. First, you have to create the tool bar yourself (see the next section for this), then add it with `addToolbar()`, which accepts a few more parameters. The second parameter is a label that is not yet used; the third indicates where you want the tool bar to dock with the main window. Possible values are `Top`, `Bottom`, `Left`, `Right`, `Unmanaged` and `TornOff`. The first four options should be obvious. The fifth does not show the tool bar, and the last one makes it "float" over the application. Currently, Qt does not allow tearing off tool bars with the mouse, but this is planned for a later release. Finally, the fourth parameter of `addToolbar()` indicates whether the tool bar should occupy a new row in the main window (pass `true`) or whether it should be set to the right of the last tool bar added if there is enough space for it (this is the default).

You can add as many tool bars as you like with `addToolbar()`, and you can also take them away with `removeToolbar()`. There are two more methods in `QMainWindow` that influence the look of all the tool bars: `setUsesBigPixmaps( true )` makes the tool bars use larger pixmaps than usual, and `setRightJustification( true )` makes the tool bar extend all the way to the right edge of the main window. Most tool bars do this now, so you might want to always use this setting.

A menu bar, tool bars, and a status bar do not make a useful application: The actual "content" is missing. You can use any widget for this, either predefined widgets from Qt, or widgets that you have written yourself. This widget should be a child of the main window, and should be registered with the latter with `setCentralWidget()`. `QMainWindow` does nothing with this widget except manage its geometry. You could, for example, put a `QMultiLineEdit` widget in as a central widget and have a text editor—which will not be useful yet, because it lacks loading and saving capabilities. These features are rather simple to add, though.

All in all, `QMainWindow` makes it easy to achieve a standard look for your applications. Unless your application has very special UI needs, you should probably use `QMainWindow`.

Tool bars

Tool bars are one of the preeminent features of today's GUI applications. Qt provides the class `QToolBar` (see Figures 4-34, 4-35, 4-36, and 4-37), which is used in conjunction with the class `QToolBarButton`.

Figure 4-34: Tool bars in Windows style

Figure 4-35: Tool bars in Motif style

Figure 4-36: Tool bars with big pixmaps in Windows style

Figure 4-37: Tool bars with big pixmaps in Motif style

When working with tool bars, you normally don't need to do anything but create objects. The parent-child relationship helps Qt figure out where to put which widget. You create a `QToolBar` object as a child of a `QMainWindow` object, and as many `QTool-Button` objects as needed as children of the `QToolBar` object. That's all. Here is some sample code:

```
...
QMainWindow* mainwindow = new QMainWindow();
QToolBar* toolbar = new QToolBar( mainwindow );
QToolButton* toolbutton1 = new QToolButton( somepixmap, "statusbartext",
```

```
                              0, this, SLOT( someSlot() ),
                              toolbar, "tooltiptext" );
    QToolButton* toolbutton2 = new QToolButton( someotherpixmap, "statusbartext",
                              0, this, SLOT( someOtherSlot() ),
                              toolbar, "tooltiptext" );
    ...
```

There are two other methods that you might want to use in `QToolBar`. The `addSepara-tor()` method inserts a bit of space that is not occupied by tool-bar buttons, and can be used to visually group tool-bar buttons together. The `setStretchableWidget()` method marks one widget as stretchable. This is used if the `QMainWindow` that contains the tool bar is configured to have one tool bar over its whole width. The marked widget then takes all remaining space. If you don't do this, the tool bar will occupy only the space needed for all its children.

`QToolButton` also has some interesting methods. Normally only the image is displayed, but when you call `setUsesTextLabel( true );` on a tool bar button, it displays text below the image. This text is set with `setTextLabel()`.

In the previous section, you saw that a whole tool bar can be configured to use large pixmaps. This can also be done for each tool-bar button by calling `setUsesBigPix-map( true );` on the button.

Finally, you can also make a tool-bar button toggle. This is rarely used, but some buttons toggle for example font styles, such as italics or bold, in word processing applications.

Status bars

A status bar (see Figures 4-38 and 4-39) contains messages for the user. These normally consist of text only. Qt, which implements status bars in the form of the class `QStatus-Bar`, distinguishes three different types of messages in the status bar:

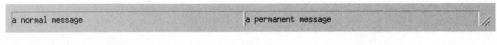

Figure 4-38: A status bar in Windows style

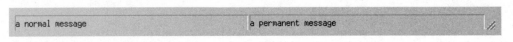

Figure 4-39: A status bar in Motif style

Temporary

Temporary messages are displayed only briefly. Most are explanatory texts for menu entries or tool-bar buttons. Temporary messages are shown by calling `QSta-tusBar::message()`. You can use the variant that accepts only the text to be shown, then remove the temporary message afterwards with `QStatus-`

`Bar::clear()`. However, it's easier to specify a time in milliseconds as the second argument. In this case, the temporary message is removed automatically. There is never more than one temporary message; if `QStatusBar::message()` is called again while the old one is still showing, the old one is deleted.

Normal

Normal messages are shown to the left of the first permanent message (see next item). They can be temporarily obscured by temporary messages. You can put any widget as a normal message into the status bar, but usually `QLabel` is used. Another widget that might be useful in a status bar is `QProgressBar`. You put a widget into a status bar as a normal message by calling `QStatusBar::addWidget()`, then passing a pointer to the widget as the first parameter. The second parameter is an integer stretch factor that is used to compute the space that is available for each normal and permanent message in the status bar. This value is not an actual width in pixels but it indicates the relative size in relation to the other widgets. The third parameter is `false`.

Normal messages are removed again with `removeWidget()`. Some things that might be useful as normal widgets are information items that are usually displayed but often change and that are not crucial for allowing the user to operate the application. Examples would be line and column indicators in a spreadsheet or a word processor or an indicator that shows whether the current document has been saved.

Permanent

From a programmer's point of view, permanent messages are used just like normal messages—except for the fact that you pass `true` as the third parameter to `addWidget()`. Permanent messages behave differently, however. They are arranged to the right of the status bar, and can never be obscured by temporary messages. It is customary to put information there that is relatively static or that is needed for the user to operate the application, such as mode indicators. Even though it does not fit the pattern, many applications also put a clock there.

Tool tips and "What's This" windows

Tool tips, also known as bubble help, quick help, or Hoover help, are small, rectangular windows with short descriptive text that pop up when you rest the mouse over a widget for a short time. The descriptive text should explain in as few words as possible the meaning of the widget the mouse is over. When the mouse is moved away or a mouse button is pressed, the tool tip disappears.

"What's This" windows (sometimes also called bubble help) have a similar purpose, but they are larger and allow more text to be shown. They bridge the gap between the low impact and low information content of tool tips and the high impact and high information content of online help systems.

Adding tool tips to a widget is very simple. You usually don't have to hassle with creating tool-tip widgets, or with sizing and showing them. All you have to do is call `QTool-Tip::add()`:

```
QLineEdit* edit = new QLineEdit( parent );
QToolTip::add( edit, "Description of edit field" );
```

This adds a tool tip to the text-entry field. If you are tired of the tool tip, you can remove it by calling `QToolTip::remove()`. Note that these two methods of `QToolTip` are static. You don't have to create `QToolTip` objects yourself, this is done internally for you.

Tool tips that are added with the method shown are always available when the mouse is over a widget. You can also restrict the area that is sensitive to tool tips to a certain rectangle within the widget:

```
QLineEdit* edit = new QLineEdit( parent );
QToolTip::add( edit, QRect( 0, 0, edit->width()/2, edit->height() ),
            "Description of edit field" );
```

This ensures that the tool tip pops up only when the mouse is over the left half of the widget.

There are cases when the text of the tool tip—or even whether a tool tip should be shown at all—can only be determined dynamically. An example would be a scroll bar in a word processor that shows the current page in a tool tip. To do this, you have to derive a class from `QToolTip` that reimplements the virtual method `maybeTip()`. A `QPoint` reference that contains the mouse position relative to the window is passed to this method. On the basis of this position, and possibly the current application state, you can decide whether a tool tip should be shown or not. You can also access the widget associated with the tool tip by calling `QToolTip::parentWidget()`. If you should decide to pop up the tool tip, you have to call `QToolTip::tip()` with a `QRect` and a `QString` that indicate size, and position, and the text to be shown, respectively. When the mouse is moved out of the widget and back to the same point, `maybeTip()` is called again. Depending on your application, you might want to do some caching to avoid expensive recalculations. The `maybeTip()` method can be called very often, and should therefore be as fast and efficient as possible.

In applications that have a status bar or other means of displaying temporary information, it could be useful to display the text shown in a tool tip in this other widget as well. You can use `QToolTipGroup` to leverage the mechanisms of deciding whether information about a widget that is in `QToolTip` should be provided. Since status bars and the like usually have more space available than tool tips, you can even show another (possibly longer) text here. To achieve this, you have to do two things: You must pass a pointer to the `QToolTipGroup` object and the second string to an overloaded form of the method `QToolTip::add()`. Then you must connect the signal `QToolTipGroup::showTip( const char* )` to a slot that will show the text and the signal `QToolTipGroup::clear()` to a slot that will remove it. These slots usually are the `setText()` and `clear()` methods of a label. Here is a code snippet that shows the whole procedure:

```
QToolTipGroup * ttgroup = new QToolTipGroup( parent );
QLabel* mylabel = new QLabel( parent ); // should be in e.g. a status bar
QObject::connect( ttgroup, SIGNAL( showTip( const char * ) ),
                  mylabel, SLOT( setText( const char * ) ) );
QObject::connect( ttgroup, SIGNAL( removeTip() ),
                  mylabel, SLOT( clear() ) );
QLineEdit* myedit = new QLineEdit( this );
QToolTip::add( myedit, "short description", ttgroup, "longer description" ):
```

Altogether, tool tips are a very efficient means of communicating to the user the meaning of the elements in a GUI. They are very easy to program, and normally don't have much overhead. You should use them liberally.

At the beginning of this section, we mentioned that you can also use What's This windows. These are represented in Qt by the class `QWhatsThis` (see Figure 4-40), and are used the same way that you use `QToolTip`. To associate a What's This window containing the text `text` with a widget `mywidget`, simply call

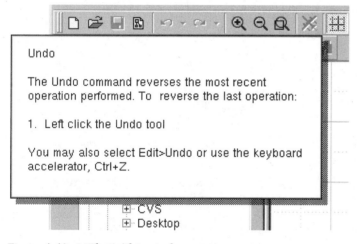

Figure 4-40: A What's This window

```
QWhatsThis::add( mywidget, text );
```

If you want to make a *deep copy*[4] of the string passed, pass `true` as the third parameter.

Another form of `QWhatsThis::add()` has the following prototype:

```
void QWhatsThis::add ( QWidget* widget, const QPixmap& icon,
                       const char *title, const char* text,
                       bool deepCopy = true )
```

---

4 A deep copy copies the actual data from one object to another, while a shallow copy only increases a reference count and copies a pointer.

Here you can specify a pixmap that is shown in the What's This window, as well as a title text that is shown as a heading of the window. Removing such an association from a widget is done by calling QWhatsThis::remove(), to which you simply pass a pointer to the widget in question.

We already know that tool-tip windows are shown automatically. What's This windows are not shown automatically, but on user request. The user can press Shift and F1 together on the keyboard, in which case the "What's This" window for the widget that has the keyboard is shown; or the user can click on a special tool-bar button and then click on the widget whose What's This window he wants to see. Such a special tool-bar button should not be created explicitly, but by calling QWhatsThis::whatsThisButton(), to which you pass the parent for the button (normally a QToolBar widget). This method creates and returns a button configured for invoking the What's This feature. You can invoke this method as many times as you like, and get a new tool-bar button each time. Here is a small example:

```
QToolBar* toolbar = new QToolBar( this );
QToolButton* contexthelpbutton = QWhatsThis::whatsThisButton( toolbar );
```

Progress bars

Figure 4-41: A progress bar in Windows style   *Figure 4-42: A progress bar in Motif style*

Progress bars are represented in Qt by the class QProgressBar (see Figures 4-41 and 4-42). They are used to show that the program is still working during lengthy operations. Normally, you will use the more convenient encapsulation QProgressDialog, which you will learn about in the "Predefined Dialogs" section. Sometimes it can be useful to integrate a progress bar into a dialog, however, or even into the top-level window of your application. In these cases, QProgressBar is used directly. Its use is restricted by the fact that it is only available horizontally. The use of QProgressBar is very simple. You create, size, and show it the usual way, and then set the total number of steps that the application will have to perform with setTotalSteps(). During this operation, call setProgress() with the number of currently completed steps. QProgressBar will automatically compute the percentage, and update the progress bar accordingly. Remember that you have to give the progress bar a chance to update its display by either returning to the event loop from time to time, or by calling QApplication::processEvents() so that the display can be refreshed and the progress bar redrawn.

Scrolled Views

A scrolled view can be any widget with a view that might be smaller than its physical size. The user is then provided with scroll bars to select the part of the widget that he wants to see. This can be cumbersome to program, but fortunately Qt provides the class `QScrollView`, which does almost everything automatically. You have already seen how to use it in the "Adding a Scrolled View" section, so we will only mention some characteristics here that have not yet been discussed or that might be less than obvious. Please note that other widgets, including `QListView` (see the "List Views" section), use `QScrollView` implicitly.

Unlike scrolled views in other toolkits, `QScrollView` can contain multiple child widgets. You add one child widget with `addChild()`, then you pass a pointer to the child as well as the x and y positions where the widget should be located on the overall canvas that the scrolled view uses. Children can be moved with `moveChild()`, removed with `removeChild()`, and made visible and invisible with `showChild()`.

If you don't want to have widgets in your scrolled view but want to draw on the canvas provided by `QScrollView` instead, you have to derive a class from `QScrollView` and reimplement `drawContentsOffset()`. The reference documentation for this method contains an example that shows how to deal with the coordinates. If you draw on the canvas this way, you might want to resize the canvas, too. This can be done with `resizeContents()`. This method can also be used when you simply add widgets to the canvas.

It might not always be obvious when to use child widgets and when to draw directly into the canvas provided by `QScrollView`. Here is a possible rule of thumb: whenever you would only put in a `QWidget` as a child (as opposed to a more specialized widget), you might just as well use the canvas directly, because the most commonly used overloaded methods for receiving low-level events are available in the methods `viewportPaint-Event()`, `viewportMousePressEvent()`, `viewportMouseReleaseEvent()`, `viewportMouseMoveEvent()`, and `viewportMouseDoubleClickEvent()`. These methods are called by `QScrollView` and you must reimplement them as needed in a class derived from `QScrollView`. If you need any special low-level events, such as `enterEvent()` or `leaveEvent()`, you must provide a widget of your own.

Scrolled views can have one of three possible scroll-bar policies. These scroll bar policies are set with `setHScrollBarMode()` and `setVScrollBarMode()` for the horizontal and vertical scroll bar, respectively. The possible values are `AlwaysOn` (scroll bar is always shown, even if it would not be necessary), `Auto` (scroll bar is shown only when the view is smaller than the physical size of the contents) and `AlwaysOff` (scroll bar is never shown, even if it is necessary). Note that `AlwaysOff` should only be used when you provide some other means of moving the view; otherwise the user will have no way to get to the parts of the view that are not visible from the beginning.

The view on the canvas can also be done programmatically. Two methods, `setContentsPos()` and `center()`, use absolute coordinates and scroll the view so that the coordinates passed as parameters are visible in the upper-left corner or in the center of the view, respectively. There is also an overloaded version of `center()` that allows you to specify some tolerance as to the center position. Finally, `scrollBy()` allows you to use relative coordinates and thus mimics what the user does when clicking on the arrows of the scroll bars. `QScrollView` has only one signal, `contentsMoving()`. It is emitted just before the contents are moved to their new position.

List Views

`QListView` (see Figures 4-43 and 4-44) is a very complex widget that can display data in rows and columns, as well as in hierarchical form. Entries that contain sub-entries can be opened and closed by the user or programmatically.

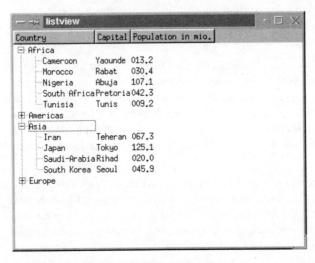

Figure 4-43: QListView in Windows style

`QListView` and its helper class `QListViewItem` have complex APIs, and it takes time and experience to master them. But if you confine yourself to the default settings at first and use some things that are done "automagically", simple operations with `QListView` are just that.

To demonstrate some features of `QListView`, we will build a list of countries, their capitals, and their populations. There will be one country per row and three columns: one each for the name of the country, the capital, and the population. In order to get some hierarchical structure into this example, we will group the countries by continent.[5] Before we dive into the workings, let's look at the code shown in Example 4-3.

---

5 If you are wondering why I chose these countries; they are the 32 nations that qualified for the world soccer championships in the summer of 1998—an event that has more than once stopped me from continuing the work on this book.

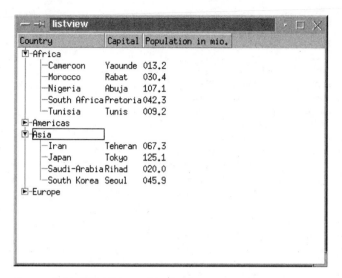

Figure 4-44: QListView in Motif style

Example 4-3: Information about countries in a list view

```
1   #include <qapplication.h>
2   #include <qlistview.h>
3
4   int main( int argc, char* argv[] )
5   {
6     QApplication a( argc, argv );
7
8     QListView* listview = new QListView();
9
10    listview->addColumn( "Country" );
11    listview->addColumn( "Capital" );
12    listview->addColumn( "Population in mio." );
13    listview->setRootIsDecorated( true );
14
15    QListViewItem* europe = new QListViewItem( listview, "Europe" );
16    QListViewItem* america = new QListViewItem( listview, "Americas" );
17    QListViewItem* africa = new QListViewItem( listview, "Africa" );
18    QListViewItem* asia = new QListViewItem( listview, "Asia" );
19
20    QListViewItem* item = new QListViewItem( america, "Brazil", "Brasilia", "161.8" );
21    item = new QListViewItem( europe, "Scotland", "Edinburgh", "057.6" );
22    item = new QListViewItem( africa, "Morocco", "Rabat", "030.4" );
23    item = new QListViewItem( europe, "Norway", "Oslo", "004.4" );
24    item = new QListViewItem( europe, "Italy", "Rome", "052.2" );
25    item = new QListViewItem( america, "Chile", "Santiago", "014.2" );
26    item = new QListViewItem( africa, "Cameroon", "Yaounde", "013.2" );
27    item = new QListViewItem( europe, "Austria", "Vienna", "008.1" );
28    item = new QListViewItem( asia, "Saudi-Arabia", "Rihad", "020.0" );
```

Example 4-3: Information about countries in a list view (continued)

```
29    item = new QListViewItem( europe, "Denmark", "Copenhagen", "005.2" );
30    item = new QListViewItem( europe, "France", "Paris", "058.0" );
31    item = new QListViewItem( africa, "South Africa", "Pretoria", "042.3" );
32    item = new QListViewItem( america, "Paraguay", "Asuncion", "005.6" );
33    item = new QListViewItem( europe, "Bulgaria", "Sofia", "008.8" );
34    item = new QListViewItem( europe, "Spain", "Madrid", "039.1" );
35    item = new QListViewItem( africa, "Nigeria", "Abuja", "107.1" );
36    item = new QListViewItem( asia, "South Korea", "Seoul", "045.9" );
37    item = new QListViewItem( america, "Mexico", "Mexico-City", "097.6" );
38    item = new QListViewItem( europe, "Netherlands", "Amsterdam", "015.6" );
39    item = new QListViewItem( europe, "Belgium", "Brussels", "010.1" );
40    item = new QListViewItem( europe, "Yugoslavia", "Belgrad", "010.8" );
41    item = new QListViewItem( asia, "Iran", "Teheran", "067.3" );
42    item = new QListViewItem( europe, "Germany", "Berlin", "081.2" );
43    item = new QListViewItem( america, "USA", "Washington", "268.0" );
44    item = new QListViewItem( europe, "England", "London", "048.5" );
45    item = new QListViewItem( africa, "Tunisia", "Tunis", "009.2" );
46    item = new QListViewItem( europe, "Romania", "Bucaresti", "022.5" );
47    item = new QListViewItem( america, "Colombia", "Bogota", "035.1" );
48    item = new QListViewItem( america, "Argentina", "Buenos Aires", "034.6" );
49    item = new QListViewItem( asia, "Japan", "Tokyo", "125.1" );
50    item = new QListViewItem( america, "Jamaica", "Kingston", "002.4" );
51    item = new QListViewItem( europe, "Croatia", "Zagreb", "004.5" );
52
53    listview->resize( 400, 300 );
54    listview->show();
55
56    a.setMainWidget( listview );
57
58    return a.exec();
59 }
```

Apart from the mass of data needed to make experimenting with the list view more interesting, this example features several interesting things. Probably the most prominent one is the lack of an explicit call to a method like `insertItem()`. The whole hierarchy is built on the normal parent-child widget hierarchy of Qt.

We have four objects of the class `QListViewItem`, which are children of the list view itself and are thus top-level items. We have 32 more `QListViewItem` objects that are each children of one of the four top-level items.

NOTE   Every piece of data displayed in a list view belongs to an object of the class `QListViewItem`. To fully exploit `QListView`, you need to master not only the API of this class, but that of `QListViewItem` as well.

For now, let's get back to our example. In the first few lines of the main function, we set up the list view by adding column headers and telling the widget that we want the top-level items to be expandable. If we did not, there would be no way for the user to get at the country entries, but you could still expand one entry programmatically by calling setOn(true) at the corresponding QListViewItem.

The headers are more than descriptions of what can be found in the columns. Clicking on them sorts the data by that column. You could also do that programmatically by calling setSorting(), where the first parameter is the number of the column and the second parameter is a Boolean value that indicates whether sorting should be in ascending (true) or descending (false) order.

Before we go into the details about how to create items for the list view, let's look at more general formatting features. One of these is column width. Column widths can be configured in two modes, Maximum and Manual. These modes are set with setColumn-WidthMode(). In Maximum mode, the column automatically gets the size needed for the widest entry in that column. In Manual mode, the width is set via setColumnWidth().

Two more methods that affect the graphical representation are setTreeStepSize() and setAllColumnsShowFocus(). The first determines how far children are indented below their parent entry (the default is 20 pixels), the second determines whether all or only the first column of an entry should be highlighted when that entry has the keyboard focus.

With the latter method, we come to the subject of keyboard focus and selection. QListView allows two selection policies, single-selection and multi-selection. The default is single-selection: selecting one entry automatically deselects the previously selected entry. You can switch to multi-selection with setMultiSelection(). With multi-selection, keyboard focus and selection are two different things, which can be set with two different methods. The setSelected() method accepts a pointer to a QList-ViewItem and a bool, which indicates whether the item in question should be selected or not. Keyboard focus, on the other hand, is set with setCurrentItem().

When you want to iterate over all items in a list view, the easiest way is to retrieve the first item with firstChild(), then use QListViewItem::itemBelow() to iterate over the items. Unfortunately, this only works, if all items with children are expanded. If you cannot guarantee this, you will have to use a combination of the various navigation functions of QListViewItem().

QListView emits several signals. The selectionChanged() signal notifies the program that more, fewer, or other items are selected. If the selection policy is single-selection, there is also selectionChanged(QListViewItem*), which makes the newly selected item readily available. currentChanged(QListViewItem*) by contrast notifies about change in keyboard focus. Since even in a multi-selection list box only one item at a time can have the keyboard focus, this signal can always pass the newly focused item.

Finally, there are three signals which could be considered lower-level and report manipulations on the items. These are `doubleClicked( QListViewItem* )`, `return-Pressed( QListViewItem* )` and `rightButtonClicked( QListViewItem*, const QPoint&, int )`. The first two should usually be connected to the same slot, because users normally expect double-clicking and pressing Enter to invoke the same functionality. The `rightButtonClicked()` signal is mainly meant for popping up context menus. The second and third parameters specify the mouse coordinates (which are a good candidate for the menu coordinates), and the column in which the mouse was clicked. Note that there is a signal `rightButtonPressed()`, but there is not `rightButtonReleased()`.

`QListViewItem` has many methods, but most of them are only useful for special cases. If you only want text entries, the constructors might be all you ever need. You pass the parent as the first argument: either a `QListView*` for top-level items, or a `QListViewItem*` for non-top-level items. In addition, you can pass up to eight strings, which serve as values for the respective columns. If you need more than eight columns, or if you want to have pixmaps in your columns, you will need some additional methods. The `setText( int, const char* )` method adds a text entry to a column specified by the first argument. The `setPixmap( int, const QPixmap& )` method does the same for pixmaps.

Three more methods allow entry configuration. The `setSelected( bool )` method selects or deselects an entry, `setExpandable( bool )` determines whether it should be possible for the user to expand or fold back the entry by means of a little icon next to it, and `setSelectable( bool )` determines whether the item can be selected by the user.

Note that when you build very large hierarchies, it may not be a good idea to create all items at startup or widget creation time, because that may take too long. For example, file systems can be very large. It would be better to create the root entries first, then create all other entries only when they are needed (for instance, when their parent is expanded). To do so, create a class derived from `QListViewItem` that reimplements `setOpen( bool )` and `setup()`. The `setup()` virtual method is called before the item is displayed at first and also after attributes like the font or the widget style have changed. You can take care of any initializations here that might have an effect on the item's visual appearance. With a file system, this might include checking whether the directory in question is empty, and calling `setExpandable( true )` if it is not, so that the user can open it. When this item is opened, `setOpen( bool )` is called, where you can read the directory and create items for the files or subdirectories. This way, there is never more file system activity than needed. Since there is already a good *dirview* example in the Qt distribution, read through it if you want to make use of `QListView`.

Widgets for Tabular Material

The widget `QListView` presented in the previous section, has a limited capability for displaying tabular data. If you need more flexibility and do not care about the possibility of having hierarchical displays, `QListView` is probably not the best choice. Qt also provides a widget especially geared toward displaying tabular material, `QTableView` (see Figures 4-45 and 4-46).

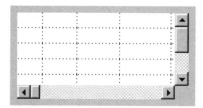

Figure 4-45: A simple table view in Windows style

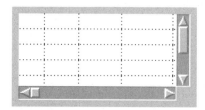

Figure 4-46: A simple table view in Motif style

`QTableView` is an abstract base class, so it cannot be used by itself. Instead, you have to derive another class from `QTableView`. There is a comprehensive example of how to use `QTableView` in the "Implementing a Browse Box" section.

`QHeader` is another very useful widget for displaying tabular material. Both `QListView` and `QTableView` use it for displaying their column or row headers, but you can also use `QHeader` for your own widgets if they display tabular data.

The most important thing to understand with `QHeader` is that you do not have one `QHeader` object per column or row, but one for all columns or rows. You add column or row headers with `addLabel()` and set the orientation (`Horizontal` for column headers and `Vertical` for rows) with `setOrientation()`. Should you need to change header labels afterwards, you can do so with `setLabel()`.

Most methods in `QHeader` deal with sizes and are seldom used, but the three signals are very important: `sectionClicked()` is emitted when one of the header parts (labels) has been clicked. It has become customary for programs to sort the data by the column or row in question when the user clicks on the header; `QListView` does exactly this. On the other hand, spreadsheets like MS-Excel simply select the column or row in question when the header is clicked.

The other two signals are emitted when headers are manipulated. When the user clicks with the mouse exactly between two header labels and then moves it, `sizeChanged ( int, int, int )` is emitted where the first parameter is the logical column or row number, the second is the old size in pixels, and the third one is the new size. If you click and drag in one label instead, you can change the physical positions of the labels. When this happens, the signal `moved( int, int )` is emitted where the first parameter specifies the column being moved, and the second its new position.

These three actions—clicking on a column or row header, resizing a header, and moving a header—can be enabled or disabled by calling `setClickEnabled( bool )`, `setResizeEnabled( bool )`, and `setMovingEnabled( bool )`, respectively. Finally, if you want the signal `sizeChanged()` to be emitted while the sizes are changed, you will have to call `setTracking( true )`. This could be useful for online resizing of columns or rows, but this feature should be used carefully, because it needs a lot of computational resources.

5

A Guided Tour Through the Qt Dialogs

Dialogs are important in every GUI-based application. Even simple applications usually have several dialogs, and in applications of medium complexity, it is not uncommon to have 50 or more dialogs. Therefore, building dialogs is something a GUI developer does often. In this chapter, we look at the facilities Qt provides for building dialogs. We start with predefined dialogs that cover a certain well-defined task, which can usually be used out of the box. Afterwards, we look at the building blocks you can use to create your own dialogs.

Predefined Dialogs

Predefined dialogs are nice for the stressed developer because you can get good results with very little coding. Often only one line of code will suffice to customize these for your purposes.

Qt currently provides three predefined dialogs that are frequently used: `QFileDialog` for specifying files, `QProgressDialog` for showing progress in lengthy operations, and `QMessageBox` for general messages. We will look at each of these in turn.

File-selection dialogs

`QFileDialog` (see Figures 5-1 and 5-2) provides a file-selection dialog. It lets the user choose a file for opening, saving, or other file-related operations. Most of the time, `QFileDialog` can be used with only one line of code:

```
QString filename = QFileDialog::getOpenFileName( "/" /* initial directory */,
                                    "*.txt" /* filename filter */ );
```

The static method `QFileDialog::getOpenFileName()` opens a file selection dialog with an initial directory / (Windows users will use something like `C:\` here) and a file-name filter `*.txt`. If the initial directory is not specified, it defaults to the current direc-

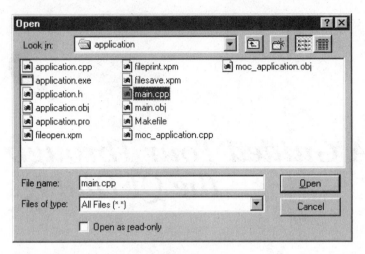

Figure 5-1: A file dialog in Windows style

Figure 5-2: A file dialog in Motif style

tory of the process the first time this method is called. Afterwards, it uses the directory shown when the last file dialog was closed.

The filename filter determines which files are shown for selection in the dialog. The user can terminate the selection by clicking either OK or Cancel, or by double-clicking a filename. If the user clicks Cancel, the returned string will be null; this can be checked with `QString::isNull()`. Notice that there is also `QFileDialog::getSaveFile-Name()`, which differs only in the text shown in the title bar.

If `getOpenFileName()` and `getSaveFileName()` don't give you the flexibility you need, you can also use a file-selection dialog the usual way by constructing it and then showing it with `QDialog::exec()`. If you inherit a class from `QFileDialog`, you can add up to three widgets to the bottom of the dialog with the method `addWidget()`.

Message boxes

Probably the most common dialog of all is the simple message box. Message boxes inform the user about any important conditions, good or bad, that arise during program execution. Message boxes are almost always *modal*, meaning that the user has to confirm whatever the message box tells them.

Like `QFileDialog`, the Qt class for message boxes, `QMessageBox` (see Figures 5-3 and 5-4) offers several static methods. First, you have to decide the level of severity of your message. `QMessageBox` supports three of these: "information", "warning", and "critical".

The next option to select is the number of buttons. `QMessageBox` objects can have one to three buttons. The buttons can be specified by their type or their text. The available types are OK, Cancel, Yes, No, Retry, Abort, and Ignore. Qt selects the text depending on the type. Note that selecting a button by type is a good idea only when you do not plan to convert your program to another language because you cannot influence the text at all. If you want to choose your text yourself, don't specify the buttons by type.

Figure 5-3: A message box in Windows style   *Figure 5-4: A message box in Motif style*

This may seem complicated now, so some examples are in order. The following shows an information dialog with only an OK button. It is specified by type, and it is also the default button (the button that is "clicked" when you press the Enter key):

```
int ret = QMessageBox::information( 0 /* parent */, "Some Caption Text",
                        "Operation complete", /* message text */
                        QMessageBox::OK | QMessageBox::Default );
```

The next example shows a warning dialog containing an OK button and a Cancel button. Both buttons are specified with their labels. The OK button should be the default button, and the Cancel button the "Escape button" (the button that is "clicked" when you press the escape key):

```
int ret = QMessageBox::warning( 0, "Some Caption Text",
                        "File is write-protected. Try to save anyway?",
                        "OK", "Cancel", 0, 0, 1 );
```

The second 0 is necessary to fill in the parameter for the third possible button. Any button whose parameter is 0 will not be shown.

Finally, here is how to show a dialog for a critical message with three buttons specified by type, one being the default and one the escape button:

```
int ret = QMessageBox::critical( 0, "Danger, Will Robinson!",
                         "This operation will set your CPU on fire. Do you\n"
                         "want to continue?",
                         QMessageBox::Yes | QMessageBox::Default,
                         QMessageBox::No,
                         QMessageBox::Cancel | QMessageBox::Escape );
```

Although this last example breaks the rule, you should always make the least destructive[1] button the default button. In addition, always set the escape button to the "cancel" function. When something unexpected happens, many users tend to hit the escape button in panic and they panic even more when this does not bring them back to normal operation.

Even though the static methods in QMessageBox are rather flexible, you can also construct and show a message box the usual way. You can set the pixmap for the icon shown with QMessageBox::setIconPixmap() or use one of the predefined icons with QMessageBox::setIcon(), to which you pass one of QMessageBox::NoIcon, QMessageBox::Information, QMessageBox::Warning, and QMessageBox::Critical. The message text can be set with setText(), the button texts with setButtonText(). The following example reimplements the dialog from the previous example, this time building the dialog "by hand" by passing the parameters to the various methods. Notice that it is not possible to specify a default and an escape button this way.[2]

```
QMessageBox* mb = new QMessageBox();
mb->setCaption( "Danger, Will Robinson!" );
mb->setText( "This operation will set your CPU on fire. Do you want to continue?" );
mb->setIcon( QMessageBox::Critical );
mb->setButtonText( 0, "Yes" );
mb->setButtonText( 1, "No" );
mb->setButtonText( 2, "Cancel" );
int ret = mb->exec();
delete mb;
```

It doesn't matter whether you use one of the static methods or show the dialog manually with exec(), the number of the button that was pressed to close the dialog will always be returned.

---

1 It is not always clear what "least destructive" means in a given situation. Try to follow the example of other well-designed programs, and use your common sense.
2 You could get default and escape buttons and still get to set everything yourself by setting the escape and the default button in the ten-argument constructor and changing the button texts afterwards.

Progress dialogs

The third predefined dialog is the progress dialog, in Qt represented by the class `QPro-gressDialog` (see Figures 5-5 and 5-6). This dialog is used to show the user how a lengthy operation progresses. "Lengthy" is here something like "more than a few seconds". A progress dialog contains a label and a progress bar, the latter showing how far the operation described by the former has progressed. In addition, a progress dialog can have a cancel button with which the user can interrupt the operation in progress. If this operation is interruptible at all, you should by all means include such a cancel button, because it gives the user a feeling of security when she can halt an over-long operation.

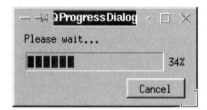
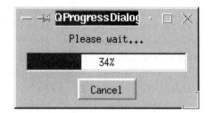

Figure 5-5: A progress dialog in
Windows style

Figure 5-6: A progress dialog in
Motif style

`QProgressDialog` has an interesting feature: Based on the time needed for one step, it estimates the total amount of time needed for the operation and only shows the dialog if at least three seconds are left. This prevents progress dialogs from flashing up for a few milliseconds, an annoying feature common to some platforms.

A progress dialog must know about the total number of steps needed to complete the operation, as well as the currently performed number of steps. Inform the dialog about these values with `QProgressDialog::setTotalSteps()` and `QProgressDialog::setProgress()`. Obviously, `setTotalSteps()` is called right after the dialog's creation while `setProgress()` is called while the operation progresses. Remember that it is not enough to call `setProgress()` during a lengthy process; you must also allow events to be processed from time to time so that the dialog has a chance to update itself. Fortunately, `setProgress()` already does this for you, if the progress dialog is modal.

You don't show a progress dialog with `exec()`, because it is not really a modal dialog, but rather a special kind of dialog. It is displayed with `show()` like modeless dialogs, but it blocks the user interface by eating up all events. Unlike a modal dialog, it does not start an event loop of its own. That means background processing (including performing the operation whose progress the dialog reports) can still occur.

`QProgressDialog` objects emit a signal called `cancelled()` whenever the cancel button is pressed. You should connect this signal to some slot in your application that stops the background operation. Please see the "Printing" section for an example of how to use `QProgressDialog` with printing.

It should be added that Qt also provides a ready-made print dialog. This is usually used in connection with the class `QPrinter` rather than in a standalone way. It is covered in the "Printing" section.

Building Blocks for Your Own Dialogs

While the predefined dialogs are nice, and accomodate most common cases, you will still have to define your own dialogs. In this section, we describe Qt's facilities for defining custom dialogs. Note that we only talk about the general frame for a dialog. You can then fill that dialog with the widgets we discussed in the previous chapter.

In most cases, you derive your own dialog class from `QDialog`. Unlike other toolkits, Qt does not make a strong distinction between modal and modeless dialogs; both kinds of dialogs inherit from `QDialog`. You pass a flag in the constructor of `QDialog` that indicates whether the dialog should be modal or not. Modal dialogs start their own event loop, and thus block the rest of the user interface until they are closed again. The most visible difference in the code between modal and modeless dialogs is that modal dialogs are shown synchronously with `exec()` which returns only after the dialog has been closed, while modeless dialogs are shown asynchronously with `show()` and `hide()`.

Defining a dialog is usually very easy. The customary procedure is to construct the widgets that make up the dialog in the dialogs constructor. You don't have to destroy them in the destructor because the dialog automatically deletes all its children that have not yet been deleted when it is destroyed itself. In most cases, you also should set a caption for the dialog in the constructor with `setCaption()`. A dialog that has been constructed can be shown with either `exec()` (modal dialogs) or `show()` (modeless dialogs). `exec()` returns an integer value that indicates how the dialog was closed. The commonly used values are `QDialog::Accepted` and `QDialog::Rejected` which usually correspond to an OK button and a Cancel button, respectively. In a modal dialog, it is easiest to close the dialog with `QDialog::accept()` or `QDialog::reject()` which set the return code correspondingly. If you want to define other return codes (rarely a good idea), you can also close the dialog with `QDialog::done( int )`, where you can pass whichever return code you want.

Note that you should never need to set a size for your dialog with `setGeometry()` or `resize()`, the base class `QDialog` automatically resizes the dialog so that it fits the contained widgets.

Example 5-1 shows a program that defines a modal dialog that only consists of a checkbox, an OK button and a Cancel button. It demonstrates how you can evaluate the settings the user has made in the dialog. The dialog is shown when you click on the button in the initial window. The interesting methods to look for are `MyDialog::MyDialog` (the constructor of the dialog) and `ClickReceiver::slotShowDialog()`. Note that the two push-buttons are saved nowhere in the dialog class—their pointers are not needed after the connect. This is no memory leak, because the dialog destroys its children when it is destroyed itself. It is not uncommon for dialogs to have no explicit destructors.

The listing is thoroughly commented, so you should be able to understand the rest of the code without further explanation.

Example 5-1: Creating and executing a modal dialog

```
 1  #include <qapplication.h>
 2  #include <qcheckbox.h>
 3  #include <qdialog.h>
 4  #include <qpushbutton.h>
 5
 6  /**
 7   * This is our dialog. Note that you cannot see from the class
 8   * declaration whether this is a modal dialog or not.
 9   */
10  class MyDialog : public QDialog
11  {
12      Q_OBJECT
13
14  public:
15      MyDialog();
16
17      bool isCheckBoxChecked() const { return _checkbox->isChecked(); }
18
19  private:
20      QCheckBox* _checkbox;
21  };
22
23
24  /**
25   * The constructor for our dialog. By passing "true" as the third
26   * parameter to the constructor of the base class, QDialog, we make
27   * it modal. It is common practice to create all widgets that make up
28   * the dialog in the constructor and set the caption there.
29   */
30  MyDialog::MyDialog() :
31      QDialog( 0, "Test dialog", true /* modal */ )
32  {
33      // Create a check-box so that the user has at least something to do.
34      _checkbox = new QCheckBox( "Check me", this );
35      _checkbox->setGeometry( 55, 10, 100, 20 );
36
37      // Create an OK button. Note how the signal/slot connection
38      // completely implements the functionality of this button without
39      // any need for user-defined code.
40      QPushButton* okbutton = new QPushButton( "OK", this );
41      okbutton->setGeometry( 10, 40, 100, 30 );
42      QObject::connect( okbutton, SIGNAL( clicked() ),
43                        this, SLOT( accept() ) );
```

Example 5-1: Creating and executing a modal dialog (continued)

```
44
45    // Create the cancel button. Similar to the OK button. Again, no
46    // user-defined functionality is needed to make this button close
47    // the dialog.
48    QPushButton* cancelbutton = new QPushButton( "Cancel", this );
49    cancelbutton->setGeometry( 120, 40, 100, 30 );
50    QObject::connect( cancelbutton, SIGNAL( clicked() ),
51                      this, SLOT( reject() ) );
52
53    // Set a caption for the dialog. Don't forget this in your dialogs.
54    setCaption( "My Test Dialog" );
55  }
56
57
58  /*
59   * This class is a kludge that is necessary because we need an object
60   * for the slot that pops up the dialog.
61   */
62  class ClickReceiver : public QObject
63  {
64    Q_OBJECT
65
66  public slots:
67    void slotShowDialog();
68  };
69
70
71  /*
72   * This is the second interesting method in this program. Note how the
73   * document is shown with exec(), how the return code is checked, and
74   * how the user settings are only evaluated when the user has pressed
75   * OK. You should never evaluate the settings in the dialog when the
76   * user has pressed cancel.
77   */
78  void ClickReceiver::slotShowDialog()
79  {
80    // create the dialog
81    MyDialog* dialog = new MyDialog();
82    // Show it. exec() only returns when the dialog is closed.
83    int ret = dialog->exec();
84    // Check how the user has closed the dialog.
85    if( ret == QDialog::Accepted )
86      {
87        // User pressed OK
88        debug( "User pressed OK; check-box was %s checked.\n ",
89          (dialog->isCheckBoxChecked() ? "" : "not") );
90      }
91    else
92      {
93        // User pressed cancel
```

Example 5-1: Creating and executing a modal dialog (continued)

```
94        debug( "User pressed cancel\n" );
95      }
96  }
97
98  #include "dialog.moc"
99
100 int main( int argc, char* argv[] )
101 {
102   QApplication myapp( argc, argv );
103
104   QPushButton* mybutton = new QPushButton( "Click for dialog" );
105   mybutton->resize( 150, 30 );
106
107   ClickReceiver clickreceiver;
108   QObject::connect( mybutton, SIGNAL( clicked() ),
109                     &clickreceiver, SLOT( slotShowDialog() ) );
110
111   myapp.setMainWidget( mybutton );
112   mybutton->show();
113   return myapp.exec();
114 }
```

Tab dialogs

If your dialogs are getting crowded, you could consider organizing the widgets in a tab dialog. Tab dialogs, in Qt represented by the class `QTabDialog` (see Figures 5-7 and 5-8), consist of several "subdialogs" ("pages"), which are accessed via "*tabs*", are small rectangles over the subdialogs labeled with a name that should express which kind of functionality the subdialog provides. Tab dialogs should always have one OK button and one cancel button for the whole dialog. Even though Qt does not stop you from doing so, you should never have a button in one of your subdialogs that closes the whole dialog. In addition to the OK button and the cancel button, tab dialogs often have a default button, which resets the settings of the dialog to sensible values if the user goofs up.

Figure 5-7: A tab dialog in Windows style   *Figure 5-8: A tab dialog in Motif style*

The subdialogs are simple QWidget objects. Often you do not even have to derive a subclass from QWidget, unless you want to bundle the slots that react to changes in a subdialog within the subdialog and not within the whole tab dialog. The usual way is to create these subdialogs in the constructor of the tab dialog and then add them to the tab dialog with QTabDialog::addTab(). addTab() accepts two parameters: a pointer to the widget, and a string that forms the label of the tab. It is important that you call add-Tab(): simply making the subdialogs children of the tab dialog does not suffice and won't show the page.

In addition to adding the subdialogs, you should add the push-buttons for the whole tab dialog. These are placed at the bottom of the tab dialog, below the subdialogs. There are four buttons available: Default, Cancel, OK, and Apply. You don't have to use these strings for the labels, though, these are just the defaults. You can pass any label of your choice to QTabDialog::setDefaultButton(), QTabDialog::setCancelButton(), QTabDialog::setOKButton() and QTabDialog::setApplyButton(). The difference between the "Apply" button and the "OK" button is that the dialog is closed upon pressing the "OK" button, but not the "Apply" button.

You should never need to explicitly set the size of a QTabDialog object, it is automatically resized to accommodate the largest contained subdialog, the tabs and the buttons at the bottom.

QTabDialog emits several signals. Three of them are emitted when one of the following buttons is clicked: applyButtonPressed() (which also covers the OK button), defaultButtonPressed(), and cancelButtonPressed(). These signals are somewhat misnamed—the signals are emitted when the button is clicked, not when it is pressed. The slots connected to these signals are usually not fundamentally different from those for normal dialogs.

Two other signals are used by Qt to notify the application that either the dialog or a certain page is about to be shown. Before the dialog is shown, the signal aboutToShow() is emitted; before a certain page is shown, Qt emits the signal selected(const char*). The parameter of the latter contains the label of the tab for that page. Unfortunately, this does not help much, since there is no method for finding the QWidget for a given tab label. Unless you keep a list of widgets and tab labels somewhere, this signal is rendered rather useless.

You can use aboutToShow() to copy your application's state into the dialog. This is mainly used for dialogs that are not created, used, and destroyed immediately after their appearance, but are kept around between invocations.

An additional feature of QTabDialog is the possibility of enabling or disabling individual pages. Do this with QTabDialog::setTabEnabled() and pass the name of the tab label and a bool parameter, which determines whether the page should be enabled (true) or disabled (false).

Here is a simple example of a constructor of a class derived from `QTabDialog`. This example is by no means complete, but it should give you an impression of how tab dialogs are set up. If you would like a complete example, see the file `pref.cpp` in the directory `examples/pref` of the Qt distribution.

```
MyTabDialog::MyTabDialog() :
  QTabDialog( 0, "MyTabDialog", true /* modal */ )
{
    // create a QWidget as the first page
    QWidget* firstpage = new QWidget( this );
    firstpage->setGeometry( ... );
    // add some widgets to firstpage here
    addTab( firstpage, "First" );
    ...
    QWidget* secondpage = new QWidget( this );
    secondpage->setGeometry( ... );
    // add some widgets to secondpage here
    addTab( secondpage, "Second" );
    ...
    // the dialog will have an OK, a Cancel, and a default button
    // for simplicity, we keep the default labels
    setOKButton();
    setCancelButton();
    setDefaultButton();

    // connect the buttons
    QObject::connect( this, SIGNAL( applyButtonPressed() ),
                      this, SLOT( applyClicked() ) );
    QObject::connect( this, SIGNAL( cancelButtonPressed() ),
                      this, SLOT( cancelClicked() ) );
    QObject::connect( this, SIGNAL( defaultButtonPressed() ),
                      this, SLOT( defaultClicked() ) );
}


MyTabDialog::~MyTabDialog()
{
}


void MyTabDialog::applyClicked()
{
    // copy the data from the dialog into the application
    ...
    accept();
}


void MyTabDialog::cancelClicked()
{
    // don't copy the data from the dialog into the application
    reject();
}
```

```
void MyTabDialog::defaultClicked()
{
    // restore the data in the dialog to some hard-coded
    // default values
    // e.g. firstpage->mytextedit->setText( "" );
}
```

Even though tab dialogs can be a good solution to overcrowded dialogs and can also bundle related things together, they are no silver bullet. The reference documentation for QTabDialog says a lot about when to choose a tab dialog. You should read it before you design your first tab dialog.

Qt tries to prevent you from misdesigning tab dialogs by allowing only one row of tabs. Multi-row tab dialogs are one of the worst design mistakes—they are very difficult for the user to understand and operate.

QTabDialog is easy to use but not very flexible. You can only have rectangular tabs with rounded corners, and you can only have them above the pages. When you want something special, like triangular tabs or tabs below the pages, you can roll your own dialog with the help of QTabBar. QTabBar contains only the tabs in one of four forms: rectangular above, rectangular below, triangular above, and triangular below. You can achieve other forms by inheriting from QTabBar and overriding some methods, but keep in mind that non-standard user interfaces are almost never a good idea.

When you don't use QTabDialog, the only support you get is the layout of the tabs in a row by QTabBar. You have to arrange the pages and buttons all by yourself. This advanced task is beyond the scope of this book, so you should read the reference documentation for QTabBar.

6

Using Layout Managers

So far, we have been very basic in how we have laid out our widgets. We have set absolute positions and sizes with `QWidget::resize` and `QWidget::move()` or `QWidget::setGeometry()`, specifying the position within the parent and the size at which a widget should be shown. This is generally not desirable. It makes the window that contains the widgets (often a dialog) look bad when it is resized. If the size of this window is increased, there will be an empty space at the right and lower borders of the window, because the widgets stay at their fixed positions and do not fill the newly available space. If, on the other hand, the size of the window is decreased, some widgets will not be visible any longer, or might be shown incompletely. Again, this occurs because the widgets do not occupy less space and use less intra-widget space to accomodate the smaller parent window.

Another disadvantage comes from internationalization. When you prepare your program for displaying text in different languages, you'll find that on-screen texts in different languages are rarely the same size. If you design your dialogs with English labels and then have your application translated into a language like Finnish, where the average word length is longer, chances are that the text will not fit into the space allocated.

Layout Manager Basics

The solution to these two problems is *geometry management*, also called *layout management*. When using geometry management, sizes and positions are not set absolutely. Instead they are set in relation to each other. The actual positions are computed according to the actual size of the parent containing the widgets by another entity, the *layout manager*. For this to work, you have to register each widget with a layout manager. Recursive management is also possible: You can have one layout manager managing other layout managers inside of another one.

Qt has four classes of layout managers; you can also write your own. The following classes are available:

`QHBoxLayout`

> Lays out the managed widgets in a row.

`QVBoxLayout`

> Lays out the managed widgets in a column.

`QBoxLayout`

> The base class of `QHBoxLayout` and `QVBoxLayout`. You need this, only when you cannot determine at compile time whether your widgets should be laid out in a row or a column—a rare situation.

`QGridLayout`

> Lays out the managed widgets in a grid.

`QLayout`

> The base class of all layout managers. You inherit from the class if you want to implement a layout manager of your own.

The basic procedure for using layout managers always follows these steps:

- Create one or more layout managers. The top-level layout manager should have the parent widget as its parent; all others should have no parent.

- Create the widgets as usual, but do not assign sizes and positions with `setGeometry()`, `resize()`, or `move()`. Instead, specify constraints like minimum or maximum sizes if needed.

- Register each widget with a layout manager by calling the `addWidget()` method of the layout manager in question.

- If you have a hierarchy of layout managers, register every layout manager except the top-level layout manager with its own layout manager by calling `addLayout()`.

- Call `activate()` on the top-level layout manager. This starts layout management. Note that you should not do this before all widgets and sublayouts have been added, to avoid unnecessary computation. `activate()` should not be called in QT 2.0.

Laying Out Widgets in Rows and Columns

To make the abstract stuff from the previous chapter easier to understand, let's start with a simple example. We want to lay out three buttons in a row, which is done with the code in Example 6-1 (see the screenshot in Figure 6-1):

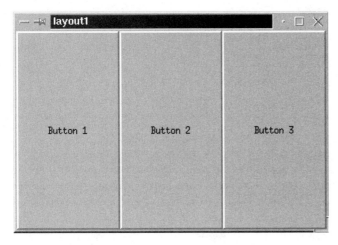

Figure 6-1: A simple layout of buttons in a dialog

Example 6-1: Laying out buttons in a dialog

```
1  #include <qdialog.h>
2  #include <qpushbutton.h>
3  #include <qlayout.h>
4  #include <qapplication.h>
5
6  class MyDialog : public QDialog
7  {
8  public:
9    MyDialog();
10 };
11
12 MyDialog::MyDialog()
13 {
14   QPushButton* b1 = new QPushButton( "Button 1", this );
15   b1->setMinimumSize( b1->sizeHint() );
16   QPushButton* b2 = new QPushButton( "Button 2", this );
17   b2->setMinimumSize( b2->sizeHint() );
18   QPushButton* b3 = new QPushButton( "Button 3", this );
19   b3->setMinimumSize( b3->sizeHint() );
20
21   QHBoxLayout* layout = new QHBoxLayout( this );
22   layout->addWidget( b1 );
23   layout->addWidget( b2 );
```

Example 6-1: Laying out buttons in a dialog (continued)

```
24   layout->addWidget( b3 );
25
26   layout->activate();
27 }
28
29 int main( int argc, char* argv[] )
30 {
31   QApplication a( argc, argv );
32
33   MyDialog* dlg = new MyDialog();
34   dlg->show();
35   a.setMainWidget( dlg );
36
37   return a.exec();
38 }
```

Let's go through the constructor of `MyDialog` step by step. First, we create a button `b1`. We do not set an actual size or position, but there is one thing we have to do: You cannot make a widget arbitrarily small. There is always a size below which you would not recognize the widget as a widget of its type, and usually there is also a larger size which you would consider the acceptable size of a widget. For push-buttons and labels, this size is determined by the size needed to display the label text. You would not want to allow the user to make the button so small that the text is not legible any longer. Therefore, we set a minimum size by calling `setMinimumSize()`. The size that we choose is the one returned from `sizeHint()`, a very useful function that returns the size at which the widget says it is displayed best.

There may also be a largest acceptable size, in which case you would set it with `setMaximumSize()`. However, this is not needed as often as a minimum size.

After we have created two more buttons, we create a layout manager. There are several layout managers in Qt, and they differ in the way they arrange the widgets. We will describe all of them later in this chapter. For now, it suffices to know that `QHBoxLayout` lays out the widgets it manages in a row. Since this layout manager is the top-level manager (there is only one in this example, after all), it is constructed with the widget as a parent for which it manages the children.

After the layout manager is created, we register our push-buttons with the layout manager by calling `addWidget()`. Finally, we initiate layout management by calling `activate()`. From now on, the `QHBoxLayout` manager will determine the size and position of the registered widgets.

You should now compile and try this little program. Try making the window as small as possible. You will see that Qt won't let you make the window smaller than the space needed for correctly displaying all three buttons with their labels. If you want to experiment, try removing the calls to `setMinimumSize()` and see what happens.

Let's experiment a little bit more. More often than not, you don't want all the widgets to have the same size changes when their parent is resized. You might have a label and an accompanying text-edit field and you want only the edit field to grow. Or you may want both to grow, but the edit field should grow "more". There are many possibilities, and they require the use of *stretch factors*. These are integer values that determine how much a widget grows or shrinks in relation to other widgets managed by the same layout manager.

The actual value of the stretch factors is of no importance, it's their ratio that counts. For example, let's assume that you want the second button to grow more than the first, and the third to grow even more than the second. You could achieve this by using the following calls to `addWidget()` (see the screenshot in Figure 6-2):

```
layout->addWidget( b1, 1 );
layout->addWidget( b2, 2 );
layout->addWidget( b3, 3 );
```

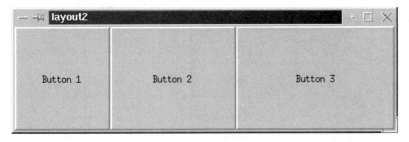

Figure 6-2: Different stretch factors for the buttons

Note that the relationships only apply for the horizontal sizes in this case, since `QHBox-Layout` is only concerned with horizontal layout. We'll see how to take care of vertical positions later.

If we had used 0 as the stretch factor for one of the widgets in this example, that widget would not have been stretched at all. In Figure 6-1 all widgets had an implicit stretch factor of 0 for fixing their horizontal size, and since the layout manager *had* to distribute the space somehow, it distributed it evenly among the widgets.

For our next example, we want to have some space between the second and third widgets. We do this by calling `addStretch()`. Again, a stretch factor can be passed. We will use a value of 2 to make the space stretch by the same factor as the widget to its left. Note that such stretchable space never has a minimum size. If you want a minimum distance between widgets, you can add space of a fixed size with `addSpacing()`. This is especially useful if you want to use a layout manager for laying out the children of a `QFrame`, such as a `QGroupBox` or a `QButtonGroup`. Just add the height of the group box's with `addSpacing()`, and pass the width of the frame as the border in the constructor:

```
QGroupBox* gb = new QGroupBox( "Some label", parent );
QVBoxLayout* vbl = new QVBoxLayout( gb, gb->frameWidth() );
```

```
    vbl->addSpacing( gb->fontMetrics().height() );
    // add children to gb and add them with addWidget to vbl
    ...
```

This ensures that neither the frame nor the label of the group box is overpainted by the widgets. Of course, if you have just a QFrame and no QGroupBox or QButtonGroup, you can skip the call to addSpacing().

Nested Layout Managers

Our next task involves layout managers that are managed by other layout managers. Again, we want to have a row of three buttons, but this time there should be another row of two more buttons below it. Both rows will be managed by a QHBoxLayout, but the two QHBoxLayout layout managers will be managed by another layout manager: a QVBoxLayout. The code is in Example 6-2, the screenshot is in Figure 6-3.

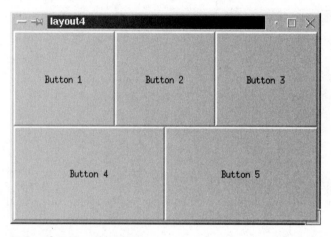

Figure 6-3: Nested layouts

Example 6-2: Two nested layouts

```
 1  #include <qdialog.h>
 2  #include <qpushbutton.h>
 3  #include <qlayout.h>
 4  #include <qapplication.h>
 5
 6  class MyDialog : public QDialog
 7  {
 8  public:
 9    MyDialog();
10  };
11
12  MyDialog::MyDialog()
```

Example 6-2: Two nested layouts (continued)

```
13 {
14   QPushButton* b1 = new QPushButton( "Button 1", this );
15   b1->setMinimumSize( b1->sizeHint() );
16   QPushButton* b2 = new QPushButton( "Button 2", this );
17   b2->setMinimumSize( b2->sizeHint() );
18   QPushButton* b3 = new QPushButton( "Button 3", this );
19   b3->setMinimumSize( b3->sizeHint() );
20   QPushButton* b4 = new QPushButton( "Button 4", this );
21   b4->setMinimumSize( b4->sizeHint() );
22   QPushButton* b5 = new QPushButton( "Button 5", this );
23   b5->setMinimumSize( b5->sizeHint() );
24
25   QVBoxLayout* vlayout = new QVBoxLayout( this );
26   QHBoxLayout* hlayout1 = new QHBoxLayout();
27   QHBoxLayout* hlayout2 = new QHBoxLayout();
28
29   vlayout->addLayout( hlayout1 );
30   vlayout->addLayout( hlayout2 );
31
32   hlayout1->addWidget( b1 );
33   hlayout1->addWidget( b2 );
34   hlayout1->addWidget( b3 );
35
36   hlayout2->addWidget( b4 );
37   hlayout2->addWidget( b5 );
38
39   vlayout->activate();
40 }
41
42 int main( int argc, char* argv[] )
43 {
44   QApplication a( argc, argv );
45
46   MyDialog* dlg = new MyDialog();
47   dlg->show();
48   a.setMainWidget( dlg );
49
50   return a.exec();
51 }
```

As described, there are three layout managers in this program. One is the vertical manager which also plays the role of the top-level layout manager. Accordingly, the parent widget is passed to the constructor, which is not done for the second-level layout managers. Passing a parent to the constructor of a second-level layout manager would result in a runtime warning from Qt, and possibly odd display results.

The two horizontal layouts are added with `addLayout()`. As with `addWidget()`, you could pass stretch factors here.

Sometimes you don't want the user to be able to resize a dialog, but you still want to use layout management for the initial layout. In this case, you can call `freeze()` after calling `activate()` on the top-level layout manager. The `freeze()` method accepts two integer parameters, the desired width and height. If you don't pass any parameters or pass two zeros, `freeze()` makes the window as small as possible.[1] Note that it is not possible to "unfreeze" ("thaw") a window again.

You might wonder if `freeze()` is a good thing to use—there is no need to use layout management if you don't want to let the user resize the window anyway, right? Of course, there is, because of the language variations. A dialog with layout management that is "frozen" still has fitting sizes for all its elements, no matter what the size of the labels may be.

Since the layout manager is not needed any more after freezing the layout, you can even delete the layout manager object to regain a little bit of memory.

We have now seen most of the features of layout management. There are more features, such as borders around the whole managed window, but they are rarely used. You can find out about these in the reference documentation. However, you have not seen the grid layout manager yet which is introduced in the next section.

Grid Layout

When creating a grid layout manager, you specify the number of rows and columns it should use. You can later increase these figures by calling `expand()`, but you can never decrease them.

When you add a widget or a sublayout, you specify the grid cell in which the widget or sublayout should be. Example 6-3 contains sample code that arranges six push-buttons in a grid with two rows of three columns (see Figure 6-4):

Example 6-3: Using a grid layout

```
 1  #include <qdialog.h>
 2  #include <qpushbutton.h>
 3  #include <qlayout.h>
 4  #include <qapplication.h>
 5
 6  class MyDialog : public QDialog
 7  {
 8  public:
 9    MyDialog();
10  };
11
12  MyDialog::MyDialog()
13  {
```

---

1   You can also freeze the layout by calling `resize( 0, 0 )` on the parent widget that is managed with a layout manager.

Example 6-3: Using a grid layout (continued)

```
14    QPushButton* b1 = new QPushButton( "Button 1", this );
15    b1->setMinimumSize( b1->sizeHint() );
16    QPushButton* b2 = new QPushButton( "Button 2", this );
17    b2->setMinimumSize( b2->sizeHint() );
18    QPushButton* b3 = new QPushButton( "Button 3", this );
19    b3->setMinimumSize( b3->sizeHint() );
20    QPushButton* b4 = new QPushButton( "Button 4", this );
21    b4->setMinimumSize( b4->sizeHint() );
22    QPushButton* b5 = new QPushButton( "Button 5", this );
23    b5->setMinimumSize( b5->sizeHint() );
24    QPushButton* b6 = new QPushButton( "Button 6", this );
25    b6->setMinimumSize( b6->sizeHint() );
26
27    QGridLayout* layout = new QGridLayout( this, 2, 3 );
28    layout->addWidget( b1, 0, 0 );
29    layout->addWidget( b2, 0, 1 );
30    layout->addWidget( b3, 0, 2 );
31    layout->addWidget( b4, 1, 0 );
32    layout->addWidget( b5, 1, 1 );
33    layout->addWidget( b6, 1, 2 );
34
35    layout->activate();
36  }
37
38  int main( int argc, char* argv[] )
39  {
40    QApplication a( argc, argv );
41
42    MyDialog* dlg = new MyDialog();
43    dlg->show();
44    a.setMainWidget( dlg );
45
46    return a.exec();
47  }
```

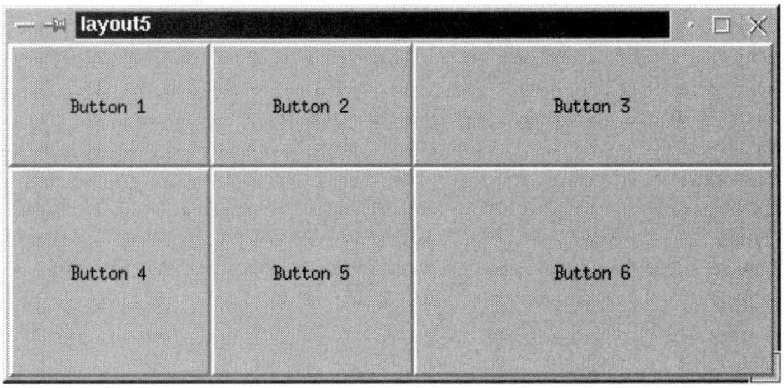

Figure 6-4: Using a grid layout

In a grid layout, you set stretch factors for whole rows and columns, not for individual widgets. This is done with the methods setRowStretch() and setColStretch(). Interestingly, you can get a rather pretty scaling if you set the minimum width of a column and its stretch factor to the same value.

Additional space can be added with addRowSpacing() and addColSpacing(). Finally, when a widget or sublayout should occupy more than one cell, you can use addMulti-CellWidget() to specify an area in the grid that the widget or sublayout should occupy. You should be careful with this method. Often, beginning users mess around with cells spanning multiple columns or rows when what they want to achieve is not really a grid. Unless you really desire a grid structure, where almost all cells span only one row and one column, you should use nested box layouts. The main use for addMultiCellWidget() should be for a table header.

If the available layout managers are not sufficient for your needs, you can always write your own. This is done by deriving a class from QLayout, the common base class of all layout managers, and implementing mainVerticalChain(), mainHorizontal-Chain(), and initGM(). Unfortunately, this is way beyond the scope of this book.

If you have problems getting the relationships between widgets and layouts straight, it can be a good idea to test things with an HTML editor like Netscape Navigator Gold. Simply use the HTML tags for creating tables and check whether they come out right in the preview window.

A box layout is nothing more than a table with either one column or one row, and a grid layout is a table with more than one column and more than one row. Once your tables look right, it is easy to transfer the layout hierarchy to Qt code.

Now you might be able to lay out a dialog properly at almost any size, make it user-resizable, and ensure that the widgets will always be at the right place. But how can you know what is the best initial size for the dialog? If your dialog contains only widgets that have a natural size, such as buttons where the natural size is a little bit larger than the label of the button, it is probably best to initially use the smallest size possible. If your dialog contains multi-line text entry fields or listboxes, however, picking the smallest possible size might not be a good idea. The user will have to manually resize the dialog to let the text-entry fields have a size where more of the text entered is visible. This is especially annoying for the growing number of users with large monitors. In these cases, it is user-friendly to make the initial size of a dialog a function of the total screen resolution. QApplication::desktop() provides the width and height of the desktop, so it is no problem to compute a size for the dialog that is adapted to the screen size and resolution. The following code starts from the minimum size of the dialog, then tries to optimize it in a sensible way. It is slightly adapted from the code used in QFile-Dialog, and could be used in the constructor of any dialog.

```
// start with the minimum size
QSize s = minimumSize();
// increase it so it will take advantage of larger monitors
if( s.width() * 3 > QApplication::desktop()->width() * 2 )
```

```
    s.setWidth( QApplication::desktop()->width() * 2 / 3 );
if( s.height() * 3 > QApplication::desktop()->height() * 2 )
    s.setHeight( QApplication::desktop()->height() * 2 / 3 );
else if( s.height() * 2 < QApplication::desktop()->height() )
    s.setHeight( QApplication::desktop()->height() / 2 );
// use the computed size as the initial size
resize( s );
```

Code like this is becoming increasingly more important, since larger monitors are more affordable nowadays.

7

Some Thoughts on GUI Design

In this chapter, we will give you some advice on GUI design. Keep in mind that these are only guidelines, and they may or may not apply to your specific application.

The initial points are general. Afterwards, we present a list of hints and guidelines for specific widgets.

If you need a more thorough description of things that can go wrong in GUI design, look at *http://www.mindspring.com/~bchayes/shame.htm*. The opposite, examples of well-done user interfaces, can be seen at *http://www.mindspring.com/~bchayes/fame.htm*.

If you are looking for something in print, try *About Face—The Essentials of User Interface Design* by Alan Cooper; *The Elements of User Interface Design* by Theo Mandel; or *The Windows Interface Guidelines for Software Design* (useful even for other platforms).

- Always try your application yourself. If you are a contract programmer writing vertical-market software, you may not have a real use for your application, but you should at least have tried to work with it for more than 10 minutes. Otherwise, you will never find out where your interface is awkward to use. Note that I am not talking about testing to find real bugs—I take it for granted that you will do so.

- Try making your application worthwhile for the casual user and the power user alike. Provide keyboard accelerators and other means of quick navigation that can be used by power users, but provide enough help and guidance for the beginner. If there is a trade-off, try to find out which type of user is more likely to use your application.

- Use the right widgets for the task at hand. Nothing is worse for the user than a developer that chooses the wrong widgets, either because she did not know what was available, or because she simply made a poor choice. A drastic example would be to use a spin box without the possibility of entering the required number for a date, forcing the user to scroll through the entire list.

Choosing the right widgets entails knowing which widgets are available. This is the main reason I provided an extensive review of Qt widgets in Chapter 4, *A Guided Tour Through the Simple Widgets*, and Chapter 5, *A Guided Tour Through the Qt Dialogs*. If you haven't yet done so, you should at least skim those chapters to know what Qt has in store for you. When a new version of Qt appears, read the changes file to see if new widgets have been added that are more suitable for a given task than those you now use.

- Be careful about inventing your own widgets. This does not mean that you should not derive your own dialogs from QDialog. You should simply be reluctant to invent completely new ways of interaction. Don't invent a new kind of button when a QPushButton would suffice. Inventing new widgets just to have a flashy interface is always a bad idea, because your users are accustomed to standard interfaces. Why should you make them learn new things when you don't have to?

  There are situations where you must invent widgets because Qt does not contain them. When we talk about writing your own widgets later in this book, we will provide you with two examples for new widgets that make sense. Each covers an interface area that has not been addressed by Qt. You will also see that we try to follow standard metaphors as closely as possible when designing these widgets.

- Provide immediate response. If the user has started a lengthy operation, at least show that the operation has been started. Don't make her wait until the operation is completed.

- Prepare for internationalization, even if you do not expect that someone who speaks and reads another language will ever use your application. This includes leaving enough room for labels because in languages other than English, words may be much longer.

  Internationalization involves much more than just translating text. Number and date formats are also different in other countries, and you must be careful with images and the use of color keys. Some images have a completely different connotation in other cultures, or are not understood at all. If you want to provide an internationalized program, you should read the standard references for this. Even though it is geared toward Macintosh programmers, the *Guide to Macintosh Software Localization* is an outstanding source of information on this subject.

- If your application involves mainly entering text via the keyboard as with a word processor, text editor, or data-entry application, make it completely usable without the mouse. It is very distracting for the user to have to move his hands from the keyboard to the mouse and then back again just to place the cursor in another text-entry field.

  Making your application "keyboard-aware" involves making all menu entries available via shortcuts, providing accelerators for the most importants menu entries, and making sure your dialogs can be sensibly traversed with the tab key. Unless you have very good reasons to do it differently, make all widgets that allow interaction (except QLabel) reachable via the tab key. On the other hand, widgets that do not allow interaction should not be accessible via the tab key.[1]

- Adhere to standards for your platform. For example, on Microsoft Windows, Close once meant to close the current window while Exit meant to close the whole application. Unfortunately, Microsoft has broken these rules itself several times—a very bad idea. Remember: Just because Microsoft, Sun, or some other big player is doing something, it may not be right or sensible. Use your own common sense. Especially on Microsoft Windows, there are some common, badly designed dialogs (like the standard file selection dialog) that might make you want to implement a dialog of your own. You should think three times before doing so, though.

- Use tool tips to explain image buttons (as in tool bars), but don't use them to explain obvious things. For example, don't assign a tool tip to a push-button that just repeats that button's label. If you have a status bar, consider repeating the tool-tip text or—even better—providing a longer description here. While the tool-tip text should only appear after the mouse rests at the same place for several seconds, the text in the status bar should appear whenever the mouse is over a widget that allows user interaction.

- Don't make your users look stupid. For example, if a user has chosen a menu entry to quit the application, don't bring up a message box asking her whether she really wants to quit, unless she could actually lose data. If she did not want to quit the application, he wouldn't have selected that menu entry in the first place.

  Don't make the computer look more stupid than it is. For example, never present the user with a dialog saying "You must enter foobar into the field blahblurb"—since this is obviously a constant, the program could easily have done so itself.

- Be as context-sensitive as possible. For example, when the user requests help by clicking the Help button in a dialog, he should be presented with the text that explains the dialog in question, not all help texts available for the application.

- Similar looking widgets should work in similar ways. Stated another way, if two operations are alike, the widgets to achieve them should also look alike. This helps the user recognize patterns in the use of the application.

- When a widget is not available for interaction because of the state of the application, disable it. It is very annoying for the user to interact with some widgets only to find out that these didn't apply for that particular situation. Hiding a widget that is not available is a bad idea. The user will think something has gone astray when a widget she is used to in a dialog is suddenly no longer there.

---

1 You might have another opinion here. Consider a data-entry application with a dialog that has five text-entry fields. Let's say that one of those fields is only available for data entry, when one of the others contains a certain text. Now imagine a user who has to change a certain field (say, the fourth) in lots of records. He would probably use the tab key to move to the fourth field (by pressing the tab key three times), make his changes, and use an accelerator to proceed to the next record, where he will again press the tab key three times. If the second text-entry field is disabled here for some reason, he will finally find himself in the fifth field instead of in the fourth as expected. You have to think about what the optimal solution for your application is.

- Always show some kind of feedback when a lengthy operation is in progress. Qt provides the ideal means to do this with `QProgressDialog` and `QProgressBar`. When you absolutely have to, you can even provide some kind of animation, but please make this removable.

The preceding points apply to most applications and user interfaces, no matter which widgets they use. Here are some points that apply to specific widgets.

- Provide shortcuts for all menu entries. Provide accelerators for the most important entries. Use the accelerator standards for your platform.

- Avoid having too many items in a menu. Work with submenus if necessary, but remember that too many levels of submenus are awkward to use (for example, see the start menu of Windows 9x/NT).

- Never execute a function when the user has clicked on an entry in the menu bar. Users expect a menu to be pulled down, not to cause an immediate action.

- When a menu entry invokes a dialog, add the common three dots to the entry. Even more important, don't add the dots when a menu executes an action directly instead of invoking a dialog. Users expect to be given a second chance when they select a menu entry with three dots by clicking on cancel in the subsequent dialog.

- Wherever possible, use pop-up menus that are invoked when the user presses the right mouse button. These pop-up menus should only provide the most common operations for the object or situation in question. Less frequently used operations can still be used via the menu bar. Pop-up menus should always be an additional means to execute a function, not the only one. Never let a pop-up menu have more than two levels of submenus—this is extremely awkward to use.

- A dialog should always have a cancel (in modal dialogs) or close (in modeless dialogs) button. The user must always have a chance to back out. Also, it is bad style to expect the user to close the dialog only via the close button of the window.

- Choose wisely between modal and modeless dialogs. Every dialog that influences the general state of the application should probably be modal. On the other hand, dialogs that the user is likely to open several times during a session with an application should be modeless. This way, the user can just leave them open and place them next to their application window for quick access. Search-and-replace dialogs are typical examples of this type of modeless dialog.

- Avoid fixed-size dialogs, especially if there are listboxes inside. It makes much more sense to be able to resize the window.

- Don't use a single-line edit field `QLineEdit` when the user is allowed to enter more than one line of text. Use a `QMultiLineEdit` instead.

- Don't use listboxes when you have space for only, say, three items. Apart from the fact that these listboxes simply look silly, they are awkward to use. When you keep pressing the mouse on one of the arrows, the list scrolls faster than the user can skim it to see whether he has found the selection he is looking for. If screen real-estate is scarce, use a combo box.

- Don't fill a listbox with more than, say, 50 elements. Apart from the fact that this will slow down the operation of the listbox, it will be almost impossible for the user to pick the correct item from a selection of 2000. When you really have to present a large number of items, use some kind of hierarchical display.

- Avoid too many push-buttons in a single dialog. A dialog that more closely resembles the control center of a spaceship than a properly designed user interface will be incomprehensible to most users. If you find yourself adding too many push-buttons to a dialog, think about whether all those functions need to be in a single dialog. You could always use a tab dialog.

- Tab dialogs are good for bundling loosely related interface elements together, but never have so many tabs in a tab dialog that they fill more than one row. It is difficult for the user to scan the available tabs and find the correct one.

- Never make dialogs scrollable. If you have so many widgets in a dialog that you need to scroll the whole contents of the dialog, the dialog is overcrowded anyway and should be split.

These points should help you a bit when designing your user interface. Unfortunately, looking at examples is not always a good idea because there are as many bad examples as there are good ones. As an inexperienced GUI designer, you may not be able to distinguish between them.

When it is possible, ask your users how they would like the interface to work. You might even provide them with several versions and let them decide which they like best. Keep in mind, though, that users do not always know what they really want. They will often say "I want everything to stay just like it is now." Change is not always good, but if this attitude prevailed, we would all still live in caves.

8

Container Classes

One of the first types of classes that were put into class libraries were container classes: classes for objects that contain other objects, such as arrays or lists. Since then, most GUI class libraries have included container classes.

Note that if you have some experience in other programming languages that are commonly used for GUI programming like Java, you might understand the notion of "container" differently. In the Java AWT, containers are objects that can hold other GUI objects. In Qt, there is no such difference; every GUI object can hold other GUI objects, even though it does not always make sense. For example, having a button contain other GUI objects would be of no use. Qt uses the classic C++ notion of containers—classes that can hold other objects in the sense of memory references, not in the more-specific sense of general containment.

With the advent of the C++ standard, another library with container classes, the Standard Template Library, has been included in the standard. This will lead to all compiler vendors including it.

Nevertheless, it still pays to learn how to use Qt's own container classes. STL is not easy to learn, and when all you want to do is put some strings in a list and iterate over it, you can just as well use the Qt classes. Of course, these are not as sophisticated as the STL classes, and there aren't quite so many of them. But if Qt contains what you need, I would suggest giving it a try. You could even save some memory in your application, since the container classes from Qt are linked to your program anyway, and it is reasonable to assume that compiler vendors will make linkage to the STL optional.

Available Container Classes

Qt provides the following container classes:

`QArray`

> This is a very restricted class that can be used only for built-in types or classes that have no constructors, destructors, or virtual methods, since it uses bitwise copy to duplicate its members. If you need something more flexible, use `QIntDict` or

QList. QArray is the only container class that stores its elements directly as a copy, all others store only pointers to their elements. There are two derived classes, QByteArray and QPointArray, for storing bytes and coordinate pairs, respectively. In addition, QString is derived from QArray, even though you usually won't use it like that.

QBitArray

This is like QArray, but contains only bits. It is useful for collecting flags in an application.

QDict

QDict provides a so-called hashtable, a structure where the elements are accessed via string keys. This is very useful when you have pairs of strings and have to look up one of the values by means of the other, for example.

QCache

Provides a hashtable like QDict, but stores only a certain amount of data in it. Entries can get lost if the cache becomes larger than a threshold, and they have to be restored by the application if necessary.

QIntCache

This class is similar to QCache, but uses long values instead of char* values for the keys.

QIntDict

This class is similar to QDict, but uses long values instead of char* values for the keys. In a way, this resembles classical arrays.

QList

This class provides doubly-linked lists, a very common data structure in computer science. It is very efficient to use when you want to access the members one after the other in insertion order (or the other way round), but not so efficient when you want to have random access to the members.

There are two classes derived from QList: QStrList and QStrIList. Both store strings, the latter uses case-insensitive compare operations.

QPtrDict

This class is similar to QDict, but uses void* values instead of char* values for the keys.

QQueue

This class implements the well-known data structure "queue", which is used when you want to put in elements at one end and take them out in the same order from the other end. You only have access to the elements whose "turn" it is at the other end of the queue.

QStack

This class implements the well-known data structure "stack", which is used when you want to put in elements at one end and take them out in the opposite order from the same end. You only have access to the end where you put the elements in.

Choosing a Container Class

It is not always easy to decide which container class to use in a given situation. QArray and QBitArray can be ruled out whenever you have non-trivial objects to store. The use of the classes mainly depends on how you put the data in and—even more so— how you plan to retrieve them again. If you know that you will retrieve the objects in exactly the same order you put them in, use QQueue. If you know that you will take them out in exactly the opposite order, use QStack. These two classes are optimized for their respective intended uses.

If you will mainly be adding new members at the end and plan to retrieve the members one after the other (and probably in the same order you put them in), use QList. On the other hand, if you need maximum flexibility for storage and retrieval of the elements, use QDict, QIntDict, or QPtrDict. Which one you should choose depends mainly on how you want to access the elements. If you access them by an integer number, use QIntDict; if you access them by a string, use QDict; if you access them by another object, use QPtrDict.

Finally, if you plan to use QDict or QIntDict, make sure there can be a very large number of entries and that it is easy for your application to restore entries no longer in the container. If this is the case, QCache or QIntCache might be a good choice, because they automatically delete the least recently used item from the cache if the size of the cache exceeds a certain threshold (see the "Caching Data" section).

Working with Container Classes

After you have chosen a container class to use, you have to know how to create objects of this class and how to insert and retrieve members.

Since most classes simply store a pointer to the contained object, it would suffice if all classes accepted void*. This would reduce type safety to a minimum when using container classes, though, so you have to define a type that accepts pointers to one kind of object. If you know about templates in C++, you probably suspect that Qt uses these as well. This is true, but to be usable with compilers that don't support templates, Qt also provides a different way which uses the preprocessor and its macro expansion capability. Use this only when your compiler does not support templates, because it will be removed in future versions of Qt.

We will explain the use of container class with the class QList. Use of the other classes is basically the same; some other classes have slightly different methods for insertion, retrieval, and removal.

For the sake of example, let's assume that you are going to write a program for managing your stamp collection. You might have already created a class Stamp, and now need a container in which to store objects of this type. Here's how you declare a type StampList with templates:

```
typedef QList<Stamp> StampList;
```

This says that `StampList` is a special kind of `QList` that accepts pointers to `Stamp` objects as its members. This works only if `Stamp` has already been defined; a forward reference is not enough. Note that you do not have to provide the asterisk to indicate that pointers are to be stored. The container classes already assume that you want to store a pointer, because that is the only thing they can store. If you used the asterisk, that would still be legal C++ code:

```
typedef QList<Stamp*> StampList;
```

This means that `StampList` stores pointers to pointers to `Stamp` objects.

If you are uncomfortable with templates, or if your compiler generates an unreasonable amount of code for template instantiation, it is still theoretically possible to use macros:

```
typedef Q_DECLARE(QListM,Stamp);
```

You can also employ `USE_TEMPLATECLASS` from *qglobal.h* to distinguish between the usage of templates and macros. Your code will compile with all compilers, and you can still use the advantages that templates offer:

```
#ifdef USE_TEMPLATECLASS
typedef QList<Stamp> StampList;
#else
typedef Q_DECLARE(QListM,Stamp) StampList;
#endif
```

It should be noted that Troll Tech has announced plans to drop support for using container classes with macros in future versions, so this is a dead end. Qt 2.0 already does not support these macros any longer.

After you have created the appropriate type, you can create an object of the container class and insert some items in it:

```
StampList stamplist;
...
Stamp stamp1;
Stamp stamp2;
Stamp stamp3;
...
stamplist.append( &stamp1 );
stamplist.insert( 0, &stamp2 );
stamplist.insert( 1, &stamp3 );
```

The `append()` method inserts items at the end. When using `insert()`, you have to pass the position at which the item should be inserted.

When you use one of the index containers `QDict`, `QIntDict`, and `QPtrDict`, you pass the key as the first parameter and the value as the second parameter to `insert()`.

Members are taken out of a collection with `remove()`—see the documentation for the correct parameters.

For retrieval in dictionary classes, you can use `find()` or the synonymous `operator[]`:

```
QDict<Stamp> stampdict;
...
Stamp stamp1;
...
stampdict.insert( "somekey", &stamp1 );
Stamp* result = stampdict["somekey"];
...
```

For `QList`, your best bet is to start at the beginning with `first()`, or at the end with `last()`, and then retrieve the elements one by one with `next()` or `prev()`. You know you are at the end of the list when one of these methods returns a 0 pointer.

All container classes support the methods `clear()`, which removes all elements from the container, and `count()`, which returns the number of stored elements.

"Auto-deletion" is a very interesting feature. By default, it is turned off, but when turned on in the constructor call or with a call to `setAutoDelete( true )`, elements that are removed from the container (either with `remove()` or when the container itself is deleted) are automatically deleted themselves. For this to work, these elements must have been created on the heap, with `new`. This allows the use of Java-style insertions:

```
typedef QList<Stamp> StampList;
...
StampList* stamplist = new StampList();
stamplist->setAutoDelete( true );
...
list->append( new Stamp( "Blue Mauritius", 3000000 ) );
list->append( new Stamp( "Tre Skilling Banco", 1800000 ) );
...
delete stamplist; // the two Stamp objects are deleted automatically
```

Caching Data

`QCache` and `QIntCache` are two useful classes that can help you reduce memory consumption by limiting the size that all the entries together may consume. On first view, they work like `QDict` and `QIntDict`, except that you pass a so-called *cost* for each entry. Apart from this, the cache classes work like the dictionary classes until the point where inserting a new item would make the sum cost of all inserted entries larger than a predefined maximum cost set with `setMaxCost()`. At this point, the cache deletes the items that have not been retrieved from the cache for the longest time to make space for the newly inserted entry. This has two consequences: First, the cache object must have ownership over the inserted objects, so that it can delete them when it needs to. You must not delete any cached objects yourself. Second, you must be able to restore cached data from some other source, because it could be deleted at any time. This other source is usually a disk file or a network connection.

By default, retrieving a cached object with either `find()` or `operator[]` makes it the least recently used entry. This assumes a cache-access pattern in which all cached objects are likely to be retrieved in turn, or all cached objects have the same probability of being retrieved. If this does not fit your application, because retrieving an object from the cache increases the probability that it will be retrieved again in the near future (or at least does not reduce the probability), you can pass `false` as the second parameter to `find()`. This prevents the cached object from being marked as the least recently used. In this case, `operator[]` cannot be used.

Iterators

Often you want to traverse all elements in a container. While you could do this using a `QList` with `next()` or `prev()`, it is better to use *iterators*. Iterators are special classes for traversing all elements in a container. They are safer, and can even work with containers that are modified at the same time without getting out of sync. For the dictionary classes, iterators are the only option for complete traversal.

An iterator's type must exactly fit the container it should iterate over. Therefore, there are iterator templates called `QDictIterator`, `QIntDictIterator`, `QPtrDictIterator`, and `QListIterator`, `QCacheIterator`, and `QIntCacheIterator`. These all have a method `toFirst()`, which can be used to get the first element in the iteration and an `operator++` for moving one element ahead. `QListIterator` also has `toLast()` and `operator--` for moving in the opposite direction. You get the current element with `current()`. This example uses a `QListIterator` to iterate over all elements in a QList:

```
typedef QList<Stamp> StampList;
StampList stamplist;
stamplist.setAutoDelete( true );
stamplist.append( new Stamp( "Blue Mauritius", 3000000 ) );
stamplist.append( new Stamp( "Tre Skilling Banco", 1800000 ) );
...
typedef QListIterator<Stamp> StampListIterator;
StampListIterator myiterator( stamplist );
for( myiterator.toFirst(); myiterator.current(); ++myiterator )
{
   debug( "%s is worth %d\n", myiterator.current()->name(),
      myiterator.current()->value() );
}
```

Note that the type of the iterator exactly fits the type of the container iterated on, and that the container is passed as an argument in the constructor of the iterator.

The dictionary containers do not have an intrinsic order, so you will never know which order the members will come back in when iterating over the container. If you need to maintain the order, use `QList`.

There is a danger associated with the incorrect use of iterators. If you retrieve the current object and do a "dangerous operation," such as removing this object from the container, incrementing the iterator will skip over the next object in question, thus leaving it out. Therefore, you should always increment the iterator right after taking the current element. Here is some boilerplate code that you can use:

```
QList<X>* mylist;
QListIterator<X> iterator( *mylist );
X *obj;

while( ( obj = iterator.current() ) ) {
    ++iterator; // iterator now points to the next object to iterate on
    obj->doAnyOperation(); // even "dangerous" ones
}
```

Stacks and Queues

Since `QStack` and `QQueue` are used a little bit differently, we treat them to a section of their own. The definition of an appropriate type and the construction of a container object work exactly the same way as in the other classes. Only insertion and retrieval are different. Since a `QStack` allows insertion and retrieval on only one end, just two methods are needed: `push()` and `pop()`. `push()` inserts one element on the stack, and `pop()` retrieves the top-most element from the stack that is no longer on the stack afterwards. The `remove()` method removes the top-most element without returning it.

`QQueue` inserts members at one end and takes them out again at the other end. But you don't have to worry about the different sides, just use `enqueue()` for insertion and `dequeue()` for deletion. If you simply want to take the frontmost element from the queue without knowing what it is, you can also use `remove()`. The methods `count()` and `clear()` are available with stacks and queues as well.

9

Graphics

Naturally, GUI programs contain a large amount of graphics code. By graphics code, we mean low-level graphics drawing code for creating things that go beyond the built-in widgets.

You already know a bit about graphics programming from the tutorial, but there is a lot more to doing it in Qt. In this chapter, you will find sections on animation, printing, basic drawing operations, and advanced drawing with two-dimensional transformations and different coordinate systems. Not all of this will be interesting to you at this time, so read intensively what you need for your current development project, and just skim the remaining sections.

Animations

Qt contains a nice little class called `QMovie` that allows programmers to include small animations in their works with a minimum of fuss.

An animation consists of several pictures or *frames*, that are shown in rapid succession. You could simply load the frames into `QPixmap` objects and show them one after the other, but `QMovie` does that for you.

While `QMovie` is designed to be independent from the animation format, it is currently not possible to use any file format other than animated GIF.[1] You can't load another animation format like AVI or FLI frame by frame and add these frames to a `QMovie` object. If you want to play these formats, you are on your own. It is likely, though, that other animation formats will be added in the future.

When the animation contains looping information, `QMovie` plays the animation again and again according to this information. It does not contain a method to force looping on an arbitrary animation, but you can easily simulate this by having it notify the pro-

---

1 I am probably required to state: The Graphics Interchange Format is the Copyright property of CompuServe Inc. GIF is a Trade Mark property of CompuServe Inc.

gram when an animation has terminated (see the following information) and restart the animation by calling `QMovie::restart()`.

`QMovie` objects are explicitly shared, so when you construct one `QMovie` object from another, you have two objects, that are programmatically, but not logically, different. When you pause the animation of one of these objects, the other will stop, too. If you want to have really different objects, construct them independently. This is usually not a problem, because you rarely want to have two objects that are independent from one another but show the same animation.

The easiest way to use `QMovie` is to assign a `QMovie` object to a label with `QLabel::setMovie()`. Since an animation starts playing as soon as the `QMovie` object is constructed and control has returned to the event loop, the following code is all you need to play a movie:

```
QMovie* mymovie = new QMovie( "animation.gif" );
QLabel* mylabel = new QLabel( parent );
mylabel->setGeometry( mymovie->getValidRect() );
mylabel->setMovie( mymovie );
mylabel->show();
```

If the animation's size changes while it runs, this code will be too simplistic, because the label won't change its size automatically with the movie. A `QMovie` object can call a slot, if the size changes when you make that slot known with `QMovie::connectResize()`. You could add the following line:

```
mymovie->connectResize( receiver,
                    SLOT( slotMovieHasResized( const QSize& ) ) );
```

and have a slot `slotMoviehasResized()` available to resize the label:

```
void MyClass::slotMovieHasResized( const QSize& size )
{
    mylabel->resize( size );
}
```

You can use `connectUpdate()` to be notified when any part of the animation's visible area changes. Even more flexible is `connectStatus()`, which informs you about errors, frame changes, and pauses in the animation. It also tells you a loop or the whole movie has terminated. See the reference documentation for `QMovie` for the full list of flags.

You can influence how an animation plays with the methods `pause()`, `unpause()`, `step()` and `restart()`. You can call `step()` without a parameter, which yields a single step; or you can pass the number of steps to be performed as an `int` parameter.

`QMovie` provides several methods for getting state information: `paused()`, `finished()`, and `running()`. If you need to be notified asynchronously about these states, you should use `connectStatus()` instead.

Printing

No matter what kind of application you write, you will probably need to provide some printing capabilities. Unfortunately, printing is notoriously platform-dependent, which makes it difficult to capture in a cross-platform toolkit like Qt. Like several other cross-platform toolkits, Qt uses an approach that has proven to be a viable solution for most needs, although it is not without problems.

In Windows, printer drivers are either shipped with the operating system or supplied by the printer vendor. In Unix, where the operating system usually does not provide printer drivers, all printing is in PostScript format. This is a reasonable choice, since PostScript is a page-description language that appropriately describes everything printable. Most printers support PostScript, and even low-cost models can often be upgraded to support it. If your printer is not PostScript-capable you can use the freely available RIP (Raster Image Processor) *ghostscript* (available from *http://www.cs.wisc.edu/~ghost/*), which can convert PostScript files to almost any current printer format. Most free Unix distributions install this transparently. You can expect your users to be able to print the PostScript output of your Qt application. If you are developing a commercial application, you might also consider bundling a commercial RIP with your application.

Adding printing support to your Qt application is easy. You use the class `QPrinter`, which inherits from `QPaintDevice` like `QWidget`, `QPixmap`, and `QPicture`. You draw whatever you want to be printed with `QPainter`, just as you would with the other classes. The only difference is that you have to handle the pagination yourself by deciding when a form-feed should occur. To do so, simply call `newPage()` at your `QPrinter` object.

You usually want to let the user change some print settings. These include whether printing should be directed to a file or directly to a printer, which pages to print, and whether printing should be in portrait (normal) or landscape (turned by 90 degrees). When you call `QPrinter::setup()`, a print-settings dialog is presented to the user.[2] In Windows, the exact appearance of the dialog is dependent on the default printer driver. On Unix systems, the dialog is provided by Qt and looks like the one pictured in Figure 9-1.

When this method returns `true`, the user has clicked the OK button and printing should proceed. If not, the user has clicked the Cancel button, and your application should refrain from printing.

You can pre-set settings for the printing dialog with several methods of the class `QPrinter`. By passing either `QPrinter::Portrait` or `QPrinter::Landscape` to `QPrinter::setOrientation()`, you can set the orientation to be selected in the dialog, for example.

---

2 In Qt 2.0, this method will be obsolete. You will call `QPrintDialog::getPrinter()` instead.

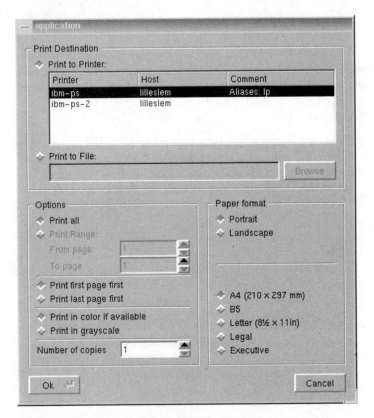

Figure 9-1: The print dialog provided by Qt on Unix systems

Some settings are taken into account by the class QPrinter. Others, notably the pages to print, have to be taken into account by the application's printer. QPrinter can restrict the range of pages to print before the user gets a chance to select them. You do this by calling QPrinter::setMinMax(). The user can then only select pages within this range for printing.

Here is some simple code that prints a red circle on the first page, and a green square on the second. Unless you have a color printer and appropriate printer drivers on your system, you won't see much red, of course.

```
QPrinter myprinter;
int ret = myprinter.setup();  // show the printing dialog
if( ret == true ) // only print if the user clicked the OK button
{
    QPainter mypainter( &myprinter );
    mypainter.setPen( red );
    mypainter.drawEllipse( 200, 200, 100, 100 );
    if( myprinter.newPage() )
        // If this fails, it is not possible to send a form feed
        // (paper empty?). This cannot happen on Unix.
```

```
                    // Also, check whether the page number is
                    // between myprinter.fromPage() and myprinter.toPage().
            {

                mypainter.setPen( green );
                mypainter.drawRect( 200, 200, 100, 100 );
                mypainter.end();
            }
        }
```

You can use any drawing command that QPainter provides for printing, with the exception of the even-odd fill algorithm used by drawPolygon when its second parameter is false. Use the winding fill algorithm by setting the second parameter to draw-Polygon() to true in this case.

Clipping can now be used in Qt when printing, but remember that it uses device coordinates instead of logical coordinates. You can read more about clipping in the "Clipping" section.

Another restriction when printing is that Qt and other toolkits depend on the font metrics provided by your operating system. QPrinter supports many fonts, but if the font metrics it gets are bad, output quality will suffer.

QPrinter is set up by default to use a resolution of 72 dots per inch, with the coordinates (0,0) in the upper left corner of the page. Accordingly, printer output should resemble screen output as closely as possible. You will learn how to change these parameters in the "Advanced QPainter: Two-dimensional Transformations and View Transformations" section.

If the printing operation will take longer because it contains complex graphics or spans more than a page, provide your users with the option to quit printing. You need to pop up a non-modal dialog containing a Cancel button before starting the printer output. A good choice would be to use the class QProgressDialog (see the "Predefined Dialogs" section) which already does this for you and contains a progress bar. Then, when the user clicks that button, call QPrinter::abort().[3] This makes QPrinter stop the printing operation, but your printing code should also periodically check QPrinter::aborted() to check whether it should stop sending printing commands.

Of course, for this to work, you need to pass control to the event loop from time to time so that the user has a chance to click the Cancel button (and the progress dialog has a chance to update its progress bar). The easiest way to do this is to call QApplication::processEvents() from time to time. Here is some code that shows you the basic set-up:

```
void MyApplication::print()
{
    // myprinter is a QPrinter object that is a member of MyApplication
    if( myprinter.setup() ) // show printer settings dialog
    {
```

---

3 It would be easiest if we could connect the cancelled() signal from QProgressDialog to QPrinter::abort(), but the latter is not a slot. Instead, we have to work with a helper slot—like in this example, printingCancelled().

```
// create a QProgressDialog
QProgressDialog progressdlg;
// the total number of steps is the number of pages to print
progressdlg.setTotalSteps( total_number_of_pages_to_print );
// connect the cancelled() signal to some slot that will
// abort the printing operation
QObject::connect( &progressdlg, SIGNAL( cancelled() ),
                  this, SLOT( printingCancelled() ) );

progressdlg.show();

// give the progress dialog a chance to appear before we start
qapp->processEvents();

// start printing the first page
int current_page = 1;
QPainter mypainter( &myprinter );
... // QPainter operations for the first page

// give the progress dialog a chance to get his signal through
qapp->processEvents();

// check whether the cancel button was pressed
if( myprinter.aborted() ) // yes, cancel was pressed
{
    myprinter.end(); // finish printing
    return; // progressdlg goes out of scope and is hidden
            // automatically
}
// if we get here, the cancel button was not pressed, continue

// inform the progress dialog about the progress
progressdlg.setProgress( current_page );
current_page++;

// continue with printing operations for the next page
...
    }
}


void MyApplication::printingCancelled()
{
    myprinter.abort(); // cancel was pressed, inform the QPrinter
}
```

In this example, the QProgressDialog object is a modeless dialog, which allows the user to continue to interact with the application. This might or might not be desirable—perhaps you want to forbid a word processor to add further text while the printing operation is in progress, so that the printout and the text on the screen are not out of sync. To do this, you can take advantage of the fact that QProgressDialog inherits from `QSemiModal`, a special kind of modal dialog that blocks events to other widgets but does not enter an event loop of its own, so that network connections or timers are still enabled. To use this, replace the line

```
QProgressDialog progressdlg;
```

in the previous example with the line

```
QProgressDialog progressdlg( 0, 0, true );
```

The third parameter in the constructor to `QProgressDialog` decides whether the dialog is semi-modal or modeless. The first parameter is the widget that the progress dialog should be centered on. For simplicity, we let it be centered on the desktop here. In your application, you might want to center it on the top level widget of your application.

Managing Colors

Working with colors is often difficult. This mainly stems from differences between graphics boards and other hardware and the operating systems. Available screen colors can also be a scarce resource. Unless you have a graphics board that is capable of True Color graphics and a driver for that board that supports this mode, you will have to make do with the available colors. Qt tries to help you here, but you still have to know what is going on to be able to use its color-management.

Color allocation

Unless you have a True Color graphics board and driver, you can only use a finite number of different colors.[4] The available number of colors depends on the *color depth*, the number of bits allocated for every pixel on the screen. If you have a color depth of eight bits, for example, you can use 256 colors.

256 colors is not much, given that you have to share these colors with other running applications. Unfortunately, you cannot assume that your users have more than 256 colors available. Most people have cheap graphics boards, which cannot provide more colors and still maintain a decent screen resolution because the amount of video memory is too small.

Perhaps the most important color-management feature in Qt is lazy color allocation. Qt does not demand allocation of a color cell from the operating or windowing system unless you really need it. You can therefore declare as many different colors as you like, and a color cell is only used when you first need it. If for some reason you do not want this feature, you can turn it off with `QColor::setLazyAllocation( false )`.

---

4   Of course, a True Color graphics board cannot give you an infinite number of colors either, but it is technically not possible to "run out of colors" because all colors are approximated to the available discrete values.

If you need many colors temporarily, you can use a *color context*. Before you start allocating the colors, call `QColor::enterAllocContext()`. When you do not need them any longer, simply call `QColor::leaveAllocContext()`, and all the colors allocated are freed. If you need to, you can even stack color contexts on top of each other.

The best thing you can do to save color cells is the reuse of cells that are already in use, by trying to use the same colors as often as possible. Of course, you cannot easily know which colors are already allocated, but Qt predefines 19 colors in the form of `QColor` objects. If you use one of these, it is very likely that some other application is already using one of these colors, so you will economize on color cells. These predefined color objects are `black`, `white`, `darkGray`, `gray`, `lightGray`, `red`, `green`, `blue`, `cyan`, `magenta`, `yellow`, `darkRed`, `darkGreen`, `darkBlue`, `darkCyan`, `darkMagenta`, `dark-Yellow`, `color0`, and `color1`. The last two colors are special colors for drawing in two-color bitmaps; you are guaranteed that these two colors contrast well.

To help Qt save color cells, you should tell it what pattern of color usage your application has. Qt differentiates between three different patterns. All of these are set with the static method `QApplication::setColorSpec()`, which must be done *before* constructing the `QApplication` object.

- `QApplication::NormalColor` is the default. Use this if your application uses mainly standard colors for widgets. On Unix systems, the standard color palette is used, so the color cells allocated by the Qt application are not available for allocation for other colors.[5] On Windows systems, all the colors are dithered[6] to the 20 predefined system colors, unless you have a True Color display.

- `QApplication::CustomColor` applies only to Windows; on Unix systems, it has the same effect as `QApplication::NormalColor`. Active applications get more colors and thus can achieve better visual results, but the visual appearance of the non-active applications will suffer.

- `QApplication::ManyColor` applies only to Unix; on Windows systems, it has the same effect as `QApplication::CustomColor`. `ManyColor` is more friendly to other applications than `NormalColor` and `CustomColor`, since colors are allocated only when needed. When a color is requested, it is compared to the closest of the 216 colors in the Netscape Navigator palette and the closest existing color in the shared palette. The closest of those two is then allocated, unless no free cells are available. In that case, the closest existing color is used. Thus, if the application is only going to use a small number of colors, `CustomColor` will give the most accurate colors. `ManyColor`, on the other hand, is careful not to grab a color if a close-enough one is already allocated by another application. The resulting colors are not quite as accurate, but the result is an application that is much more friendly to other applications when it comes to color cells.

---

5   Of course, other applications can use the same color cells if they want to use the same colors.
6   Dithering is a method of reducing the number of colors needed in an image while keeping the overall impression of the image as close to the original as possible.

Color models

The next thing you need to know is how you specify colors in Qt. Qt provides three ways to specify the color of a QColor object: the RGB (Red Green Blue) color model, the HSV (Hue Saturation Value) color model, and named colors.

The RGB color model reflects how computer monitors and TV sets put colors together on the screen. Each color in this model consists of a red, a green, and a blue component. You can specify minimum and maximum values for each component, but usually (and in Qt), the range is from 0 to 255. If you specify 0 for all three components, you get black. If you specify 255 (or whatever the maximum value is) for all three components, you get white. Specifying the same value for all three components gives you some kind of gray (the lesser the value, the darker the gray), and specifying 255 for one component and 0 for the others gives you plain red, plain green, or plain blue. It takes a while to determine which values you have to choose for a certain color, but most systems have a color-selection application that lets you pick a color and read the values for this color.

You construct a QColor object from RGB values by simply passing the values for red, green, and blue as int values to the constructor like this:

```
QColor myColor( 128, 128, 128 ); // medium gray
```

The HSV model splits a color into its hue, its saturation, and its value. In Qt, the range for the hue is from -1 to 360, and the range for the saturation and value is from 0 to 255. Determining the HSV values for a certain color is even more difficult than working with RGB, but the HSV model is good for calculating one color from the values of another.

To construct a QColor object from HSV values, pass the HSV values as int values to the constructor and add QColor::Hsv as the fourth parameter:

```
QColor myColor( 214, 100, 50, QColor::Hsv ); // whatever color this is
```

You can even specify the color by name, because all X11 systems have a color database that maps color names to RGB values. On Windows, this database is shipped with Qt as the file *rgb.txt*. The purpose of this database is to encourage reuse of color cells, because it is likely that a color cell with a color from that database already exists. Unfortunately, the database is simply too large, which sometimes foils this plan. Nevertheless, it is easier to name a color than it is to use three numbers. Here's how you construct a color from a name:

```
QColor myColor( "MidnightBlue" );
```

Color groups and palettes

Applications that don't use colors consistently are awkward to use. Imagine a word processor in which one menu entry is red and the next one is green, just because the application designer thought that would look nice. Qt has two concepts that are meant to ensure a consistent use of colors in an application: *color groups* and *palettes*.

A color group consists of eight colors. The idea behind this is that no widget needs more than eight colors, and that colors should be used by function rather than by their absolute numeric values. The eight members of a color group are:

background
> The general background color of the widget (default: light gray).

foreground
> The foreground color for drawing graphics, such as lines, in the widget (default: black).

light
> A color lighter than the background color that is used for shadow effects (default: white).

midlight
> A color between background and light, which is used for shadow effects (default: a medium gray).

dark
> A color darker than the background color that is used for shadow effects (default: a dark gray).

medium
> A color between the background color and dark, which is used for shadow and contrast effects.

text
> Used for drawing text like labels into a widget. This is usually the same as the foreground color, but some widgets may have different colors for drawing text and graphics (default: black).

base
> Used as the background color in some widgets. This is usually a color that contrasts well with the text color (default: white).

The class QColorGroup groups these colors together.

Three objects of the class QColorGroup form a palette, which is represented by the class QPalette. Again, the three color groups have functional rather than physical descriptions. Their purposes are:

active
> This color group is used when the widget has the focus. This should normally be the same color group as the normal group (see the following description) in order to avoid overloading the user interface with too many colors.

disabled
> This color group is used when the widget is not available for user input.

normal
> This color group is used for all other purposes.

You can construct a palette by passing three color group objects to the constructor, or by calling `QPalette::setNormal()`, `QPalette::setDisabled()`, or `QPalette::setActive()`, but you should do this only if you are knowledgable about color design. It is easy to create an awkward user interface. Your best bet is to simply pass one color to the `QPalette` constructor, which in this case is used as the background color of the normal color group. All other colors in the three color groups are then computed automatically, so that the contrasts are sharp and colors in the whole user interface have a nice look.

Qt always creates a standard palette for you, which is used as a default by all widgets if you don't set a palette yourself. This palette is stored with the `QApplication` object. If you want to use a palette of your own, you can pass this palette to a widget with `QWidget::setPalette()`. This will make your interface inconsistent, because only this widget will use this palette. This is a good idea only in rare circumstances—for example, you might want to create a warning label that is based on red.

When you want to change the palette for the whole application, use `QApplication::setPalette()`. This method expects a `QPalette` object as its first parameter, which is then used as the default palette for all widgets that haven't received a palette of their own with `QWidget::setPalette()`. If you pass `true` as the second optional parameter, all widgets in your application will be instantaneously redrawn to use the new colors. Here's how you set the whole application to a blueish look, in contrast to the default grayish look:

```
QPalette mypalette( blue );          // compute the whole palette based on blue
qApp->setPalette( mypalette, true ); // make all widgets
                                     // accept this palette and redraw them
```

Note that you should normally not do this. The default look based on gray has many advantages, and it works for visually impaired people who cannot distinguish colors. On the other hand, some window systems allow setting default "themes" that also contain colors, and your application might want to follow these to better integrate with the desktop.

Basic QPainter: Drawing Figures

`QPainter`, Qt's drawing engine, can do many amazing things, some of which we will talk about in the next section. Of course, you also need to know the basics, which means selecting colors, brushes, and pens; and drawing basic geometric figures.

Selecting brushes, colors and pens

Each `QPainter` object comes with defaults for brushes, colors, pens, and fonts. These are initialized with `QPainter`. For example, the default pen draws solid lines with a thickness of one pixel.

You can change these parameters. To start with the color, select a *pen*. It is possible (and sometimes necessary), to create an object of the class `QPen` and pass that to the method `setPen()` of the `QPainter` object. However, you can simply pass a color to another variant of `setPen()`, which then creates a suitable pen on-the-fly for you. Like-wise, you can select a pen style by passing this to yet another variant of `setPen()`.

The full list of available pen styles can be found in the reference documentation for `QPen`. If you think that solid lines are boring and you would rather have dashed lines, you can use the pen style `QPen::DashLine`—and there is also the pen style `NoPen` to draw nothing at all. These shortcuts don't work if you want to set both the pen style and the color. In this case, you'll have to create a `QPen` object. This can easily be done with code like the following:

```
painter.setPen( QPen( red, 3, QPen::DashLine ) );
```

This creates a pen that makes red lines that are three pixels wide and in a dashed-line style, and assigns this pen to the `QPainter`.

While the pen is used for drawing lines and outlines, the *brush* is used for drawing filled shapes. For example, if you draw a rectangle, the outline will be drawn with the pen, but the inside will be filled with the brush. Like a pen, a brush has a color and a style, and can be set when passed to `setBrush()`. If you don't want your shapes to be filled, choose the brush style `NoBrush`, which is also the default brush. If you want to set both the color and the brush style, you will have to create a brush. The brush style determines how the shape is filled. For example, `QBrush::SolidPattern` creates plain fills, while `QBrush::VerPattern` fills your shapes with vertical lines. The full list of available brush styles is in the reference documentation for `QBrush`.

If you want to set a font for text-drawing operations, you can do that with `QPainter::setFont()`.

Drawing operations in `QPainter`

`QPainter`'s drawing operations cover all basic geometric shapes, and then some. Most come in more than one variant; they often differ only in the way the coordinates are specified. For example, you can specify the start and end points for a line to be drawn with `QPainter::drawLine()` by passing four integer values that specify the x- and y-coordinates of the points, or by passing two `QPoint` objects. The following table contains Qt's drawing operations:

Method	Shape
`drawRect()`	rectangle
`drawRoundRect()`	rectangle with rounded corners
`drawTiledPixmap()`	rectangle tiled with a pixmap
`drawEllipse()`	circle and ellipse
`drawArc()`	arc

Method	Shape
drawPie()	pie slice of a circle
drawChord()	chord of a circle
drawLineSegments()	draws a number of independent lines
drawPolyline()	draws connected lines
drawPolygon()	draws connected lines and connects the last with the first point
drawQuadBezier()	bezier curve
drawText()	text
drawPixmap()	pixmaps
drawImage()	images

The two variants of the drawText() method look as if they are almost identical in the reference documentation, but they aren't. The first accepts two integer values as the coordinate, which it uses to specify the left end of the baseline of the text to be drawn. The baseline is the line on which all letters reside that don't extend further down, such as p and q do. The second variant accepts four integer values as coordinates, which are used to specify a rectangle into which the text is drawn. You can specify whether the text should be clipped at the bounds of this rectangle or whether it can extend the rectangle. You can also decide how it should be aligned, if it is shorter than the rectangle, among other parameters.

It is not very difficult to use these drawing methods. You should experiment with them a little.

Advanced QPainter: Two-dimensional Transformations and View Transformations

QPainter, the drawing engine of Qt, is a very advanced piece of software. It goes far beyond the simple drawing of lines or pie slices. In this section, we cover some advanced features. These might be difficult to understand, initially. First, we talk about classic two-dimensional transformations, such as rotating and translating, and then generalize this to general view transformations. View transformations allow for powerful drawing methods.

If you want to dive deeper into graphics programming, consult *Introduction to Computer Graphics* and *Computer Graphics in C: Principles and Practice*, both by J. Foley et al.

Two-dimensional transformations

Two-dimensional transformations allow you to adjust the view of some graphics, for example by rotating or scaling it. In general, two-dimensional transformations can be described by a 3x3 matrix, and affect only one place. The most common of these—translating, rotating, scaling, and shearing—are directly supported by methods of their own. However, you can achieve all possible two-dimensional transformations by specifying a transformation matrix.

You usually do so by calling the respective method at your `QPainter` object, as shown in the following code:

```
...
QPainter painter( mywidget );
painter.rotate( 30.0 );
painter.drawLine( 10, 10, 10, 100 );
...
```

The vertical line in this example will be turned by thirty degrees.

Most often, you use `rotate()` and friends when copying bitmap data from a `QPixmap` into a `QWidget`. This lets you keep the original pixmap, while still displaying it as transformed. The code for this might look roughly like:

```
void MyWidget::paintEvent( QPaintEvent* )
{
    QPainter painter( this );
    painter.rotate( 90.0 );
    painter.drawPixmap( 0, 0, bufferpixmap );
}
```

Another interesting application is drawing rotated text. There is no method `QPainter::drawRotatedText`, but you can emulate one easily with the following code:

```
void drawRotatedText( QPainter* painter, float degrees, int x, int y,
                      const char* text )
{
    // we assume that begin() has already been called on painter
    painter->rotate( degrees ); // rotate the coordinate system
    QPoint pos( x, y );
    pos = painter->xFormDev( pos );
    painter->drawText( pos, text );
    painter->rotate( -degrees );
}
```

This is not as straightforward as you might think, but it's relatively uncomplicated. The variable `pos` is needed because the client of this function will pass the coordinates `x` and `y` in the coordinate system that are current when `drawRotatedText()` is called. Therefore, we have to compute the coordinates for the new coordinate system, which is done with `QPainter::xFormDev()`. After drawing the text, we finally revert the rotation so that `painter` is not affected by this function (except for the text drawn).

Another method that achieves the same result is using `save()` and `restore()`. These two `QPainter` methods save and restore the current state of the painter, respectively, and must always come in pairs. Using these methods, the code (`translate( float, float )` moves the coordinate system by the values passed as arguments:

```
void drawRotatedText( QPainter* painter, float degrees, int x, int y,
                      const char* text )
{
    // we assume that begin() has already been called on painter
    painter->save();
    painter->translate( x, y );
    painter->rotate( degrees ); // rotate the coordinate system
    painter->drawText( 0, 0, text );
    painter->restore();
}
```

The other methods for two-dimensional transformations are `shear( float, float )` for shearing and `scale( float, float )` for scaling.

If this is not enough, you can define your own transformations by using an object of class `QWMatrix`. You do this by creating such an object and applying transformation methods to this object. These have the same names as in `QPainter`. You then call `QPainter::setWorldMatrix` and pass your transformation matrix. For example, if you want to draw something in a coordinate system that is first rotated by 30 degrees and then scaled up by 10% in both dimensions, you could use the following code:

```
...
QWMatrix matrix;
matrix.rotate( 30.0 );
matrix.scale( 1.1, 1.1 );
painter.setWorldMatrix( matrix );
// drawing operations go here
...
```

You can also rewrite the `drawRotatedText()` function again. Since two transformations (a rotation and a translation) are involved, it is slightly faster to first build a matrix that is the mathematical representation of those two transformations applied one after the other and then apply that matrix to the `QPainter` object. Here is the code:

```
void drawRotatedText( QPainter* painter, float degrees, int x, int y,
                      const char* text )
{
    // we assume that begin() has already been called on painter
    QWMatrix oldmatrix = painter->worldMatrix();
    QWMatrix matrix = painter->worldMatrix();
    matrix.translate( x, y );
    matrix.rotate( degrees );  // rotate the coordinate system
    painter->setWorldMatrix( matrix );
    painter->drawText( 0, 0, text );
    painter->setWorldMatrix( oldmatrix );
}
```

Note that we do not create an empty `QWMatrix` object from scratch, but instead retrieve it from the `QPainter` object. This is necessary, because other transformations might already be in place. We keep a backup copy of the current transformation state in the variable `oldmatrix`, and reset the old matrix after drawing the text. We could have used the `save()`/`restore()` pair here, instead.

If this is still not flexible enough, you can also build the transformation matrix completely on your own. There is a method `QWMatrix::setMatrix()` with which you can set all nine values of the 3x3 transformation matrix. See the reference documentation of `QWMatrix` for a discussion of how to use these. You need to understand analytical geometry to make good use of this capability.

As we have already seen, it can be useful to be able to transform coordinates to and from the new coordinate system. `QPainter` provides methods for doing so for points (`QPoint`), rectangles (`QRect`), and arrays of points (`QPointArray`). `QPainter::xForm` transforms coordinates from the current coordinate system to the default coordinate system, and `QPainter::xFormDev` transforms coordinates from the default coordinate system to the current coordinate system.

If you have set up a complicated transformation but need to perform a few drawing operations in the default coordinate system, you can temporarily disable the transformations by calling `QPainter::setWorldXForm( false );` and then reenabling it with `QPainter::setWorldXForm( true );`. By default, transformations are disabled but automatically are enabled as soon as the first transformation is applied.

View transformations

View transformations are different from coordinate system transformations. They are also called *world transformations*. View transformations do not change the relative arrangement of the coordinates; instead, they change the coordinates as a whole. There are two kinds of view transformations: viewport transformations and window transformations. Both can be done using the world matrix transformations that you already know, but they are easier to understand if you look at them separately. Also, your code will be easier to read and maintain if you use the specialized methods.

Viewport transformations are used when you want to draw on only part of a `QPaint-Device`. Let's say that you are writing a presentation program that can put borders around slides. When drawing the inner graphics of a slide, you have to compute the border size to keep the graphics within the border. This is a cumbersome and error-prone job, which is why `QPainter` can do it for you. By calling `QPainter::setViewport()` and passing the starting coordinates, the width, and the height, the normal coordinates are recomputed automatically to fit into the viewport. The problem is that even fonts and pixmaps are scaled, which might give bad results. If you want to use a viewport but don't want the fonts and pixmaps to be scaled, do the transformation manually by using a `QWMatrix` object. Note that viewport use is different from simple clipping, in that drawing operations that would extend over the desired area are simply chopped off with clipping (see the "Clipping" section). Here is some sample code:

```
...
QPainter painter( mywidget );
painter.setViewport( leftmargin, topmargin,
                     totalwidth - leftmargin - rightmargin,
                     totalheight - topmargin - bottommargin );
/// your drawing operations go here
```

You can still use the same coordinates as you would without setting the viewport, but these coordinates are transformed so that all drawing operations take place only in the viewport specified.

Window transformations can be used to normalize the coordinate system of a `QPaint-Device`. Say that you want to draw a logo into various `QPaintDevices`, all of which have different sizes. Instead of computing the needed coordinates for each paint device, you can normalize all the paint devices to one virtual coordinate system. Often, this will simply be the coordinate system of one paint device that happens to be "more equal than others", but this is not necessary. For example, this code transforms the coordinate system of `mywidget` to a coordinate system that starts at (0,0) and has a size of (100,100), regardless of the original coordinate system size. Drawing operations in this widget can assume this new coordinate system, and `QPainter` will take care of all necessary transformations.

```
QPainter painter( mywidget );
painter.setWindow( 0, 0, 100, 100 );
// your drawing operations go here
```

You can also combine viewport and window transformations. If you want to draw your logo into a virtual coordinate system you have to take the unprintable margin into account as well when drawing onto a printer; here's what you could do:

```
QPainter painter( myprinter );
painter.setWindow( 0, 0, 100, 100 );
painter.setViewport( leftmargin, topmargin,
                     pagewidth - leftmargin - rightmargin,
                     pageheight - topmargin - bottommargin );
// your drawing operations go here
```

Of course, it's also possible to apply the two view transformations the other way around, but we can't think of an example where that would make sense.

As with world transformations, you can turn view transformations on and off at your leisure by calling `QPainter::setViewXForm( true )` and `QPainter::setViewXForm ( false );`. It is not possible to enable or disable only viewport *or* window transformations.

Finally, view transformations and world transformations can be combined. No matter in which order you set them, world transformations are always applied after the view transformations.

Clipping

Clipping is not a transformation, but it fits here because it also affects how drawing operations work in QPainter.

Clipping restricts the output of drawing operations to a certain area. While nothing bad happens when you try to draw pixels outside the clipping area, any pixels that lie outside the clipping area are simply not drawn. Often it is easier to define a clipping area that protects other parts of a drawing from being overpainted than it is to compute exactly how far the drawing operations should extend.

Since clipping can be computationally expensive, it must be explicitly turned on. This is done by calling setClipping(true); on the QPainter object in question. Set the clipping area with either setClipRect(), for a rectangle-shaped area, or setClipRegion() for a clipping area with an arbitrary shape.

Note that clipping coordinates are always physical coordinates, and are never transformed. All underlying window systems do it this way and, depending on your graphics board and its driver, clipping may be done in the hardware, which is faster.

Double Buffering and Other Nifty Techniques

We used double-buffering in the tutorial example, but now it is time to introduce it more formally.

When you draw a complex graphic into a widget with QPainter, you will notice that the resulting image is unsteady. This effect is called *flicker*. Programs that flicker are not only a strain on the eyes, but also are considered unprofessional. Fortunately, the *double buffering* technique for getting rid of flicker is not difficult to implement.

There is, however an even simpler technique for reducing flicker. This technique can be used when you have changed the state of a widget you have written, and therefore want to repaint the widget. By passing the Boolean parameter false to the repaint method, you tell Qt not to erase the widget background before calling the paintEvent() method of the widget. This results in a faster repainting operation that might be less visible to the eye. Qt allows you to further fine-tune the operation by calling QWidget:setBackgroundMode(). This method tells Qt how to fill the background before repainting a widget. The advantage of setBackgroundMode() is that it applies even when the request to repaint the widget comes from the window system, not from the program itself. The setBackgroundMode() method takes one parameter, which describes how to fill the widget. If you pass NoBackground, the background is not cleared. This means that you have to fill the widget completely by yourself. Other values that can be passed to setBackgroundMode() are listed in the reference documentation of QWidget, and each specifies one of the palette colors with which the widget is filled. The default is PaletteBackground, which defaults to gray.

The `NoBackground` trick works, because what really produces flicker is one pixel being drawn two or more times within a short interval. Without setting `NoBackground` or passing `false` to `repaint()`, the pixel is drawn the first time when the widget is cleared and a second time when the actual drawing is done. If you don't clear, the pixel is drawn only once.

Even if you use this trick, you can still get flicker if you aren't careful about your drawing code. Let's say you want to draw a scroll bar. If you first draw the trunk, then the arrows, and then the knob, you are sure to get flicker. Regardless of whether the area of the widget on the screen has been cleared before or not, all the pixels that make up the knob and the arrows are drawn twice. You have to make sure that your drawing code never paints a pixel twice. Clipping (see the "Clipping" section) is one technique that can help.

But now let's get back to double-buffering. As the name implies, this technique uses two buffers. One buffer is the widget itself, and the other is a `QPixmap` object that normally has the same size. If your widget is very large, like the canvas in a drawing program, this might exceed memory restrictions. In this case, you might only be able to double-buffer a part of the widget. When you consider memory requirements, however, keep in mind that you need to double-buffer only the visible part. For example, if you have a widget inside a `QScrollView` widget, your buffer pixmap needs to be only the size of the viewport. You do not even need to know the size of the viewport, because the paint event will tell you how much needs to be repainted, and areas that are not currently visible never need to be repainted.

There are several different varieties of double buffering, but they all boil down to copying the contents of the pixmap buffer to the widget in the `paintEvent()` method, or in another method that is called from the `paintEvent()` method. This can be done by calling `QPainter::drawPixmap()`, or `bitBlt()`. We'll examine each of these in turn. Please keep in mind that using pixmaps as buffers can lead to large memory consumption, so be careful, and explore the alternatives.

The `bitBlt()` function is very fast and powerful. It is specifically designed to copy data from pixmaps to widgets and back. It has the following signature:

```
void bitBlt( QPaintDevice* dst, int dx, int dy,
             const QPaintDevice* src, int sx = 0, int sy = 0,
             int sw = -1, int sh = -1, RasterOp rop = CopyROP,
             bool ignoreMask = false )
```

As in the function `strcpy()` from the standard C library, the destination is mentioned first. The first three parameters describe the destination with a pointer to the paint device (for double-buffering, this is a pointer to a `QWidget`), and the coordinates of the upper-left corner of the area into which the graphics are copied. The next five parameters describe the source with a pointer to a paint device (for double-buffering, this is a pointer to a `QPixmap`), the coordinates of the starting point, and the size of the area that is to be copied. The last two parameters specify a raster operation for the copying, and declare whether the mask of a `QPixmap` should be ignored, if it has one.

You might get the impression from the number of parameters that double buffering with `bitBlt` is difficult to use, but that is not true. You usually employ the same parameters over and over again, and most have reasonable defaults. Here is the most typical usage of `bitBlt`, already embedded in a `paintEvent()` method:

```
void MyWidget::paintEvent( QPaintEvent* )
{
    bitBlt( this, 0, 0, &bufferpixmap );
}
```

Note that no `QPainter` is used here, and that we use default arguments that have suitable values. This looks simple, but it is less efficient than it could be. The parameter passed to `paintEvent()` tells us which part of the widget needs to be repainted, so we can use that information and copy over only the part that is needed:

```
void MyWidget::paintEvent( QPaintEvent* e )
{
    bitBlt( this, e->rect().topLeft(), &bufferpixmap, e->rect() );
}
```

Here we use an overloaded form of `bitBlt()` that uses a `QPoint` and a `QRect` rather than integer parameters for the coordinates.

If `bitBlt()` is not flexible enough—for example, if you want to copy the buffer rotated and you don't want to rotate the buffer with `QPixmap::xForm()`—you can use `QPainter::drawPixmap()` instead. This method has the following signature:

```
void QPainter::drawPixmap( int x, int y, const QPixmap& pixmap,
                           int sx=0, int sy=0, int sw=-1, int sh=-1 )
```

Again, there are also overloaded versions that use `QPoint` and `QRect`. Putting this method in context leads to the following code:

```
void MyWidget::paintEvent( QPaintEvent* e )
{
    QPainter painter( this );
    painter.drawPixmap( 0, 0, bufferpixmap );
}
```

Here we use the default values, which leads to the whole buffer being copied over. We can make the repainting operation more effective by copying only the needed rectangle:

```
void MyWidget::paintEvent( QPaintEvent* e )
{
    QPainter painter( this );
    painter.drawPixmap( e->rect().topLeft(), bufferpixmap, e->rect() );
}
```

If you want to use raster operations with `drawPixmap()`, as you can do with `bitBlt()`, you need to use `QPainter::setRasterOp()`.

The simple implementations of `paintEvent()` shown so far only work when the pixmap buffer already contains the desired graphics. In a paint program like the one in our tutorial, where you can perform all drawing operations once in the widget and once in the pixmap buffer, this will work. If pixmap first needs to be computed itself, you have to do a little bit more in `paintEvent()`. The data for repainting the pixmap might come from an object list in a CAD-like vector-graphics program, or from state variables in a widget you wrote. In the latter case, you can either update the pixmap in the methods that implement event handlers, update it in `paintEvent()`, or update it in a drawing method called from `paintEvent()`. For both options it is usually preferable to update `paintEvent()`, because it keeps all drawing code in one place.

The following sample code first updates the buffer pixmap, then copies the data to the widget. Note the use of the "dirty" flag. We assume that the methods that change the state of the widget set this flag to true whenever the buffer pixmap has to be updated from internal data. After updating the buffer pixmap, this `paintEvent()` implementation clears the flag. If `paintEvent()` is called with the flag being `false`, no state changes have been made to the widget since it was last repainted. In other words, `paintEvent()` is called because the window system reported that the widget had been obscured by another window, and is now at least partly visible again. In this case, we need to update only the widget, and can simply copy the buffer pixmap to the widget as we did before.

```
void MyWidget::paintEvent( QPaintEvent* e )
{
    if( dirty ) {
        QPainter painter( &bufferpixmap );
        // perform any needed painting operations on the bufferpixmap
        dirty = false; // updating of buffer pixmap is done
    }
    // copy the buffer pixmap over to the widget
    bitBlt( this, e->rect().topLeft(), &bufferpixmap, e->rect() );
}
```

In addition, font and palette changes have to be considered. Overloading `setFont()` and `setPalette()`, and then setting the dirty flag in these methods before calling `set-Font()` or `setPalette()` in the base class should do the job.

One detail is still missing. The buffer pixmap needs to have a size that is large enough to hold all the pixels—ideally, it should have the same size. To make sure this is always the case, we simply overload the `resizeEvent()` method and ensure that the pixmap is resized to the size of the widget whenever the size of the widget changes. Since `resizeEvent()` is also called when the widget is created, it is not even necessary to initialize the size of the buffer pixmap in a special case.

You have two options for resizing the buffer pixmap. You can either do it directly in the `resizeEvent()` method:

```
void MyWidget::resizeEvent( QResizeEvent* )
{
    bufferpixmap.resize( size() );
}
```

Or, you can just set the `dirty` flag there, and resize the buffer pixmap in `paint-Event()`:

```
void MyWidget::resizeEvent( QResizeEvent* )
{
    dirty = false;
}

void MyWidget::paintEvent( QPaintEvent* )
{
    if( dirty ) {
        bufferpixmap.resize( size() );
        ... // rest as before
    }
}
```

If the drawing operations do not fill every pixel of the buffer pixmap, you probably should first fill the pixmap with the background color of the widget to remove any trace of the previous graphics from the pixmap:

```
void MyWidget::paintEvent( QPaintEvent* )
{
    if( dirty ) {
        bufferpixmap.resize( size() );
        bufferpixmap.fill( backgroundColor() );
        ... // rest as before
    }
}
```

To further reduce memory consumption, you do not even need to have one buffer pixmap for each widget. Since the buffer pixmap is needed and valid only within `paint-Event()`, and since there can never be more than one `paintEvent()` method running at the same time[7], it is enough to have one buffer pixmap for a whole class or—even more extreme—for all widgets that you define yourself. The idea is to let the pixmap have the size of the largest repaint so far, so that it does not have to be reallocated all the time. Then you use translations to copy exactly the right parts of it. This code assumes that there is a `QPixmap` object `sharedpixmap` available somewhere:

```
void MyWidget::paintEvent( QPaintEvent* e )
{
    // make sure the pixmap is large enough
    sharedpixmap.resize(
        QMAX( e->rect().width(), sharedpixmap.width() ),
        QMAX( e->rect().height(), sharedpixmap.height() )
    );

    // Create a painter for the pixmap
    QPainter painter( sharedpixmap );
    // Translate the coordinate system so that you can paint
```

---

7   Unless you have a multi-threaded program, but Qt does not yet support more than one thread that services the UI.

```
// into the pixmap with the usual coordinates
painter.translate( -e->rect().x(), -e->rect().y() );
// your drawing operations go here
...
painter.end();

// Copy the buffer pixmap over to the widget with bitBlt()
// or drawPixmap()
...
```

Double-buffering is a powerful technique for reducing flicker, thus making your applications look more professional. If you are writing a bitmap-graphics drawing program like the one in the tutorial, you probably already use a buffer pixmap to repaint your application's work area. In this case, you get double-buffering practically for free.

Loading and Saving Custom Image Formats

The two methods `QPixmap::load()` and `QPixmap::save()` are convenient and practical for loading and saving bitmap graphics. Qt already supports many image formats, including GIF[8], BMP, XBM, XPM, and the various PNM formats (PBM, PGM, PPM, PBM-RAW, PGMRAW and PPMRAW). The class that manages image input and output operations, `QImageIO`, provides a feature for adding your own image-reading or -writing code to the system, and for automatically invoking it when an image of this format is to be read or written.

We first draw your attention to the image I/O extension. With this extension, which you can find in the directory *$QTDIR/extensions/imageio*, the Qt developers provide additional image-file formats. These should not bloat Qt, because they are rarely used. Currently, filters for reading and writing JPEG and PNG images are provided. Just compile that extension and link the resulting library to your code if you need it. You then need only to call the function `qInitImageIO()`, or if you only need one of the filters, call either `qInitJpegIO()` or `qInitPngIO()` to make these image filters available for `QPixmap::load()` and `QPixmap::save()`. More image formats will probably be added in the future, so calling `qInitImageIO()` might give you additional image formats if you have upgraded your version of Qt. This might not be desirable in all cases[9] so it might be a good idea to link the image I/O extension statically.

Now let's go back to adding your own image-file formats. Let's imagine that you want to add a filter for reading and writing TIFF (Tagged Image File Format) images. Of course, we cannot include the (huge) code for reading and writing TIFF files here, but you can use the freely available TIFF library on Unix systems. On Windows systems, you might have to buy a third-party product if you don't want to write the actual reading and writing code yourself.

---

8   Read-only, due to patent restrictions. GIF support might be removed in the future.
9   Especially since the image filters might need external libraries, as the JPEG and the PNG filter do, which would require you to also have those shared libraries on your system.

Let's assume that you have already written this code, and want to integrate it into the image I/O system. Your code is in two handler functions, void `read_TIFF(` `QImageIO* )` and void `write_TIFF( QImageIO* )`. Note that you are bound to these signatures; the `QImageIO` object whose pointer is passed here will provide your code with access to both the file and the memory location where the image data is stored, or will be stored.

Now you have to register your handlers by calling the static method `QImageIO::defineIOHandler()`. This method has the following signature:

```
void QImageIO::defineIOHandler ( const char* format,
                                 const char* header,
                                 const char* flags,
                                 image_io_handler read_image,
                                 image_io_handler write_image )
```

The first argument, `format`, is a string that identifies the format. This string is used to specify the format in `QPixmap::save()` and `QPixmap::load()`—use the latter only if you do not want the format to be auto-detected. The second argument, `header`, is a string that contains a regular expression for detecting the graphics file format. When you use `QPixmap::load()` with the auto-detection feature, all the regular expressions of registered image-read handlers are matched against the first few bytes of the file, one after another, until a matching format is found. This is then used for reading the image file. You can use the full syntax made available here by the class `QRegExp` (see the "Working with Regular Expressions" section).

To determine a good regular expression that identifies files of the desired type but rules out files of all other types, you need some knowledge of the file format in question. For TIFF, a good regular expression would be `MM\x00\x2a` for big-endian images and `II\x2a\x00` for little-endian images. Unfortunately, `QRegExp` can't combine these two regular expressions, but you can easily circumvent this problem by calling `QImageIO::defineIOHandler()` twice.

The third parameter, `flags`, can be either `"T"` for text-based image file formats like PBM or `0` for all others. Finally, the fourth and fifth parameters are pointers to the handler functions for reading and writing the image, respectively.

To put all of this together, here is how we would register the TIFF handlers:

```
QImageIO::defineIOHandler( "TIFF-LE", "II\0x2a\0x01", 0,
                           &read_TIFF, &write_TIFF );
QImageIO::defineIOHandler( "TIFF-BE", "MM\0x01\0x2a", 0,
                           &read_TIFF, &write_TIFF );
```

Wait a moment! Why does it say `0x01` instead of `0x00` in the previous code example? There's a little bug in the regular expression routines: zero bytes are never parsed correctly. The file-format detection routines work around this by expecting a `0x01` instead of a `0x00`. In this special case only, `0x01` is interpreted as `0x00` or `0x01`.

Once you have called `QImageIO::defineIOHandler()`, you can use your new image-filters just like built-in ones—under the assumption, of course, that your image-file filters are correct, and that they correctly pass the data to Qt.

The question remains of how you actually get your data correctly into and out of the image mechanisms of Qt. The class that you use is `QImage`. A `QImageIO` object is passed to your read or write procedure. You can access a `QIODevice`, which is usually a `QFile` that represents the file from which or to which the data is being read or written, by calling `ioDevice()`. The QImage object that encapsulates the pixel data is retrieved with `image()`. Once you have this image, you can get the pixels out of it for writing, or you can put them in for reading.

`QImage` objects have a width, a height, and a depth. In addition, there is a color table and, of course, the actual pixels. You can also handle alpha channels—explaining this is beyond the scope of this book, but you can learn more at *http://developer.kde.org/qt-useful/alpha-channel.txt*.

There are three possible depths: 1 bit per pixel (for monochrome images), 8 bits per pixel, and 32 bits per pixel. With the last color depth, only the three least significant bytes are used for the color value, while the most significant byte is reserved for the alpha channel (transparency). In 8-bit mode, an index into the color table is stored; in 32-bit mode, the RGB value is stored. You can construct such a RGB value with the function `qRgb()` (defined in *qcolor.h*). The individual values available are `qRed()`, `qGreen()` and `qBlue()`, all defined in the same header file.

You can also change the depth of a `QImage` object after construction with `convertDepth()`, but when you reduce the color depth, you may lose information.

Check the documentation for the file format to see how you get at the individual pixels in the disk file and how to store them there. Here are six functions that also help you access individual pixels within a `QImage` object. These functions read and write pixels in each of the three possible color depths. Note that these functions need to take into account that the length of each scanline is aligned to a multiple of 32. If you want to implement the pixel access yourself, you will also have to make any scanline alignment adjustments.

```
// value is either true (set the pixel) or false (clear the pixel)
void setPixel1BPP( QImage& image, int x, int y, bool value )
{
    if( value )
        if ( image.bitOrder() == QImage::LittleEndian )
            *( image.scanLine( y ) + ( x >> 3 ) ) |= 1 << ( x & 7 );
        else
            *( image.scanLine( y ) + ( x >> 3 ) ) |= 1 << ( 7 - ( x & 7 ) );
    else
        if ( image.bitOrder() == QImage::LittleEndian )
            *( image.scanLine( y ) + ( x >> 3 ) ) &= 254 << ( x & 7 );
        else
            *( image.scanLine( y ) + ( x >> 3 ) ) &= 254 << ( 7 - ( x & 7 ) );
}
```

```
bool getPixel1BPP( const QImage& image, int x, int y )
{
    if( image.bitOrder() == QImage::LittleEndian )
        return *( image.scanLine( y ) + ( x >> 3 ) ) & 1 << ( x & 7 );
    else
        return *( image.scanLine( y ) + ( x >> 3 ) ) & 1 << ( 7 - ( x & 7 ) );
}



// value is an index into the color table
void setPixel8BPP( QImage& image, int x, int y, unsigned char value )
{
    *( image.scanLine( y ) + x ) = value;
}



unsigned char getPixel8BPP( const QImage& image, int x, int y )
{
    return *( image.scanLine( y ) + x );
}



// red, green and blue form the color value together
void setPixel32BPP( QImage& image, int x, int y, uint red, uint green, uint blue )
{
    uint *p = (uint *)image.scanLine( y ) + x;
    *p = qRgb( red, green, blue );
}



void getPixel32BPP( const QImage&, int x, int y, uint& red, uint&green, uint&blue )
{
    uint *p = (uint *)image.scanLine( y ) + x;
    red = qRed( *p );
    green = qGreen( *p );
    blue = qBlue( *p );
}
```

With this information and the reference documentation for `QImage`, you now know enough to write your own image-file format filters. Qt also provides a mechanism for incremental image loading, as used when you load an image via a network connection, but implementing this is well beyond the scope of this book. If you wish to know more, read the documentation for `QImageFormatType` in the reference documentation.

Note that for loading animations, `QMovie` is the class of choice.

Setting a Cursor

Sometimes you want to set a special mouse cursor for all widgets in an application, such as an hourglass that indicates that the application is busy with some long task. Setting the cursor with `setCursor` on every widget would be very cumbersome, especially with large applications. Therefore, Qt provides two static methods `QApplication::setOverrideCursor()` and `QApplication::restoreOverrideCursor()`, that do this task for you. In the aforementioned case, you would do something like the following:

```
QApplication::setOverrideCursor( waitCursor );
... // some long calculation
QApplication::restoreOverrideCursor();
```

The new cursor stays in effect until you call `restoreOverrideCursor()` or set another one with a new call to `setOverrideCursor`. Note that these two functions must come in pairs, or the cursor stack will get out of sync.

To find out if an override cursor is in effect, you can use the static method `QApplication::overrideCursor()`, which returns a pointer to the current `QCursor` that serves as override cursor, or returns `0` if no override cursor is in effect.

10

Text Processing

This chapter covers some topics in the area of text processing. The first section tells you how to validate the input that users enter into a text field, and the second explains how to use the class QRegExp for regular expression matching.

Validating User Input

It often happens that the user is required to enter text into a text field that must conform to special formatting requirements. Examples include phone numbers and ISBNs. It is possible to check for validity when the user closes the dialog containing the edit field, but it is much more user-friendly when the user gets immediate response, and can fix things right away.

Qt provides a class called QValidator which works with the three classes that allow the input of single-line text: QLineEdit, QSpinBox, and QComboBox. These all have a method setValidator(), with which a QValidator object may be added. If there is such a QValidator object, all input is subject to validation. The validator can reject input of a character, accept it, or perhaps even fix defective input. Note that QValidator has a loophole: Only text entered via the keyboard or programmatically is subject to validation—text pasted via the clipboard is not.

In addition to acceptance and non-acceptance, QValidator can also tell the user that the input is not acceptable, but could be made acceptable with more entered characters. In this case, the text-entry field accepts the character, but refuses to emit the returnPressed() signal when the user presses Enter.

QValidator is an abstract base class, so you cannot instantiate objects of type QValidator but have to derive your own subclasses from it. Qt comes with two simple subclasses, QIntValidator and QDoubleValidator, which will suffice for most common cases. These don't attempt to fix faulty input.

Example 10-1 shows how to use QValidator, including its text-fixing features. It shows a field in which the user is supposed to enter an ISBN[1]. This number is of the form x-xxxxxxxxx-x, where the first digit encodes the country of origin of the book[2] and the last one is a checksum. The eight digits in between represent the publisher and its article number. If we added a full list of publisher codes to our program, it would even be possible to determine, where the third dash that usually separates the publisher from the article number should be, if desired. Since people usually don't enter the dashes, we just check for the digits during input, and add dashes later—although dashes at the correct positions are allowed in the input, too. In a more sophisticated program, we could use the checksum to validate the input.

Example 10-1: Using QValidator to validate ISBNs

```
 1  #include <qapplication.h>
 2  #include <qlineedit.h>
 3  #include <qvalidator.h>
 4  #include <ctype.h>
 5
 6  /**
 7    * A class that validates ISBN numbers. See text for the
 8    * specification.
 9    */
10  class ISBNValidator : public QValidator
11  {
12  public:
13    ISBNValidator() : QValidator( 0 ) {};
14    virtual State validate( QString&, int& );
15    virtual void fixup( QString& );
16  };
17
18
19  /**
20    * This method is called after every input. Since we can check every
21    * character as soon as it is entered, we only need to check one
22    * character at a time for validity. To determine whether
23    * the whole string is acceptable, we must look at the whole
24    * string.
25    * Note that input can also be deleted. This makes it useless
26    * to save state (like the number of entered digits) between
27    * invocations of validate(), because we would have to keep an extra
28    * copy of the last string.
29    */
30  QValidator::State ISBNValidator::validate( QString& text, int& pos )
31  {
32    /* An empty string could be made acceptable */
33    if( !text.length() )
34      return Valid;
```

---

1   International Standard Book Number, a worldwide unique identification code for every book in print.

2   There are, of course, more than ten languages or countries, which is why there can also be *two* digits for the country/language. For simplicity's sake, we don't consider this possibility here.

Example 10-1: Using QValidator to validate ISBNs (continued)

```
35
36     /* Protect against spurious calls to validate() */
37     if( (unsigned int)pos >= text.length() )
38       return Valid;
39
40     /* Anything but decimal digits and dashes is invalid. We only need
41      * to check the character at the cursor positions. This speeds
42      * things up massively.
43      */
44     if( !isdigit( text[pos] ) && ( text[pos] != '-' ) )
45       {
46         debug( "Typed character is neither digit nor dash\n" );
47         return Invalid;
48       }
49
50     /* Dashes are only valid at position 1 (the second position),
51      * position 8 (if there was no dash at position 1), or position 9 (if
52      * there was a dash at position 1).
53      */
54     if( text[pos] == '-' )
55       {
56         if( pos != 1 && pos != 8 && pos != 9 )
57           {
58             debug( "Dash at wrong position\n" );
59             return Invalid;
60           }
61
62         if( ( pos == 8 && text[1] == '-' ) ||
63             ( pos == 9 && text[1] != '-' ) )
64           {
65             debug( "Dash at wrong position\n" );
66             return Invalid;
67           }
68       }
69
70     /* If the characters entered so far are valid, but the string
71      * contains less than ten digits, it could be made acceptable, but
72      * is not yet.
73      */
74     int numdigits = text.length();
75     if( text.length() > 1 && text[1] == '-' ) numdigits--;
76     if( text.length() > 8 && text[8] == '-' ) numdigits--;
77     if( text.length() > 9 && text[9] == '-' ) numdigits--;
78
79     if( numdigits < 10 )
80       {
81         debug( "Less than ten digits; input valid but not yet acceptable\n" );
82         return Valid;
83       }
84
```

Example 10-1: Using QValidator to validate ISBNs (continued)

```
85      /* More than ten digits is always invalid */
86      if( numdigits > 10 )
87          {
88              debug( "More than ten digits; input invalid\n" );
89              return Invalid;
90          }
91
92      /* If we have exactly ten digits but the dashes are not in place,
93       * we don't declare the input Acceptable, but Valid only. In this
94       * case, the text-entry field will call fixup(), where we can add the
95       * missing dashes.
96       */
97      if( text[1] != '-' || text[9] != '-' )
98          {
99              debug( "Ten digits, but dashes not in the right places."
100                     "Could be fixed up\n" );
101             return Valid;
102         }
103
104     /* Everything is as it should be. */
105     debug( "Input acceptable\n" );
106     return Acceptable;
107 }
108
109
110 /**
111   * This method is called when the user has pressed return, but
112   * validate() has judged the string valid but not acceptable. Note
113   * that fixup() is not required to return an acceptable string. It is
114   * guaranteed that the caller will validate() the string once again
115   * after the call to fixup().
116   */
117 void ISBNValidator::fixup( QString& text )
118 {
119     /* We can fix the input only if the dashes are missing,
120      * since we cannot implement the missing digits. (We could at least
121      * compute the last one with the checksum algorithm, but won't do so
122      * here.)
123      */
124
125     /* If at least one digit has been entered but there is no dash at
126      * position 1, insert one.
127      */
128     if( text.length() && text[1] != '-' )
129         text.insert( 1, '-' );
130
131     /* If at least nine digits have been entered but there is no dash
132      * at position 10 (because of the last two lines, we can safely
133      * assume that the first dash is already in place), insert one.
134      */
```

Example 10-1: Using QValidator to validate ISBNs (continued)

```
135   if( text.length() >= 10 /* nine digits plus dash */ && text[10] != '-' )
136     text.insert( 10, '-' );
137 }
138
139
140 /**
141  * This class only serves as a receiver for the returnPressed()
142  * signal, so we can know when the input has been accepted.
143  */
144 class ReturnReceiver : public QObject
145 {
146   Q_OBJECT
147
148 public slots:
149   void slotReturnPressed();
150 };
151
152
153 void ReturnReceiver::slotReturnPressed()
154 {
155   /* When this string appears, the input was acceptable. */
156   debug( "return pressed - input accepted\n" );
157 }
158
159 #include "validator.moc"
160
161 int main( int argc, char* argv[] )
162 {
163   QApplication myapp( argc, argv );
164
165   // create a line edit
166   QLineEdit* myedit = new QLineEdit();
167   myedit->resize( 100, 30 );
168
169   // create and assign a validator for the line edit
170   ISBNValidator* myvalidator = new ISBNValidator();
171   myedit->setValidator( myvalidator );
172
173   // set up a receiver for the returnPressed() signal
174   ReturnReceiver receiver;
175   QObject::connect( myedit, SIGNAL( returnPressed() ),
176                     &receiver, SLOT( slotReturnPressed() ) );
177
178   myapp.setMainWidget( myedit );
179   myedit->show();
180   return myapp.exec();
181 }
```

Look closely at this program to see what is done to ensure that only valid input is entered. Note that even though it is already quite complex, the validator is not bullet-proof. One problem is that the validator checks whether a dash has been entered at a valid position, but it does not check later to see if that dash was moved to an invalid position when more characters were inserted before it. It's not difficult to fix this, but it does require more code.

To help you understand what's going on here, some words about the collaboration between QLineEdit and QValidator and about QComboBox and QSpinBox are in order. Whenever a key is pressed and a validator is set for the QLineEdit object, the validate() method of the assigned validator is called with the current input text plus the new character and the current input position (again taking the new character into account). When QValidator::validate() returns Invalid, but did not return Invalid the last time, the key is simply discarded and the old value is kept. This effectively prevents the user from entering invalid keys, as long as validate() works correctly.

When the user presses Enter, QLineEdit calls validate() again. This time, a return value of Valid is not enough: the return value must be Acceptable. If this is not the case, the QLineEdit object calls QValidator::fixup(), which might or might not repair the defective input. Since it is not guaranteed that fixup() can help, validate() is called once again. If it does not return Acceptable this time either, the signal returnPressed() is not emitted. Otherwise, it is emitted.

Working with Regular Expressions

If you followed the design of the ISBN checking program in the previous section, you might think that there must be an easier way. Fortunately, there is. The magic words are *regular expressions*. Regular expressions are a concept from the theory of automata, a subject from theoretical computer science. They are extremely useful for most text-processing tasks, and are frequently used in Unix systems. In the Windows world, they are still not used very much, although programs geared toward developers, such as editors and Integrated Development Environments, do make some use of regular expressions.

We can't explain all the intricacies of regular expressions here. If you want to know more, see *Mastering Regular Expressions* by J. Friedl, published by O'Reilly & Associates.

To begin with, a regular expression is a string that describes a number of other strings (even an infinite number of them). For example, the string a*bcd describes a set of strings that all start with an arbitrary number of a's (even zero) and are followed by the characters b, c, and d. This set of strings is already infinite, because you can have an arbitrary number of a's at the beginning. We say that a*bcd *matches* the strings bcd, abcd, aabcd, aaabcd, and many more like them. Usually we are not interested in the set of all strings that a regular expression matches, but in the question of whether a regular expression matches one certain string.

A regular expression consists of literal characters that match exactly the same character, and special characters that are often called *meta characters*. In Qt, a regular expression is described by an object of the class `QRegExp`. This implementation of regular expressions in Qt does not support all the many meta characters found in other implementations, such as those of Emacs or Perl. For example, it does not support backreferences[3], but it has most of the things you need for your daily work. The meta characters from Table 10-1 are available in `QRegExp`.

Table 10-1: Meta characters in Qt regular expressions

Metacharacter	Meaning	Example	Matches
.	Matches any character	`a.b`	An a, followed by any character, followed by a b
^	Matches the start of a string	`^ab`	aba, but not bab
$	Matches the end of a string	`ab$`	bab, but not aba
[]	Matches any character in the brackets	`[abc]`	An a or a b or a c.
*	Matches any number of the preceding character	`a*b`	Any number of a's (or even none), followed by a b.
+	Matches any number greater than zero of the preceding character	`a+b`	At least one a, followed by one b.
?	Matches zero or one occurrence of the preceding character	`a?b`	ab and b.

Apart from literal characters, `QRegExp` also knows about special *escape sequences* that stand for one literal character. These escape sequences are listed in Table 10-2.

Table 10-2: Escape sequences in Qt regular expressions

Sequence	Meaning
*	A literal *
\+	A literal +
\?	A literal ?
\.	A literal .
\^	A literal ^
\$	A literal $
\[	A literal [
\]	A literal]

---

3   Strictly speaking, backreferences leave the realm of regular expressions anyway, because they add much more expressive power.

Table 10-2: Escape sequences in Qt regular expressions (continued)

Sequence	Meaning
\b	The bell character (ASCII 7)
\t	The tab character (ASCII 9)
\n	The newline character (ASCII 10)
\r	The return character (ASCII 13)
\s	Any whitespace character (ASCII characters 9, 10, 11, 12, 13 and 32)
\x*nn*	The character with the hexadecimal ASCII value *nn*
\0*nn*	The character with the octal ASCII value *nn*

After all this theory it's time to see some code. The following code example checks whether characters stored in the QString variable checkthis consist of an arbitrary number of a's, followed by bcd:

```
QRegExp regexp( "a*bcd" );
int ret = regexp.match( checkthis );
if( ret != -1 )
    debug( "Value of checkthis matches at position %d\n", ret );
else
    debug( "Value of checkthis does not match." );
```

As you can see, the actual matching is done with the method match(). You can also pass a second parameter of type integer to match that indicates that match() should start searching at this position. If you want to know how many characters the longest match contained, you can also pass a pointer to an integer variable as the third parameter. The match() method then stores the length of the longest match in this variable.

In our example, matching is case-sensitive, so a does not match A. If you want to disregard case, you can pass false as the second argument of the constructor of QRegExp, as in the following example, or you can call setCaseSensitive() later.

```
QRegExp regexp( "a*bcd", false );
// rest as before
```

The class QRegExp also supports a different kind of text matching, often called *file globbing*, because it is used by command-line processors or shells to expand wildcards in filenames. Windows and Unix have slightly different conventions here, and Qt follows the Unix conventions. With file globbing, there are only four metacharacters: ?, *, [and]. The bracket pair ([]) has the same meaning as with regular expressions. The question mark (?) is a wildcard for exactly one character. In other words, it has the same meaning as the dot (.) in regular expressions. The asterisk (*), like in regular expressions, is a wildcard for any number of characters. Unlike in regular expressions, however, it does not work with the preceding character to constrain the characters it can stand for. In regular expressions, the asterisk means "any number of the preceding character"; in file globbing, it means "any number of any character in any order". Thus, to get the meaning that * has in file globbing in regular expressions, you write .*.

You turn on file globbing matching by passing `true` as the third parameter to the constructor of `QRegExp`. Calling `setWildcard( true )` allows you to do this even after construction.

11

Working with Files and Directories

There are few programs that don't deal with files and directories in some way. File system manipulation is another inherently platform-dependent area. If you don't plan to make your application available on multiple platforms and you are absolutely sure that nobody will ever ask you to, you can use the native functions for accessing files and directories provided by your operating system or development environment. However, if you need or want to be portable, using the classes that Qt provides might be a better choice. Even if portability is not important for you, the Qt classes might be useful because they provide easy, and type-safe access to this functionality.

The Qt API for accessing files and directories mainly consists of the classes QIODevice, QFile, QFileInfo, and QDir. There are also two classes, QDataStream and QText-Stream, for writing binary and text data to files.

We explain how to use these classes by means of three examples: reading a text file, recursing over a directory tree, and outputting information about one file.

Reading a Text File

To read a text file, you create a QFile object, assign the file name to this object, and open it. You then create a QTextStream object that works with the QFile object, and read the data by means of the normal C++ input operators or with QText-Stream::readLine(). Example 11-1 contains the complete code.

Example 11-1: Reading textual data from a file

```
1 #include <qapplication.h>
2 #include <qfile.h>
3 #include <qtextstream.h>
4
5 int main( int argc, char* argv[] )
```

Example 11-1: Reading textual data from a file (continued)

```
 6 {
 7   QApplication a( argc, argv );
 8
 9   QFile file( "/etc/passwd" ); // use something like C:\\AUTOEXEC.BAT for Windows
10   if( !file.open( IO_ReadOnly ) )
11       return 1;
12   QTextStream stream( &file );
13   QString line;
14   while( !stream.eof() ) {
15     line = stream.readLine();
16     debug( "%s\n", line.data() );
17   }
18   file.close();
19
20   return 0;
21 }
```

This program follows exactly the pattern described earlier. First a `QFile` object is created. In this case, we pass the name of the file that this object should encapsulate in the constructor. It is also possible to construct a `QFile` object without a filename, and set the name later with `setName()`.

The freshly created `QFile` object is then opened. This maps directly to the `open()` operation of the operating system. Fortunately, the flags that `QFile::open()` uses—`IO_Raw`, `IO_ReadOnly`, `IO_WriteOnly`, `IO_ReadWrite`, `IO_Append`, `IO_Truncate`, and `IO_Translate`—are much easier to memorize than their native counterparts on both Unix and Windows systems. The last of these might not be obvious. `IO_Translate` turns on carriage return/linefeed translation for text files on Windows systems.

We then create a `QTextStream` object that is passed a pointer to our `QFile` object in the constructor. The main objective of `QTextStream` is to provide type-safe operations for reading and writing data. This is done with the overloaded operators `<<` and `>>`. If you know C++ standard IO streams, this should be nothing new. In this example we don't use these operators, though, because the file that we plan to read is line-oriented. Therefore, the method `QTextStream::readLine()` is more suitable, because code like this:

```
stream >> line;
```

would slurp the entire string into memory at once rather than reading one line. Note that `readLine()` removes the trailing newline character, which we therefore have to add again before outputting the line to standard error. If you want to see the full list of input and output operators supported by `QTextStream`, please see the reference documentation. You can safely assume that all basic types are there, however.

The output in this example is done via the Qt function `debug()`, which sends the output to standard error on Unix systems and to the debugger on Windows. Where exactly you can read this output on Windows depends on your development environment.

`QFile` itself contains many more methods than the simple `open()` and `close()` that we have used here, but these are the two methods you need in any program that uses `QFile` objects. Some more interesting methods are `at()`, which allows random access to the file by setting or retrieving the file pointer; and `readBlock()` and `writeBlock()` which let you read or write raw data block-wise (although you might lose portability of your data format if you do so). Finally, there are the methods `exists()`, with which you can query whether the file you want to work on exists; and `remove()`, which lets you remove a file. These two methods also exist as static variants that accept the name of the file to check for the file's existence or to delete it.

In this example, we have read textual data. If you work with binary data, you can use `QDataStream` instead of `QTextStream`. Like `QTextStream`, it provides many overloaded input or output operators. Files that are written exclusively with `QDataStream` are portable across all platforms that Qt supports. You need to write code for reading and writing your data files only once, and you can even exchange the data files thus produced. This works between Windows and Unix systems, and between little-endian systems, like Intel-based machines, and big-endian systems, like SPARC computers and other fast workstations.

If you look at the reference documentation for `QDataStream`, you'll only find operators for reading and writing standard data types. Many other Qt classes provide operators for reading and writing their objects from and to `QDataStream` objects, however. Examples of these include `QFont` and `QColor`.

Before we go on, we should mention that `QFile` is derived from `QIODevice`, which is a general abstraction of objects to which you can write data, and from which you can read data. `QBuffer` is another class that inherits from `QIODevice`, and emulates "in-memory files". This might be useful for caching operations. You could, for example, read image files into a `QBuffer`, then retrieve the image data from there as needed.

Traversing a Directory

Our next example traverses a directory tree. It starts at a hard-coded directory, then recursively displays all the files, subdirectories and their contents in that directory. If you start this program in the root directory of a large filesystem or partition, the output may be quite lengthy. Let's first look at the code in Example 11-2:

Example 11-2: Traversing a directory tree

```
1  #include <qapplication.h>
2  #include <qdir.h>
3  #include <qfileinfo.h>
4
5  void traverse( const char* dirname );
6
7  void traverse( const char* dirname )
8  {
```

Example 11-2: Traversing a directory tree (continued)

```
 9    QDir dir( dirname );
10    dir.setFilter( QDir::Dirs | QDir::Files | QDir::NoSymLinks );
11
12    const QFileInfoList* fileinfolist = dir.entryInfoList();
13    QFileInfoListIterator it( *fileinfolist );
14    QFileInfo* fi;
15    while( ( fi = it.current() ) ) {
16      if( fi->fileName() == "." || fi->fileName() == ".." ) {
17        ++it;
18        continue;
19      }
20      if( fi->isDir() && fi->isReadable() )
21        traverse( fi->absFilePath() );
22      else
23        debug( "%s\n", fi->absFilePath().data() );
24
25      ++it;
26    }
27
28    delete fileinfolist;
29  }
30
31
32  int main( int argc, char* argv[] )
33  {
34    QApplication a( argc, argv );
35
36    traverse( "/" ); // for Windows, use something like "C:\\"
37
38    return 0;
39  }
```

Obviously, the best choice for recursively traversing a filesystem is a recursive function, in our case `traverse()`. This function first creates a `QDir` object, which encapsulates the directory this instance of `traverse()` is working on. In line 11, `QDir` is told only to report files and directories, but not symbolic links, to avoid endless loops on Unix systems. Then, in line 13, we demand a `QFileInfoList`. This is a list of `QFileInfo` objects.

We come to `QFileInfo` in the next example. For now, it suffices to know that `QFileInfo` can tell us whether a directory entry is a file or a directory. An iterator (for more information about iterators see the "Iterators" section) traverses all the entries in this list, and calls `traverse()` recursively if the current entry is a directory. Otherwise, it just prints the filename. Unreadable directories are skipped. Note that we explicitly skip the entries for the current directory and the parent directory, to avoid an endless loop.

`QDir` is a class with a large number of methods. Probably its most interesting feature is the capability to filter and sort its entries. You can filter the entries either by type or by name. Filter by type by calling `setFilter()`, as in our example. You can ask for direc-

tories, files, no symbolic links, drives, readable, writable and executable entries, modified, hidden, and system entries, or a combination of any of these. The correct values
are in the reference documentation. Note that not all of these filters apply to all operating systems: for example, there are no special system files on Unix systems, and no
symbolic links on Windows.

If you want to filter by name, call `setFilterName()` and pass a filter string. You can
use the wildcards * and ?. It is also possible to combine filtering by type and filtering by
name.

Sometimes, you want to filter file names but not directories. If so, you can call `set-
MatchAllDirs(true)`. In this case, the directories are not affected by name or type
filters.

`QDir` can also sort its entries. Call `setSorting()` and pass one of the following values:
`QDir::Name`, `QDir::Time`, `QDir::Size`, or `QDir::Unsorted`. The latter uses the operating system order. You can further change these sorting specifications by or-ing the
previous values with one or more of `DirsFirst` (which always puts directories first),
`Reversed`, or `IgnoreCase`.

Filtering and sorting the entries would be of no use if you didn't do anything with them.
We have already seen `entryInfoList()` in our example, which returns a pointer to a
`QFileInfoList` to provide information about the entries in the directory. If you are
only interested in the names themselves, you can also call `entryList()`, which returns
a pointer to a `QStrList` object containing the names of the directory entries.

By the way, when specifying a path for `QDir`, you normally do not need to use different
paths for Unix and Windows because of the different path-separation characters. You
can always use / as the path-separation character, and Qt will convert your path specification to whatever is applicable to the current platform. Should you need to know
what the path-separation character is, you can call the static method `QDir::separa-
tor()`.

Two more interesting static methods are `QDir::rootDirPath()` and `QDir::homeDir-
Path()`, which return the absolute path to the root directory and the user's home direc-
tory, respectively.

File Information

Let's leave `QDir` for now, and look a little bit more at `QFileInfo`. An object of this class
encapsulates various bits of information about a certain file. Normally you construct a
`QFileInfo` by passing a string with the file name to the constructor, but you can also
pass a `QFile` object. You can then call various methods to get information about the file
in question. Example 11-3 contains a small program that outputs information about a
certain file:

Example 11-3: Getting information about a file

```
1  #include <qfileinfo.h>
2
3  int main( int argc, char* argv[] )
4  {
5    QFileInfo fi( "/etc/passwd" ); // use something like "C:\\AUTOEXEC.BAT on windows
6
7    debug( "%s:\n", fi.filePath() );
8
9    if( fi.isFile() )
10     debug( "is a file\n" );
11   if( fi.isDir() )
12     debug( "is a directory\n" );
13   if( fi.isSymLink() )
14     debug( "is a symbolic link and points to %s\n ", fi.readLink().data() );
15
16   debug( "The size is %d\n", fi.size() );
17   if( fi.isReadable() )
18       debug( "is readable\n" );
19   else
20     debug( "is not readable\n" );
21   if( fi.isWritable() )
22     debug( "is writable\n" );
23   else
24     debug( "is not writable\n" );
25   if( fi.isExecutable() )
26     debug( "is executable\n" );
27   else
28     debug( "is not executable\n" );
29
30   if( fi.owner() )
31     debug( "is owned by %s\n", fi.owner() );
32   if( fi.group() )
33     debug( "belongs to group %s\n", fi.group() );
34
35   debug( "was last modified at %s\n", fi.lastModified().toString().data() );
36   debug( "was last read at %s\n", fi.lastRead().toString().data() );
37
38   return 0;
39 }
```

On a Linux system, this program outputs for `/etc/passwd`:

```
/etc/passwd:
is a file
The size is 1354
is readable
is not writable
is not executable
is owned by root
belongs to group root
was last modified at Fri May 15 20:02:53 1998
was last read at Thu Jun 18 14:34:37 1998
```

and if we run it on a Windows system for C:\\AUTOEXEC.BAT, we get:

```
C:/AUTOEXEC.BAT:
is  a file
The size is 1775
is readable
is writable
is executable
was last modified at Sat Jul 11 20:36:50 1998
was last read at Sun Jul 12 00:00:00 1998
```

QFileInfo caches its data to improve performance. Thus, if you create a QFileInfo object and your program, or even another program, changes the file in question in the meantime, you must call refresh() to update the data. You could call setCaching (false); on your QFileInfo object instead, which completely turns off caching for this object.

12

Inter-Application Communication

In this chapter, we will see how two applications can exchange data with each other—except for writing data to a file and then reading it back, of course. This communication can be done between two Qt applications, and between Qt applications and other applications that support the same protocols.

There are two techniques for user-invoked transfer of data from one running application to another: using the clipboard, and using drag-and-drop. We will examine each of these in turn.

Using the Clipboard

The clipboard is an area provided by the operating system or the window system in which data can be deposited. Other applications can then pick up this data. The type of data that can be put in the clipboard depends on the operating or window system, but the less common the data type, the less likely it is that other applications can use it. Currently, Qt only supports text data for transfers via the clipboard, but there is a little workaround that we will show you later in this chapter.

All clipboard operations are done via the class `QClipboard`. This class follows the singleton pattern, which means there can never be more than one instance of this class. You cannot create an object of this class yourself, because its constructor and destructor are private. Instead, ask your `QApplication` for the QClipboard object by calling `QApplication::clipboard()`.

Let's first look at how you get data from the clipboard. To make this easier to understand, imagine that there is not only one `QClipboard` object in one application, but there is one in all applications—even those not written with Qt. Now, whenever another application puts some data into the clipboard (which, after all, is accessible to all applications), the `QClipboard` object emits the signal `dataChanged()`. You can then get the data with `text()`.

The other way works by calling `setText()`, then passing it the text you want to put into the clipboard. Note that the method `setPixmap()` is not implemented yet. Thus, it is not easy to use the clipboard for graphics.

The code in Example 12-1 is not optimal, but it works.

Example 12-1: Copying data from application to application via the clipboard

```
 1 #include <qapplication.h>
 2 #include <qclipboard.h>
 3 #include <qmultilinedit.h>
 4 #include <qpopupmenu.h>
 5
 6 class ClipboardMultiLineEdit : public QMultiLineEdit
 7 {
 8   Q_OBJECT
 9
10 public:
11   ClipboardMultiLineEdit( QWidget* parent = 0, const char* name = 0 );
12
13 protected:
14   void mouseReleaseEvent( QMouseEvent* event );
15
16 private slots:
17   void myCut();
18   void myCopy();
19   void myPaste();
20   void clipboardChanged();
21
22 private:
23   QPopupMenu* _menu;
24   QClipboard* _clipboard;
25   int _pasteitem;
26 };
27
28
29 ClipboardMultiLineEdit::ClipboardMultiLineEdit( QWidget* parent,
30                                                 const char* name ) :
31   QMultiLineEdit( parent, name )
32 {
33   _menu = new QPopupMenu();
34   _menu->insertItem( "Cut", this, SLOT( myCut() ) );
35   _menu->insertItem( "Copy", this, SLOT( myCopy() ) );
36   _pasteitem = _menu->insertItem( "Paste", this, SLOT( myPaste() ) );
37   _menu->setItemEnabled( _pasteitem, false );
38
39   _clipboard = QApplication::clipboard();
40   connect( _clipboard, SIGNAL( dataChanged() ),
41            this, SLOT( clipboardChanged() ) );
42 }
43
44
45 void ClipboardMultiLineEdit::mouseReleaseEvent( QMouseEvent* event )
```

Example 12-1: Copying data from application to application via the clipboard (continued)

```
46 {
47   if( event->button() == RightButton )
48     _menu->popup( mapToGlobal( event->pos() ) );
49 }
50
51
52 void ClipboardMultiLineEdit::myCut()
53 {
54   if( hasMarkedText() ) {
55     _clipboard->setText( markedText() );
56     del();
57   }
58 }
59
60
61 void ClipboardMultiLineEdit::myCopy()
62 {
63   if( hasMarkedText() )
64     _clipboard->setText( markedText() );
65 }
66
67
68 void ClipboardMultiLineEdit::myPaste()
69 {
70   int x, y;
71   cursorPosition( &x, &y );
72   insertAt( _clipboard->text(), x, y );
73 }
74
75
76 void ClipboardMultiLineEdit::clipboardChanged()
77 {
78   if( strlen( _clipboard->text() ) )
79     _menu->setItemEnabled( _pasteitem, true );
80   else
81     _menu->setItemEnabled( _pasteitem, false );
82 }
83
84
85 #include "clipboard.moc"
86
87 int main( int argc, char* argv[] )
88 {
89   QApplication a( argc, argv );
90
91   ClipboardMultiLineEdit* edit = new ClipboardMultiLineEdit();
92   a.setMainWidget( edit );
93   edit->show();
94
95   return a.exec();
96 }
```

The new widget in this example, `ClipboardMultiLineEdit`, inherits from `QMulti-LineEdit` and pops up a context menu when the right mouse button is pressed. Choosing "Copy" leads to `QClipboard::setText()` being called, and thus the text is transferred to the clipboard. When "Cut" is called, the marked text is additionally deleted with `del()`, a protected method available only for subclasses of `QMultiLineEdit`.

Pasting retrieves the data from the clipboard object with `QClipboard::text()`. `QMultiLineEdit::cursorPosition()` is used to determine the cursor position in the text-entry field, and the new text is then inserted at that position.

To try this program, you can start two instances of it and copy text back and forth between the two windows. Also try copying and pasting text to and from other applications that are not Qt-based.

As already mentioned, this program is not optimal, because it implements a functionality that is already there. The program in Example 12-2 does just the same, but uses the built-in methods `cut()`, `copyText()`, and `paste()` from `QMultiLineEdit`.

Example 12-2: Using the built-in methods from `QMultiLineEdit` *for clipboard operations*

```
 1 #include <qapplication.h>
 2 #include <qclipboard.h>
 3 #include <qmultilinedit.h>
 4 #include <qpopupmenu.h>
 5
 6 class ClipboardMultiLineEdit : public QMultiLineEdit
 7 {
 8   Q_OBJECT
 9
10 public:
11   ClipboardMultiLineEdit( QWidget* parent = 0, const char* name = 0 );
12
13 protected:
14   void mouseReleaseEvent( QMouseEvent* event );
15
16 private slots:
17   void clipboardChanged();
18
19 private:
20   QPopupMenu* _menu;
21   QClipboard* _clipboard;
22   int _pasteitem;
23 };
24
25
26 ClipboardMultiLineEdit::ClipboardMultiLineEdit( QWidget* parent,
27                                                 const char* name ) :
28   QMultiLineEdit( parent, name )
29 {
30   _menu = new QPopupMenu();
31   _menu->insertItem( "Cut", this, SLOT( cut() ) );
```

Example 12-2: Using the built-in methods from QMultiLineEdit for clipboard operations

```
32    _menu->insertItem( "Copy", this, SLOT( copyText() ) );
33    _pasteitem = _menu->insertItem( "Paste", this, SLOT( paste() ) );
34    _menu->setItemEnabled( _pasteitem, false );
35
36    _clipboard = QApplication::clipboard();
37    connect( _clipboard, SIGNAL( dataChanged() ),
38             this, SLOT( clipboardChanged() ) );
39 }
40
41
42 void ClipboardMultiLineEdit::mouseReleaseEvent( QMouseEvent* event )
43 {
44    if( event->button() == RightButton )
45      _menu->popup( mapToGlobal( event->pos() ) );
46 }
47
48
49 void ClipboardMultiLineEdit::clipboardChanged()
50 {
51    if( strlen( _clipboard->text() ) )
52      _menu->setItemEnabled( _pasteitem, true );
53    else
54      _menu->setItemEnabled( _pasteitem, false );
55 }
56
57
58 #include "clipboard2.moc"
59
60 int main( int argc, char* argv[] )
61 {
62    QApplication a( argc, argv );
63
64    ClipboardMultiLineEdit* edit = new ClipboardMultiLineEdit();
65    a.setMainWidget( edit );
66    edit->show();
67
68    return a.exec();
69 }
```

So far, we have only talked about copying and pasting text, since that's the only kind of data directly supported by QClipboard. If you wrote both applications that want to participate in the clipboard operation, however, you can transfer any kind of data by converting it to text. The word "text" is not to be taken literally here: any data taken as an array of bytes can be considered text for this purpose. All you have to do is get at the raw bytes of the data you want to transfer and pass this to setText(). Just make sure that there is a trailing null byte.

To make this more practical, let's copy and paste a pixmap, represented by a `QPixmap` object.

`QPixmap`—like many other classes in Qt—has operators for reading and writing pixmaps from and to a `QDataStream` object. In turn this object can be used on a `QFile` (see Chapter 11, *Working with Files and Directories*), on a `QBuffer`, or (even more useful for us) on a `QByteArray`. `QString` is derived from `QByteArray`, so we can go ahead and stream our object into a string. Thus, copying a `QPixmap` object to the clipboard could be done like this:

```
QPixmap pixmap; // this pixmap should be copied to the clipboard
...
QString buffer;
QDataStream stream( buffer, IO_WriteOnly );
stream << pixmap;
QApplication::clipboard()->setText( buffer );
```

On the other side, this only has to be reverted:

```
QPixmap pixmap; // this pixmap will be filled from the clipboard
QString buffer;
buffer = QApplication::clipboard()->text();
QDataStream stream( buffer, IO_ReadOnly );
stream >> pixmap;
```

For copying into the clipboard, the pixmap is written into a `QDataStream`, which is then passed to the clipboard. For pasting back, the clipboard data is first read into a `QDataStream`, and then the pixmap is recreated from this stream.

Drag and Drop

Drag and drop is a newer technique for transferring data from one application to another. Since it provides more direct feedback than cutting and pasting via the clipboard, it is generally considered more user-friendly.

Alas, this user-friendliness has a price. Adding drag and drop to an application is notoriously difficult, even though Qt makes it easier than, for example, the Win32 API or Motif.

If you want to drag and drop one of the predefined data types in Qt (currently text and images), implementing drag and drop consists of two steps: Writing code for the drag source (determining when the user wants to start a drag and invoking it) and writing code for the drag sink (determining whether a drop is acceptable at a certain location and retrieving the data that is dropped). If you need to drag and drop other types of data, such as sound files or URLs, you will have to implement a drag object for this type in the first step.

As an example, we will adapt the application from the previous section. Here are the specifications: The application consists of a multi-line text-entry field, which serves as both a drag source and a drop sink. The user can drag the text as a whole over to another instance of the application. When a text object is dropped over this application, the text is inserted at the current cursor position.

It's difficult to decide which mouse button should initiate a drag and drop operation. This depends on the operating system or the windowing system, and on other factors. In Windows, drag and drop is always done with the first (usually the left) mouse button. This might be a good choice if you only want to drag around icons on a desktop, but it's a bad choice for more general operations. We followed this convention and used the left mouse button, which means the left mouse button can no longer be used for selecting text in the text field. Therefore, in Windows style only selecting with the keyboard is possible.

Also, when you start to drag in Windows, the selection disappears again. Drag and drop and selections (or text-entry fields in general) don't really mix in Windows.

In Unix, there is no standard for drag and drop. Motif, the most popular GUI toolkit, defines a drag and drop protocol, and also mandates in its styleguide that drag and drop operations are to be done with the middle mouse button. This is not very good either, because in Unix the middle mouse button is also customarily used for pasting operations. You usually don't invoke it specifically from a menu as in Windows, but simply by pressing the middle mouse button. Since the use of the middle mouse button is not as cemented as the left mouse button's function is in Windows, we decided to use the right button for the drag and drop operation in Motif style.

It should be mentioned here that Qt on Unix does not use the overly complex and rarely correctly implemented Motif drag and drop protocol, but the more modern *XDND* drag and drop. This is supposed to replace the Motif protocol in the future.

Example 12-3: Drag and Drop Operations with Qt

```
 1  #include <qapplication.h>
 2  #include <qdragobject.h>
 3  #include <qdropsite.h>
 4  #include <qmultilinedit.h>
 5
 6  class DragDropMultiLineEdit : public QMultiLineEdit, public QDropSite
 7  {
 8  public:
 9    DragDropMultiLineEdit( QWidget* parent = 0, const char* name = 0 );
10
11  protected:
12    void mousePressEvent( QMouseEvent* event );
13    void mouseMoveEvent( QMouseEvent* event );
14    void dragEnterEvent( QDragEnterEvent* event );
15    void dropEvent( QDropEvent* event );
16
17  private:
18    QPoint _presspos;
19    int _dragdropbutton;
```

Example 12-3: Drag and Drop Operations with Qt (continued)

```
20  };
21
22
23  DragDropMultiLineEdit::DragDropMultiLineEdit( QWidget* parent,
24                                                const char* name ) :
25    QMultiLineEdit( parent, name ),
26    QDropSite( this )
27  {
28    // determine which button will invoke dragging
29    if( style() == WindowsStyle )
30      _dragdropbutton = LeftButton;
31    else
32      _dragdropbutton = RightButton;
33  }
34
35
36  void DragDropMultiLineEdit::mousePressEvent( QMouseEvent* event )
37  {
38    // record the position
39    if( event->button() == _dragdropbutton )
40      _presspos = event->pos();
41
42    QMultiLineEdit::mousePressEvent( event );
43  }
44
45
46  void DragDropMultiLineEdit::mouseMoveEvent( QMouseEvent* event )
47  {
48    if( event->state() & _dragdropbutton )
49      if( QABS( event->pos().x() - _presspos.x() ) >= 3 ||
50          QABS( event->pos().y() - _presspos.y() ) >= 3 ) {
51        // Mouse has been dragged for three pixels or more, start
52        // dragging operation
53        QTextDrag* drag = new QTextDrag( text(), this );
54        drag->dragCopy();
55      }
56
57    QMultiLineEdit::mouseMoveEvent( event );
58  }
59
60
61  void DragDropMultiLineEdit::dragEnterEvent( QDragEnterEvent* event )
62  {
63    if( QTextDrag::canDecode( event ) )
64      event->accept();
65  }
66
67
68  void DragDropMultiLineEdit::dropEvent( QDropEvent* event )
69  {
```

Example 12-3: Drag and Drop Operations with Qt (continued)

```
70    QString droptext;
71    if( QTextDrag::decode( event, droptext ) ) {
72      int row, col;
73      cursorPosition( &row, &col );
74      insertAt( droptext, row, col );
75    }
76 }
77
78
79 int main( int argc, char* argv[] )
80 {
81   QApplication a( argc, argv );
82
83   DragDropMultiLineEdit* edit = new DragDropMultiLineEdit;
84   a.setMainWidget( edit );
85   edit->show();
86
87   return a.exec();
88 }
```

Let's start with the dragging. In the constructor, we define which mouse button will do the dragging. As detailed earlier, we will use the first (left) button in Windows style and the third (right) button in Motif style. The two methods that together implement the dragging functionality are the two mouse event handlers `mousePressEvent()` and `mouseMoveEvent()`. The `mousePressEvent()` event handler records only the position where a mouse button was pressed if this button was the designated drag button. This position is then used in `mouseMoveEvent()`, because we want to start a dragging operation only when the mouse has been moved with the button pressed for at least three pixels. This value comes from the Macintosh tradition, and is a good compromise between ease of dragging on one hand, and avoiding accidental and unwanted drag operations on the other.

If it has been determined that a dragging operation should be started, we create an object of the class `QTextDrag`. This is one of the two predefined types in Qt. The constructor accepts the text to be transferred, for which we simply use the selected text and a pointer to the drag source—the widget in which the drag was initiated. You then call either `drag()`, `dragCopy()`, or `dragMove()`. The `dragCopy()` method indicates that the data should be copied to the destination, and `dragMove()` indicates that it should be moved (removed from the source after a successful operation). The `drag()` method can do both, depending on where the data is dropped. Both `drag()` and `dragMove()` return `true` if the data should be removed from the source; even with `dragMove()`, the drag and drop operation may not be completed, in which case the source data must not be removed.

After you have called one of the three drag methods, control stays there until the drag and drop operation has been completed.

Dropping, on the other hand, is always done into a `QWidget`. To enable a widget to accept drops, it must be derived from `QDropSite` in addition to the widget it inherits from, with `QDropSite` being last on the inheritance list.[1] You must always implement your own widget class if you want to accept drops.

Your drop site has to reimplement two methods: `dropEvent()` and either `dragEnter-Event()` or `dragMoveEvent()`. Reimplement `dragEnterEvent()` if the whole widget can accept drops, and `dragMoveEvent()` if you accept drops only over certain parts of the widget or if you need to provide special visual feedback during the drag, such as moving a cursor to show exactly where the drop will go.

In any case, when you want to accept a drop, you call `accept()` at the event that is passed into the event handler. If this is `dragMoveEvent()`, make this dependent on the position available from the event pointer.

Usually your widget cannot handle all types of data that can be dropped over it. Therefore, you can ask for the type of the data to be dropped. For all the kinds of data that you can accept, you call the static method `canDecode()` of the corresponding drag class. If it returns true, this is data of that class. In our case, where we can only handle text data, we only call `QTextDrag::canDecode()`.

After `accept()` has been called, the drop handler `dropEvent()` is called. This is the place where the data is retrieved from the drag object, by calling the static `decode` method of the drag object for the type you expect. If your widget can handle more than one data type, call more than one of those `decode()` methods that return `true` if the data could be decoded. Then you can do whatever you want with the data.

For dragging and dropping text and images, this is basically all you need to know. If you want to define your own drag types, however, you need to know a little more. We will only cover drag types with no more than one representation; drag types with more than one representation are harder to deal with and beyond the scope of this book. Looking at the implementation of the class `QImageDrag`, which uses several implementations (in this case, image-file formats), should give you an idea of what is required.

For drag types with one representation, use the base class `QStoredDrag`, which stores the data to be transported. The minimum you have to implement is the two static methods `decode()` and `canDecode()`. The `decode()` method should accept a pointer to a `QDropEvent`, and a reference of an object of a class suitable for storing the data transmitted. For strings with `QTextDrag`, this is `QString`; for images with `QImageDrag`, this is either `QImage` or `QPixmap`; and for your own drag type, it might be a class of your own. The `decode` method should take the raw data available via the `data()` method of the `QDropEvent` pointer in the form of a `QByteArray` and convert it to the desired type. This data is then stored in the object whose reference is passed to `decode()` as the second argument.

---

1   This latter requirement has nothing to do with drag and drop, but is a general requirement when using *moc*: Classes that contain the `Q_OBJECT` macro must come first in the inheritance list.

To give an example, let's say we want to implement a drag type for URLs called URLDrag. To keep it simple, we treat the URL more like a string, but in a full-featured implementation, you could adapt the URL to the drop sink by changing from relative to absolute URLs. We assume a MIME type (a string-format description of the data to be transferred; there's more information on MIME types in the "Writing Netscape Plugins" section) of application/x-url. Here is what decode() might look like:

```
bool URLDrag::decode( QDropEvent* event, QFile& file )
{
    // data is transferred
    QByteArray rawdata = event->data( "application/x-url" );
    // make it a string
    rawdata.resize( rawdata.size() + 1 );
    rawdata[ rawdata.size() - 1 ] = 0;
    QString str( rawdata.data() );
    // and construct a file form it
    file.setName( str );

    // We accept the drop if the file exists at the drop site
    if( file.exists() ) {
        event->accept();
        return true;
    } else
        return false;
}
```

The other obligatory method is the static canDecode() to which a pointer to a QDrag-MoveEvent is passed. This method should then return true if the data associated with this event can be decoded by this class with the already described method decode(), and false if otherwise. Since the event carries around the MIME type, this method is usually a one-liner: It suffices to call provides() at the event, and pass the MIME type that this class could handle. Here's the code:

```
bool URLDrag::canDecode ( QDragMoveEvent* event )
{
    return event->provides( "application/x-url" );
}
```

When writing your own drag types, remember to always check whether you can reuse an existing MIME type instead of inventing one of your own.

Implementing these two static methods is the absolute minimum, but makes the new drag type awkward to use. You should at least provide a constructor that accepts the data to be transferred as its first argument, and stuffs it into the space provided by QStoredDrag by calling setEncodedData() and passing the data in the form of a QByteArray. This constructor must also initialize the constructor of the base class QStoredData by passing the MIME type as the first argument. Of course, the parent argument should be passed as usual. Here is the code:

```
URLDrag::URLDrag( const QString& urlstring, QWidget* parent, const char* name )
    : QStoredDrag( "application/x-url", parent, name )
{
    QByteArray data( urlstring );
    setEncodedData( data );
}
```

13

Working with Date
and Time Values

Date and time values are inherently hard to make portable. Therefore, it's a good idea to use the classes provided by Qt when you work with this kind of data.

There are three Qt classes in this area: QDate, QTime, and QDateTime. Their purposes are obvious: QDate encapsulates a date value, QTime encapsulates a time value, and QDateTime encapsulates both. You can either pass the scalar values that make up a date (day, month, and year) or a time value (hour, minute, and optional second and millisecond), or set these values later.

For computations with date and time values, use the methods QTime::addSecs(), QTime::addMSecs(), QDate:addDays(), QDateTime::addSecs(), and QDateTime::addDays(). There are also many comparison operators, and you can stream date and time values to and from QDataStream streams.

Getting the current time and date is a popular feature. All three classes provide static methods for this: QDate::currentDate(), QTime::currentTime(), and QDate-Time::currentDateTime().

QTime can also be used as a stop watch: start() sets the time value to the current time, and elapsed() returns the number of milliseconds since start(). You could use it like this:

```
QTime t;
t.start();
// some lengthy operation
debug( "%d\n", t.elapsed() );
```

If you want to take repeated measurements, you can use restart(), which returns the number of milliseconds since the last start() or restart(), and then resets the timer:

```
QTime t;
t.start();
for( int i = 0; i < verymuch; i++ ) {
```

```
    // some lengthy operations
    debug( "%n th loop: %d\n", i, t.restart() );
}
```

One last thing: In case you need to output date or time values, all three classes provide a method `toString()`, which returns a `QString` with a representation suitable for printing. If you don't like the format or it does not fit your cultural customs, you are on your own, although your operating system probably has some functions that can help you.

14

Writing Your Own Widgets

In this chapter, you will learn how to write your own widgets. We first introduce you to the basics of widget writing and then present two widgets written for use with Qt: a coordinate selector and a browse box.

There are times when the widgets that Qt provides are not enough. You may have an application with special user-interaction needs or you may be required to support some fancy new interaction paradigm that Qt does not support (yet). Qt makes it very easy to write your own widgets, especially if you compare its procedure to those of the MFC or Motif. Nevertheless, you should be reluctant to write widgets unless you absolutely need to do so. As explained in Chapter 7, *Some Thoughts on GUI Design*, non-standard user interfaces are usually a bad thing, because users will have to unlearn the standard interaction procedures. Programmers tend to invent new ways of user interaction because that is more creative than simply exploiting the available mechanisms. Marketing people also tend to demand new UI features to distinguish the application from its competitors. Remember, however, that usability and stability should always be the foremost criteria when writing an application.

A widget can be as little as a check-box, or as complex as a complete HTML widget in a Web browser. Almost all of the "little" widgets that could be thought of when creating a GUI are already in Qt, but the appearance of a new UI paradigm could drive the need for more "small", focused widgets. The two custom widgets presented in this chapter are what I call "small" widgets.

Then, there are the really big widgets. The HTML widget in a web browser mentioned previously is one example, as is the terminal-emulation widget in a terminal emulator, whose GUI is really just the terminal-emulation widget, a menu bar, and some dialogs for configuring the terminal widget. Mail programs can have a widget for displaying the contents of one mail-message or the contents of a mail folder. These are all real Qt widgets that exist somewhere.

Which part of your application should be implemented as a widget of its own depends a lot on your application, and perhaps even more so on its design.

Here is the basic procedure for writing a widget:

- Decide on a base class. If your planned widget is unlike any other widget in Qt, pick `QWidget` as your base class. If it is similar to existing Qt widgets, you can save a lot of work by deriving your widget from a more-specialized one, such as `QButton` for a button-like widget or `QFrame` for a widget with a frame around it. `QTableView` is suitable as a base class for widgets with a tabular representation. We will see the usage of `QTableView` in the "Implementing a Browse Box" section.

- Reimplement the event handlers for events that your widget has to react to. This will almost always be at least `mousePressEvent()` and `mouseReleaseEvent()` and, if your widget accepts any keyboard input, also `keyPressEvent()`. In the latter case, it might also be useful to implement `focusInEvent()` and `focusOutEvent()` to change the widget's appearance when it gets and loses focus. For example, any widget that provides text-input facilities will probably want to display some kind of cursor if the widget has the keyboard focus. Qt's focus-handling mechanisms are slightly unusual and a topic in their own right. We have devoted Chapter 15, *Focus Handling*, to this topic.

- Reimplement `paintEvent()` to draw the widget's appearance. Unless your widget is static, like `QLabel`, the drawing operations depend on some state variables in the widget whose values are changed in response to user interaction in the other event handlers.

- Decide which signals you want to emit. The emitting of signals is usually done in response to some user interaction. For example, a button-like widget emits a signal like `clicked()` in response to the user pressing the mouse over the widget. Depending on the exact specification of your widget, this would be in your reimplementation of `mousePressEvent()`, `mouseReleaseEvent()`, or `mouseDoubleClickEvent()`.

- Decide which state variables you want to make accessible from the outside. Usually these are variables that are non-volatile: those that change their value because of user interaction. For example, you usually do not want to make information about which part of the widget the mouse is currently over accessible, but if your widget can react to either single or double clicks, you should provide two methods for getting and setting this state.

  Note that you should follow the Qt convention of starting all method names with a lower-case letter, and methods that set a variable in the widget should start with `set`. On the contrary, methods that retrieve some state should not begin with `get`. To stay with the example of single and double clicks, you could provide two methods `void setDoubleClick( bool )` and `bool doubleClick() const`. Following these conventions is not necessary for making your widget work, but they do make it easier for you and others who might use the widget to write code with it.

- Decide which methods that set states in your widget should be public slots. Generally, methods that have only one parameter of an integral type, such as `bool`, `int`, or `const char*`, are good candidates for being slots.[1]

- Decide whether it should be possible to subclass your widget. If you decide this would be useful, you probably want to make some methods protected that you planned to make private.

These concepts are implemented in the examples in the next two sections.

Implementing a Coordinate Selector

Our first self-made widget is a coordinate selector, `QKCoordSel`[2]. This is a rectangular widget that lets you select x and y coordinates with the mouse. The user provides the range of x and y coordinates that should be available, and the widget translates a mouse-click in its area into a coordinate pair. In addition, it displays the current coordinates below the widget. The mouse cursor changes to a crosshair when it is over the widget. Figure 14-1 shows what it should look like.

Figure 14-1: The coordinate selector

You might extend this widget yourself by implementing tick marks at the margins. Making it usable with the keyboard is another good idea. There are many possibilities.

The first thing we have to decide on is the base class. There is no widget similar to this one in Qt, so we choose `QWidget`. Since we are selecting a value from a certain range, we could make `QRangeControl` an additional base class, but this does not work out too well since we have two values and two ranges, one for each dimension. Therefore, we decided to make two `QRangeControl` objects members of `QKCoordSel`.

---

1   This guideline does not apply only to widgets.
2   The prefix QK was chosen because it is a class for use with Qt written by the author.

The next thing to decide is which event handlers to implement. Obviously, since we want to emit a signal when the user has chosen a coordinate pair, we have to reimplement mouseReleaseEvent(). To display the translated coordinates while the mouse is moving or has just been pressed, we also reimplement mousePressEvent() and mouseMoveEvent(). Since the translation from mouse coordinates to logical coordinates depends on the mouse coordinates, the minimum and maximum values selected, and the width and height of the widget, we need to know when the size of the widget changes. We could also compute the ratio whenever we need it, but that would not be the best style. Thus, we reimplement resizeEvent(). For reasons explained later, we also reimplement setFont(), which is not an event handler but is reimplemented for the same purposes: to ensure notification when something important changes.

Our widget emits one signal, valueChanged(int, int). This signal is emitted whenever the user clicks into our widget. We make all the methods that set minimum, maximum, or current value slots, for maximum reusability.

Now we can write the class declaration. We explain the protected methods and the private fields as we go through the implementation. See Example 14-1.

Example 14-1: The header file for the coordinate selector

```
 1  #ifndef _QKCOORDSEL_H
 2  #define _QKCOORDSEL_H
 3
 4  #include <qwidget.h>
 5  #include <qrangecontrol.h>
 6  #include <qpoint.h>
 7
 8  class QKCoordSel : public QWidget
 9  {
10      Q_OBJECT
11
12  public:
13      QKCoordSel( QWidget* parent = 0, const char* name = 0, WFlags flags = 0 );
14      virtual ~QKCoordSel();
15
16      int xMinValue() const;
17      int yMinValue() const;
18      int xMaxValue() const;
19      int yMaxValue() const;
20      QPoint value() const;
21
22      virtual QSize sizeHint() const;
23      virtual void setFont( const QFont& );
24
25  public slots:
26      void setXMinValue( int );
27      void setXMaxValue( int );
28      void setYMinValue( int );
29      void setYMaxValue( int );
30      void setValue( int, int );
```

Example 14-1: The header file for the coordinate selector (continued)

```
31   void setValue( const QPoint& );
32
33 signals:
34   void valueChanged( int, int );
35
36 protected:
37   virtual void paintEvent( QPaintEvent* );
38   virtual void mousePressEvent( QMouseEvent* );
39   virtual void mouseReleaseEvent( QMouseEvent* );
40   virtual void mouseMoveEvent( QMouseEvent* );
41   virtual void resizeEvent( QResizeEvent* );
42
43 protected:
44   QPoint mouseToLogical( QPoint );
45   int labelHeight();
46   void computeRatio();
47
48 private:
49   QRangeControl _xrange;
50   QRangeControl _yrange;
51   QPoint _tempvalue;
52   int _labelheight;
53   double _xratio, _yratio;
54 };
55
56 #endif
```

For easier reference, look at the complete implementation in Example 14-2; we then comment on the interesting parts by repeating a few code snippets.

Example 14-2: The implementation of the coordinate selector

```
 1 #include "qkcoordsel.h"
 2 #include "qkcoordsel.moc"
 3 #include <qpainter.h>
 4 #include <qfontmetrics.h>
 5
 6 QKCoordSel::QKCoordSel( QWidget* parent, const char* name, WFlags flags ) :
 7   QWidget( parent, name, flags )
 8 {
 9   // default for the ranges is 0-100
10   _xrange.setRange( 0, 100 );
11   _yrange.setRange( 0, 100 );
12
13   // initial value is (0, 0)
14   _xrange.setValue( 0 );
15   _yrange.setValue( 0 );
16
17   // calculate the space to set apart for the label
18   _labelheight = labelHeight();
19
```

Example 14-2: The implementation of the coordinate selector (continued)

```
20    // compute the ratios
21    computeRatio();
22
23    // set a cursor for this widget
24    setCursor( crossCursor );
25  }
26
27
28  QKCoordSel::~QKCoordSel()
29  {
30  }
31
32
33  int QKCoordSel::xMinValue() const
34  {
35    return _xrange.minValue();
36  }
37
38
39  int QKCoordSel::xMaxValue() const
40  {
41    return _xrange.maxValue();
42  }
43
44
45  int QKCoordSel::yMinValue() const
46  {
47    return _yrange.minValue();
48  }
49
50
51  int QKCoordSel::yMaxValue() const
52  {
53    return _yrange.maxValue();
54  }
55
56
57  QPoint QKCoordSel::value() const
58  {
59    return QPoint( _xrange.value(), _yrange.value() );
60  }
61
62
63  void QKCoordSel::setXMinValue( int value )
64  {
65    _xrange.setRange( value, _xrange.maxValue() );
66  }
67
68
69  void QKCoordSel::setXMaxValue( int value )
```

Example 14-2: The implementation of the coordinate selector (continued)

```
 70 {
 71    _xrange.setRange( _xrange.minValue(), value );
 72 }
 73
 74
 75 void QKCoordSel::setYMinValue( int value )
 76 {
 77    _yrange.setRange( value, _yrange.maxValue() );
 78 }
 79
 80
 81 void QKCoordSel::setYMaxValue( int value )
 82 {
 83    _yrange.setRange( _yrange.minValue(), value );
 84 }
 85
 86
 87 void QKCoordSel::setValue( int x, int y )
 88 {
 89    _xrange.setValue( x );
 90    _yrange.setValue( y );
 91 }
 92
 93
 94 void QKCoordSel::setValue( const QPoint& point )
 95 {
 96    _xrange.setValue( point.x() );
 97    _yrange.setValue( point.y() );
 98 }
 99
100
101 void QKCoordSel::resizeEvent( QResizeEvent* )
102 {
103    computeRatio();
104 }
105
106
107 void QKCoordSel::paintEvent( QPaintEvent* e )
108 {
109    QPainter painter( this );
110    painter.drawLine( 0, height()-_labelheight, width(), height()-_labelheight );
111    QString coordstext;
112    coordstext.sprintf( "%d x %d", _tempvalue.x(), _tempvalue.y() );
113    painter.drawText( 0, height(), coordstext );
114 }
115
116
117 void QKCoordSel::mousePressEvent( QMouseEvent* e )
118 {
119    _tempvalue = mouseToLogical( e->pos() );
```

Example 14-2: The implementation of the coordinate selector (continued)

```
120   repaint();
121 }
122
123
124 void QKCoordSel::mouseReleaseEvent( QMouseEvent* e )
125 {
126   if( rect().contains( e->pos() ) ) {
127     QPoint coords = mouseToLogical( e->pos() );
128     emit valueChanged( coords.x(), coords.y() );
129     _xrange.setValue( coords.x() );
130     _yrange.setValue( coords.y() );
131     _tempvalue.setX( coords.x() );
132     _tempvalue.setY( coords.y() );
133     repaint();
134   }
135 }
136
137
138 void QKCoordSel::mouseMoveEvent( QMouseEvent* e )
139 {
140   QPoint oldtempvalue = _tempvalue;
141   _tempvalue = mouseToLogical( e->pos() );
142   if( _tempvalue.x() < _xrange.minValue() )
143     _tempvalue.setX( _xrange.minValue() );
144   if( _tempvalue.y() < _yrange.minValue() )
145     _tempvalue.setY( _yrange.minValue() );
146   if( _tempvalue.x() > _xrange.maxValue() )
147     _tempvalue.setX( _xrange.maxValue() );
148   if( _tempvalue.y() > _yrange.maxValue() )
149     _tempvalue.setY( _yrange.maxValue() );
150
151   repaint();
152 }
153
154
155 void QKCoordSel::setFont( const QFont& font )
156 {
157   QWidget::setFont( font );
158   _labelheight = labelHeight();
159   repaint();
160 }
161
162
163
164 QPoint QKCoordSel::mouseToLogical( QPoint point )
165 {
166   return QPoint( point.x() * _xratio + _xrange.minValue(),
167                  point.y() * _yratio + _yrange.minValue() );
168 }
169
```

Example 14-2: The implementation of the coordinate selector (continued)

```
170
171 int QKCoordSel::labelHeight()
172 {
173   QFontMetrics fm( font() );
174   return fm.height();
175 }
176
177
178 void QKCoordSel::computeRatio()
179 {
180   _xratio = (double)( _xrange.maxValue() - _xrange.minValue() ) / (double)width();
181   _yratio = (double)( _yrange.maxValue() - _yrange.minValue() ) / (double)(height()-\
_labelheight);
182 }
183
184
185 QSize QKCoordSel::sizeHint() const
186 {
187   return QSize( _xrange.maxValue() - _xrange.minValue(),
188                 _yrange.maxValue() - _yrange.minValue() + _labelheight );
189 }
```

The first part, the constructor and the accessor methods, is not very interesting. The only things that happen here are assigning values to and retrieving values from the two QRangeControl objects, and setting a cross-hair mouse cursor for the widget with set-Cursor().

Now let's tackle the event handlers, and look at the mouse events that are related to coordinate selections. First, some more specifications. A changed coordinate should only be reported when the mouse is pressed over the widget and released over the widget. If not released in between, it may be moved temporarily out of the widget. No coordinate change should be reported when the mouse is pressed outside the widget and released inside, or pressed inside and released outside. The former case is handled automatically: no mouse release is reported when the mouse is pressed outside the widget. The latter case is different: Even if the mouse is moved outside the widget while being pressed, mouse-release events are still being reported to the widget. This is called a "mouse grab". Because of this, we have to check in mouseReleaseEvent() whether the mouse was inside the widget when being released. This is done with the following code:

```
if( rect().contains( e->pos() ) ) {
    // mouse was released inside the widget
```

If the condition evaluates to true, the following code is executed:

```
QPoint coords = mouseToLogical( e->pos() );
emit valueChanged( coords.x(), coords.y() );
_xrange.setValue( coords.x() );
_yrange.setValue( coords.y() );
```

```
_tempvalue.setX( coords.x() );
_tempvalue.setY( coords.y() );
repaint();
```

The method QMouseEvent::pos() returns the position of the hot spot of the mouse cursor relative to the widget in question. We pass that widget to mouseToLogical, which computes the logical coordinates by taking the widget size, and the minimum and maximum values, for both dimensions. These logical coordinates then form the parameters for the signal valueChanged, which is emitted next. Finally, we update both the actual selected value stored within the QRangeControl objects _xrange and _yrange, and the variable _tempvalue from which the coordinate text at the lower margin of the widget is generated. We use separate values for this, because the text should already be updated when the mouse is moved over the widget with the button pressed, but this should not yet update the value of the widget itself. At the end, repaint() is called so that the new coordinates are drawn.

The mouseMoveEvent() method does the same things, except for emitting the signal and updating _xrange and _yrange. The signal is not emitted here because we want the user to explicitly click somewhere to make a selection. We don't want spurious signals to be sent when the user simply moves the mouse over the widget.

In addition, mouseMoveEvent() makes sure the new value does not lie outside the boundaries, since the mouse grab ensures that mouseMoveEvent() is also called if the mouse moves outside the widget, as long as the mouse button had been clicked in the widget.

The mousePressEvent() method is very simple, and it's also not really needed. We have only added it so that the coordinates are already shown after the mouse is clicked the first time in the widget.

All those calls to repaint() lead to paintEvent() being called (of course, this method is called on request from the window system). First, a line is drawn to separate the label area from the clickable area, then a string for output is computed and drawn.

Some small things remain that have not been mentioned yet. The first is the height of the label. We want to use exactly the height that is needed, not a fixed height. This height is computed in labelHeight() and stored in the member variable _labelheight. Apart from the construction time, this has to be done every time the font is changed. We need to reimplement setFont() for this purpose, because then we can record that the font has been changed. By simply calling the base class setFont(), we don't have to fiddle around with the font-related stuff ourselves. All we do is recompute the label height and have the widget repainted.

Since the ratio of mouse coordinates to logical coordinates depends on the width and height of the widget, and we don't want to recompute this ratio every time the mouse is moved, we have to make sure that it is always correct. This is done by reimplementing resizeEvent(), the event handler called whenever the widget is resized—either by the user or by calling `setGeometry()` or `resize()`. We simply call `computeRatio()` there, the method that computes the ratio and takes into account the room for the coordinates label.

Finally, we reimplement the method `sizeHint()` like this:

```
QSize QKCoordSel::sizeHint() const
{
   return QSize( _xrange.maxValue() - _xrange.minValue(),
                 _yrange.maxValue() - _yrange.minValue() + _labelheight );
}
```

The `sizeHint()` method is mainly used for layout management, and returns the size that the widget *would like* to have. If this method is not reimplemented, the implementation in `QWidget` is used. This returns an invalid size that indicates that the widget does not provide a size hint. In our case, we take a 1:1 ratio between the mouse coordinates and the logical coordinates as the optimal size, augmented in the vertical dimension by the space for the coordinates label.

Finally, we need a test program. A good test program should exercise every line of code, because of space constraints we won't test all the accessor methods in ours. It is pretty straightforward, so there should be no explanation necessary. The code is in Example 14-3.

Example 14-3: A test program for the coordinate selector

```
 1 #include "qkcoordsel.h"
 2 #include <qapplication.h>
 3
 4 class Receiver : public QObject
 5 {
 6   Q_OBJECT
 7 public slots:
 8   void received( int, int );
 9 };
10
11 #include "testqkcoordsel.moc"
12
13 void Receiver::received( int x, int y )
14 {
15   debug( "New value selected: (%d, %d)\n", x, y );
16 }
17
18
19 int main( int argc, char* argv[] )
20 {
21   QApplication a( argc, argv );
22
23   QKCoordSel* selector = new QKCoordSel();
24   selector->resize( 200, 200 );
25   selector->setXMinValue( 20 );
26   selector->setXMaxValue( 130 );
```

Example 14-3: A test program for the coordinate selector (continued)

```
27    selector->setYMinValue( 50 );
28    selector->setYMaxValue( 150 );
29    selector->show();
30
31    Receiver* receiver = new Receiver();
32    QObject::connect( selector, SIGNAL( valueChanged( int, int ) ),
33                      receiver, SLOT( received( int, int ) ) );
34
35    a.setMainWidget( selector );
36    return a.exec();
37 }
```

Implementing a Browse Box

In this section, we will implement another widget with a different specification. Naturally, it focuses on other concepts, so the two widget implementations taken together should give you a nice overview of the tasks related to implementing your own widgets.

The first thing we'll look at in this section is how to implement a tabular, grid-like representation. The second is how to implement menu-like pop-up behaviour. Both result immediately from the specification. In addition, you will learn how to draw a widget in Motif style and in Windows style.

A *browse box* is a little window that presents the user with a number of choices. These choices can be represented by text, a pixmap, or both. They are arranged in a rectangular grid. When the user clicks on one of the choices, a signal is emitted with the x and y coordinates of the choice and the window pops down. If the user clicks outside the window or hits the escape key, the window pops down without emitting any signal. Figure 14-2 shows the browse box in action.

Figure 14-2: A browse box

The widget should exhibit synchronous menu-like behavior. Not unlike a modal dialog, it is popped up by calling `exec()`. Control returns to the application only after the window has popped down. The choice that the user has made is available to the application by two means: The signal `selected( int, int )` is emitted, and `exec()` returns the absolute position number.

Let's go through our usual design choices. The first is deciding on a class from which to inherit. In order to get menu-like behaviour, it would be very nice to use `QPopup-Menu`—if only it lent itself to subclassing. We will have to implement this behavior ourselves, but that's not as difficult as it may seem. There is another class that is very suitable, given our specifications: `QTableView`, an abstract base class that works for all kinds of tabular representations where you can distinguish columns and rows. Instead of reimplementing `paintEvent()`, with `QTableView` you take the default implementation of this method and implement `paintCell()` instead. The `paintCell()` method is called once for every cell that has to be repainted, and the row and column positions of the cell to be currently painted are passed as arguments. In addition, a pointer to a `QPainter` is passed that is already prepared for painting on that cell.

Apart from `paintCell()`, we will implement four more event handlers. First, `mouse-MoveEvent()` is used to highlight the cell over which the mouse currently resides. This makes it easier to distinguish which cell would be chosen by clicking now when the cells are rather small. The `mouseReleaseEvent()` event handler takes care of actually selecting a cell which finally leads to popping down the browse-box window. The `resizeEvent()` event handler is overloaded to adapt the cells to the new widget size, while the only task of `keyPressEvent()` is popping down the window when the escape key is pressed.

We provide three overloaded `exec()` methods for popping up the widget at a certain position. The first two, `exec( int, int )` and `exec( const QPoint& )`, just pop up the widget at the global position specified by the coordinates as two integer values or by a `QPoint`. The `exec( QWidget* )` method is more interesting. It is mainly meant for popping up the browse box from a tool-bar button or other buttons. You pass a pointer to the widget that has triggered the browse box, and the browse box is aligned with this widget. We will see that the code makes sure the browse box fits on the screen, if possible, and chooses to pop up the browse box where it looks best.

To specify the choices presented in the browse box, various `insertItem()` methods are provided for setting a string or a pixmap at a certain position. Any cell can have both a string and a pixmap; the pixmap is then drawn in the background, with the string drawn over it. You can remove the value passed to a single cell by calling `removeItem()`, and clear all cells by calling `clear()`. This is consistent with `QMenu-Data`. It is also possible to ask for the text or the pixmap at any given cell.

These design decisions lead to the header file in Example 14-4.

Example 14-4: The header file for the browse box

```
 1  #ifndef _QKBROWSER_H
 2  #define _QKBROWSER_H
 3
 4  #include <qwidget.h>
 5  #include <qtableview.h>
 6  #include <qarray.h>
 7
 8  class QString;
 9  class QPainter;
10  class QPixmap;
11
12  class QKBrowseBox : public QTableView
13  {
14    Q_OBJECT
15  public:
16    QKBrowseBox( int x, int y,
17              QWidget* parent=0, const char* name=0, WFlags f=0 );
18    ~QKBrowseBox();
19
20    void insertItem( const char* text, int x, int y )
21    void insertItem( QPixmap pixmap, int x, int y );
22    void removeItem( int x, int y );
23    void clear();
24
25    QString text( int x, int y );
26    QPixmap pixmap( int x, int y);
27
28    int exec( const QPoint& pos );
29    int exec( int x, int y );
30    int exec( const QWidget* trigger );
31
32  signals:
33    void selected( int, int );
34
35  protected:
36    virtual void keyPressEvent( QKeyEvent* e );
37    virtual void resizeEvent( QResizeEvent* e );
38    virtual void mouseReleaseEvent( QMouseEvent* e );
39    virtual void mouseMoveEvent( QMouseEvent* e );
40    virtual void paintCell( QPainter *, int, int );
41
42  private:
43    int coordsToIndex( int x, int y );
44
45    QString* _texts;
46    QPixmap* _pixmaps;
47    QPoint _activecell;
48    bool _firstrelease;
```

Example 14-4: The header file for the browse box (continued)

```
49  };
50
51  #endif
```

The member variables `_texts` and `_pixmaps` hold the arrays of QString and QPixmap objects, respectively, that contain the strings or labels set for a certain cell. The `_activecell` variable contains the cell that would be returned to the caller and emitted via the signal in case the mouse is clicked now. The method `coordsToIndex()` computes the scalar cell coordinate (the x and y coordinates of a cell boiled down to a single integer) from mouse coordinates, and we'll come to `_firstrelease` in a minute.

The full code of the implementation is in Example 14-5.

Example 14-5: The implementation of the browse box

```
 1  #include <qstring.h>
 2  #include <qpixmap.h>
 3  #include <qkeycode.h>
 4  #include <qpainter.h>
 5  #include <qapplication.h>
 6  #include <qdrawutil.h>
 7
 8  #include <stdio.h>
 9  #include <math.h>
10
11  #include "qkbrowser.h"
12  #include "qkbrowser.moc"
13
14  QKBrowseBox::QKBrowseBox( int x, int y, QWidget* parent, const char* name,
15                            WFlags f ) :
16    QTableView( parent, name, WType_Popup )
17  {
18    setNumCols( x );
19    setNumRows( y );
20    setCellWidth( width()/x );
21    setCellHeight( height()/y );
22    setTableFlags( Tbl_clipCellPainting );
23
24    _texts = new QString[x*y];
25    _pixmaps = new QPixmap[x*y];
26
27    _activecell.setX( -1 );
28    _activecell.setY( -1 );
29    setMouseTracking( true );
30    if( style() == MotifStyle )
31      setFrameStyle( QFrame::Panel | QFrame::Sunken );
32    else
33      setFrameStyle( QFrame::WinPanel | QFrame::Sunken );
34  }
35
```

Example 14-5: The implementation of the browse box (continued)

```
36
37
38  QKBrowseBox::~QKBrowseBox()
39  {
40    delete[] _texts;
41    delete[] _pixmaps;
42  }
43
44
45  int QKBrowseBox::coordsToIndex( int x, int y )
46  {
47    if( x < 0 || x > numCols() || y < 0 || y > numRows() )
48      debug( "coordsToIndex: invalid coords (%d, %d)\n", x, y );
49
50    return y * numCols() + x;
51  }
52
53
54  void QKBrowseBox::insertItem( const char* text, int x, int y )
55  {
56    _texts[ coordsToIndex( x, y ) ] = text;
57  }
58
59
60  void QKBrowseBox::insertItem( QPixmap pixmap, int x, int y )
61  {
62    _pixmaps[ coordsToIndex( x, y ) ] = pixmap;
63  }
64
65
66  void QKBrowseBox::removeItem( int x, int y )
67  {
68    _texts[ coordsToIndex( x, y ) ] = "";
69    _pixmaps[ coordsToIndex( x, y ) ].resize( 0, 0 );
70  }
71
72
73  void QKBrowseBox::clear()
74  {
75    for( int x = 0; x < numCols(); x++ )
76      for( int y = 0; y < numRows(); y++ )
77        removeItem( x, y );
78  }
79
80
81  QString QKBrowseBox::text( int x, int y )
82  {
83    if( x < 0 || x >= numCols() || y < 0 || y >= numRows() )
84      return "";
85
```

Example 14-5: The implementation of the browse box (continued)

```
86    return _texts[ coordsToIndex( x, y ) ];
87  }
88
89
90  QPixmap QKBrowseBox::pixmap( int x, int y )
91  {
92    static QPixmap empty;
93
94    if( x < 0 || x >= numCols() || y < 0 || y >= numRows() )
95      return empty;
96
97    return _pixmaps[ coordsToIndex( x, y ) ];
98  }
99
100
101 int QKBrowseBox::exec( const QPoint& pos )
102 {
103   return exec( pos.x(), pos.y() );
104 }
105
106
107 int QKBrowseBox::exec( const QWidget* trigger )
108 {
109   QPoint globalpos = trigger->parentWidget()->mapToGlobal( trigger->pos() );
110
111   // is there enough space to put the box below the trigger?
112   if( globalpos.y() + trigger->height() + height() + 1 <
113       QApplication::desktop()->height() )
114     {
115       // is there enough space to set the box left-justified with the trigger
116       if( globalpos.x() + width() < QApplication::desktop()->width() )
117         // put the box left-justified below the trigger
118         return exec( globalpos.x(), globalpos.y()+trigger->height() + 1 );
119       else
120         // put the box below the trigger, extending to the left
121         return exec( globalpos.x() - width() - 1,
122                      globalpos.y()+trigger->height() + 1 );
123     }
124   else
125     {
126       // not enough space below: put the box above the trigger
127       // is there enough space to set the box left-justified with the trigger
128       if( globalpos.x() + width() < QApplication::desktop()->width() )
129         // put the box left-justified above the trigger
130         return exec( globalpos.x(), globalpos.y() - height() - 1 );
131       else
132         // put the box above the trigger, extending to the left
133         return exec( globalpos.x() - width() - 1,
134                      globalpos.y() - height() + 1 );
135     }
```

Example 14-5: The implementation of the browse box (continued)

```
136 }
137
138
139 int QKBrowseBox::exec( int x, int y )
140 {
141   _firstrelease = true;
142
143   move( x, y );
144   show();
145   repaint();
146   qApp->enter_loop();
147   hide();
148
149   if( _activecell.x() != -1 && _activecell.y() != -1 )
150     return _activecell.x() + _activecell.y() * numCols();
151   else
152     return -1;
153 }
154
155
156 void QKBrowseBox::keyPressEvent( QKeyEvent* e )
157 {
158   if( e->key() == Key_Escape )
159     {
160       qApp->exit_loop();
161     }
162 }
163
164
165 void QKBrowseBox::mouseReleaseEvent( QMouseEvent* )
166 {
167   if( _firstrelease )
168     _firstrelease = false;
169   else {
170     emit selected( _activecell.x(), celly );
171     qApp->exit_loop();
172   }
173 }
174
175
176 void QKBrowseBox::paintCell(class QPainter * painter, int y, int x )
177 {
178   bool ispixmap = false;
179   if( !(_pixmaps[ coordsToIndex( x, y ) ].isNull()) )
180     {
181       painter->drawPixmap( 0, 0, _pixmaps[ coordsToIndex( x, y ) ] );
182       ispixmap = true;
183     }
184
185   bool bActive = ( ( _activecell.x() == x ) && ( _activecell.y() == y ) );
```

Example 14-5: The implementation of the browse box (continued)

```
186   if( style() == MotifStyle )
187     {
188       if( bActive )
189         {
190           if( ispixmap )
191             qDrawShadeRect( painter, 0, 0, cellWidth(), cellHeight(),
192                             colorGroup(), false, 2 );
193           else
194             qDrawShadePanel( painter, 0, 0, cellWidth(), cellHeight(),
195                             colorGroup(), false, 2 );
196         }
197       else
198         qDrawPlainRect( painter, 0, 0, cellWidth(), cellHeight(),
199                         colorGroup().background(), 2 );
200     }
201   else
202     if( bActive )
203       {
204         if( ispixmap )
205           qDrawShadeRect( painter, 0, 0, cellWidth(), cellHeight(),
206                           colorGroup(), false, 1 );
207         else
208           qDrawShadePanel( painter, 0, 0, cellWidth(), cellHeight(),
209                           colorGroup(), false, 1 );
210       }
211
212   if( !_texts[ coordsToIndex( x, y ) ].isEmpty() )
213     {
214       painter->drawText( 0, 0, cellWidth(), cellHeight(), AlignCenter,
215                          _texts[ coordsToIndex( x, y ) ] );
216     }
217
218 }
219
220
221 void QKBrowseBox::resizeEvent( QResizeEvent* )
222 {
223   setCellWidth( width()/numCols() );
224   setCellHeight( height()/numRows() );
225 }
226
227
228 void QKBrowseBox::mouseMoveEvent( QMouseEvent* e )
229 {
230   int x = e->pos().x();
231   int y = e->pos().y();
232
233   int cellx, celly;
234   if( x < 0 || y < 0 || x > width() || y > height() ) // outside the box
235     {
```

Example 14-5: The implementation of the browse box (continued)

```
236          cellx = -1;
237          celly = -1;
238        }
239     else
240        {
241          cellx = (int)floor( ((double)x) / ((double)cellWidth()) );
242          celly = (int)floor( ((double)y) / ((double)cellHeight()) );
243        }
244
245     if( (_activecell.x() != cellx) || (_activecell.y() != celly) )
246        {
247          // mouse has been moved to another cell
248          int oldactivecellx = _activecell.x();
249          int oldactivecelly = _activecell.y();
250          _activecell.setX( cellx );
251          _activecell.setY( celly );
252          updateCell( oldactivecelly, oldactivecellx ); // remove old highlighting
253          updateCell( _activecell.y(), _activecell.x() ); // set new highlighting
254        }
255 }
```

This is a lot of code, and we will go through it slowly. First, let's look at the constructor that is repeated here:

```
QKBrowseBox::QKBrowseBox( int x, int y, QWidget* parent, const char* name,
                          WFlags f ) :
   QTableView( parent, name, WType_Popup )
{
   setNumCols( x );
   setNumRows( y );
   setCellWidth( width()/x );
   setCellHeight( height()/y );
   setTableFlags( Tbl_clipCellPainting );

   _texts = new QString[x*y];
   _pixmaps = new QPixmap[x*y];

   _activecell.setX( -1 );
   _activecell.setY( -1 );
   setMouseTracking( true );
   if( style() == MotifStyle )
     setFrameStyle( QFrame::Panel | QFrame::Sunken );
   else
     setFrameStyle( QFrame::WinPanel | QFrame::Sunken );
}
```

Note that for the first time in this book, we use a widget flag, the flag WType_Popup. This flag makes sure that the window looks like a pop-up menu, mainly by omitting the decorative frame that the window manager would usually put around the window.

The first five lines of code set up the `QTableView` by assigning the number of rows and columns, and their respective widths. In addition, we set the flag `Tbl_clipCellPainting`, which tells `QTableView` to make sure that we never paint over the border of the cell in question.

Afterwards, space is allocated for the texts and pixmaps, and the variable `_activecell` is initialized to `(-1,-1)`, which indicates that no item has been selected yet. We call `setMouseTracking( true )`, so that `mouseMoveEvent` is called even when the mouse button is not pressed while moving. This is needed so that we can always highlight the cell the mouse is over.

NOTE   Text strings and pixmaps are stored in a C++ array here. In this example, this is a simple and efficient solution since the number of rows and columns is known from the start. If these were variable, a good strategy would be to use `QDict` or `QIntDict` (see Chapter 8, *Container Classes*), and employ a value computed from the row and the column number as an index. This way, the structure can be resized without the items having to be repositioned.

The last four lines, then, show how to deal with different widget styles. `style()` always returns the widget style, which is either `MotifStyle` or `WindowsStyle`. We want the whole browse box to appear sunken, but use different frame styles depending on the widget style used.

The following methods should be obvious, but the `exec()` methods get interesting again. The variant with the two `int` parameters does the actual popping up, but the variant with the `QWidget*` does some calculations for determining the position where the browse box should be popped up. The code is well-documented, but some methods used here deserve attention. The first line, which is repeated here:

```
QPoint globalpos = trigger->parentWidget()->mapToGlobal( trigger->pos() );
```

computes the position of the trigger widget by calling `mapToGlobal()` on its parent. `QWidget::mapToGlobal()` is a general method that maps coordinates relative to a widget to global coordinates, which are relative to the whole screen. It is most often used with mouse positions. Note that there is also a method for computing the relative position from a global position which is called `QWidget::mapFromGlobal()`.

To check whether there is enough screen real estate for the browse box, we retrieve the size of the whole screen with the static method `QApplication::desktop()`.

With the positions computed, it's time to actually pop up the browse box. This is done in `exec( int, int )`:

```
int QKBrowseBox::exec( int x, int y )
{
  _firstrelease = true;
```

```
        move( x, y );
        show();
        repaint();
        qApp->enter_loop();
        hide();

        if( _activecell.x() != -1 && _activecell.y() != -1 )
          return _activecell.x() + _activecell.y() * numCols();
        else
          return -1;
    }
```

The widget is first moved to the computed position, then shown. The line `qApp->enter_loop()` is the crucial part of the whole widget. It sets up a secondary event loop. While this loop is running, our browse box and its child widgets are the only widgets that get events. This is a convenient way to synchronously pop up widgets. The same technique is used within Qt for modal menus and modal dialogs. At first glance, it looks as if the statement following the call to `enter_loop()`, the call to `hide()`, immediately pops the widget down again, but this is not the case. The call to `enter_loop()` only returns when the whole secondary event loop is terminated, which happens later.

The last part of this method just checks whether an item has been selected and computes a scalar value indicating that item which is then returned from `exec()`.

The next two methods, `keyPressEvent()` and `mouseReleaseEvent()`, are both responsible for popping the browse box down again. Implementing `keyPressEvent()` is very simple. If the pressed key was the escape key, `qApp->exit_loop()` is called. This exits the secondary event loop and returns control to the function from which `enter_loop()` was called—in our case, `exec( int, int )`. At this place, `hide()` effectively removes the widget from the screen.

The `mouseReleaseEvent()` method is not much different but also takes into account whether this was the first release event. If this is the case, the widget should not be popped down yet, because clicking on the button that triggers popping up the browse box would just show the browse box and then immediately hide the button again. Before this happens, we emit the signal `selected( int, int )`, in case the user of the widget wants to be informed about the selected item via a signal and not via the return value of `exec()`.

The `mouseMoveEvent()` method looks complicated, but the main part of it deals with computing cell coordinates. If the mouse has arrived in another cell, we record the new cell coordinates in `_activecell`, and then call `updateCell()` on the old cell and the new cell to remove the old highlighting rectangle and draw the new one. Calling `updateCell()` leads to calling `paintCell()`, just as a call to `repaint()` leads to a call to `paintEvent()`.

Let's finish the discussion of the browse box with its longest method, `paintCell()`. As already mentioned, this method is called once for each cell that needs repainting. Note that unlike other methods in Qt, the row comes before the column in this method.

The implementation of `paintCell()` can be divided into three parts. First, the pixmap (if any) is painted; then the cell to paint is highlighted, if it is the one below the mouse painter. Finally, the text (if any) is drawn.

Drawing the pixmap and the text is straightforward, but the highlighting procedure is interesting. It distinguishes between Motif widget style and Windows widget style, and determines whether the cell contains a pixmap. If it contains a pixmap, a rectangle is drawn around the pixmap; if it does not, a simple panel is drawn to serve as the background for the text. In Motif style, a rectangle is drawn even if the cell is not the one below the mouse pointer.

For drawing, `paintCell()` uses some convenience functions: `qDrawShadeRect()`, `qDrawShadePanel`, and `qDrawPlainRect`. These are very convenient, because you don't have to worry about shading and picking the correct colors. There are three more functions of this type: `qDrawShadeLine()`, `qDrawWinButton()`, and `qDrawWinPanel()`). All six of these functions are documented in the reference documentation for QPainter.

The last remaining method, `resizeEvent()`, just recomputes the width and height of the cells.

Now that we have completed our browse box, it is time to test it. You can find a test program in Examples 14-6 and 14-7.

Example 14-6: A test program for the browse box

```
 1 #include <qapplication.h>
 2 #include <qpushbutton.h>
 3 #include <qfont.h>
 4 #include <qpixmap.h>
 5 #include <qcolor.h>
 6 #include "qkbrowser.h"
 7 #include "browsertest.h"
 8
 9 #include <stdio.h>
10
11 MyWidget::MyWidget( QWidget *parent, const char *name, WFlags flags )
12         : QWidget( parent, name, flags )
13 {
14   setMinimumSize( 200, 120 );
15   setMaximumSize( 200, 120 );
16
17   quit = new QPushButton( "BrowseBox", this, "quit" );
18   quit->setGeometry( 62, 40, 75, 30 );
19   quit->setFont( QFont( "Times", 14 ) );
20
21   connect( quit, SIGNAL(pressed()), this, SLOT(buttonClicked()) );
22 }
23
24
25 void MyWidget::buttonClicked()
```

Example 14-6: A test program for the browse box (continued)

```
26  {
27      QKBrowseBox* browsebox = new QKBrowseBox( 7, 4 );
28      browsebox->resize( 100, 100 );
29      browsebox->insertItem( "A", 0, 0 );
30      browsebox->insertItem( "B", 0, 1 );
31      browsebox->insertItem( "C", 0, 2 );
32      browsebox->insertItem( "D", 0, 3 );
33      QPixmap pixmap( 32, 32 );
34      pixmap.fill( white );
35      browsebox->insertItem( pixmap, 1, 0 );
36      pixmap.fill( red );
37      browsebox->insertItem( pixmap, 1, 1 );
38      pixmap.fill( green );
39      browsebox->insertItem( pixmap, 1, 2 );
40      pixmap.fill( yellow );
41      browsebox->insertItem( pixmap, 1, 3 );
42      browsebox->insertItem( "I", 2, 0 );
43      pixmap.fill( magenta );
44      browsebox->insertItem( pixmap, 2, 0 );
45      browsebox->insertItem( "J", 2, 1 );
46      pixmap.fill( cyan );
47      browsebox->insertItem( pixmap, 2, 1 );
48      browsebox->insertItem( "K", 2, 2 );
49      pixmap.fill( blue );
50      browsebox->insertItem( pixmap, 2, 2 );
51      browsebox->insertItem( "L", 2, 3 );
52      pixmap.fill( darkYellow );
53      browsebox->insertItem( pixmap, 2, 3 );
54      browsebox->insertItem( "M", 3, 0 );
55      browsebox->insertItem( "N", 3, 1 );
56      browsebox->insertItem( "O", 3, 2 );
57      browsebox->insertItem( "P", 3, 3 );
58      browsebox->insertItem( "Q", 4, 0 );
59      browsebox->insertItem( "R", 4, 1 );
60      browsebox->insertItem( "S", 4, 2 );
61      browsebox->insertItem( "T", 4, 3 );
62      browsebox->insertItem( "U", 5, 0 );
63      browsebox->insertItem( "V", 5, 1 );
64      browsebox->insertItem( "W", 5, 2 );
65      browsebox->insertItem( "X", 5, 3 );
66      browsebox->insertItem( "Y", 6, 0 );
67      browsebox->insertItem( "Z", 6, 1 );
68      browsebox->insertItem( "!", 6, 2 );
69      browsebox->insertItem( "?", 6, 3 );
70      int ret = browsebox->exec( quit );
71      debug( " Item chosen: %d\n", ret );
72      QEvent ev( Event_Leave );
73      QMouseEvent mev ( Event_MouseButtonRelease,
74                        QCursor::pos(), LeftButton, LeftButton );
75      QApplication::sendEvent( quit, &ev );
```

Example 14-6: A test program for the browse box (continued)

```
76   QApplication::sendEvent( quit, &mev );
77   delete browsebox;
78 }
79
80 #include "browsertest.moc"
81
82 int main( int argc, char **argv )
83 {
84     QApplication a( argc, argv );
85
86     MyWidget* w = new MyWidget();
87     w->setGeometry( 100, 100, 200, 120 );
88     a.setMainWidget( w );
89     w->show();
90     return a.exec();
91 }
```

Example 14-7: Header file for Example 14-6

```
1 #ifndef _BROWSERTEST_H
2 #define _BROWSERTEST_H
3
4 #include <qwidget.h>
5
6 class QPushButton;
7
8 class MyWidget : public QWidget
9 {
10    Q_OBJECT
11
12 public:
13    MyWidget( QWidget *parent = 0, const char *name = 0, WFlags flags = 0 );
14
15 public slots:
16    void buttonClicked();
17
18 private:
19    QPushButton* _quit;
20 };
21
22 #endif
```

The only interesting thing you will find in this test program is the following code sequence:

```
QEvent ev( Event_Leave );
QMouseEvent mev ( Event_MouseButtonRelease,
                  QCursor::pos(), LeftButton, LeftButton );
QApplication::sendEvent( _quit, &ev );
QApplication::sendEvent( _quit, &mev );
```

Since the button that makes the browse box pop up never gets the mouse release event, it would not be drawn in its normal state again if didn't fake two events: leaving the button and releasing the mouse. This is done by creating two events, and then sending these fake events to the widget with the static application `QApplication::send-Event()`. We will come back to this in the "Sending Synthetic Events" section.[3]

---

3   The necessity of this code is likely to be removed in future versions of Qt.

15

Focus Handling

Focus handling is one of the most difficult topics in GUI programming, and few programs get it completely right. Focus handling is all about having the keyboard focus where the user expects it to be and allowing the user to navigate through the GUI elements that can accept keyboard focus without using the mouse (and thus having to take the hands away from the keyboard). Normally, this operation of moving the keyboard focus is invoked by the Tab key.

The main concept to understand about focus handling in Qt is the *focus policy*. This attribute is set separately for each widget. It controls whether the widget can receive keyboard focus and how it can happen. A `QWidget` disables focus by default, but all widgets that want to get keyboard focus enable it in their constructors. Thus, the constructor of your widget is the correct place to set the focus policy. You rarely need to override the focus policy that built-in widgets in Qt have set for themselves.

The following focus policies are available:

NoFocus
> The widget does not accept the keyboard focus at all.

ClickFocus
> The widget accepts the focus when the user explicitly clicks into the widget with the mouse.

TabFocus
> The widget accepts the focus when the user moves the focus to it by means of the tab key.

StrongFocus
> A combination of `ClickFocus` and `TabFocus`.

You can ask a widget whether it accepts focus by calling `isFocusEnabled()`. This method returns `false` when the focus policy is `NoFocus` and `true` if it is otherwise.

There is one exception to these focus policies: A top-level widget has the focus policy NoFocus by default, but it still gets focus and key events so it can be used without calling any focus-related functions.

Here are some guidelines for choosing a focus policy. NoFocus should be used for widgets that only display information, or when you want to move focus around some widgets with the Tab key, but want to exclude some other widgets from this. These widgets should then have a shortcut to ensure they are reachable via the keyboard. An example of a built-in widget that uses the NoFocus policy is QLabel. ClickFocus should normally not be used if you want your program to be usable without a mouse. It is mainly available for completeness. TabFocus is useful for widgets that assist other widgets. For example, you might have a text-entry field for entering a file name, and a button next to it that invokes a file-selection dialog from which the selected filename is later filled into the text field. This button would be a good candidate for TabFocus. Finally, StrongFocus should be used for all other widgets.

Another focus-related topic that has a large influence on the usability of an application is the *tab order*. This is the order in which the widgets receive keyboard focus when the user presses repeatedly the Tab key. Normally, the tab order is the order in which the widgets are inserted into their parent, the order in which they are created. You can change this, by calling setTabOrder(). This static method accepts two pointers to QWidget objects. The second widget is moved in the tab order so that pressing Tab while the focus is in the first widget moves the keyboard focus to the second one. You have to be careful not to break the tab ring with this method.

It pays off to spend some time thinking about and experimenting with different tab orders. This is especially true for complex dialogs, where most of the fields have to be filled out, or that are invoked over and over again (such as a data-entry mask). Make sure that the tab traversal through the various widgets that can accept keyboard focus is done in the order in which the user naturally uses the widget. This most often is a left-to-right or top-to-bottom order.

If QWidget::setTabOrder() is still not flexible enough for you, you might consider using focusNextPrevChild(). This is a low-level function that implements in QWidget the standard tab order just described. You can override this method to change the tab traversal to your needs. Child widgets ask this method in their parent widget where to put the focus. The focusNextPrevChild() method accepts a Boolean parameter, which when true indicates that the tab movement should be "forward" for some definition of forward. Otherwise it should go "backward". The method is expected to return true when it can find a suitable new widget, and false otherwise. To construct an example, imagine a dialog that contains a check-box and two edit fields in this order. When the check-box is not checked, the first edit field should not be editable. In this case, you can simply call setEnabled(false) on the first edit field, and tab traversal automatically jumps from the check-box to the second edit field. When the check-box is not checked, it is *unlikely* that the user will enter something into the first edit field, but it's not completely impossible. In this case, you cannot disable the first edit field, but you want to exclude it from tab traversal. Here is a possible implementation for `focus-NextPrevChild()`, assuming that there are no other widgets in the dialog:

```
bool MyDialog::focusNextPrevChild( bool forward )
{
    QFocusData* focusdata = focusData();
    QWidget* current = focusdata->home();

    if( current == _checkbox ) {
        if( !forward )
            _edit2->setFocus(); // cycles backwards
        else
            if( _checkbox->isChecked() )
                _edit1->setFocus(); // check-box is checked, edit1->jump to first
edit field
            else
                _edit2->setFocus(); // else jump to the second
    } else // nothing special with the other widgets
        if( !forward )
            focusdata->prev()->setFocus();
        else
            focusdata->next()->setFocus();

    return true;
}
```

We use the class `QFocusData` here to get information about the currently focused widget, as well as to get the next or previous widget in the keyboard traversal ring. If the current widget is the check-box, we implement the specification mentioned previously; for all other widgets, nothing fancy is needed. In any case, the focus is moved to another widget by calling `setFocus()` on the widget that should get the focus now.

If this looks complicated, console yourself with the knowledge that special focus management is rarely needed. With the natural tab order, the focus policies, and sometimes a change in the tab order with `setTabOrder()`, you should be okay in most cases.

16

Advanced Event Handling

So far, you have seen how to respond to events by connecting to signals or by reimplementing event handlers. This suffices for most applications, but there are cases in which you need a little bit more. In this chapter, we will discover ways to override the standard event-handling mechanisms, notably by using event filters and synthetic events.

Event Filters

An *event filter* is an object that gets all events for another object, and has the chance to react to an event before the original addressee of the event can do so. This is useful if you want override the behavior of an object but do not want to or cannot change the class of that object itself. Another possible scenario for using an event filter is when you want to add a certain function to a lot of widgets in your application, but don't want to subclass every class used there. We will see such an application in a moment.

There are two steps to using an event filter: Writing the event-filter code, and installing it. You write an event filter by reimplementing the method `eventFilter()` in a class derived from `QObject`. Often, this is a widget itself. This method has two parameters: a pointer to the object for which the event was originally meant, and a pointer to an object of the class `QEvent` that encapsulates the event data.

The event handler can do anything it wants. It can even delete the object for which the event was meant. When it is done with the event, it must return a Boolean value. If this value is `true`, the event is no longer dispatched; if it is `false`, normal event processing happens. Of course, you should never delete the receiver of the event and then return control back to it—this leads to a very quick exit of your application.

Once you have such an event handler, you can install it by calling `installEventFilter()` on the object for which you want to filter the events. Note that you pass a pointer to an object for which the event filter is implemented, not the address of the method itself. You can even install more than one event filter for an object and, unlike signals and slots, the order of filter execution is defined: The event filter installed last is executed first. Only the execution of the first event filter is guaranteed, since this filter can break the event chain by returning `true`.

Event filters filter every event, so if you install an event filter for a widget that always returns `true`, breaking the event chain, you should not be too astonished if you do not see your widget—it simply will not get its paint events.

Example 16-1 demonstrates the use of event filters. It can help you get rid of your destructive energies. At the beginning, there are four widgets (a push-button, a check box, a radio button, and a text-entry field) with hard-coded positions. Clicking with the right mouse button on any of these does not invoke a slot connected to the `clicked()` signal of the slot, but deletes the widget. This is done, of course, in an event filter. All other events, including mouse clicks with the other mouse buttons, are passed on to the respective widget.

Example 16-1: Killing widgets with the right mouse button

```
 1  #include <qapplication.h>
 2  #include <qpushbutton.h>
 3  #include <qlineedit.h>
 4  #include <qradiobutton.h>
 5  #include <qcheckbox.h>
 6
 7  class KillerFilter : public QObject
 8  {
 9  protected:
10    bool eventFilter( QObject* object, QEvent* event ) {
11      if( event->type() == Event_MouseButtonPress )
12        if( ((QMouseEvent*)event)->button() == RightButton ) {
13          delete object;
14          return true;
15        }
16        else
17          return false;
18      else
19        return false;
20    }
21  };
22
23
24  int main( int argc, char* argv[] )
25  {
26    QApplication a( argc, argv );
27
28    QWidget* toplevel = new QWidget();
29    toplevel->resize( 230, 130 );
30
31    QObject* killerfilter = new KillerFilter();
32
33    QPushButton* pb = new QPushButton( toplevel );
```

Example 16-1: Killing widgets with the right mouse button (continued)

```
34    pb->setGeometry( 10, 10, 100, 50 );
35    pb->setText( "pushbutton" );
36    pb->installEventFilter( killerfilter );
37
38    QLineEdit* le = new QLineEdit( toplevel );
39    le->setGeometry( 10, 70, 100, 50 );
40    le->setText( "Line edit" );
41    le->installEventFilter( killerfilter );
42
43    QCheckBox* cb = new QCheckBox( toplevel );
44    cb->setGeometry( 120, 10, 100, 50 );
45    cb->setText( "Check-box" );
46    cb->installEventFilter( killerfilter );
47
48    QRadioButton* rb = new QRadioButton( toplevel );
49    rb->setGeometry( 120, 70, 100, 50 );
50    rb->setText( "Radio button" );
51    rb->installEventFilter( killerfilter );
52
53    a.setMainWidget( toplevel );
54    toplevel->show();
55    return a.exec();
56 }
```

This is one of those examples where you want to add a certain feature (in this case, destruction upon clicking) to several objects without having to subclass each of them. If we had not used an event filter here, we would have had to write four new classes, one for each widget class used.

Sending Synthetic Events

Sometimes the events that the windowing system sends to your application are not enough, and you would like to fake events. There is no need to go through low-level events of the Win32 or X11 API, since Qt provides the necessary functionality.

When you seem to need such a functionality, it is often because of bad design. The occasions when you really need a fake event (also called a *synthetic event*) are rare, and you should always look for alternatives.

We have already seen an example in which a synthetic event was necessary and useful, although we haven't stressed on it so far. In the test program for the browse box in the "Implementing a Browse Box" section, we had the following lines of code:

```
QEvent ev( Event_Leave );
QMouseEvent mev ( Event_MouseButtonRelease,
                  QCursor::pos(), LeftButton, LeftButton );
QApplication::sendEvent( _quit, &ev );
QApplication::sendEvent( _quit, &mev );
```

In this case, the button that invoked the browse box would have continued to be drawn pressed in, because the leave event and mouse release event are swallowed by the browse box. Thus, we regenerated these events so that they could also be sent to the invoking push-button.

There are two static methods for sending synthetic events: `QApplication::send-Event()` and `QApplication::postEvent()`. Both accept a pointer to the addressee object, and a pointer to the event to be sent. The latter can simply be constructed as usual, and may be of any subclass of `QEvent`—or, of course, of the class `QEvent` itself.

The difference between `sendEvent()` and `postEvent()` is that `sendEvent()` sends the event immediately to the receiver and waits until it has been processed. The `postEvent()` method places the event in the event queue, just as though it came from the windowing system, and returns immediately. This means that all events already in the event queue are processed before the synthetic event.

In case you later want to enforce that all or some queued synthetic events come first, you can call `QApplication::sendPostedEvents()`. This static method expects a pointer to a `QObject` and an event type as its arguments. It then passes all events that have the named type and are directed to the named object directly to that object.

You might ask why you could not simply pass the event handler itself. In some cases, this is indeed possible, but it is rarely advisable because it surpasses any installed event filter (see the "Event Filters" section) and thus might lead to unexpected results.

17

Advanced Signals and Slots

In this chapter, we'll cover some more topics concerning signals and slots. In the first section, we'll look at additional methods of connecting signals to slots, and afterwards we will show you some useful tricks to help you get even more out of signals and slots.

Signals and Slots Revisited

You have already learned the basics about signals and slots in Chapter 2, *First Steps in Qt Programming*, but there are a few things we haven't told you yet. You probably won't need this information very often, but from time to time it can come in handy.

First, you do not need to use the static method `QObject::connect()` when you are in a method of a class that is derived from `QObject` (which is usually the case when you program with Qt). So, instead of writing:

```
QObject::connect( myslider, SIGNAL( valueChanged( int ) ),
                  mylcdnum, SLOT( display( int ) ) );
```

you could write:

```
connect( myslider, SIGNAL( valueChanged( int ) ),
         mylcdnum, SLOT( display( int ) ) );
```

if this code is located in a method of a class derived from `QObject`. Apart from a few less characters to type, you don't save anything here, though.

To save even more typing, you can also leave out the receiver if the code is in a method of the object that is to receive the signal. For example, you could write the following:

```
class MyLCDNum : public QLCDNumber
{
   ...
}
```

```
MyLCDNumber::MyLCDNumber( ... )
{
  ... // create myslider somewhere here

  connect( myslider, SIGNAL( valueChanged( int ) ),
          SLOT( display( int ) ) );
  ...
}
```

To be honest, we would not advise you to use this. It saves only a few characters and it is harder to read.

Sometimes a signal and a slot that you want to connect do not really fit: The signal provides more information than the slot wants to handle. For example, let's say that you want to know when a toggle button has been toggled, but you are not interested in whether the new state is on or off, either because you already have that value from somewhere else or because you just want to play a beep or something. In this case, you just leave out the corresponding parameter in the SLOT clause:

```
connect( mytogglebutton, SIGNAL( toggled( bool ) ),
        myreceiverobject, SLOT( slotBeep() ) );
```

If you controlled the source code for the class of which `myreceiverobject` is a pointer to an object, you could just add that Boolean parameter to the method declaration, and not use it in the method body. But if you aren't, or if you do not have access to the source code because you bought that class as part of a commercial library for which no source code was shipped, this is a viable alternative.

While the tricks we have told you about so far are not much more than syntactic sugar, the following really helps make your programs faster and more elegant. Do you remember the "signal forwarding" technique we introduced in Chapter 2? We had a slot that did not do much more than emit another signal, just to pass it on.[1] If you ever have such a case in your program, you can connect a signal to a signal. This sounds odd, and we won't explain here why it works since that would mean digging very deep into the implementation of signals and slots in Qt, but it does work—and often it leads to elegant solutions.

For example, let's say that you have a dialog subclassed from `QDialog` that will serve as a "search and replace" dialog in a word processor. It should emit a signal `continueSearch()` whenever the "search" button is clicked. Without connecting signals to signals, you would end up with roughly the following code:

```
SearchAndReplaceDialog::SearchAndReplaceDialog( ... ) : QDialog( ... )
{
  ...
  QPushButton* searchbutton = new QPushButton( "Search", this );
  connect( searchbutton, SIGNAL( clicked() ),
```

---

1 If you look back, you will see that we did a little bit more: We changed a color code into a pointer to a color object. But we could have just passed on the code.

```
               this, SLOT( slotSearchClicked() ) );
  ...
}
  ...
{
void SearchAndReplaceDialog::slotSearchClicked()
{
  emit continueSearch();
}
```

But when you connect a signal to a signal, you simply save the method `slotSearch-Clicked()`:

```
SearchAndReplaceDialog::SearchAndReplaceDialog( ... ) : QDialog( ... )
{
  ...
  QPushButton* searchbutton = new QPushButton( "Search", this );
  connect( searchbutton, SIGNAL( clicked() ),
         this, SIGNAL( continueSearch() ) );
}
```

What we are doing here is saying "if the search button emits a `clicked()` signal, make it look like the dialog emitted the `continueSearch()` signal." This can be a very powerful technique, especially when you are designing dialog interfaces.

It is also possible to remove a connection between a signal and slot when you don't need it any longer. The method you need is called `QObject::disconnect()`, and it expects exactly the same parameters as `QObject::connect()` in its simplest form. Usually you don't need it, because all connections are automatically disconnected for you when an object is destroyed, but sometimes it can be desirable to disable a signal-slot connection for a while.

You can specify the signals and slots to disconnect explicitly:

```
QObject::disconnect( myslider, SIGNAL( valueChanged( int ) ),
                 mylcdnum, SLOT( display( int ) ) );
```

or you can disconnect all signals that might be connected with a slot by only passing the receiving object and the slot name:

```
disconnect( myslider, SIGNAL( valueChanged( int ) ) );
```

This example does not make much sense, because you would probably never connect more than one slider to a number display. We don't like these implicit parameters much anyway, so we suggest you just stick with the first syntax and explicitly disconnect all signals that you want to disconnect.

If you want to stop a slot from being called for a short time, you do not need to explicitly disconnect signals and slots with `disconnect()`. Instead, you can call the method `blockSignals( true )` on the object that is emitting the signals. This prevents all signals from being emitted from the object until you call `blockSignals( false )` on that same object. This is useful, when you want to programmatically change a widget state in a way you would normally do from the user interface. For example, you might want to check a check-box from your program code, but don't want the `toggled( bool )` signal to be emitted because of this. You could the do the following:

```
mycheckbox->blockSignals( true );
mycheckbox->setChecked( true );
mycheckbox->blockSignals( false );
```

Here is one more thing that you might have been wondering about if you are a Unix programmer: Qt signals are not Unix signals! These have nothing to do with each other. Unix signals are asynchronous notifications about things that happen and that need the immediate attention of your application. Often, these signals are sent in reaction to an event that occurred outside the address space of your process, like the `SIGINT` signal that is sent when the user types Ctrl-C. Qt signals, on the other hand, are just a synchronous notification that something has happened in your application that some other part of your application might be interested in.

Connecting Several Buttons to One Slot

Sometimes several buttons in a dialog trigger similar functions, and you would like to connect all of these to one slot because the code for the reactions to the button-clicks is very similar. This is not possible with the signal `clicked()`, because this signal does not pass any information about the button that was pressed, forcing you to use a different slot for every button:

```
QPushButton* button1 = new QPushButton( "text1", parent );
QObject::connect( button1, SIGNAL( clicked() ),
                  receiver, SLOT( slotForButton1() ) );
QPushButton* button2 = new QPushButton( "text2", parent );
QObject::connect( button2, SIGNAL( clicked() ),
                  receiver, SLOT( slotForButton2() ) );
QPushButton* button3 = new QPushButton( "text3", parent );
QObject::connect( button3, SIGNAL( clicked() ),
                  receiver, SLOT( slotForButton3() ) );
...
```

The trick here is to use a `QButtonGroup` object. Normally you use this class to visually group buttons (for example, a set of mutually exclusive radio buttons), but it is not necessary to show the `QButtonGroup` object. Simply call `QButtonGroup::insert()` to add the buttons, and connect to the signal `clicked( int )` that the group emits:

```
QButtonGroup* bgroup = new QButtonGroup( parent );
QPushButton* button1 = new QPushButton( "text1", parent );
bgroup->insert( button1 );
QPushButton* button2 = new QPushButton( "text2", parent );
bgroup->insert( button2 );
QPushButton* button3 = new QPushButton( "text3", parent );
bgroup->insert( button3 );
QObject::connect( bgroup, SIGNAL( clicked( int ) ),
                  receiver, SLOT( slotForAllButtons( int ) ) );
```

You can then use the `int` parameter to `slotForAllButtons()` to distinguish which button has been pressed.

You might just want to take advantage of the single signal, but not have a frame around your buttons. In this case, you can call `QButtonGroup::hide()`. The button group will no longer have a visual representation, but will still do its work.

You can generalize on this concept by using the class `QSignalMapper`. See the Qt reference documentation for how to do this.

18

Debugging

This is not a chapter about general debugging techniques—there are already plenty of good books about that out there. Instead, this is a list of features that Qt provides specifically to help with debugging.

First, Qt provides the functions `debug()`, `warning()`, and `fatal()`, which are all declared in *qapplication.h*. These functions work just like `printf()`, in that they accept a format string and a variable number of parameters. The advantage of these functions is that they work equally well with Unix or with Windows. In Unix, the output is written to standard error. With Windows, it is sent to the debugger. In addition to printing the message, `fatal()` also exits the program. All three functions restrict the text output to no more than 512 characters, including the trailing zero byte.

If you want to redirect the output from these functions, you can install your own message handler. This is especially interesting, because Qt contains hundreds of warning messages. Most warn the developer about invalid function parameters. Even though you should take all efforts to avoid provoking these warnings, you might want to rule out any possibility that your users will see them. A custom message handler can solve this problem.

Such a message handler is installed with the function `qInstallMsgHandler()`. As its only argument, it expects the address of a function—the message handler itself—with the following signature:

```
void (*)( QtMsgType type, const char *msg );
```

The second parameter is the message, and the first parameter tells your message handler what type of message it was. Possible values are `QtDebugMsg`, `QtWarningMsg` and `QtFatalMsg`.

In *qglobal.h*, two macros are defined that might be useful when you are debugging. `ASSERT()` accepts a Boolean expression and prints a warning message if this expression does not evaluate to `true`. `CHECK_PTR()` expects a pointer and prints a warning message if this pointer is 0, because memory allocation failed. Note that these macros do nothing fancy—you might have better stuff in your programmer's toolchest, and you shouldn't hesitate to use the tools you are accustomed to. Of course, when you use these macros, all the usual warnings about using macros for debugging apply, like not executing code in assertions that is needed afterwards.

The last debugging feature for your source code is also Qt-specific. You have already seen that you can pass a name to the constructor of each widget. This can be very useful when you need to identify your widgets later in the debugger. If the debugger stops program execution at a breakpoint, or simply because the program has crashed, you might not know which widget you can currently see in a variable that is nothing but a `QWidget*`. If you have given names to all your widgets, however, and your debugger has the facility to call arbitrary functions from its command-line, you can call `QObject::name()` to get the name of the widget. It's good for this name to be unique, but that's up to you. Or, you can simply look at all the members of the `QWidget` and search for its name. As you can already see, this feature is not restricted to widgets, but applies to every object of a class that is derived from QObject—in other words, most objects that float around in a Qt program. Qt 2.0 features two additions to `QObject::name()`: If no name is set for the object, this method returns "unnamed", but if you pass 0 to this method, it returns a null pointer in this case.

Another method in `QObject` can be very useful during debugging. When you are unsure that you have gotten the parent-child relationships right, call `dumpObjectTree()` at your top-level object (for example, the top level widget, when you want to debug widget hierarchies). This method prints out the hierarchy all the way down to the last object.

Finally, the last method useful for debugging is `QObject::dumpObjectInfo()`, which prints various internal information about any object of a class derived from `QObject`, including the signals and slots connected to it.

A common mistake in Unix/X11 programming is trying to debug code that grabs the server. This inevitably locks up the whole server. The server is grabbed by the application, the application is stopped in the debugger waiting for a command, but you cannot enter commands in the debugger because the server is locked. In Qt, you can avoid this problem by passing the command-line parameter `-nograb` to any Qt application. This parameter is parsed and understood by Qt, and leads to no server grabs being executed.

On Linux systems, Qt applications even detect automatically if they are run inside a debugger, and automatically assume the `-nograb` switch. Should you ever wish to have grabbing turned on while running inside the debugger (be very careful with that and make sure that no grabs can be active when the program is stopped by the debugger), you can pass the `-dograb` parameter to turn off the automatic debugger detection.

Another nice feature on X11 systems is that Qt applications understand the `-sync` command-line switch, which is very common with X11 applications. It turns off buffering of X requests, and thus helps you debug low-level X errors. Note that when you use only Qt and no native X11 calls in your code, this should not happen. If it does, it should be reported as a bug to *qt-bugs@troll.no*.

19

Portability

One of the great advantages of Qt is that you can write your programs on one platform, and then simply recompile them to run on another one. Of course, you need to take some precautions.

Qt is not the only platform-independent library that allows you to deploy your programs on Windows and Unix systems. Some other libraries, like *wxWindows*, even support OS/2, the Macintosh and other platforms. What is so interesting about Qt is that it does not simply use the widgets that the platform in question provides and encapsulate them in its own structures, but it emulates them. Thus, you can run your program on Unix, but make it look like a Windows program. Of course, this also works the other way round. This is very useful when your users migrate from one platform to the other. With Qt, you can provide them with a familiar look-and-feel that can reduce migration costs since users will be more secure about how the application works on the new platform.

Why Portability Is Desirable

If you are a software contractor hired to design and implement one specific product for one specific client on one specific platform, portability is not of much use to you. If you sell your applications to a larger market, however, being able to deploy your application on a wider scale can be a great benefit. All of a sudden, you can reach a large number of potential customers for a rather low price. You still need some knowledge about all supported platforms, the needed hardware and the like, but the cost-gain ratio could be quite favorable. No matter whether you are currently a Windows or a Unix developer, don't underestimate the "other" market. Windows is the most widespread platform of all, but Unix—after years of decline—is gaining a lot of market share, especially as the "free" operating systems like Linux and FreeBSD gain acceptance in the corporate world. In fact, Linux (a Unix clone developed by the Internet community) is currently the operating system with the highest growth rate of all.

Another benefit of a portable development environment is that it can help you reduce development costs. If you currently have, 10 developers developing on Windows, you have to purchase 10 licenses of the operating system and ten licenses for the compiler. On the other hand, with operating systems like Linux, the operating system, compiler, debugger, editor, and other development tools are free for the taking—and equal in quality to those for Windows. If you move 8 of your 10 developers to a free operating system, they can continue to develop the same application at a lower cost because you avoid paying high upgrade fees when new compiler or operating system versions are released. The remaining two Windows developers can then make sure that your application is really portable, and package the application for Windows deployment.

There is one more reason, which may sound unlikely to you if you have never tried it: Portable programs tend to have fewer bugs. If you think about this a bit, the reason becomes obvious. Most programs have bugs lurking deep in their source code, bugs that crash or otherwise influence your application only in rare situations. It is unlikely that your QA department will find these bugs before one of your customers does. If you have run your programs on other platforms on a regular basis, bugs are more likely to be found, because other operating systems have other memory access patterns, other timing values, etc. Also, some quality assurance tools, like memory or API checkers, are often available either only on Windows or only on Unix. Portability allows you to use more of these helpful tools.

Still, there are times when it does *not* make sense to write your programs portably. If you develop device drivers and use Qt only to write configuration programs for those drivers, you needn't care much about portability. Device drivers are inherently unportable. But then again, if you manufacture the hardware yourself and want to provide drivers and configuration programs for both Windows and Unix systems, you could still save time and money by writing your configuration program to be portable.

Another situation where portability is difficult to achieve is integration with the surrounding environment, such as supporting OLE/COM on Windows, or Tooltalk on Unix. If the code needed for this makes up a large part of your application, you won't be able to program very portably. But the more this integration is just a sideline of your application, the more it pays off to write portable programs.

How to Write Portable Programs

There are several rules that can help you design your programs to be portable. They are easy to understand and often astonishingly easy to follow.

Avoid calling native API functions.

> The rationale behind this rule is obvious: Native API functions like those from the Win32 API or the Unix C library are normally not available on other platforms.
>
> Of course, following this rule is only possible if Qt provides what you need. Remember that Qt has many features other than those for creating user interfaces. Qt also provides classes for portable drawing (`QPainter`), portable printing

(QPrinter) and, most notably, portable file and directory access (classes QDir, QFile, QDataStream, QTextStream and QFileInfo—see Chapter 11, *Working with Files and Directories*). QDataStream can be especially useful, because it can help you develop file formats that are portable as well: Your Windows word processor could read files saved from the Unix version of your word processor, for example. If you use the streaming operations provided with the standard C++ library, this might not be the case because of differently sized built-in types, such as int, different alignment requirements, and other factors. If you need to deal with input sources other than mice and keyboards (network sockets, for example), QSocketNotifier provides a portable means of reacting to input from these channels. Unfortunately, you still have to create your socket or whatever you use in a platform-specific manner. You will learn how to use QSocketNotifier in Chapter 21, *Qt Network Programming*.

If the classes Qt provides do not suffice, try to stick with POSIX.

POSIX (an acronym for *IEEE Portable Operating System Interface for Computing Environments*) is a standard for accessing operating system-specific files, processes, and other items in a portable manner.[1] Nowadays, virtually all Unix systems and Windows NT support POSIX. Thus, if you don't have to support Windows 95, but only Windows NT and Unix, sticking with POSIX ensures that your programs are still portable.

While POSIX maps almost directly to operating system calls on Unix systems, in Windows NT it is an extra layer, which could result in a performance penalty. If you want to learn more about POSIX, read *POSIX Programmer's Guide* by Donald Lewine.

If POSIX is not an option, isolate the platform-specific calls in special classes and files.

Sometimes you just have to access operating system-specific functions to achieve a certain functionality. It is important that these calls are not scattered all over your source code, but grouped together in one or more classes and source files. This way, you will have to rewrite these classes for the other platform when you port your program and know exactly when you are done. Otherwise, you would have to search through all of your source code for platform-specific code. Of course, to make this technique really useful, you should never include platform-specific header files in your header files, because your header files represent your internal API that separates the platform-specific parts from the platform-independent ones. Therefore, always include those header files in the source files. You can then have one source file for each platform, and use a common header for both. Depending on the platform, you compile the correct source file for that platform. If you want to implement networking functionality, for example, you could have a header file *networking.h* and source files *networking-win.cpp* and *networking-x11.cpp*, which both include *networking.h* and implement the classes and functions defined there.

---

1 When we talk about POSIX here, we really mean POSIX.1, the part of the POSIX specification that deals with function-level access to operating system-specific features.

Danger Ahead: When Even Qt Is Not Portable

There are very few methods in Qt that behave differently on Windows and Unix. If you want to write portable programs, you have to watch out for these. Table 19-1 sums up these methods, and includes some hints about when these problems could apply to your application.

Table 19-1: Qt Methods That Behave Differently on Windows and Unix

Method	Comment
`debug()`, `warning()`, `fatal()`	These methods, which are meant for outputting debugging messages for the developer (not for the user), send the data to stderr on Unix and to the debugger on Windows. Since you don't want these messages to be printed in the final version (they indicate problems, or at least confuse the user), this is not really a problem.
`QApplication::flushX()`	This method flushes the event queue on Unix systems. On Windows, it does nothing.
`QApplication::setColor-Spec()`	The possible values for the parameter this method accepts depend on the platform. See the "Managing Colors" section in the Chapter "Graphics" for a detailed description.
`QApplication::setDouble-ClickInterval()`	On Windows, this value is ignored; the value from the command panel is taken instead.
`QApplication::setMainWid-get()`	On Unix systems, this method also resizes the main widget, if the command-line switch –geometry was given.
`QApplication::syncX()`	On Unix systems, this processes all outstanding events and flushes all queues. On Windows, it does nothing.
`QCursor::handle()`	This method returns a handle to the native data that represents the mouse cursor represented by `QCursor`. Calling this method itself is not unportable, but using the handle is.
`QDir::convertSeparators()`	On Windows systems, this method converts slashes to backslashes, the path separator used on Windows systems. On Unix, this method does nothing. This is usually a portability advantage, not a problem, because you can always use slashes as path separators in your application, and call `QDir::convertSeparators()` when you want to hand over such a path to a native function. Also, `QDir::separator()` returns the character used as the separator on the current platform.
`QDir::setFilter()`	If you use the parameters `Modified` or `System`, nothing happens on Unix, because Unix file systems have neither archive nor system bits.

Table 19-1: Qt Methods That Behave Differently on Windows and Unix (continued)

Method	Comment
`QFile::open()`	On Windows systems, the flag `IO_Translate` enables translation of carriage return/linefeed pairs to single line-feeds and back. On Unix, this is not necessary, so the flag does nothing.
`QFont::handle()`	This method returns a handle to the native data that represents the font represented by `QFont`. Calling this method itself is not unportable, but using the handle is.
`OObject::startTimer()` and classes `QTime` and `QTimer`	On Windows 95, the granularity is not better than 55 milliseconds. On Windows NT and Unix, the granularity is usually 1 millisecond.
`QPaintDevice::handle()`	This method returns a handle to the native data that represents the paint device represented by `QPaintDevice`. Calling this method itself is not unportable, but using the handle is.
`QPaintDevice::x11Display()`	On Unix systems, this returns a pointer to the `Display` structure of the display with which the paint device is associated. Calling this method itself is not unportable, but using the return value is. This method returns 0 on Windows systems.
`QPainter::handle()`	This method returns a handle to the native data structure that is used for the drawing performed by `QPainter`. Calling this method itself is not unportable, but using the handle is.
`QWidget::setSizeIncrement()`	Calling this method has no effect under Windows. On Unix systems, it may be ignored by the window manager, although most window managers respect it.
`QWidget::winId()`	This method returns the ID of the native window in the window system. Calling this method itself is not unportable, but using the handle is.

Building Projects Portably with tmake

When your projects exceed a certain size, you will need to use some tools to manage your project. We won't talk about the various Integrated Development Environments (IDEs) that come with your compiler (see Chapter 23, *Using the Visual C++ IDE for Qt Programs*, for learning how you can use the Visual Studio from the Visual C++ Compiler), can be purchased separately, or are available as freeware. These products can help you to a certain extent, but which one can help most depends very much on your project and on your work habits. Something to watch out for is that IDEs that are shipped with compilers are often awkward to use if you want to use a tool like Qt instead of that compiler vendor's class library. Often a versatile and powerful editor with integrated compilation and debugging facilities, such as Emacs (available for both Unix and Windows), can help you more when programming with Qt.

Organizing your makefiles allows your program to be built on various platforms from one source tree. In larger corporate installations, you might even have the same source tree that you checked out from whatever version-control software you use for Windows and Unix. Accordingly, you might want to—or have to—build your program for Windows and Unix in the same directory.

With their diversity, Unix systems have a long tradition of tools that allow building a program on several Unix-like platforms. The two best-known tools are Autoconf/Automake from the Free Software Foundation (available from *ftp://ftp.gnu.org/pub/gnu/automake-1.3.tar.gz* and *ftp://ftp.gnu.org/autoconf-2.12.tar.gz*), and Metaconfig (see *http://www.oasis.leo.org/perl/exts/date-time/scripts/devel/dist.dsc.html*). Alas, these tools won't help you at all if you are building on Unix *and* on Windows.

Troll Tech, the makers of Qt, provide a very useful tool called *tmake*. It allows you to easily define the structure of your project, and generates makefiles for your platform. You only have to write a *project file*. *tmake* then takes this project file and combines it with a predefined set of templates suitable for the platform in question to form a makefile. *tmake* already comes with template sets for most platforms that Qt runs on, so you will rarely have to define a template set of your own (even though it's not terribly difficult to do so).

What's so nice about *tmake* is that it knows about Qt, and that it automatically generates makefile rules for moc-generated files. Thus, you cannot forget to include these, which often happens if you add them to your makefiles by hand. In addition, *tmake* automatically computes the dependencies for you.

The *tmake* tool is written in Perl, a very powerful scripting and programming language. If you are working on a Unix system, chances are that you already have the Perl interpreter installed. If not, you can get it from *http://www.perl.com*. If you are working on Windows, check *http://www.activeware.com*. Perl is free software. You can download either a precompiled binary or the sources, install it, and be ready to run Perl programs like *tmake*. You do not have to know Perl to use *tmake*, unless you want to write your own template sets.

The *tmake* tool itself is also freeware, and is available from *http://www.troll.no/freebies/tmake.html*.

tmake comes in a compressed tar file or a zip file. To install, unpack it and set the environment variable TMAKEPATH to the subdirectory suitable for your platform. For example, if you are using the Microsoft Visual C++ compiler, the appropriate directory is *tmake\lib\win32-msvc*. You set the environment variable as follows:

```
set TMAKEPATH=c:\tmake\lib\win32-msvc
```

If you have unpacked *tmake* somewhere else, you will have to adapt the path to your situation.

The *tmake* tool supports other Windows compilers, including the Borland compiler, the Symantec compiler, and the Win32 G++ compiler, so chances are that you will find suitable template sets for your development environment. For Unix systems, template sets for several Unix variants, each for the native compiler and the GNU compiler g++, are provided. For example, if you are running Irix and want to use the native compiler, you would use

```
TMAKEPATH=/usr/local/tmake/lib/irix-dcc
export TMAKEPATH
```

if you are using the Bourne shell or

```
setenv TMAKEPATH /usr/local/tmake/lib/irix-dcc
```

if you are using the C-shell. On Windows, this would be

```
TMAKEPATH=c:\tmake\lib\win32-msvc
```

for the Visual C++ compiler, and something similar for other compilers.

The last thing you have to do is make the *tmake* command available in your path either by copying it into a directory that is already in your path, or by adding the directory *tmake/bin* to your PATH environment variable.

Now you need to know how to write a project file. This is very easy. Let's first write a project file for the first scribble application from the tutorial in Chapter 2, *qtscribble1*. This project does not have any header files, and consists of one source file, *qtscribble1.cpp*. Therefore, we can make do with the following project file, *qtscribble1.pro*:

```
SOURCES = qtscribble1.cpp
TARGET  = qtscribble1
```

That's all there is to it. Run *tmake* with

```
tmake -o Makefile qtscribble.pro
```

The *tmake* tool automatically detects whether you want to generate a makefile for Windows or Unix from the template files, and reads the compiler options from these. We won't show the generated makefile here, since it is long and uninteresting for now.

There are many options in *tmake*, but fortunately most of these have sensible defaults. For example, if you are building an application, you do not have to specify that, because this is *tmake*'s default. On the other hand, if you are building a library, you must tell *tmake* about it by including the following two lines in the project file:

```
TEMPLATE = lib
VERSION  = 1.9
```

The VERSION tag applies only to Unix systems, and indicates the version number of the shared library that will be built.

The CONFIG tag lets you fine tune how *tmake* should generate your makefile. The valid options are shown in Table 19-2.

Table 19-2: tmake Options

Option	Meaning
qt	Tells *tmake* this is a Qt-based project, and that support for moc-generated files should be included. This is the default.
opengl	Tells *tmake* you want to use the OpenGL extension.
warn_on	Tells *tmake* the compiler should emit as many warnings as possible. This is the default, if no CONFIG entry is present.
warn_off	Tells *tmake* the compiler should emit as few warnings as possible. This is not recommended.
release	Tells *tmake* the code should be optimized for production. This is the default, if no CONFIG entry is present.
debug	Tells *tmake* the compiler should include debugging symbols, and not use optimization.

For example, you could use the following CONFIG line:

```
CONFIG = qt warn_off debug
```

If you want to add a *tmake* project file to an existing application, it is tiresome and error-prone to list all sources and header files by hand. *tmake* comes with another utility called progen, which can scan your source files in one directory and automatically build a template file for you to start with. You run progen like this:

```
progen -n projectname -o project file
```

If you want to know all the nitty-gritty details about using *tmake*, check out the documentation in *tmake/doc/tmake.html* and the reference documentation in *tmake/doc/tmake_ref.html*. The latter also tells you how to write your own template files, if you want to port *tmake* to a platform that is not yet supported.

We don't want to finish this section without mentioning a little trick that is useful when working with *tmake*. Often you want to compile your project as a release or as a debugging version, and you want to be able to determine on the command line which version to build. Since a project file can be configured for building either version, but not for both of them, it is not possible to adapt the project file for this. Since *tmake* runs fast, however, why not keep two project files around and generate the makefile before each build on-the-fly? For the *qtscribble1* program, you could have the following two project files:

```
# qtscribble-release.pro
CONFIG  = qt release warn-off
SOURCES = qtscribble1.cpp
TARGET  = qtscribble-release
```

```
# qtscribble-debug.pro
CONFIG  = qt debug warn-on
SOURCES = qtscribble1.cpp
TARGET  = qtscribble-debug
```

Then, write two shell scripts or batch files, like the following `rmake`:

```
tmake -o Makefile qtscribble-release.pro
make
```

and `dmake`:

```
tmake -o Makefile qtscribble-debug.pro
make
```

Modern command-line interpreters (shells) also allow you to write these as aliases, which would be even better. Now you only have to call either `rmake` or `dmake` in order to build a release or a debugging version.

This procedure has one disadvantage: When you add source or header files, you have to add them to both project files. On the other hand, this gives you more flexibility, since you can have source files that are only compiled for one of the versions. For example, special debug routines that are replaced by dummy stubs in the release version. If the only thing you want to change is the `CONFIG` line and you don't need the additional flexibility, you don't need to have two project files around. You can help yourself with a call like:

```
tmake -o Makefile qtscribble.pro "CONFIG+=debug"
```

or

```
tmake -o Makefile qtscribble.pro "CONFIG+=release"
```

tmake is an outstanding tool, and when you want to keep your makefiles portable across both platforms, Unix and Windows, it is almost indispensable.

20

Using GUI Builders

When you are writing a program that contains a lot of dialogs, you might get tired of having to program all those dialogs, getting the positions and sizes right, and struggling with layout management (see Chapter 6, *Using Layout Managers*). This might be the moment for using a GUI builder. No GUI builder ships with Qt, nor is one available separately from the makers of Qt, Troll Tech. But if you are using Unix, there are at least three free GUI builders available. We will introduce these later in this chapter.

Before we look at these GUI builders, it is worthwhile to explain what GUI builders can and cannot do for you. We need to stress the difference between a GUI builder and an application builder. A GUI builder helps you write dialogs, or even other windows, and can provide editors for other GUI elements, such as menu bars or pixmaps. An application builder, on the other hand, helps you set up the structure of the application. It usually generates a complete, albeit empty, application at the click of a button, complete with a makefile. Of course, there is no reason why GUI builders and application builders should not be integrated into one program (as with the Visual Studio on Windows), but this is not always the case.

If you write your dialogs with hard-coded positions, GUI builders can help you figure out the correct positions, so that all GUI elements have an acceptable size and none overlap. Unfortunately, not all GUI builders let you build parent-child hierarchies in a dialog. Some require you to make all GUI elements children of the top level window.

If you want to use layout management, there is much less support from GUI builders. Some of the available GUI builders for Qt support layout management, but it is usually very rudimentary support.

What a GUI builder cannot do is help you design your GUI to look consistent, cohesive, and logical to the user. The builder can help you decide whether it is better to put the text-entry field 10 or 20 pixels away from a pushbutton, but it cannot help you decide whether it is obvious to the user that they have some logical relationship.

Most GUI builders do not allow you to switch between the builder and a normal editor, because the two would mutually overwrite the changes. One GUI builder for Qt, *QtArchitect*, has a mechanism for avoiding this. Another one, *QtEZ*, at least provides built-in editors for adding additional source code. Most of the GUI builders also provide editors for setting up the signal/slot connections. Of course, this can only work for GUI elements that you have designed or used in the GUI builder itself, not in code written somewhere else.

Before we go through the available GUI builders, please note that all of these are written by voluntary programmers in their spare time, and that they make their work freely available. They all appreciate reports about bugs and missing features, but please be polite, and always remember that the developers are doing this for free.

QtArchitect

QtArchitect, written by Jeff Harris and Klaus Ebner and available from *http://www.primenet.com/~jtharris/qtarch*, was the first GUI builder available for Qt. It supports all the widgets that are in Qt 1.4x.

QtArchitect contains some features that make designing dialogs easier. For example, by default all widgets positioned in a dialog automatically snap to a grid, thus helping with the alignment of the buttons. After you have positioned a widget, you can open an Attributes dialog, where you set everything that you could usually set programmatically from Qt. Figure 20-1 shows a widget being added to an otherwise empty dialog, together with the tab dialog that lets you set the properties of the widget. The page visible in that tab dialog is one of the pages that contains settings that apply to all widgets. All properties tab dialogs are set up this way: The first pages contain settings, such as geometry and signals and slots that apply to all widgets, and the last page contains widget-specific properties.

QtArchitect provides a means for using box layout management, but not grid layout management. I did not find it particularly easy to use, but this is not the fault of QtArchitect. It stems from the complexity inherent to layout management.

QtArchitect allows you to integrate your own widgets, but lets you specify only the class names of the widgets. It makes no attempt to set their characteristics.

QtArchitect provides a means for two-way editing or jumping back and forth between the dialog editor and any source code editor without losing changes. This is achieved by generating two classes for every dialog. The first class contains the widgets, their positions, and their settings and should never be edited by hand. The second class is derived from the first, and is the place where you should add your own code. After the initial code generation, the source and header file for this class are never touched by QtArchitect again.

QtArchitect also has a pixmap editor (see Figure 20-2) that is useful for such tasks as designing pixmaps for tool-bar buttons. It also allows you to group dialogs and pixmaps into a project, so that you can load and save them all together.

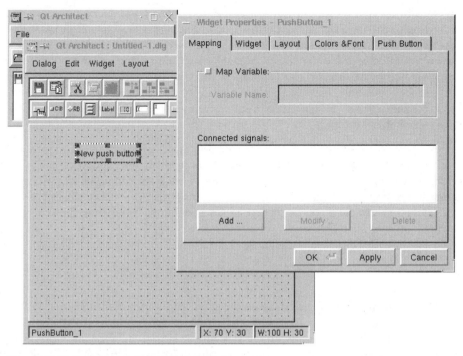

Figure 20-1: Building a dialog with QtArchitect

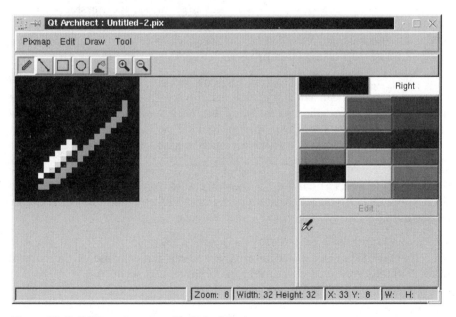

Figure 20-2: Editing pixmaps with QtArchitect

One thing we do not like about QtArchitect is the generated code. Machine-generated code is never very readable, but the code from QtArchitect seems worse than most. For one thing, this comes from the separation into two source and header files, which is needed for QtArchitect's implementation of two-way editing.[1] The other factor is that enumeration constants are emitted to the source code with the numerical values instead of their symbolic constants. For example, instead of `setFrameStyle( QFrame::Sunken | QFrame::Panel );`, it emits `setFrameStyle( 50 );`, which makes the code unnecessarily hard to read.

Despite these points, QtArchitect is a great tool for rapid prototyping. You can put together a dialog very fast, and then have your users try it. If you and your users are happy with the way the dialog is designed, you can go back and implement it by hand, adding complete layout management, too. The daunting task of writing dialogs is not writing the actual lines of code (cut and paste helps a lot here), but getting the sizes and positions right.

QtEZ

QtEZ, written by Sam Magnuson and available from *http://qtez.commkey.net*, comes closest to being a complete application builder. Besides having editors for dialogs and menu bars (see Figure 20-3 for the latter), it can also generate a *main* function and a makefile, and compile, run, and debug your program all from within QtEZ. In addition, QtEZ contains simple source editors for your classes, making it possible to add small pieces of code to the generated classes. This makes up a bit for the missing two-way capability, but you would probably not want to edit larger chunks of code in these editors without the usual conveniences of syntax coloring and automatic indentation. Like QtArchitect, QtEZ can group dialogs to a project.

Figure 20-4 shows QtEZ editing a dialog, and setting the properties of a push-button just added to the dialog. You can see at a glance that, unlike QtArchitect, QtEZ does not let you edit the settings of a widget in a tab dialog, but rather uses a property editor similar to those in Visual Basic or Java development tools. This lets you see all settings at once, but it might be more difficult to find a certain setting, because they are sorted alphabetically rather than by function.

QtEZ adds new GUI elements as children of the current active GUI element, which can lead to strange results when you add something by accident as a child of a `QLineEdit` or another widget that is not meant to have child widgets.

Most dialogs have a help button that displays a question mark. When you click on the help button, a message box opens that informs you about the purpose of the current editor window, and tells you what you can do in the individual sections.

---

1   The other way to implement two-way editing, as used by Visual Studio from Microsoft, is embedding special characters into comments. This makes the code look just as ugly.

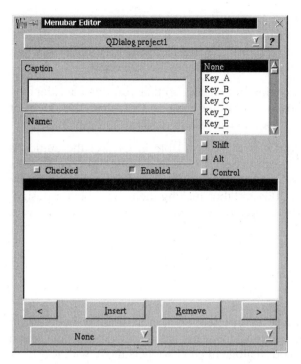

Figure 20-3: Editing menus with QtEZ

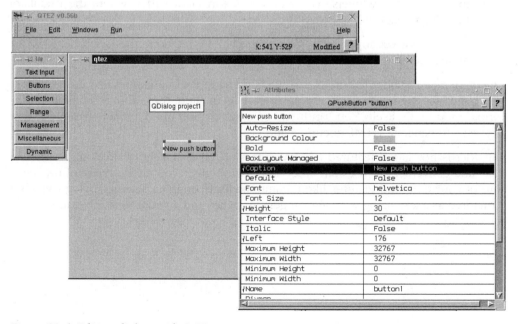

Figure 20-4: Editing dialogs with QtEZ

Every configuration dialog also has a combo box from which you can choose the part of your application that you wish to configure. You don't have to leave the configuration dialog, select another widget, and reenter that widget's configuration dialog when you want to switch between widgets or other parts that need configuring.

Finally, you can lock a widget to its position in a dialog, so that you don't accidentally move it around while changing the positions of other widgets. Of course, this does not prevent the widget from being moved programmatically at runtime.

QtEZ does not yet contain support for all widgets available in Qt, but the author is actively pursuing development, so you can expect a version supporting more widgets by the time this book goes to press. In addition, QtEZ provides a mechanism for dynamically linking new widgets into QtEZ and thus making them available for designing your dialog. This is very useful when you have written your own widgets and want to include them in your dialogs.

EBuilder

EBuilder, written by Ernie van der Meer and available from *http://www.fys.ruu.nl/~meer/Ebuilder*, is a dialog editor whose main intention was to simplify building up widget hierarchies from parent-child relationships. This has the advantage that when you move a parent widget around in your dialog, all child widgets move with it.

To enforce this, the main window of EBuilder contains a tree view that shows the relationship between the widgets. You can see this in Figure 20-5, where the calculator project has been loaded.

EBuilder does not yet support all widgets in Qt 1.33, let alone the new ones from Qt 1.4x, but like the other GUI builders, it is being actively developed.

One very nice EBuilder feature is that it lets you add documentation text to the dialogs you build (see Figure 20-6). When the code is generated, these form comments in the format used by Qt itself. You can then use another tool, the documentation generator *doxygen*, to generate HTML documentation.

EBuilder is not as full-featured as QtArchitect or QtEZ, but the dialog builder itself is easy and convenient to use. The tree view always gives you an overview of the structure of your GUI, and features like the automatically opening settings dialog (which is structured as a tab dialog with several general pages and a widget-specific page) add to its usability.

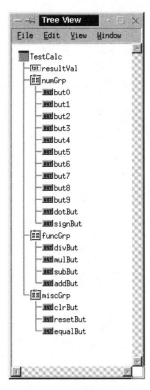

Figure 20-5: The tree view window of EBuilder

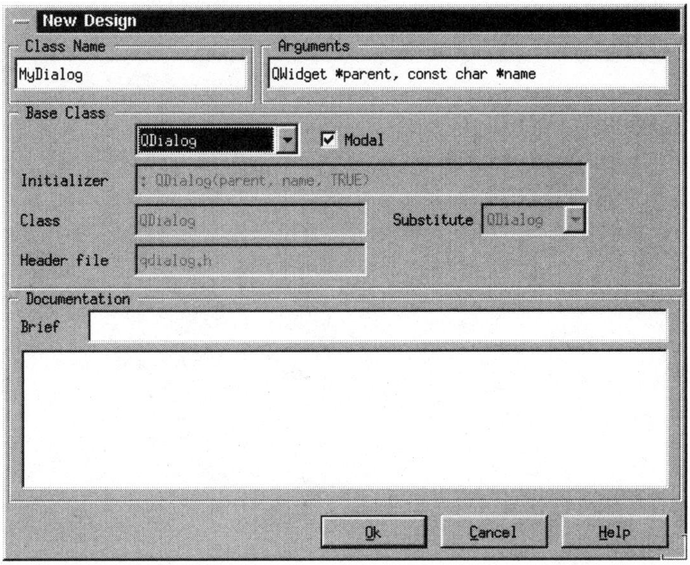

Figure 20-6: The mask for creating a new dialog in EBuilder

21

Qt Network Programming

Until now, we have only been talking about using Qt for GUI programming. This is Qt's main mission, but you can also use its classes for other things. To prove this, we will write a simple HTTP server in this chapter. Naturally, this will not be a full-featured web server like Apache or Netscape FastTrack. Instead, our server will simply echo the HTTP header that the client sends to it. This can be useful when you want to debug a client and need to check out what it actually sends to the server when it makes a request. We will provide an example of how to use the server later in this chapter.

Unfortunately, Qt does not provide all the classes that are needed for this project, so we will have to add some platform-specific code. We will encapsulate this code in special classes so that porting efforts to other platforms need to port only these classes.

Due to space constraints, we cannot provide a general introduction to network programming here. We will therefore assume that you have a basic understanding of what a socket is and how connections are set up in a TCP/IP-based network. The standard book for network programming on Unix systems is *Unix Network Programming* by W. Richard Stevens; for Windows you could try *Windows Sockets Network Programming* by Bob Quinn and Dave Shute.

The central Qt class in this example will be QSocketNotifier. This class is rather simple, but very useful when dealing with alternate input sources like sockets or named pipes. Objects of this class "watch" a certain file descriptor and emit the signal activated(int) when something happens on that descriptor. You can choose whether you want to be notified about the socket being ready for reading, writing, or exceptional conditions.

In addition to QSocketNotifier, we will mainly use the string processing capabilities of QString. Before we go more deeply into the details of the server, see Example 21-1 to get a first impression of the code.

Example 21-1: A simple HTTP server with Qt

```
 1 /*
 2  * A simple mirroring HTTP server in Qt.
 3  *
 4  * Copyright 1998, Matthias Kalle Dalheimer
 5  */
 6
 7 #define PORT 8080
 8
 9 #include <qapplication.h>
10 #include <qfile.h>
11 #include <qintdict.h>
12 #include <qsocketnotifier.h>
13 #include <qstring.h>
14 #include <qtextstream.h>
15
16 /* Platform-specific includes. */
17 #ifdef _WS_X11_
18 #include <netinet/in.h>
19 #include <sys/socket.h>
20 #include <sys/types.h>
21 #include <unistd.h>
22 #elif _WS_WIN_
23 #include <winsock2.h>
24 #include <io.h>
25 #endif
26
27 class Socket
28 {
29 public:
30   Socket();
31   ~Socket();
32
33   void close();
34   int handle() { return fd; }
35
36   void read( QString& text );
37   void write( const char* text );
38
39   void setFd( int fd );
40
41 private:
42   int _fd;
43   QFile* _file;
44   QTextStream* _tstream;
45 };
46
47
48 class ServerSocket : public Socket
49 {
50 public:
```

Example 21-1: A simple HTTP server with Qt (continued)

```
51   ServerSocket( int port );
52
53   Socket* accept();
54 };
55
56
57 class HTTPMirrorServer : QObject
58 {
59   Q_OBJECT
60
61 public:
62   HTTPMirrorServer();
63   ~HTTPMirrorServer();
64
65 private slots:
66   void connectionWanted( int );
67   void dataArrived( int );
68
69 private:
70   ServerSocket* _serversocket;
71   QSocketNotifier* _notifier;
72   QIntDict<Socket> _socketlist;
73   QIntDict<QSocketNotifier> _notifierlist;
74 };
75
76
77 #include "httpserv.moc"
78
79 /* The Socket constructor only initializes the member variables. */
80 Socket::Socket()
81 {
82   _file = 0;
83   _tstream = 0;
84   _fd = -1;
85 }
86
87
88 /* Close the socket when destroyed in case this has not been done
89    yet. Delete the QFile and the QTextStream. */
90
91 Socket::~Socket()
92 {
93   close();
94
95   delete _file;
96   delete _tstream;
97 }
98
99
100 /* Close the socket. */
```

Example 21-1: A simple HTTP server with Qt (continued)

```
101 void Socket::close()
102 {
103   ::close( _fd );
104   _file->close();
105 }
106
107
108 /* Sets the _fd member and creates QFile/QTextStream pair for easier I/O. */
109 void Socket::setFd( int newfd )
110 {
111   _fd = newfd;
112
113   // Close and delete the old _file and _tstream in case it had already
114   // been opened.
115   delete _file;
116   delete _tstream;
117
118   // Open with the new file descriptor
119   _file = new QFile();
120   _file->open( IO_ReadWrite, newfd );
121
122   // Create a QTextStream object on that file
123   _tstream = new QTextStream( _file );
124 }
125
126
127
128 /* Read one line of data from the socket. */
129 void Socket::read( QString& text )
130 {
131   text = _tstream->readLine();
132 }
133
134
135 /* Write data to the socket. */
136 void Socket::write( const char* text )
137 {
138   *_tstream << text;
139 }
140
141
142
143 /* Create a server socket that binds the port passed in the
144    argument. After creation, the socket is already set up for
145    accepting connections. */
146 ServerSocket::ServerSocket( int port )
147 {
148   // create a OS-level socket
149   int newfd = socket( AF_INET, SOCK_STREAM, 0 );
150
```

Example 21-1: A simple HTTP server with Qt (continued)

```
151    struct sockaddr_in serverAddress;
152    memset( &serverAddress, 0, sizeof( serverAddress ) );
153    serverAddress.sin_family = AF_INET;
154    serverAddress.sin_addr.s_addr = htonl( INADDR_ANY );
155    serverAddress.sin_port = htons( port );
156
157    // bind the socket to the port
158    bind( newfd, (sockaddr*)&serverAddress, sizeof( serverAddress ) );
159
160    // and listen (allow up to five backlogged connections)
161    listen( newfd, 5 );
162
163    setFd( newfd );
164 }
165
166
167 /* Accept a connection by creating a new socket for passing data
168    between client and server. It is the caller's responsibility to
169    delete the Socket object. */
170 Socket* ServerSocket::accept()
171 {
172    struct sockaddr client_addr; /* will contain the client's address,
173                                      not used here */
174    int len;
175    // accept the connection
176    int newfd = ::accept( handle(), &client_addr, &len );
177    Socket* newSocket = new Socket();
178    newSocket->setFd( newfd );
179
180    return newSocket;
181 }
182
183
184
185
186 /* Constructs the server by creating a QKServerSocket on a
187    (hard-coded) port.  */
188 HTTPMirrorServer::HTTPMirrorServer()
189 {
190    // create the socket
191    _serversocket = new ServerSocket( PORT );
192
193    // demand notification when there is data to be read from the socket
194    _notifier = new QSocketNotifier( _serversocket->handle(),
195                                      QSocketNotifier::Read );
196    connect( _notifier, SIGNAL( activated( int ) ),
197             this, SLOT( connectionWanted( int ) ) );
198 }
199
200
```

Example 21-1: A simple HTTP server with Qt (continued)

```
201 /* Destroys the server by removing the notifier and the server
202    socket. */
203 HTTPMirrorServer::~HTTPMirrorServer()
204 {
205   delete _notifier;
206   delete _serversocket;
207 }
208
209
210 /* This slot is called whenever data is coming from the server socket,
211    as when a client demands a connection. It accepts the connection and
212    sets a socket that will do the actual communication.*/
213 void HTTPMirrorServer::connectionWanted( int )
214 {
215   // Accept the connection. This automatically creates a new socket
216   // for the communication.
217   Socket* socket = _serversocket->accept();
218
219   // Enter the socket/file descriptor pair into a list so we can
220   // find the address of the socket later.
221   _socketlist.insert( socket->handle(), socket );
222
223   // Demand notification for this socket as well.
224   QSocketNotifier* dataNotifier = new QSocketNotifier( socket->handle(),
225                                                        QSocketNotifier::Read );
226   connect( dataNotifier, SIGNAL( activated( int ) ),
227            this, SLOT( dataArrived( int ) ) );
228
229   // Enter the notifier in a list as well so that it can be deleted
230   // later on.
231   _notifierlist.insert( socket->handle(), dataNotifier );
232 }
233
234
235 /* This slot is called when data arrives via one of the data
236    sockets. It reads the header until an empty line occurs, and
237    echoes it back to the client. */
238 void HTTPMirrorServer::dataArrived( int handle )
239 {
240   // Retrieve the Socket object that corresponds to the handle. After
241   // this slot has run, we don't need the socket any longer, so we can
242   // now use take() to remove it from the list.
243   Socket* socket = _socketlist.take( handle );
244
245   if( !socket )
246     // Something strange has happened, better back out of here.
247     return;
248
249   // Read the data line by line, and echo it back until a blank line
250   // (which marks the end of the header) occurs.
```

Example 21-1: A simple HTTP server with Qt (continued)

```
251    QString line;
252    socket->read( line );
253    while( !line.isEmpty() )
254      {
255        // Echo back
256        line += '\n';
257        socket->write( line );
258        // Get next line
259        socket->read( line );
260      }
261
262    // We do not need the socket any longer. Remove its
263    // notifier from the list, and delete the socket itself and the
264    // notifier. The socket has already been removed from the list a few
265    // lines up.
266    delete socket;
267    delete _notifierlist.take( handle );
268 }
269
270
271 int main( int argc, char* argv[] )
272 {
273    // We need a QApplication object, but there won't be any widgets.
274    QApplication a( argc, argv );
275
276    // Creating a server object starts the server.
277    HTTPMirrorServer server;
278
279    return a.exec();
280 }
```

The server is organized in three classes. `Socket` provides basic services, like reading from and writing to a socket. It encapsulates the file descriptor that identifies the socket to the operating system and holds a `QFile` and a `QTextStream` object. Their only task it is to facilitate input and output.

`ServerSocket` inherits from `Socket`, and binds to a port passed in the constructor. The additional method `accept()` can accept a connection from a client, and returns a pointer to a `Socket` object. If we wrote a client as well, we would derive another class `ClientSocket` from `Socket`, which would be able to connect to a `ServerSocket` object.

The work is done in the class `HTTPMirrorServer`. In the constructor of this class, a `ServerSocket` is created, and a `QSocketNotifier` is used to notify the application when a client wishes to connect. In this case, `QSocketNotifier` emits the `activated ( int )` signal which is connected to `HTTPMirrorServer::connectionWanted`. Here, `ServerSocket::accept()` is called to create a new socket over which all data is passed. As with the `ServerSocket` object, a `QSocketNotifier` object is created to notify the application when the client has sent some data. In contrast to the *server socket* there can be more than one socket for data connections, since more than client can connect at the same time. We will have to save the association between the file descriptor, which is the parameter of the `activated( int )` signal, and both the `Socket` object and the `QSocketNotifier` object. This is done in two `QIntDict` objects, which are members of `HTTPMirrorServer`.

When new data arrives from a client, the slot `HTTPMirrorServer::dataArrived ( int )` is called. This method reads data from the client until it receives an empty line, a sure sign that the header is finished. At the same loop in which the data is read, it is echoed back to the client. Finally, both the socket that is no longer needed and the notifier are deleted.

The `main()` method is very simple in this case. We still need a `QApplication` object; because otherwise `QSocketNotifier` would not work. We do not need any widgets, however. By simply creating the `HTTPMirrorServer` object, we make the server ready for accepting connections.

Note that the only places where platform-dependent code can be found are the methods of `ServerSocket`; everything else should be portable, provided that all platforms have a `close()` function in their system libraries and identify file descriptors via `int`s. This is the case for all platforms that Qt supports.

To test this example, use any web browser. The server does not listen on the default port 80 for HTTP connection requests, because binding this port is usually possible only for priviliged processes. Instead, it uses port 8080, which should be available to everyone.[1]

If you want to use another port, just change the value of the `PORT` pre-processor symbol at the beginning of the listing.

If you use the default `PORT` value of 8080, you can simply point any web browser to *http://localhost:8080/*. Note that you do not need a web server running on your machine, because this program *is* the web server. You should see some lines like the following ones in your browser window, although some browsers run all the text in a single row:

```
Read GET / HTTP/1.0
Read Connection: Keep-Alive
Read User-Agent: Mozilla/4.03 [en] (X11; I; Linux 2.0.33 i586; Nav)
Read Host: localhost:8080
Read Accept: image/gif, image/x-xbitmap, image/jpeg, image/pjpeg, */*
Read Accept-Language: de-DE,sv
Read Accept-Charset: iso-8859-1,*,utf-8
```

We used Netscape Communicator 4.03 for Linux to test this example.

---

1   Unless someone else has bound to that port, of course.

22

Interfacing Qt with Other Languages and Libraries

Qt comes with several *extensions*. These provide additional features that are not in the normal Qt library. These extensions are only needed for special applications and thus should not bloat "normal" applications. You have to compile these extensions separately, since they are not included in the normal Qt build process. This is no problem, since compiling normally means no more than calling *make* on Unix, or *nmake* on Windows, in the respective directories.

We will describe three of those extensions in this chapter. We'll also discuss the possibility of integrating Qt with other programming languages. Programmers who like Qt but don't like C++ have written language bindings for other languages, such as Perl, and made these freely available on the Internet. We will look at how to use these, and how programming with Qt looks in Perl.

Please note that these sections require additional knowledge that is not directly related to Qt and, therefore, not covered in this book. For example, to use the OpenGL extension, you need to know how to use OpenGL. To call Qt from Perl programs, you will obviously need some Perl knowledge.

OpenGL Programming with Qt

Then OpenGL extension of Qt makes it possible to write OpenGL programs and still use Qt for the GUI. OpenGL is a platform- and language-independent API standard for three-dimensional vector graphics, and is used on many platforms. Windows NT comes with OpenGL libraries, as do some Unix systems, including Irix. For other Unix systems, there are commercial implementations of OpenGL available. There is also a free implementation of OpenGL for Unix, MESA, which might not include all the latest features and might not exploit your 3D graphics board to the fullest, but it is a cheap alternative that's well-suited for getting started with OpenGL graphics programming—and even for doing "real" work.

No matter which OpenGL implementation you choose, it might always be a good idea to compile the OpenGL extension and the sample programs that come with it, and then run the samples to ensure that everything works smoothly. Depending on your implementation, you might have to change some include paths or library names in the makefiles that come with Qt. If you use MESA on Unix or you use Windows NT, no changes should be necessary.

WARNING   We cannot include a course on OpenGL programming here, because that would be enough material for another book. We therefore assume that you have some knowledge about OpenGL programming and know crucial terms like display lists, or that you can read up on them. If you are the "learning-by-doing" type, it might also be a good idea to read through the examples provided with your OpenGL implementation, and then try to make them run inside a Qt application.

Being able to use OpenGL and Qt together is a great advantage, because it takes away the burden of having to implement UI elements from scratch again from OpenGL programmers. The Qt OpenGL extension integrates nicely into Qt by providing a widget for OpenGL drawing. Altogether, the OpenGL extension consists of these three classes:

QGLWidget
> To its parents, this widget behaves just like any other Qt widget. You create it in the usual window hierarchy, and it is even suitable for layout management. Inside the widget, however, you paint with Open GL functions, not Qt painter. If you don't have any special needs, QGLWidget is the only class from the OpenGL extension you will explicitly use.

QGLContext
> This is an OpenGL context, a collection of OpenGL state variables. QGLWidget automatically creates such a context for you, but if you want to switch between multiple contexts, you can create objects of this class, and set and retrieve them with QGLWidget::setContext() and QGLWidget::context().

QGLFormat
> If the default settings of QGLWidget are not sufficient, you can use an object of this class to configure and set options like alpha blending, double buffering, or stencil buffering. Objects of this class are set and retrieved from QGLWidget with QGLWidget::setFormat() and QGLWidget::format().

Let's look at what is needed to use OpenGL functions in Qt. First, you need a class that is derived from QGLWidget. Create an object of this class just like any other widget, and put it in your widget hierarchy.

In your class that is derived from `QGLWidget`, reimplement the three methods `initializeGL()`, `paintGL()`, and `resizeGL()`. Note that you do not reimplement `paintEvent()` and `resizeEvent()` in this case. The `initializeGL()` method is used for setting up the OpenGL subsystem. For example, you could create your display lists here, if you don't change them at runtime. Note that all OpenGL-specific initialization should be done here and not in the widget's constructor. The `repaintGL()` method is called each time the widget is resized (and thus also before it is shown first), and should be used for setting up size-specific parameters, such as viewports and matrix modes. Finally, `paintGL()` is where you actually perform the OpenGL drawing—just as you perform `QPainter` drawing in `paintEvent()`.

It is only possible to call OpenGL functions directly inside the three methods `initializeGL()`, `paintGL()`, and `resizeGL()`. Everywhere else, including in the constructor, you first have to call `QGLWidget::makeCurrent()` to make the widget the current OpenGL output.

To finish this section, Example 22-1 contains a program that draws a Sierpinski Gasket, a classic in graphics programming. It's not 3D, but unfortunately most 3D examples are either too boring or too long to be printed here. The example is adapted from the very recommendable *Interactive Computer Graphics* by Edward Angel. Figure 22-1 shows the output.

Example 22-1: Using OpenGL within Qt

```
 1 #include <qapplication.h>
 2 #include <stdlib.h>
 3 #include <qgl.h>
 4
 5 class SierpinskiWidget : public QGLWidget
 6 {
 7 public:
 8   virtual void paintGL();
 9   virtual void initializeGL();
10   virtual void resizeGL( int w, int h );
11 };
12
13 void SierpinskiWidget::paintGL()
14 {
15   typedef GLfloat point2[2];
16   point2 vertices[3] = {{ 0.0,.0},{200.0,175.00},{400.0,0.0}}; // triangle
17   point2 p = { width()/2.0, height()/2.0 }; // initial point
18
19   glClear( GL_COLOR_BUFFER_BIT );
20
21   /* Compute and plot 5000 new points */
22   for( int k = 0; k < 5000; k++ ) {
23     int j = rand() % 3; // pick a random vertex
24
25     // Compute the point between the vertex and the old point
26     p[0] = ( p[0] + vertices[j][0] ) / 2.0;
```

Example 22-1: Using OpenGL within Qt (continued)

```
27      p[1] = ( p[1] + vertices[j][1] ) / 2.0;
28
29      // Plot new point
30      glBegin( GL_POINTS );
31      glVertex2fv( p );
32      glEnd();
33    }
34
35    glFlush();
36 }
37
38
39 void SierpinskiWidget::initializeGL()
40 {
41    glClearColor( 1.0, 1.0, 1.0, 1.0 );
42    glColor3f( 1.0, 0.0, 0.0 );
43 }
44
45
46 void SierpinskiWidget::resizeGL( int w, int h )
47 {
48    glMatrixMode( GL_PROJECTION );
49    glLoadIdentity();
50    gluOrtho2D( 0.0, w, 0.0, h );
51    glMatrixMode( GL_MODELVIEW );
52
53    updateGL();
54 }
55
56 int main( int argc, char* argv[] )
57 {
58      QApplication::setColorSpec( QApplication::CustomColor );
59      QApplication a(argc,argv);
60
61      SierpinskiWidget* w = new SierpinskiWidget();
62      w->resize( 400, 350 );
63      a.setMainWidget( w );
64      w->show();
65      return a.exec();
66 }
```

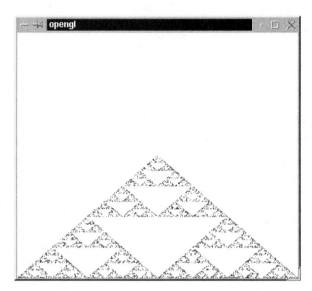

Figure 22-1: A Sierpinski gasket with the Qt OpenGL extension

Writing Netscape Plugins

Plugins are little pieces of code that are loaded at runtime by the web browser Netscape Navigator[1]. They enhance the capabilities of the browser by, for example, providing new graphics formats or other features that are not built in. Plugins are not new, nor are they an invention of Netscape. Programs like Adobe Photoshop have used plugin technology in the past. Note that the different plugin interfaces are incompatible: You cannot use a plugin written for Netscape Navigator in Photoshop.

Technically, a plugin is a Dynamic Link Library (DLL) on Windows platforms, and a Shared Object on Unix systems. The plugin has to be copied into a special directory so that it can be found by the browser. In addition, special linking conventions have to be followed on Windows. On Unix systems, no special linker flags are necessary, as long as a Shared Library is built and all necessary symbols are exported.

Since the building and installation procedures can differ greatly on the platforms, and might even change from browser to browser version, we won't go into much detail about this here. Read the release notes and the instructions for your platform. There are many platform-related idiosyncrasies, like the fact that you have to name your plugin np*name*.dll on Windows because the browser won't recognize it otherwise.

The first thing you should do before you try to develop plugins with Qt is download the Plugin Software Development Kit (Plugin SDK) from Netscape's FTP server (*ftp. netscape.com*), read the intructions contained therein, and compile and install one of

---

1   Many plugins also work in Microsoft Internet Explorer.

the sample plugins. There is one Plugin SDK for every platform, so make sure you get the correct one. The makefiles contained therein should already be appropriate for your platform, and can be used as templates for plugins built with Qt.

After you have compiled and installed one of the sample plugins from the Plugin SDK, quit and then restart your browser. Next, select About Plugins from the Help menu. Your sample plugin should be listed there. If it is not listed, go through the documentation provided with the Plugin SDK, and make sure you followed all instructions. Check that your plugin has an accepted name, and has been copied to the correct directory.

The next thing you need to know about plugins is that the selection is based on MIME types. A MIME (Multimedia Internet Mail Extension) type is a description of the content of some piece of data. It is divided into a major type and a minor type, which are separated by a slash. For example, text/html is the MIME type for HTML pages.

Netscape plugins register one or more MIME types that they can handle. Whenever the browser receives data tagged with this MIME type, it activates the plugin and forwards the data to it. The MIME types that a plugin declares are shown in the page you get when choosing About Plugins, but the real assignment between MIME types, plugins, external applications, and internal browser code is done on the Navigator/Plugins page of the Preferences dialog of Netscape Navigator 4.

Since the server determines the MIME type of a piece of data, and since you might not have the rights to configure a server so that it delivers the desired MIME type for your plugin, it is a good thing that plugins can also register a file extension.[2] If you had a plugin for displaying PNG images, you would probably register the MIME type image/png and the extension *.png. The extensions that a plugin has registered are also listed in the About Plugins page.

Now that you know how and when the browser invokes your plugin, it's time to look at what is needed to actually write one. The plugin API consists of two sets of functions and some structures. The functions that start with NPP_ are provided by the plugin, and are called by the browser when it needs information about the plugin (for example, which extension and MIME type it wants to serve on Unix platforms), when it passes data into the plugin, or when it wants to invoke some functions within in the plugin. The functions in the other set start with NPN_. These contain services that the browser provides for the plugin. To develop a plugin, you have to implement all the NPP_ functions, and you can use the NPN_ functions for help.

Writing plugins can be very cumbersome, because there are a lot of details to consider, such as registration. This is where Qt comes in. The Qt Netscape plugin extension provides a framework with which you can develop plugins much faster than you could by simply using the plugin API. The extension consists of a static library that you must link to your plugin code. In addition to making writing plugins easier, the Qt plugin extension also lets you use all the power of Qt in your plugins.

---

2   A caveat: Netscape Navigator never looks at the filename extensions for files retrieved via HTTP, it always believes the web server. Filename extensions are used only for local files and documents retrieved via FTP.

The Qt plugin extension consists of four classes, of which you have to subclass at least three:

QNPlugin

As the documentation says, "this class is the heart of the plugin". The browser calls the static method QNPlugin::create(), which is supposed to return a pointer to a subclass of QNPlugin. There is never more than one object of this class; multiple plugins of a class are dealt with by means of *instances*, which are covered by the next class, QNPInstance. QNPlugin is also the class that tells the browser which MIME types at which file extensions the plugin can handle. This is done by reimplementing getMIMEDescription(), and returning a string that contains the MIME type and the extension. The format of this string is shown later in this section. The browser then calls this function and parses the string. There are two more functions with which the browser queries information about the plugin: getPluginNameString() and getPluginDescriptionString(). Reimplementing these is not obligatory.

Please note that getMIMEDescription(), getPluginNameString() and getPluginDescriptionString() are declared and necessary only on Unix systems. On Windows systems, the same information comes from a resource file.[3]

QNPInstance

There is one object of this class per plugin instance. Once the plugin is setup, this class takes over communication with the browser. It declares several methods that must be reimplemented in a subclass and are called by the browser. Probably the most important of these methods is newWindow() which is called once by the browser when the plugin should go ahead and display itself for the first time. All plugins that have a visual representation[4] should reimplement this method and return a pointer to their widget, which must be a subclass of QNPWidget. Another important method is newStreamCreated(), which the plugin must also overload. The browser calls this method to tell the plugin that there is data available for it, and to ask whether the plugin wants to have the data in parts as a stream or as a whole file. The browser either calls writeReady() and write() for streaming data, or streamAsFile() for whole files.

QNPWidget

This widget provides the event and drawing interface between the browser and the plugin. You create a subclass of this class, which can then be used either as a drawing area or as a container for child widgets. The only place where you should create an instance of a subclass of QNPWidget is in a reimplementation of QNPInstance::newWindow(), because plugin windows are always created on demand.

This widget makes all the event methods, such as paintEvent() and resizeEvent(), available. You can use them as you would with any other widget.

---

3 Yes, this is a bad idea, because you need different code and unnecessarily complex makefiles on Windows.

4 There are plugins that don't have any visual representation, for example, audio players.

QNPStream

QNPStream is the abstraction of data being streamed into the plugin from the browser. Since our example uses only file-based data for the plugins, we won't use this class.

Writing plugins is cumbersome not because the coding is especially difficult, but because it is hard to debug plugins. You cannot just start the plugin program. Even if you start the browser itself in the debugger, you cannot set a breakpoint on the plugin entry code, because the plugin is loaded dynamically at runtime. In addition, if your plugin crashes, the whole browser crashes with it, because they share the same address space. Therefore, it is advisable to develop a plugin as an ordinary widget, test and debug it, and make it a plugin only afterwards. Here is some sample code from the reference documentation that requires no modifications to the previously coded widget:

```
class MyPluginWindow : public NPWidget
{
    QWidget* _child;
public:
    MyPluginWindow()
    {
        // Some widget that is normally used as a top-level widget
        _child = new MyIndepentlyDevelopedWidget();

        // Use the bckground color of the web page
        _child->setBackgroundColor( backgroundColor() );

        // Fill the plugin widget
        _child->setGeometry( 0, 0, width(), height() );
    }

    void resizeEvent( QResizeEvent* )
    {
        // Fill the plugin widget
        _child->resize( size() );
    }
};
```

As an example, we will now write a little plugin for displaying GIF graphics. But instead of only displaying it (Netscape could do that all on its own), we will also provide a slider above the plugin with which you can rotate the image. As always, we start with the complete listing in Example 22-2 and then look at the details.

Example 22-2: A Netscape plugin for rotating GIFs

```
1 #include <qnp.h>
2 #include <qimage.h>
3 #include <qpainter.h>
4 #include <qpixmap.h>
5 #include <qslider.h>
6 #include <stdio.h>
7
8 class ViewWidget : public QWidget
```

Example 22-2: A Netscape plugin for rotating GIFs (continued)

```
 9 {
10   Q_OBJECT
11
12 private:
13   QPixmap _pm;
14   QPixmap _pmScaledRotated;
15   int _angle;
16
17 public:
18   ViewWidget( QWidget* parent = 0, const char* name = 0, WFlags flags = 0 ) :
19     QWidget( parent, name, flags ) { _angle = 0; }
20
21   void paintEvent( QPaintEvent* event )
22     {
23       QPainter p( this );
24       p.setClipRect( rect() );
25
26       if ( ( _pm.size() == size() ) && ( _angle == 0 ) ) {
27         p.drawPixmap( 0, 0, _pm );
28       } else {
29         QWMatrix m;
30         m.scale( (double)width() / _pm.width(),
31                  (double)height() / _pm.height() );
32         m.rotate( _angle );
33         _pmScaledRotated = _pm.xForm( m );
34         p.drawPixmap( 0, 0, _pmScaledRotated );
35       }
36     }
37
38   void showImage(const QImage& image)
39     {
40       _pm.convertFromImage( image, QPixmap::Color );
41       repaint( false );
42     }
43
44 public slots:
45   void newAngle( int newangle )
46     {
47       _angle = newangle;
48       repaint( true );
49     }
50 };
51
52
53 class RotateGIFView : public QNPWidget
54 {
55 public:
56   RotateGIFView()
57     {
58       _slider = new QSlider( 0, 360, 10, 0, QSlider::Horizontal, this );
```

Example 22-2: A Netscape plugin for rotating GIFs (continued)

```
59          _slider->show();
60          _view = new ViewWidget( this );
61          _view->show();
62
63          connect( _slider, SIGNAL( valueChanged( int ) ),
64                   _view, SLOT( newAngle( int ) ) );
65       }
66
67    void resizeEvent( QResizeEvent* event )
68       {
69         _slider->setGeometry( 0, 0, event->size().width(), _slider->height() );
70         _view->setGeometry( 0, _slider->height(),
71                             event->size().width(),
72                             event->size().height()-_slider->height() );
73       }
74
75    void showImage( const QImage& image )
76       {
77         _view->showImage( image );
78       }
79
80 private:
81    QSlider* _slider;
82    ViewWidget* _view;
83 };
84
85 class RotateGIFLoader : public QNPInstance
86 {
87    RotateGIFView* _view;
88    QImage _image;
89
90 public:
91    RotateGIFLoader() :
92      _view(0)
93      {
94      }
95
96    QNPWidget* newWindow()
97       {
98         _view = new RotateGIFView;
99         imageToGIF();
100        return _view;
101      }
102
103   void imageToGIF()
104      {
105        if (!_view || _image.isNull()) return;
106
107        _view->showImage(_image);
108        _image.reset();
```

Example 22-2: A Netscape plugin for rotating GIFs (continued)

```
109      }
110
111   bool newStreamCreated( QNPStream*, StreamMode& smode )
112   {
113       smode = AsFileOnly;
114       return true;
115   }
116
117   void streamAsFile( QNPStream*, const char* fname )
118   {
119       _image = QImage( fname );
120       if ( _image.isNull() )
121         debug( "Could not convert file: %s\n", fname );
122       imageToGIF();
123   }
124 };
125
126
127 class RotatePlugin : public QNPlugin
128 {
129 public:
130   RotatePlugin()
131   {
132   }
133
134   QNPInstance* newInstance()
135   {
136      return new RotateGIFLoader;
137   }
138
139   const char* getMIMEDescription() const
140   {
141       return "image/gif:gif:GIF Image";
142   }
143
144   const char * getPluginNameString() const
145   {
146       return "GIF Qt-based Image Plugin";
147   }
148
149   const char * getPluginDescriptionString() const
150   {
151   return "Lets you view and rotate a GIF image";
152   }
153 };
154
155 QNPlugin* QNPlugin::create()
156 {
157     return new RotatePlugin;
```

Example 22-2: A Netscape plugin for rotating GIFs (continued)

```
158 }
159
160 #include "plugin.moc"
```

Since we have lumped all the code into one file and defined all the methods inline, the classes appear here in reverse order of their use. To make it easier for you to follow the code, we'll describe the code from the bottom to the top.

The browser first calls the method `RotatePlugin::create()`, which in turn creates an instance of the class `RotatePlugin`. The browser then retrieves the information about the plugin by calling `RotatePlugin::getMIMEDescription()`, `RotatePlugin::getPluginNameString()`, and `RotatePlugin::getPluginDescriptionString()` (if it runs on Unix—otherwise it gets this information from the version resource of the DLL). Information from the last two methods is just displayed in the `About Plugins` page, but the string returned from the first method informs the browser about which MIME types and file extensions the plugin can handle. The string consists of three fields separated by colons: The first field contains the MIME type, the second the extension, and the third a description of this kind of data. If a plugin can serve more than one kind of data, such as different image-file formats there can be more groups of these three fields, each group separated by a semicolon.

`RotatePlugin::create()` is only called once, and therefore there is only one instance of this class. For each use of this plugin, however, there is one instance of the class `RotateGIFLoader`, which the browser demands by calling `RotatePlugin:: newInstance()`.

`RotateGIFLoader` uses standard Qt techniques for converting the image data into something usable with `QImage`. The two interesting things here are the collaboration of `newStreamCreated()` and `streamAsFile()` on the one hand, and the call to `newWindow()` on the other. The browser uses `streamAsFile()` to tell the plugin that data is available. By assigning a value to the second parameter, the plugin tells the browser whether it wants this data as a stream or as a file. Working with files is easier, but streams provide for incremental processing. This is especially useful when you have to process large amounts of data, or when you have data that is inheritly incremental, like audio or video data. In our case, a file suffices. The browser therefore first collects all the data, saves it into a temporary file, and then calls `streamAsFile()` where the name of the temporary file is passed. Finally, `newWindow()` is called when the browser wants to display the plugin. This method should return a pointer to an instance of a subclass of `QNPWindow` if the plugin has any visual appearance.

The widget `RotateGIFView` just contains ordinary Qt code, as should be fairly obvious by now. It has two child widgets, a slider for determining the angle, and a widget that finally displays the image.

The only thing that restricts this plugin from displaying graphics file formats other than GIF is the registration of this plugin as GIF-only. Since it uses the default Qt image-loading mechanisms, it could load and display other graphics file formats, like BMP or XPM, if it registered those.

To try this plugin, compile it and copy it into the directory where your browser looks for plugins. Then restart the browser and try to open a GIF file. You should now see your plugin in action. Note that Netscape seems to use a plugin declared for `image/gif` only for URLs pointing to GIF files, but not to embedded GIFs. See the information about the EMBED tag in the documentation of the Plugin SDK for more information.

The Qt Netscape plugin extension makes plugin writing a lot easier. You still have to know how plugins work and how the control flows back and forth between the browser and the plugin, but you don't have to deal with low-level X11 or Win32 event handling and drawing code—and you can use all available Qt widgets.

Integrating Xt Widgets

NOTE   This section applies only to using Qt on Unix systems. If you are using Qt on Windows only, or are using Unix, but are not concerned with reusing legacy applications, you do not need to read this.

Despite its quality, Qt is not yet in widespread use on Unix systems. A lot of legacy programs are written in Motif/Xt, and porting those applications to Qt would be a large effort. Sample porting projects like QtMozilla (see *http://www.troll.no/qtmozilla*) have shown that by using Qt, performance gains and reduced memory consumption can be achieved in comparison to using Motif/Xt, but porting a whole application might still be too much work. This is where the Qt Xt extension comes in. It allows you either to integrate Motif/Xt widgets into Qt programs or to integrate Qt widgets into Motif/Xt programs. This could also be useful if you need certain widgets in your Qt application that are not yet available for Qt, but are available for Motif/Xt.

The Qt Xt extension consists of two classes, `QXtApplication` and `QXtWidget`. `QXtApplication` has to be used instead of `QApplication` whenever you want to integrate Qt and Xt widgets. `QXtWidget` encapsulates either a Qt widget for use in Xt applications or an Xt widget in a Qt application. Because of the way Xt widgets are created and managed, a `QXtWidget` must have nothing but other `QXtWidgets` or Xt widgets as ancestors all the way to the top-level widget. This is not a great restriction, since it is easy to encapsulate Qt widgets in `QXtWidget` objects.

Since working with Qt always means working with C++ on the one hand, but Xt/Motif applications are usually written in C on the other, your first porting task is making sure that the old C code compiles with a C++ compiler. The most common problem is that strings like `private` or `class` are keywords in C++, but not in C, where they might have been used as identifiers.

Let's first look at integrating Qt widgets into legacy Motif/Xt applications. No matter what you do, when you want to use Qt widgets you need a `QApplication` object. This time, however, it is constructed differently than normal, because the command-line parameters have already been parsed by Xt, and the connection to the X display has been established as well. Therefore you use the constructor of QXtApplication that expects a pointer to an X11 Display structure. Such a pointer has been returned from XtOpenDisplay() or XOpenDisplay(). Once you have done this, you can either write a subclass of QXtWidget, or simply create an object of QXtWidget and make your desired widgets children of this widget.

On the other hand, if you want to integrate Motif/Xt widgets into an application that consists mainly of Qt code, the procedure is slightly different. Again, a QApplication object is not sufficient. You need an object of the class QXtApplication, since this class contains the necessary glue code, but this time you can use the "ordinary" type of constructor that expects argc and argv as its first two arguments. In addition, you can pass Xt-specific information: a string naming the application class for the resource database, a pointer to a structure of the type XrmOptionDeskRec for hard-coded resources, an integer value that specifies the number of options in the previous parameter, and finally a string array with hard-coded fallback resources. For an exact description, please see the manual page for XtAppInitialize.

When you have created your application object like this, you can go ahead and encapsulate Xt widgets in an object of the class QXtWidget. This is done by using the following constructor of QXtWidget:

```
QXtWidget::QXtWidget( const char* name, WidgetClass widget_class,
                      QXtWidget* parent, ArgList args, Cardinal num_args,
                      bool managed)
```

The first parameter is the ordinary Qt name. The second parameter is the widget class as used by Xt. For example, for using the Motif text-edit widget, you would pass xmTextWidgetClass here. parent is the Qt parent. As mentioned before, all ancestors until the top-level widget must be QXtWidget objects. You cannot fail here, because the compiler ensures that this constraint is met. The fourth and fifth parameters are the typical Xt resource parameters, as used by XtCreateWidget() and similar functions. Finally, when the sixth parameter is true, the widget is managed (shown) automatically.

It's hard to come up with an example that sufficiently illustrates the integration of Qt and Xt and still fits in one or two book pages. Since this topic is probably of interest to few readers anyway, we suggest that you read the three Qt distribution examples *mainlyMotif*, *mainlyXt*, and *mainlyQt*. These are in the directory *extensions/xt/examples*. All of these have two multi-line text-entry fields, where one of these is always a QMulti-LineEdit, and the other is either an Athena or a Motif text entry widget. There is one example of integrating the Athena widget into Qt, and one example each for integrating the Qt widget into both Xt and Motif.

Interfacing Qt with Perl

Qt is inherently a C++ toolkit, but this does not mean that it can only be used with C++. Ingenious programmers have made *language bindings* available, so Qt can be used with other languages. Among these are bindings for C, Python, and Perl. Since Perl is probably the most interesting of these, we'll describe what programming with Qt in Perl looks like.

Perl is a scripting language invented by Larry Wall, and now developed and maintained by volunteers via the Internet. Born on Unix systems, Perl long ago became a platform-independent language and is now at home on Windows systems and the Macintosh. Perl is also the language behind most of the CGI servers on the Web, and has therefore been dubbed "the glue of the Internet".

We don't have the space to teach you Perl here, but in case you want to learn Perl (good idea!), we recommend *Learning Perl,* by Tom Christiansen and Randal L. Schwartz. If you want to dive deeper into Perl programming, have a look at *Advanced Perl Programming,* by Sriram Srinivasan. Finally, the best reference manual is *Programming Perl,* by Larry Wall, Randal L. Schwartz, and Tom Christiansen.

PerlQt, the Perl language bindings for Qt, is written by Ashley Winters who has made it freely available. You can get it from your nearest CPAN (Comprehensive Perl Archive Network, see *http://www.perl.com/CPAN*) mirror from the directory *authors/Ashley_Winters*. It comes with build instructions, and since the configuration script is written in Perl itself, you should be able to install it on any Unix platform where Perl and a C++ compiler are installed. PerlQt is not yet ported to Windows, although this should not be too difficult and might even be done before this book hits the book-shops. Of course, you need to have Perl installed. If you use a system where Perl does not come with the operating system (like Windows or some outdated Unix systems), you can also get Perl from the CPAN.

At time of this writing, the current version of PerlQt supports only Qt 1.2. This does not mean that you cannot use the current version of Qt, but you will not be able to use any widgets introduced after Version 1.2. The author of PerlQt has promised, to make an updated version available, and it might be out by the time you read this. If you are a fairly skilled Perl programmer, you might even be able to add the missing bindings yourself by looking at the glue code for the widgets that is already available.

Once you have Perl and PerlQt installed, try to run the example programs. When these work, try one of the examples from this book. As an example, we have converted the program from Example 2-1 to Perl, see Example 22-3.

Example 22-3: Using Qt from Perl: A small example

```
1 use Qt;
2 use QLabel;
3
4 $mylabel = new QLabel( "Hello world" );
```

Example 22-3: Using Qt from Perl: A small example (continued)

```
 5 $mylabel->resize( 100, 30 );
 6
 7 $qApp->setMainWidget( $mylabel );
 8 $mylabel->show();
 9
10 exit $qApp->exec();
```

This looks so similar to the corresponding C++ code that it doesn't even need much explanation. Perl's object-oriented syntax is used here to make the code look just like it does in C++. The first line, `use Qt;`, is needed in any PerlQt program. It is not necessary to create a `QApplication` object, because PerlQt does this for you. Note that you still need to import the Qt widgets that you want to use.

What about signals and slots? Well, connecting them is trivial, because the usual connect() method is available with PerlQt as well. Assuming that you have replaced QLabel with `QPushButton` in the previous example, adding the following line would quit the application when the button is pressed:

```
$qApp->connect( $mybutton, 'clicked()', 'quit()' );
```

Defining your own class with slots and signals is easy, too. To declare a slot, use a statement like the following:

```
use slots 'myslot(arguments)';
```

and for signals:

```
use signals 'myslots(arguments)';
```

The slots are then implemented as normal subroutines within the Perl package that forms the class. There is nothing like calling *moc* when using PerlQt, because it does not need it.

To finish this chapter, Examples 22-4, 22-5, and 22-6 contain a longer PerlQt program. Together, they are a port to Perl of the program in Example 3-2. Most of the things shown here are not specific for PerlQt, but are simply part of object-oriented programming in Perl. For example, look at the constructor method called `new()`, where you can see how member variables are declared and accessed. Freestanding functions like `bitBlt()` have been integrated into the package where they fit most, `QPaintDevice` in this case.

Example 22-4: The class ScribbleArea as a Perl package

```
1 package ScribbleArea;
2
3 use QColor;
4 use QPixmap;
5 use QWidget;
6 use QPaintDevice;
7
```

Example 22-4: The class ScribbleArea as a Perl package (continued)

```perl
 8 @ISA = qw( QWidget );
 9
10 use slots 'setColor(QColor)';
11
12 #
13 # The constructor. Initializes the member variables.
14 #
15 sub new {
16    my $class = shift;
17    my $self = $class->SUPER::new(@_);
18
19    # initialize member variables
20    $$self{'_last'} = new QPoint;
21    $$self{'_currentcolor'} = $black;
22    $$self{'_buffer'} = new QPixmap;
23
24    # don't blank the window before repainting
25    $self->setBackgroundMode( $BackgroundMode{NoBackground} );
26
27    return $self;
28 }
29
30 #
31 # The destructor. Does nothing in this version.
32 #
33 sub DESTROY {
34 }
35
36
37 #
38 # This slot sets the current color for the scribble area. It will be
39 # connected with the colorChanged(QColor) signal from the
40 # ScribbleWindow.
41 #
42 sub setColor {
43    my $self = shift;
44    $$self{'_currentcolor'} = shift;
45 }
46
47
48 #
49 # This virtual method is called whenever the user presses the mouse
50 # over the window. It just records the position of the mouse at the
51 # time of the click.
52 #
53 sub mousePressEvent {
54    my $self = shift;
55    my $event = shift;
56    $$self{'_last'} = $event->pos();
57 }
```

Example 22-4: The class ScribbleArea as a Perl package (continued)

```perl
58
59
60  #
61  # This virtual method is called whenever the user moves the mouse
62  # while the mouse button is pressed. If we had called
63  # setMouseTracking( true ) before, this method would also be called when
64  # the mouse was moved without any button pressed. We know that we
65  # haven't, and thus don't have to check whether any buttons are
66  # pressed. One caveat: If you use tool tips, mouse tracking is turned on
67  # automatically.
68  #
69  sub mouseMoveEvent {
70    my $self = shift;
71    my $event = shift;
72
73    # create a QPainter object for drawing onto the window
74    my $windowpainter = new QPainter;
75    # and another QPainter object for drawing into an off-screen pixmap
76    my $bufferpainter = new QPainter;
77
78    # start painting
79    $windowpainter->begin( $self ); # this painter paints onto the window
80    $bufferpainter->begin( $$self{'_buffer'} ); # and this one in the
81                                                 # buffer
82
83    # set a standard pen with the currently selected color
84    $windowpainter->setPen( $$self{'_currentcolor'} );
85    $bufferpainter->setPen( $$self{'_currentcolor'} );
86
87    # draw a line in both the window and the buffer
88    $windowpainter->drawLine( $$self{'_last'},
89                              $event->pos() );
90    $bufferpainter->drawLine( $$self{'_last'},
91                              $event->pos() );
92
93    # done with painting
94    $windowpainter->end();
95    $bufferpainter->end();
96
97    # remember the current mouse position
98    $$self{'_last'} = $event->pos();
99  }
100
101
102 #
103 # This virtual method is called whenever the widget needs painting,
104 # such as when it has been obscured and then revealed again.
105 #
106 sub paintEvent {
107   my $self = shift;
```

Example 22-4: The class ScribbleArea as a Perl package (continued)

```
108
109   # copy the image from the buffer pixmap to the window
110   my $buffer = $$self{'_buffer'};
111   $self->bitBlt( 0, 0, $buffer );
112 }
113
114
115 #
116 # This virtual method is called whenever the window is resized. We
117 # use it to make sure that the off-screen buffer is always the same
118 # size as the window.
119 # To retain the original scribbling, it is first copied
120 # to a temporary buffer. After the main buffer has been resized and
121 # filled with white, the image is copied from the temporary buffer to
122 # the main buffer.
123 #
124 sub resizeEvent {
125   my $self = shift;
126   my $event = shift;
127
128   my $buffer = $$self{'_buffer'};
129   my $save = new QPixmap( $buffer );
130   $buffer->resize( $event->size() );
131   $buffer->fill( $white );
132   bitBlt( $buffer, 0, 0, $save );
133 }
```

Example 22-5: ScribbleWindow.pm: The class ScribbleWindow as a Perl package

```
 1 package ScribbleWindow;
 2
 3 use Qt;
 4 use QWidget;
 5 use QColor;
 6 use QMenuBar;
 7 use QPopupMenu;
 8 use QScrollView;
 9 use QMessageBox;
10 use ScribbleArea;
11
12 use slots 'slotAbout()', 'slotAboutQt()', 'slotColorMenu(int)';
13 use signals 'colorChanged(QColor)';
14
15 @ISA = qw(QWidget);
16
17 $COLOR_MENU_ID_BLACK = 0;
18 $COLOR_MENU_ID_RED = 1;
19 $COLOR_MENU_ID_BLUE = 2;
20 $COLOR_MENU_ID_GREEN = 3;
21 $COLOR_MENU_ID_YELLOW = 4;
22
```

Example 22-5: ScribbleWindow.pm: The class ScribbleWindow as a Perl package (continued)

```
23  #
24  # Constructor
25  #
26  sub new {
27    my $class = shift;
28    my $self = $class->SUPER::new(@_);
29
30    # The next few lines build the menu bar. We first create the menus
31    # one by one and add them afterwards to the menu bar.
32    my $filemenu = new QPopupMenu; # create a file menu
33    $filemenu->insertItem( '&Quit', $self, 'hide()' );
34
35    my $colormenu = new QPopupMenu; # create a color menu
36    $colormenu->insertItem( 'B&lack', $COLOR_MENU_ID_BLACK );
37    $colormenu->insertItem( '&Red', $COLOR_MENU_ID_RED );
38    $colormenu->insertItem( '&Blue', $COLOR_MENU_ID_BLUE );
39    $colormenu->insertItem( '&Green', $COLOR_MENU_ID_GREEN );
40    $colormenu->insertItem( '&Yellow', $COLOR_MENU_ID_YELLOW );
41    QObject::connect( $colormenu, 'activated(int)', $self, 'slotColorMenu(int)' );
42
43    my $helpmenu = new QPopupMenu; # create a help menu
44    $helpmenu->insertItem( '&About QtScribble', $self, 'slotAbout()' );
45    $helpmenu->insertItem( 'About &Qt', $self, 'slotAboutQt()' );
46
47    my $menubar = new QMenuBar( $self ); # create a menu bar
48    $menubar->insertItem( '&File', $filemenu );
49    $menubar->insertItem( '&Color', $colormenu );
50    $menubar->insertSeparator();
51    $menubar->insertItem( '&Help', $helpmenu );
52
53    # We create a QScrollView and a Scribble Area. The ScribbleArea will
54    # be managed by the scroll view.
55    my $scrollview = new QScrollView( $self );
56    $scrollview->setGeometry( 0, $menubar->height(), $self->width(),
57                              $self->height() - $menubar->height() );
58    my $scribblearea = new ScribbleArea();
59    $scribblearea->setGeometry( 0, 0, 1000, 1000 );
60    $scrollview->addChild( $scribblearea, 0, 0 );
61    QObject::connect( $self, 'colorChanged(QColor)',
62                      $scribblearea, 'setColor(QColor)' );
63
64    @$self{ '_menubar', '_filemenu', '_colormenu', '_helpmenu',
65            '_scrollview', '_scribblearea' } =
66              ( $menubar, $filemenu, $colormenu, $helpmenu,
67                $scrollview, $scribblearea );
68
69    return $self;
70  }
71
72
```

Example 22-5: ScribbleWindow.pm: The class ScribbleWindow as a Perl package (continued)

```
 73  sub DESTROY {
 74  }
 75
 76
 77  sub resizeEvent {
 78    my $self = shift;
 79    my $event = shift;
 80
 81    # When the whole window is resized, we have to rearrange the
 82    # geometry in the ScrihbleWindow as well. Note that the ScribbleArea
 83    # does not need to be changed.
 84    my ( $scrollview, $menubar ) = @$self{ '_scrollview', '_menubar' };
 85    $scrollview->setGeometry( 0, $menubar->height(),
 86                              $self->width(),
 87                              $self->height() - $menubar->height() );
 88  }
 89
 90  sub slotAbout {
 91    my $self = shift;
 92
 93    QMessageBox::information( $self, 'About QtScribble 3',
 94                              "This is the QtScribble 3 application in Perl\n" .
 95                              "Copyright 1998 by Matthias Kalle Dalheimer\n" );
 96  }
 97
 98
 99  sub slotAboutQt {
100    my $self = shift;
101
102    QMessageBox::aboutQt( $self, "About Qt" );
103  }
104
105
106  sub slotColorMenu {
107    my $self = shift;
108    my $item = shift;
109
110    if( $item == $COLOR_MENU_ID_BLACK ) {
111      emit $self->colorChanged( $black );
112    } elsif( $item == $COLOR_MENU_ID_RED ) {
113      emit $self->colorChanged( $darkRed );
114    } elsif( $item == $COLOR_MENU_ID_BLUE ) {
115      emit $self->colorChanged( $darkBlue );
116    } elsif( $item == $COLOR_MENU_ID_GREEN ) {
117      emit $self->colorChanged( $darkGreen );
118    } elsif( $item == $COLOR_MENU_ID_YELLOW ) {
119      emit $self->colorChanged( $yellow );
120    }
121  }
```

Example 22-6: The driver program

```
1 use Qt;
2 use ScribbleWindow;
3
4 $mywidget = new ScribbleWindow();
5 $mywidget->setGeometry( 50, 500, 400, 400 );
6 $qApp->setMainWidget( $mywidget );
7 $mywidget->show();
8 exit $qApp->exec();
```

23

Using the Visual C++ IDE for Qt Programs

If you are working on a Windows system and use Microsoft Developer Studio/Visual Studio, you might want to use the IDE for your Qt work. Even though the IDE is mainly geared towards writing MFC programs, it is possible to use it for writing Qt programs and even benefit from a lot of its integration features, albeit with some additional work on your part.

Basically, there are three possibilities: importing an already existing makefile, creating your own project from scratch, and having *tmake* create a project for you. All have their advantages and disadvantages.

Importing an Existing Makefile

Importing an existing makefile is easy. Either write that makefile yourself, or have *tmake* (see the "Building Projects Portably with tmake" section) write one for you. Make sure that the makefile has the extension *.mak*. Now, open Developer Studio, choose "Open Workspace" from the "File" menu, and select the makefile. Developer Studio will ask whether you want to create a new project. Say "yes" here, and save your project afterwards.

While this is very easy to do, it has several severe disadvantages:

- Developer Studio does not know about the source files that make up your project, thus you won't find the usual list of files in the File View tab.

- Consequently, the source files will not be scanned for class definitions and such. In other words, the browser is not very useful in this project.

- You cannot change compiler and other settings via the IDE.

- Your project has the name of the makefile, which is probably something like `Makefile` and thus not very informative.

Creating Your Own Project from Scratch

We list this possibility here mainly for completeness. You probably won't use it, because it entails a lot of boring, manual work. Its only advantage is that it gives you the most control over every aspect of your project settings.

Choose the File/New menu item, and then `Win32 Application` as the type of the project to build. Also enter the name of the project and the path where it should be located. Then press "OK". Next, right-click on the project name in the project view, and select "Add files to project". Add all your source files here. Then you have to add all the moc files needed for your application. If you have already created your moc files, you can add these files the same way you added the source files. Otherwise, choose File/New for each moc file and create an empty file for each.

The next step involves setting up the dependencies for the moc files. Developer Studio does not know anything about moc, so you have to make sure that moc is called correctly yourself. For this, right-click on each moc file in turn and choose "Settings". In the general tab, activate the check-box "User-defined build step". Go to the next tab and enter the data for calling moc:

- In the description field, put something like "Running moc...". This text will be shown in the Build Progress window at the bottom of Developer Studio.

- In the "commands" field, enter the command you would usually enter on the command line to invoke moc, perhaps something like:

  ```
  moc -o myfile.moc myfile.h
  ```

- In the "output files" box, enter the name of the moc file generated—the file for which you invoked this dialog in the first place. In the previous example, this would be *myfile.moc*.

- Click on "Dependencies", and add the name of the file from which the moc file is built. In our example, this is `myfile.h`.

Compared to the first method, you have the advantage that you can use most of the features of Developer Studio. For example, you can use the class browser, jump around to class definitions, or set compiler settings via the IDE. The main disadvantage is the amount of work you have to do, because you have to repeat the previous procedure for every file involved.

Using tmake to Create a Project File

If you have tried following the second method, you might have thought that there must be a way to automate the manual work involved. This is indeed possible, and fortunately somebody has already done the hard work of working it out for you. This solution involves using *tmake*, a makefile generator. If you have not read the "Building Projects Portably with tmake" section about *tmake*, do so now and come back to this section afterwards.

To use *tmake* to create a project file for Developer Studio, you use either the vcapp or vclib template to generate a Win32 application or a library. The result is a .dsp file that you can open from Developer Studio to jump to your freshly generated project. If you are curious, right-click on a moc file and choose to check the settings *tmake* has generated for you.

We can recommend using this method only if you want to use Developer Studio. Like the second method, it gives you almost all of the features of the IDE, but with a lot less work. The only drawback occurs when you want to create something other than a Win 32 application or a library, for example, a console application or a DLL. In this case, you either have to hack *tmake*, which requires some Perl knowledge, or generate the project and then change it accordingly afterwards.

24

Sample Qt Projects

In this chapter, we present two projects where people have used Qt in real-world work. This might be interesting for you if you are still unsure about whether Qt is the right tool for your project.

The KDE Project

The KDE (K Desktop Environment, see *http://www.kde.org*) is a freeware project whose aim is to provide a user-friendly, stable, good-looking, and consistent desktop for Unix systems. Approximately 60 developers are working on various parts of this project like, including a window manager, a launch pad, lots of productivity tools, and even a complete office productivity software suite. Please see figure 24-1 with a screenshot of the KDE desktop.

KDE is aimed at Unix systems, so Qt's cross-platform capabilities are not needed here. The KDE developers value the flexibility of Qt and the support from the Qt developers anyway. Large parts of the KDE consist of simply putting Qt widgets together. Except for the collection classes, the non-GUI parts of Qt are scarcely used, and for some programs (like the window manager), it was necessary to bypass Qt and use direct X11 calls.

The KDE project has some special widget needs, like a date-entry field, so it was highly appreciated that writing your own widgets is made so easy in Qt. The KDE contains many widgets that might be useful in other projects.

Since it is possible to create complex user interfaces in a short time with Qt, it has been valuable for this large freeware project. Programmers who do not get paid for their work at least want to see fast, high-quality results.

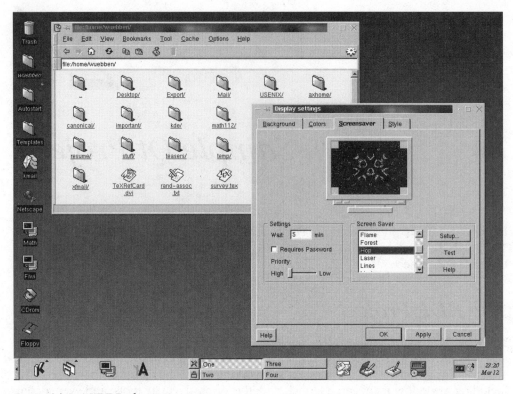

Figure 24-1: A KDE Desktop

OrthoVista

OrthoVista (see the screenshot in Figure 24-2) from Stellacore (*http://www.stella core.com*) is a commercial program for the aerial mapping and photography market. It takes ortho photos and, through a variety of corrections and adjustments, creates seamless mosaics of the images so that they appear to be a single photo. The program is sold for use on various platforms: SGI Irix, Windows NT/Intel, Windows NT/Alpha, Linux/Intel, Linux/Alpha, and Solaris/SPARC.

The designer and lead programmer of OrthoVista, Valient Gough, reported that compared with other toolkits he was experienced with, Qt had several large advantages. Among these were the availability of source, which makes it possible to compile a patch on all needed platforms so that you don't have to wait for the vendor to do so; the price, which is rather cheap compared with other commercial GUI toolkits; the stability of the code; the easy to use signal/slot mechanism; and the rather complete API, which covers GUI operations and also file I/O and data structures. He also appreciated the comprehensive set of graphics operations, like affine transformations, rotations, scales, and shifts.

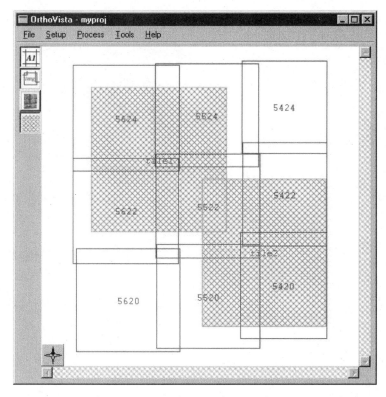

Figure 24-2: OrthoVista, an Application for Aerial Mapping and Photography Written With Qt

One of the main drawbacks Gough identified while working on the OrthoVista product was the lack of device-independent graphics primitives. Depending on rounding errors, an object with coordinates that are not full integers might show up differently on the screen and the printer. This is mainly a result of the design choice in Qt to represent all coordinates in integers instead of floats. The developers of OrthoVista solved this problem by writing a middle-layer GUI library that transforms world coordinates to pixel coordinates. That way, all objects that use these libraries can draw in floating-point coordinates, and only this middle layer needs to deal with the transformations necessary to convert the coordinates to pixel units. There are other toolkits that can handle this themselves.

The other main disadvantage of Qt, according to Gough, is the fact that the developers of Qt chose not to break binary compatibility between the minor versions. While this is valuable and necessary for freeware development, it is not so useful for developing vertical-market commercial applications, which are usually linked statically anyway. In such a project, you would prefer new features over binary compatibility.

All in all, Gough noted, OrthoVista's developers consider Qt to be an "extremely well done product".

25

A First Look at Qt 2.0

When this book has hit the shelves, it is likely that the new version of Qt, version 2.0, will already be available. While 99.9% of the information you can find in this book applies to Qt 1.4x as well as Qt 2.0, there are a few new additions that might be interesting for you. It is very likely that the programs you have written or will write for Qt 1.4x will compile without problems with Qt 2.0. For the few cases where source incompatibilities can arise, Qt 2.0 includes a converter script that helps you change your source code.

Unicode Support and Improved QString

The string abstraction, `QString`, has been improved a lot. While for most of you the most important thing might be the performance improvements, it is also very interesting that `QString` now supports Unicode. This means that you can use `QString` to represent strings made up with Unicode characters as well as classic strings made up with 8bit characters. Unicode is an international standard for representing characters of all scripts of the earth in one encoding. A Unicode character has a size of 16 bits, and there are more than 40,000 characters and space for more than 10,000 more. Unicode is intended to cover all fonts used in printing today's languages.

There are classes, so-called codecs (coder-decoder), that can handle conversion from Unicode to 8 bit strings and vice versa for the most general encodings. If you use a common encoding like ASCII or ISO-Latin-1, you will not have to do any extra work in order to make use of Unicode. It should be noted, though, that your operating system must also be able to handle Unicode strings. Of the supported operating/windowing systems, all Unix/X11 systems and Windows NT support Unicode in principle while Windows 95/98 does not. It is not sufficient if the operating/windowing system can accept 16 bit strings, though. In order to display those strings you must also have the fonts needed, otherwise you might see nothing or only replacement characters. Fortunately, Qt provides a lot of character conversions according to standards like EUC-JP or KOI8-R so that you might even get along with a limited number of fonts available.

In order to use those improvements, most methods in Qt that expected a `const char*` now expect a `QString`.[1] Since there were always operators for automatically converting classic C strings into `QString` objects and vice versa, you should probably not experience any problems with this change. The only case where you might get in trouble is when you have overloaded one of the very few methods that expect a `const char*` reference or if you make signal/slot connections involving `const char*`—all those now use `const QString&`.

Improved Layout Management

The layout management classes in Qt which have been the target of a lot of criticism have been completely rewritten. You can still use the old API and benefit from the more robust implementation, the more sensible defaults and the more comprehensible warning and error messages. On the other hand, you can also work with the new class `QSizePolicy` which will be easier to understand for most users than the old API. Using `QSizePolicy`, you can tell the layout management system that a widget may for example only shrink, only grow or do both.

In addition, there are now widgets called `QGrid`, `QHBox` and `QVBox` which are ordinary `QWidgets` that have a layout manager set by default.

Internationalization Support

Qt 2.0 finally contains support for internationalization. While it was already possible to use external internationalization systems like Windows resources on Windows systems and `gettext` on Unix systems, this tended to be awkward and to "uglify" the code.

With the new internationalization system, every `QObject` can translate strings by means of the new method `QObject::tr()`. This method takes a `QString` and returns a translated `QString`. The translations come from an instance of the class `QMessageFile`. As the programmer, you have very little to do; in fact, all you need to do is wrap the strings that should be translated with `tr()`.

An example will clarify this: If you have written so far:

```
okbutton->setText( "OK" );
```

you should now write:

```
okbutton->setText( tr( "OK" ) );
```

Depending on what your current language settings are and which translations are available, `QMessageFile` determines the translation from the class name of the dialog the button is in, the current language and the translation string (`OK` in this case), and returns a proper translation, for example `V redu` if the current language is Slovenian.

---

1 Actually, they expect a `const QString&`; `QString` is used for return values.

Of course, you also need the translations, but Qt makes it easy for the translators to translate the applications: Qt provides a program to edit those translation strings at runtime which the translators use and which automatically generates translation files for the language in question.

Themability

Something that developers developing visually appealing applications with a lot of graphics have wished for for a long time while others consider it unnecessary or even evil are themes. Themes[2] are sets of colors (like `QColorGroup` always was), combined with special ways of drawing widgets. A well designed theme is a visually appealing mixture of drawing styles and colors. Qt 2.0 comes with a few predefined themes like `QMotifStyle`, `QWindowsStyle` and `QPlatinumStyle`, of which the first two correspond to the classic widget styles "Motif" and "Windows".

In order to implement a new theme, you design a class that inherits from `QStyle` and reimplements `QStyle::polish()` which is called for each widget after it has been constructed and before it is shown the first time. For example, if you want your widgets to look like crystal glass, you would probably set a background pixmap.

New or Improved Widgets

Qt 2.0 contains another predefined dialog, the `QColorDialog` which lets you graphically select colors; `QSplitter` has been improved and can now handle more than two child widgets. In addition, there is now the long awaited edit field for styled text, an edit field that can show different fonts, colors, images and multiple columns.

Debugging Help

If you have already used `QObject::dumpObjectTree()` to understand which object or widget trees your application constructs at runtime, you will be happy to see `QDeveloper` in action. This class implements a GUI version of `dumpObjectTree()` and lets you visually inspect your object or widget trees. It is supposed to be further improved in subsequent releases of Qt. You can get an impression of what `QDeveloper` can do for you by looking at the screenshot in Figure 25-1.

---

2 You could argue that a theme includes much more like window manager settings, sound effects and other things that are beyond the scope of Qt. This is why the Qt developers prefer the term "generalized styles", but since "theme" is the more common term, we use it here.

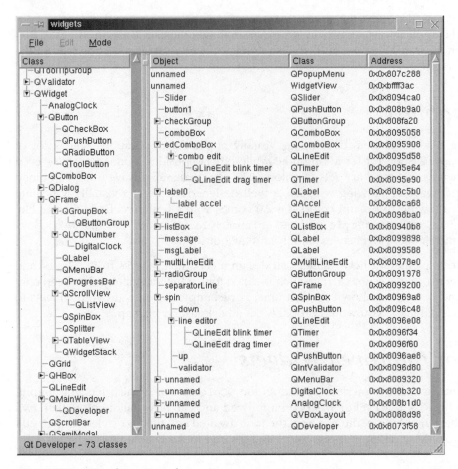

Figure 25-1: QDeveloper at work

Preventing Namespace Pollution

Qt developers, especially those working on the Unix/X11 platform have been struggling with namespace pollution and name clashes for a long time. Some symbol names were used in Qt as well as in the X11 header files at the top level which was a bad idea from both the Qt developers and the X Consortium. With Qt 2.0, those clashes should disappear, because those symbols have been moved into a new class `Qt` which leads to a source code incompatibility. Instead of `red`, you would now use `Qt::red`, but since most Qt classes inherit from the class `Qt`, you can almost always leave your source code as it is. In classes that do not inherit from `Qt` or in non-member functions, you have to prefix those constants with `Qt::`. Qt 2.0 comes with a clever script that compiles your source code, parses the compiler output and looks for errors that might be a result of this change in Qt. It then offers to automatically fix your source code.

You might wonder why Qt does not use the `namespace` feature of the new C++ standard. The reason for this is that not all compilers implement this feature yet, and of those that do, not all implement it correctly. Thus, it is better for Qt to stick with a simple albeit a little bit awkward solution so that it still compiles with all compilers that have been supported before.

Miscellaneous Changes

There are a few other minor changes which we sum up here:

- It is no longer possible to use the macro versions of the container classes; only the template versions are now available.

- A large number of methods have been made virtual and several methods have been made slots. This increases the suitability of the classes in Qt to serve as base classes.

- `QObject::name()` now returns "unnamed" by default, for ease of debugging messages. `name( 0 )` returns a null pointer if the object is unnamed.

- All remaining support for OS/2 Presentation Manager has been removed, but this was never officially supported anyway.

The Future of Qt

Like every maintained piece of software, Qt evolves. There are always new Qt features to wish for, like new widgets, new graphics filters, and more. You can participate in the discussion of these ideas on the mailing list *qt-interest@troll.no*. If you know what you want, you can also mail feature requests to this list. The mailing list is often read by the Qt developers—and while Qt is a product of those developers, it is also a product of *us*, its users!

A

Answers to Exercises

Answers to Exercises in Chapter 2

Answers to Exercises in the "Hello World!" section

1. Of course, there is not much to write as a solution here. The actual commands to compile Qt applications are indicated in the "Hello World!" section. Try some of the example programs from the Qt distribution first.

Answers to Exercises in the "Using the Qt Reference Documentation" section

1. You can find the documentation for QApplication in *html/qapplication.html* in your Qt installation.

2. QFrame is derived from QWidget. Other classes in Qt that are derived from QFrame are QGroupBox, QLCDNumber, QLabel, QMenuBar, QProgressBar, QScrollView, QSpinBox, QSplitter, QTableView, and QWidgetStack.

   Since QLabel inherits from QFrame, all public and protected methods of QFrame, including setFrameStyle(), are available for QLabel objects. You can see all methods available in a class (including those inherited from base classes) in the "list of all member functions" in the class documentation.

Answers to Exercises in the "Adding an Exit Button" section

1. The following code adds another button. There is nothing new here. Note that we have also increased the size of the top-level widget to accommodate for the additional widget.

```
#include <qapplication.h>
#include <qlabel.h>
#include <qpushbutton.h>

int main( int argc, char* argv[] )
```

```
    {
        QApplication myapp( argc, argv );

        QWidget* mywidget = new QWidget();
        mywidget->setGeometry( 400, 300, 120, 130 );

        QPushButton* anotherquitbutton = new QPushButton( "Click me", mywidget );
        anotherquitbutton->setGeometry( 10, 10, 100, 30 );
        QObject::connect( anotherquitbutton, SIGNAL(clicked()), &myapp, SLOT(quit()) );

        QLabel* mylabel = new QLabel( "Hello world", mywidget );
        mylabel->setGeometry( 10, 50, 80, 30 );

        QPushButton* myquitbutton = new QPushButton( "Quit", mywidget );
        myquitbutton->setGeometry( 10, 90, 100, 30 );
        QObject::connect( myquitbutton, SIGNAL(clicked()), &myapp, SLOT(quit()) );

        myapp.setMainWidget( mywidget );
        mywidget->show();
        return myapp.exec();
    }
```

2. In the following code, we have only replaced the signal `clicked()` from the first
    push-button, `anotherquitbutton`, with the signal `pressed()`.

```
    #include <qapplication.h>
    #include <qlabel.h>
    #include <qpushbutton.h>

    int main( int argc, char* argv[] )
    {
        QApplication myapp( argc, argv );

        QWidget* mywidget = new QWidget();
        mywidget->setGeometry( 400, 300, 120, 130 );

        QPushButton* anotherquitbutton = new QPushButton( "Click me", mywidget );
        anotherquitbutton->setGeometry( 10, 10, 100, 30 );
        QObject::connect( anotherquitbutton, SIGNAL(pressed()), &myapp, SLOT(quit()) );

        QLabel* mylabel = new QLabel( "Hello world", mywidget );
        mylabel->setGeometry( 10, 50, 80, 30 );

        QPushButton* myquitbutton = new QPushButton( "Quit", mywidget );
        myquitbutton->setGeometry( 10, 90, 100, 30 );
        QObject::connect( myquitbutton, SIGNAL(clicked()), &myapp, SLOT(quit()) );

        myapp.setMainWidget( mywidget );
        mywidget->show();
        return myapp.exec();
    }
```

Answers to Exercises in the "Introduction to Signals and Slots" section

1. Along with the signal `sliderMoved()`, QSlider, also emits `valueChanged()` which is only emitted when the user releases the knob. This leads to the following code:

```
#include <qapplication.h>
#include <qslider.h>
#include <qlcdnumber.h>

int main( int argc, char* argv[] )
{
  QApplication myapp( argc, argv );

  QWidget* mywidget = new QWidget();
  mywidget->setGeometry( 400, 300, 170, 110 );


  QSlider* myslider = new QSlider( 0,                  // minimum value
                                   9,                  // maximum value
                                   1,                  // step
                                   1,                  // initial value
                                   QSlider::Horizontal, // orientation
                                   mywidget            // parent
                                 );
  myslider->setGeometry( 10, 10, 150, 30 );

  QLCDNumber* mylcdnum = new QLCDNumber( 1,        // number of digits
                                         mywidget // parent
                                       );
  mylcdnum->setGeometry( 60, 50, 50, 50 );
  mylcdnum->display( 1 ); // display initial value

  // connect slider and number display
  QObject::connect( myslider, SIGNAL( valueChanged( int ) ),
                    mylcdnum, SLOT( display( int ) ) );

  myapp.setMainWidget( mywidget );
  mywidget->show();
  return myapp.exec();
}
```

2. The following code adds two push-buttons, and connects their `clicked()` signals to the slots `subtractStep()` and `addStep()`, respectively, of the QSlider. We want the QLCDNumber widget to change its value, too. To achieve this, we have to change the signal of the slider connected with the LCD display from slider-Moved() to `valueChanged()`, because only the latter is emitted when the value of the slider is updated programmatically which is done by calling `addStep()`, substractStep(), or `setValue( int )`. The latter method is is probably most common, but is not used in this example.

```cpp
#include <qapplication.h>
#include <qpushbutton.h>
#include <qslider.h>
#include <qlcdnumber.h>

int main( int argc, char* argv[] )
{
  QApplication myapp( argc, argv );

  QWidget* mywidget = new QWidget();
  mywidget->setGeometry( 400, 300, 170, 150 );


  QSlider* myslider = new QSlider( 0,                       // minimum value
                                   9,                       // maximum value
                                   1,                       // step
                                   1,                       // initial value
                                   QSlider::Horizontal,     // orientation
                                   mywidget                 // parent
                                 );
  myslider->setGeometry( 10, 10, 150, 30 );

  QLCDNumber* mylcdnum = new QLCDNumber( 1,        // number of digits
                                         mywidget  // parent
                                       );
  mylcdnum->setGeometry( 60, 50, 50, 50 );
  mylcdnum->display( 1 ); // display initial value

  // connect slider and number display
  QObject::connect( myslider, SIGNAL( valueChanged( int ) ),
                    mylcdnum, SLOT( display( int ) ) );

  // create two push-buttons for deincrementing and
  // incrementing the slider values
  QPushButton* decrement = new QPushButton( "<", mywidget );
  decrement->setGeometry( 10, 110, 50, 30 );

  QPushButton* increment = new QPushButton( ">", mywidget );
  increment->setGeometry( 110, 110, 50, 30 );

  // connect the clicked() signal of the buttons to the slots that
  // increment and decrement the slider value
  QObject::connect( decrement, SIGNAL( clicked() ),
                    myslider, SLOT( subtractStep() ) );
  QObject::connect( increment, SIGNAL( clicked() ),
                    myslider, SLOT( addStep() ) );

  myapp.setMainWidget( mywidget );
  mywidget->show();
  return myapp.exec();
}
```

Answers to Exercises in the "Event Handling and Simple Drawings with QPainter" section

1. The solution to this exercise involves two steps. First, you have to distinguish between the different mouse buttons. The QMouseEvent object passed to each mouse event handler has two methods for retrieving the button that was pressed: button() and state(). Normally, button() would be just right, but in this case it does not work since we need the button in the handler mouseMoveEvent(). For some reason unknown to me, this method always returns NoButton in this handler, no matter which mouse button was pressed. Therefore, we have to use state(). This method not only reports the buttons, but also reports the modifiers that might have been pressed with the mouse button, such as the Shift, Alt, and CTRL keys. We will have to mask out only the information that we need, like this:

    ```
    if( event->state() & RightButton )
    ```

    The next thing we need is a QPen object that has a width other than the default width of 1. We achieve this by creating a default pen and then calling setWidth (10) to get a pen with a width of 10 pixels. Since the rest of the program is just like Example 2-4, we only show the new mouseMoveEvent() handler here:

    ```
    void ScribbleWindow::mouseMoveEvent( QMouseEvent* event )
    {
      // create a QPainter object for drawing onto the window
      QPainter windowpainter;
      // and another QPainter object for drawing into an off-screen pixmap
      QPainter bufferpainter;

      // start painting
      windowpainter.begin( this );     // this painter paints onto the window
      bufferpainter.begin( &_buffer ); // and this one in the buffer

      if( event->state() & RightButton ) {
        QPen pen;
        pen.setWidth( 10 );
        windowpainter.setPen( pen );
        bufferpainter.setPen( pen );
      }

      // draw a line in both the window and the buffer
      windowpainter.drawLine( _last, event->pos() );
      bufferpainter.drawLine( _last, event->pos() );

      // done with painting
      windowpainter.end();
      bufferpainter.end();

      // remember the current mouse position
      _last = event->pos();
    }
    ```

2.   Again, solving this exercise involves two steps. The key-presses have to be evalu-
     ated, and a pen with the chosen color has to be used. Starting with the first point,
     you need to reimplement the method `keyPressEvent()`. The class `QKeyEvent` a
     pointer to an object of which is passed to `keyPressEvent()` has a method called
     `key()`, which returns a keycode. The complete list of keycodes that Qt works with
     is contained in *qkeycode.h*. All keycodes are symbolic names that start with `Key_`.
     The only thing we do in `keyPressEvent()` is assign one of the predefined colors
     to a new member of the `ScribbleWindow`, `_color`, like this:

```
void ScribbleWindow::keyPressEvent( QKeyEvent* event )
{
  switch( event->key() ) {
  case Key_F1:
    _color = black;
    break;
  case Key_F2:
    _color = darkGray;
    break;
  case Key_F3:
    _color = gray;
    break;
  ...
  }
}
```

Next, we have to use `_color` in `mouseMoveEvent()` where the actual drawing is
done. This is very easy, since `QPainter` has a method `setPen()` to which you can
pass a color, and that automatically constructs a pen for you. Here is the new
`mouseMoveEvent()`

```
void ScribbleWindow::mouseMoveEvent( QMouseEvent* event )
{
  // create a QPainter object for drawing onto the window
  QPainter windowpainter;
  // and another QPainter object for drawing into an off-screen pixmap
  QPainter bufferpainter;

  // start painting
  windowpainter.begin( this );     // this painter paints onto the window
  bufferpainter.begin( &_buffer ); // and this one in the buffer

  // set the color
  windowpainter.setPen( _color );
  bufferpainter.setPen( _color );

  // draw a line in both the window and the buffer
  windowpainter.drawLine( _last, event->pos() );
  bufferpainter.drawLine( _last, event->pos() );

  // done with painting
  windowpainter.end();
  bufferpainter.end();
```

```
  // remember the current mouse position
  _last = event->pos();
}
```

If you want to key this in instead of compiling the file that is available online, remember to add the following lines to the class declaration of `ScribbleWindow`:

```
protected:
    void keyPressEvent( QKeyEvent* );

private:
    QColor _color;
```

3. One more time, you need a new event handler. This time it is `mouseDouble-ClickEvent()` which is called when the user double-clicks into the widget. The implementation of this method is trivial:

```
void ScribbleWindow::mouseDoubleClickEvent( QMouseEvent* )
{
  qApp->quit();
}
```

If you want to key this in, remember to also declare this method in the class declaration of the class `ScribbleWindow`.

Answers to Exercises in Chapter 3

Answers to Exercises in the "Adding Menus" section

1. Using pixmaps instead of strings in menus is very easy, since most overloaded versions of `QMenuData::insertItem()` that insert a text menu item also exist as versions that insert a pixmap. Here is the constructor for the class `ScribbleWindow`, the rest is as in Example 3-1:

```
ScribbleWindow::ScribbleWindow()
{
  // initialize member variables
  _currentcolor = black;

  // don't blank the window before repainting
  setBackgroundMode( NoBackground );

  /* The next lines build the menu bar. We first create the menus
   * one by one, then add them to the menu bar. */
  _filemenu = new QPopupMenu; // create a file menu
  _filemenu->insertItem( "&Quit", qApp, SLOT( quit() ) );

  _colormenu = new QPopupMenu; // create a color menu
  QPixmap blackpixmap( 20, 20 );
  blackpixmap.fill( black );
  _colormenu->insertItem( blackpixmap, COLOR_MENU_ID_BLACK );
```

```
    QPixmap redpixmap( 20, 20 );
    redpixmap.fill( red );
    _colormenu->insertItem( redpixmap, COLOR_MENU_ID_RED );
    QPixmap bluepixmap( 20, 20 );
    bluepixmap.fill( blue );
    _colormenu->insertItem( bluepixmap, COLOR_MENU_ID_BLUE );
    QPixmap greenpixmap( 20, 20 );
    greenpixmap.fill( green );
    _colormenu->insertItem( greenpixmap, COLOR_MENU_ID_GREEN );
    QPixmap yellowpixmap( 20, 20 );
    yellowpixmap.fill( yellow );
    _colormenu->insertItem( yellowpixmap, COLOR_MENU_ID_YELLOW );
    QObject::connect( _colormenu, SIGNAL( activated( int ) ),
                      this, SLOT( slotColorMenu( int ) ) );

    _helpmenu = new QPopupMenu; // create a help menu
    _helpmenu->insertItem( "&About QtScribble", this, SLOT( slotAbout() ) );
    _helpmenu->insertItem( "About &Qt", this, SLOT( slotAboutQt() ) );

    _menubar = new QMenuBar( this ); // create a menu bar
    _menubar->insertItem( "&File", _filemenu );
    _menubar->insertItem( "&Color", _colormenu );
    _menubar->insertSeparator();
    _menubar->insertItem( "&Help", _helpmenu );
}
```

2. This is not much more difficult than the previous exercise, since there are also
    some methods that allow you to add menu items that consist of both a pixmap and
    text. Here is the new constructor for `ScribbleWindow`; again, the rest is just like in
    Example 3-1.

```
ScribbleWindow::ScribbleWindow()
{
  // initialize member variables
  _currentcolor = black;

  // don't blank the window before repainting
  setBackgroundMode( NoBackground );

  /* The next lines build the menu bar. We first create the menus
   * one by one, then add them to the menu bar. */
  _filemenu = new QPopupMenu; // create a file menu
  _filemenu->insertItem( "&Quit", qApp, SLOT( quit() ) );

  _colormenu = new QPopupMenu; // create a color menu
  QPixmap blackpixmap( 20, 20 );
  blackpixmap.fill( black );
  _colormenu->insertItem( blackpixmap, "B&lack", COLOR_MENU_ID_BLACK );
  QPixmap redpixmap( 20, 20 );
  redpixmap.fill( red );
  _colormenu->insertItem( redpixmap, "&Red", COLOR_MENU_ID_RED );
  QPixmap bluepixmap( 20, 20 );
  bluepixmap.fill( blue );
```

```
    _colormenu->insertItem( bluepixmap, "&Blue", COLOR_MENU_ID_BLUE );
    QPixmap greenpixmap( 20, 20 );
    greenpixmap.fill( green );
    _colormenu->insertItem( greenpixmap, "&Green", COLOR_MENU_ID_GREEN );
    QPixmap yellowpixmap( 20, 20 );
    yellowpixmap.fill( yellow );
    _colormenu->insertItem( yellowpixmap, "&Yellow", COLOR_MENU_ID_YELLOW );
    QObject::connect( _colormenu, SIGNAL( activated( int ) ),
                      this, SLOT( slotColorMenu( int ) ) );

    _helpmenu = new QPopupMenu; // create a help menu
    _helpmenu->insertItem( "&About QtScribble", this, SLOT( slotAbout() ) );
    _helpmenu->insertItem( "About &Qt", this, SLOT( slotAboutQt() ) );

    _menubar = new QMenuBar( this ); // create a menu bar
    _menubar->insertItem( "&File", _filemenu );
    _menubar->insertItem( "&Color", _colormenu );
    _menubar->insertSeparator();
    _menubar->insertItem( "&Help", _helpmenu );
}
```

3. The solution to this exercise is not really difficult, but it involves several steps:

   - Add two member variables, QPopupMenu* _widthmenu and int _width, to the class ScribbleWindow.

   - Add a new private slot, slotWidthMenu(int), to the class ScribbleWindow that will be called when an item in the width menu is selected.

   - Add code to the constructor to ScribbleWindow that creates the pen width menu. Since the item IDs are integer values and the widths are as well, you can save yourself some work by using the width are values for the item IDs.

   - Implement the slot slotWidthMenu; assign suitable values to the member variables _width.

   - Use the _width value when painting in mouseMoveEvent().

   For your reference, here is the complete code:

```
#include <qapplication.h>
#include <qmenubar.h>
#include <qmessagebox.h>
#include <qpainter.h>
#include <qpixmap.h>
#include <qpopupmenu.h>
#include <qwidget.h>

enum MenuIDs{
    COLOR_MENU_ID_BLACK,
    COLOR_MENU_ID_RED,
    COLOR_MENU_ID_BLUE,
    COLOR_MENU_ID_GREEN,
    COLOR_MENU_ID_YELLOW };
```

```
/**
  * A class that lets the user draw with the mouse. The
  * window knows how to redraw itself.
  */
class ScribbleWindow : public QWidget
{
  Q_OBJECT  // necessary because ScribbleWindow contains slots

public:
  ScribbleWindow();
  ~ScribbleWindow();

protected:
  virtual void mousePressEvent( QMouseEvent* );
  virtual void mouseMoveEvent( QMouseEvent* );
  virtual void paintEvent( QPaintEvent* );
  virtual void resizeEvent( QResizeEvent* );

private slots:
  void slotAbout();
  void slotAboutQt();
  void slotColorMenu( int );
  void slotWidthMenu( int );

private:
  QPoint _last;
  QColor _currentcolor;
  int _width;

  QPixmap _buffer;
  QMenuBar* _menubar;
  QPopupMenu* _filemenu;
  QPopupMenu* _colormenu;
  QPopupMenu* _widthmenu;
  QPopupMenu* _helpmenu;
};

#include "exercise-3-1-3.moc"

/** The constructor. Initializes the member variables and the menu
  * system.
  */
ScribbleWindow::ScribbleWindow()
{
  // initialize member variables
  _currentcolor = black;
  _width = 1;

  // don't blank the window before repainting
  setBackgroundMode( NoBackground );
```

```
   /* The next lines build the menu bar. We first create the menus
    * one by one, then add them to the menu bar. */
   _filemenu = new QPopupMenu; // create a file menu
   _filemenu->insertItem( "&Quit", qApp, SLOT( quit() ) );

   _colormenu = new QPopupMenu; // create a color menu
   _colormenu->insertItem( "B&lack", COLOR_MENU_ID_BLACK );
   _colormenu->insertItem( "&Red", COLOR_MENU_ID_RED );
   _colormenu->insertItem( "&Blue", COLOR_MENU_ID_BLUE );
   _colormenu->insertItem( "&Green", COLOR_MENU_ID_GREEN );
   _colormenu->insertItem( "&Yellow", COLOR_MENU_ID_YELLOW );
   QObject::connect( _colormenu, SIGNAL( activated( int ) ),
                     this, SLOT( slotColorMenu( int ) ) );

   _widthmenu = new QPopupMenu; // create a pen-width menu
   _widthmenu->insertItem( "&1", 1 );
   _widthmenu->insertItem( "&2", 2 );
   _widthmenu->insertItem( "&3", 3 );
   QObject::connect( _widthmenu, SIGNAL( activated( int ) ),
                     this, SLOT( slotWidthMenu( int ) ) );

   _helpmenu = new QPopupMenu; // create a help menu
   _helpmenu->insertItem( "&About QtScribble", this, SLOT( slotAbout() ) );
   _helpmenu->insertItem( "About &Qt", this, SLOT( slotAboutQt() ) );

   _menubar = new QMenuBar( this ); // create a menu bar
   _menubar->insertItem( "&File", _filemenu );
   _menubar->insertItem( "&Color", _colormenu );
   _menubar->insertItem( "&Pen width", _widthmenu );
   _menubar->insertSeparator();
   _menubar->insertItem( "&Help", _helpmenu );
}


/**
 * The destructor. Does nothing for now.
 */
ScribbleWindow::~ScribbleWindow()
{
}


/**
 * This virtual method is called whenever the user presses the
 * mouse over the window. It just records the position of the mouse
 * at the time of the click.
 */
void ScribbleWindow::mousePressEvent( QMouseEvent* event )
{
   _last = event->pos(); // retrieve the coordinates from the event
}
```

```
/**
  * This virtual method is called whenever the user moves the mouse
  * while the mouse button is pressed. If we had called
  * setMouseTracking( true ) before, this method would also be called
  * when the mouse was moved without any button pressed. We know that
  * we haven't, and thus don't have to check whether any buttons are
  * pressed. One caveat: If you use tool tips, mouse tracking is
  * turned on automatically.
  */
void ScribbleWindow::mouseMoveEvent( QMouseEvent* event )
{
    // create a QPainter object for drawing onto the window
    QPainter windowpainter;
    // and another QPainter object for drawing into an off-screen pixmap
    QPainter bufferpainter;

    // start painting
    windowpainter.begin( this );     // this painter paints onto the window
    bufferpainter.begin( &_buffer ); // and this one in the buffer

    // set a standard pen with the currently selected color
    windowpainter.setPen( QPen( _currentcolor, _width ) );
    bufferpainter.setPen( QPen( _currentcolor, _width ) );

    // draw a line in both the window and the buffer
    windowpainter.drawLine( _last, event->pos() );
    bufferpainter.drawLine( _last, event->pos() );

    // done with painting
    windowpainter.end();
    bufferpainter.end();

    // remember the current mouse position
    _last = event->pos();
}


/**
  * This virtual method is called whenever the widget needs
  * painting, as when it has been obscured and then revealed again.
  */
void ScribbleWindow::paintEvent( QPaintEvent* event )
{
    // copy the image from the buffer pixmap to the window
    bitBlt( this, 0, 0, &_buffer );
}


/**
  * This virtual method is called whenever the window is resized. We
  * use it to make sure that the off-screen buffer always has the same
  * size as the window.
```

```
 * In order to retain the original scribbling, it is first copied
 * to a temporary buffer. After the main buffer has been resized and
 * filled with white, the image is copied from the temporary buffer to
 * the main buffer.
 */
void ScribbleWindow::resizeEvent( QResizeEvent* event )
{
  QPixmap save( _buffer );
  _buffer.resize( event->size() );
  _buffer.fill( white );
  bitBlt( &_buffer, 0, 0, &save );
}


void ScribbleWindow::slotAbout()
{
  QMessageBox::information( this, "About QtScribble 2",
                           "This is the QtScribble 2 application\n"
                           "Copyright 1998 by Matthias Kalle Dalheimer\n"
                           );
}


void ScribbleWindow::slotAboutQt()
{
  QMessageBox::aboutQt( this, "About Qt" );
}


void ScribbleWindow::slotColorMenu( int item )
{
  switch( item )
    {
    case COLOR_MENU_ID_BLACK:
      _currentcolor = black;
      break;
    case COLOR_MENU_ID_RED:
      _currentcolor = darkRed;
      break;
    case COLOR_MENU_ID_BLUE:
      _currentcolor = darkBlue;
      break;
    case COLOR_MENU_ID_GREEN:
      _currentcolor = darkGreen;
      break;
    case COLOR_MENU_ID_YELLOW:
      _currentcolor = yellow;
      break;
    }
}
```

```
void ScribbleWindow::slotWidthMenu( int item )
{
  _width = item;
}


int main( int argc, char* argv[] )
{
  QApplication myapp( argc, argv );

  ScribbleWindow* mywidget = new ScribbleWindow();
  mywidget->setGeometry( 50, 500, 400, 400 );

  myapp.setMainWidget( mywidget );
  mywidget->show();
  return myapp.exec();
}
```

Answers to Exercises in the "Adding a Scrolled View" section

1.   The solution to this exercise involves nothing more than connecting the two hints
     given in the question: You reimplement the key event handler **keyPressEvent()**
     in ScribbleWindow, and call the method **scrollBy()** at the QScrollView object
     with suitable parameters. In the following sample implementation of Scrib-
     bleWindow::keyPressEvent(), the cursor keys move the contents by 10 pixels,
     and the page up and page down keys move the contents by either one-tenth of the
     contents height, or 10 pixels, whatever is more. For your application, other values
     might be more suitable.

```
void ScribbleWindow::keyPressEvent( QKeyEvent* event )
{
    switch( event->key() ) {
    case Key_Up:
    _scrollview->scrollBy( 0, -10 );
    break;
    case Key_Down:
    _scrollview->scrollBy( 0, 10 );
    break;
    case Key_Left:
    _scrollview->scrollBy( -10, 0 );
    break;
    case Key_Right:
    _scrollview->scrollBy( 10, 0 );
    break;
    case Key_PageUp:
    _scrollview->scrollBy( 0, - QMAX( _scrollview->contentsHeight() / 10,
                           10 ) );
```

```
        break;
        case Key_PageDown:
        _scrollview->scrollBy( 0, QMAX( _scrollview->contentsHeight() / 10,
                            10 ) );
        break;
        }
    }
```

If you want to key this in manually, remember to also add a declaration of `key-PressEvent()` to the class declaration of `ScribbleWindow`, and to include the header file *qkeycode.h*. *qkeycode.h* is the include file for the key definitions line `Key_Up`.

2. If you use `AlwaysOff` and the contents are larger than the viewport, you have no way to get to the invisible part of the contents, unless you implement some kind of custom scrolling, like the key-based scrolling shown in the previous exercise.

Answers to Exercises in the "Adding a Context Menu" section

1. The solution to this exercise involves two steps: First, the pop-up menu must be created, and then its signals must be connected to some slot. Here is the creation code contained in the constructor of `ScribbleArea`:

```
ScribbleArea::ScribbleArea()
{
  // initialize member variables
  _currentcolor = black;

  // don't blank the window before repainting
  setBackgroundMode( NoBackground );

  // create a pop-up menu
  _popupmenu = new QPopupMenu();

  QPopupMenu* subpopup1 = new QPopupMenu();
  subpopup1->insertItem( "&Clear", this, SLOT( slotClearArea() ) );
  _popupmenu->insertItem( "Popup &1", subpopup1 );

  QPopupMenu* subpopup2 = new QPopupMenu();
  subpopup2->insertItem( "B&lack", COLOR_MENU_ID_BLACK );
  subpopup2->insertItem( "&Red", COLOR_MENU_ID_RED );
  subpopup2->insertItem( "&Blue", COLOR_MENU_ID_BLUE );
  subpopup2->insertItem( "&Green", COLOR_MENU_ID_GREEN );
  subpopup2->insertItem( "&Yellow", COLOR_MENU_ID_YELLOW );
  QObject::connect( subpopup2, SIGNAL( activated( int ) ),
                    this, SIGNAL( colorMenuSelected( int ) ) );
  _popupmenu->insertItem( "Pop-up &2", subpopup2 );
}
```

You also need to add the lines

```
signals:
        void colorMenuSelected( int );
```

to the class declaration of `ScribbleArea`

For actually changing the color, it seems like a good idea to reuse the slot `slot-ColorMenu()` from the class `ScribbleWindow`. Unfortunately, we neither have a pointer to the `ScribbleWindow` object in the class `ScribbleArea` nor a usual parent/child relationship in the case of a scrolled view and the scrolled contents. Since we want the classes decoupled as much as possible anyway, we use a nifty technique: As you can see in the previous code, we connect the `activated( int )` signal from the pop-up menu to another signal that is defined for this purpose, `colorMenuSelected( int )`. In the constructor of `ScribbleWindow`, we can then connect this signal to the existing slot `slotColorMenu( int )`:

```
QObject::connect( _scribblearea, SIGNAL( colorMenuSelected( int ) ),
                  this, SLOT( slotColorMenu( int ) ) );
```

Answers to Exercises in the "File-I/O" section

1. Since we have not passed a file format to the method `QPixmap::load()`, but used the auto-detection of the file format instead, the code does not need to be changed at all. GIF and XPM support are built into Qt, so you can simply select a GIF or XPM file in the file-selection dialog, and it will be loaded.

2. Adding three calls to `setCaption()` is all it takes to solve this exercise. At the end of the constructor of `ScribbleWindow`, add the line:

    ```
    setCaption( "QtScribble: unnamed" );
    ```

    `ScribbleWindow::slotLoad()` is shown next, `slotSave()` has to be changed equivalently:

    ```
    void ScribbleWindow::slotLoad()
    {
      /* Open a file dialog for loading. The default directory is the
       * current directory, the filter *.bmp.
       */
      QString filename = QFileDialog::getOpenFileName( ".", "*.bmp", this );
      if( !filename.isEmpty() ) {
          emit load( filename );
          setCaption( "QtScribble: " + filename );
      }
    }
    ```

3. There are several steps required for this exercise:
    *   Declare a `bool` member variable `_dirty` in the class `ScribbleArea` that is true in case the drawing is changed but not saved.
    *   Add a method `bool isDirty() const` to the class `ScribbleArea` that returns whether the dirty flag is `false`. An inline method is a good choice here.
    *   Initialize `_dirty` to `false` in the constructor of `ScribbleArea`.
    *   Change `_dirty` to `true` when a line is drawn in `ScribbleArea::mouseMoveEvent()`.
    *   In `ScribbleArea::slotSave()`, set back `_dirty` to `false` since the drawing is now saved.

- In `ScribbleWindow::slotLoad()`, add code that checks whether the drawing is dirty and pops up a message box instead that asks whether the user wants to save. If this is the case, call `slotSave()`.

- Add a new slot, `slotQuit()`, to `ScribbleWindow` that checks whether the drawing is dirty, asks the user whether she wants to save, and calls `slotSave()` in this case. At the end of this method, `QApplication::quit()` should be called.

- Change the connection of the "Quit" menu entry in the constructor of `ScribbleWindow` from `QApplication::quit()` to `ScribbleWindow::slotQuit()`.

For your reference, here are all the changed pieces. The rest is just like Example 3-4. Note that this code has two drawbacks: If the application is closed via the window system (for example from the system menu), rather than the menu, `slotQuit()` will not be called. If missing disk space or permissions prevent the user from saving, the drawing will be discarded nevertheless. These are problems trivial to fix, though.

```
class ScribbleArea : public QWidget
{
  Q_OBJECT

public:
  ScribbleArea();
  ~ScribbleArea();

  bool isDirty() const { return _dirty; }

public slots:
  void setColor( QColor );
  void slotLoad( const char* );
  void slotSave( const char* );

protected:
  virtual void mousePressEvent( QMouseEvent* );
  virtual void mouseMoveEvent( QMouseEvent* );
  virtual void paintEvent( QPaintEvent* );
  virtual void resizeEvent( QResizeEvent* );

private slots:
  void slotClearArea();

private:
  QPoint _last;
  QColor _currentcolor;

  QPixmap _buffer;
  QPopupMenu* _popupmenu;

  bool _dirty;
};
```

```
...

class ScribbleWindow : public QWidget
{
  Q_OBJECT

public:
  ScribbleWindow();
  ~ScribbleWindow();

private slots:
  void slotAbout();
  void slotAboutQt();
  void slotColorMenu( int );
  void slotLoad();
  void slotSave();
  void slotQuit();

signals:
  void colorChanged( QColor );
  void load( const char* );
  void save( const char* );

protected:
  virtual void resizeEvent( QResizeEvent* );

private:
  QMenuBar* _menubar;
  QPopupMenu* _filemenu;
  QPopupMenu* _colormenu;
  QPopupMenu* _helpmenu;
  QScrollView* _scrollview;
  ScribbleArea* _scribblearea;
};

...

ScribbleArea::ScribbleArea()
{
  // initialize member variables
  _currentcolor = black;

  // don't blank the window before repainting
  setBackgroundMode( NoBackground );

  // create a pop-up menu
  _popupmenu = new QPopupMenu();
  _popupmenu->insertItem( "&Clear", this, SLOT( slotClearArea() ) );

  // initially, drawing is not changed
  _dirty = false;
}

...
```

```
void ScribbleArea::slotSave( const char* filename )
{
  if( !_buffer.save( filename, "BMP" ) )
      QMessageBox::warning( 0, "Save error", "Could not save file" );
  else
      _dirty = false;
}

...

void ScribbleArea::mouseMoveEvent( QMouseEvent* event )
{
  // create a QPainter object for drawing onto the window
  QPainter windowpainter;
  // and another QPainter object for drawing into an off-screen pixmap
  QPainter bufferpainter;

  // start painting
  windowpainter.begin( this );    // this painter paints onto the window
  bufferpainter.begin( &_buffer ); // and this one in the buffer

  // set a standard pen with the currently selected color
  windowpainter.setPen( _currentcolor );
  bufferpainter.setPen( _currentcolor );

  // draw a line in both the window and the buffer
  windowpainter.drawLine( _last, event->pos() );
  bufferpainter.drawLine( _last, event->pos() );

  // done with painting
  windowpainter.end();
  bufferpainter.end();

  // remember the current mouse position
  _last = event->pos();

  // record the scribble as dirty (changed), but not saved
  _dirty = true;
}

...

ScribbleWindow::ScribbleWindow()
{
  /* The next few lines build the menu bar. We first create the menus
   * one by one and add them afterwards to the menu bar. */
  _filemenu = new QPopupMenu; // create a file menu
  _filemenu->insertItem( "&Load", this, SLOT( slotLoad() ) );
  _filemenu->insertItem( "&Save", this, SLOT( slotSave() ) );
  _filemenu->insertSeparator();
  _filemenu->insertItem( "&Quit", this, SLOT( slotQuit() ) );

  _colormenu = new QPopupMenu; // create a color menu
  _colormenu->insertItem( "B&lack", COLOR_MENU_ID_BLACK );
```

```cpp
_colormenu->insertItem( "&Red", COLOR_MENU_ID_RED );
_colormenu->insertItem( "&Blue", COLOR_MENU_ID_BLUE );
_colormenu->insertItem( "&Green", COLOR_MENU_ID_GREEN );
_colormenu->insertItem( "&Yellow", COLOR_MENU_ID_YELLOW );
QObject::connect( _colormenu, SIGNAL( activated( int ) ),
                  this, SLOT( slotColorMenu( int ) ) );

_helpmenu = new QPopupMenu; // create a help menu
_helpmenu->insertItem( "&About QtScribble", this, SLOT( slotAbout() ) );
_helpmenu->insertItem( "About &Qt", this, SLOT( slotAboutQt() ) );

_menubar = new QMenuBar( this ); // create a menu bar
_menubar->insertItem( "&File", _filemenu );
_menubar->insertItem( "&Color", _colormenu );
_menubar->insertSeparator();
_menubar->insertItem( "&Help", _helpmenu );

/* We create a QScrollView and a ScribbleArea. The ScribbleArea will
 * be managed by the scroll view.*/
_scrollview = new QScrollView( this );
_scrollview->setGeometry( 0, _menubar->height(),
                          width(), height() - _menubar->height() );
_scribblearea = new ScribbleArea();
_scribblearea->setGeometry( 0, 0, 1000, 1000 );
_scrollview->addChild( _scribblearea );
QObject::connect( this, SIGNAL( colorChanged( QColor ) ),
                  _scribblearea, SLOT( setColor( QColor ) ) );
QObject::connect( this, SIGNAL( save( const char* ) ),
                  _scribblearea, SLOT( slotSave( const char* ) ) );
QObject::connect( this, SIGNAL( load( const char* ) ),
                  _scribblearea, SLOT( slotLoad( const char* ) ) );
}

...

void ScribbleWindow::slotLoad()
{
    /*
     * Check if the scribble is dirty, and ask the user whether he wants to
     * save.
     */
    if( _scribblearea->isDirty() ) {
    if( !QMessageBox::information( this, "Save?",
                    "Your drawing is not saved yet",
                    "Save", "Don't save" ) )
        slotSave();
    }

    /* Open a file dialog for loading. The default directory is the
     * current directory, the filter *.bmp.
     */
    QString filename = QFileDialog::getOpenFileName( ".", "*.bmp", this );
    if( !filename.isEmpty() )
      emit load( filename );
```

```
}

...

/**
 * Ask the user whether he wants to save if the drawing is changed,
 * but not saved. Then quit.
 */
void ScribbleWindow::slotQuit()
{
    /*
     * Check if the scribble is dirty, and ask the user whether he wants to
     * save.
     */
    if( _scribblearea->isDirty() ) {
    if( !QMessageBox::information( this, "Save?",
                        "Your drawing is not saved yet",
                        "Save", "Don't save" ) )
        slotSave();
    }

    // now really quit
    qApp->quit();
}
```

Bibliography

[1] Apple Computer Inc., *Guide to Macintosh Software Localization,* 1992, Addison-Wesley, Reading, Mass.
Contains a wealth of information about software localization, including pitfalls like cultural differences, and has lots of details about specific locales, their script systems, and cultural properties. The technical information is only useful for Macintosh programmers, but the general information is much more important here anyway (and fills many more pages).

[2] Edward Angel, *Interactive Computer Graphics,* 1996, Addison-Wesley, Reading, Mass.
This book teaches not only the functions that make up the OpenGL API, but also explains the theory and the mathematical foundations of 3D computer graphics. It is beautifully typeset, and contains color pages with 3D images.

[3] Alan Cooper, *About Face—The Essentials of User Interface Design,* 1995, IDG Books, Foster City, Calif.
The seminal book about user interface design. Contains lots of examples of how to and how not to design interfaces and covers topics like installation and help.

[4] J. Foley, A. v. Dam, et al., *Computer Graphics in C: Principles and Pratice,* 1995, Addison-Wesley, Reading, Mass.
Contains a large number of graphics algorithms and their implementation in C.

[5] J. Foley, et al., *Introduction to Computer Graphics,* 1994, Addison-Wesley, Reading, Mass.
A readable introduction to concepts and algorithms in computer graphics.

[6] Jeffrey E. Friedl, *Mastering Regular Expressions,* 1997, O'Reilly & Associates, Sebastopol, Calif.
This book teaches you all you ever wanted to know about regular expressions—and probably a lot more that you ever thought would exist.

[7]   Donald Lewine, *POSIX Programmer's Guide,* 1992, O'Reilly & Associates, Sebastopol, Calif.
A reference documentation to the POSIX.1 standard.

[8]   Theo Mandel, *The Elements of User Interface Design,* 1997, John Wiley, New York, N.Y.
Another book about designing user interfaces that especially stresses design as a process, and covers advanced topics like multimedia.

[9]   Microsoft Press, *The Windows Interface Guidelines for Software Design,* 1995, Microsoft Press, Redmond, Wash.
This book covers the basics of user interface in a very detailed manner. Every UI element is mentioned, together with information about when each should and should not be used. Fundamental topics like keyboard navigation and focus are also covered. Despite the title, this book is also a valuable resource for programmers and designers targeting platforms other than Windows.

[10] Bob Quinn, Dave Shute, *Windows Sockets Network Programming,* 1996, Addison-Wesley, Reading, Mass.
Explains how to use sockets on Windows; also covers Windows NT.

[11] Gregory Satir, Doug Brown, *C++: The Core Language,* 1995, O'Reilly & Associates, Sebastopol, Calif.
An introduction to C++ for C programmers that does not aim to present every feature of the language, but restricts itself to the most often-used language constructs. Knowledge of the language topics covered herein is completely sufficient for starting Qt programming.

[12] Randal L. Schwartz, Tom Christiansen, *Learning Perl,* 2. ed., 1997, O'Reilly & Associates, Sebastopol, Calif.
The classic introduction to Perl, this book features exercises with complete solutions.

[13] Sriram Srinivasan, *Advanced Perl Programming,* 1997, O'Reilly & Associates, Sebastopol, Calif.
This is a very good book for people who have mastered the basics of Perl and want to learn more. It is especially strong in its coverage of object-oriented programming with Perl.

[14] W. Richard Stevens, *Unix Network Programming, Vol. 1,* 2. ed., 1997, Prentice-Hall, Upper Saddle River, N.J.
This series is made up of the standard books about Unix network programming. As this book goes to print, only the first volume of the second edition has appeared, but this volume already contains most of the things you will need to know.

[15] Larry Wall, Randal L. Schwartz, Tom Christiansen, *Programming Perl,* 2. ed., 1996, O'Reilly & Associates, Sebastopol, Calif.
The first book about Perl and still one of the best, especially because of the very extensive reference section. Contains a wealth of material about all aspects of Perl programming, and documents the standard modules.

Index

3D graphics programming 279

A
abort()
  QPrinter 155
aborted()
  QPrinter 155
aboutQt()
  QMessageBox 45
aboutToShow()
  QTabDialog 122
accept()
  QDialog 118
  QDropSite 206
Accepted
  QDialog 118
access methods see C++, access methods
activate()
  QLayout 126
activated()
  QComboBox 84
  QMenuBar 44
  QPopupMenu 44, 55, 90
  QSocketNotifier 271
add()
  QToolTip 101
  QWhatsThis 103
addChild()
  QScrollView 53, 88, 105
addColSpacing()
  QGridLayout 132
addDays()
  QDate 209
  QDateTime 209

addLabel()
  QHeader 111
addLayout()
  QLayout 126
addMSecs() 1525
  QTime 209
addMultiCellWidget()
  QGridLayout 132
addRowSpacing()
  QGridLayout 132
addSecs()
  QDateTime 209
  QTime 209
addSeparator()
  QToolBar 100
addStretch()
  QBoxLayout 129
  QHBoxLayout 129
  QVBoxLayout 129
addTab()
  QTabDialog 121
addToolbar()
  QMainWindow 98
addWidget()
  QGridLayout 132
  QHBoxLayout 128
  QVBoxLayout 128
  QLayout 126
  QStatusBar 101
  QWidgetStack 93
AlignLeft
  QLabel 95
AlignVCenter
  QLabel 95

animations 151–152
API emulation 4–5
API layering 4–5
append()
    QDict 146
    QIntDict 146
    QList 146
    QPtrDict 146
applyButtonPressed()
    QTabDialog 122
arrangers 91–94
arrays 145
ASSERT() 251
at()
    QFile 190

B
begin()
    QPainter 34
bitBlt() 36, 169
black 158
blockSignals()
    QObject 247
blue 158
BMP (graphics file format) 173
bool see C++, bool
bounded range input widgets 85–87
brush 162
bubble help see tool tips
bubble help see what's this windows
buffer 34
buffering, double- see double-buffering
building projects 257
button groups 81
buttons 79–81

C
C++ 9–10
    access methods 10
    bool 10
    classes 9
    inheritance 10
    operator overloading 10
    templates 10
    virtual functions 10
caches 147–148
callback functions 21
cancelButtonPressed()
    QTabDialog 122

cancelled()
    QProgressDialog 117
canDecode()
    QStoredDrag 206
    QTextDrag 206
CDE 1
center()
    QScrollView 89, 105
CHECK_PTR() 251
check-boxes 80–81
checkOverFlow()
    QLCDNumber 97
classes see C++, classes
clear()
    QDict 147
    QIntDict 147
    QList 147
    QPtrDict 147
    QQueue 149
    QStack 149
    QStatusBar 100
    QToolTipGroup 102
clicked()
    QButton 20, 79, 80
    QButtonGroup 248
clipboard 197–202
    built-in operations in QMultiLineEdit 200
    transferring non-textual data 200
clipboard()
    QApplication 197
clipping 168
close()
    QFile 190
collection classes see containers
color groups see colors, groups
color0 158
color1 158
colorChanged()
    ScribbleWindow 54
colors 157–161
    allocation 157–158
        lazy 157
    groups 159–161
    models 159
    palettes 159–161
combo boxes 83–84
    vs. list boxes 84
command-line parameters 14

communication
    inter-application see inter-application
        communication
connect()
    QObject 25, 27, 44, 54, 245, 246
connectItem()
    QMenuData 44
connectResize()
    QMovie 152
connectStatus()
    QMovie 152
connectUpdate()
    QMovie 152
container classes
    arrays 145
    caches 147
    choosing 145
    hash tables 145
    iterators 148
    lists 145
    with macros 146
    queues 145, 149
    stacks 145, 149
    templates 146
    using 145
containers 143–149
contentsMoving()
    QScrollView 105
contentsRect()
    QFrame 91
context()
    QGLWidget 280
context menus 55
    invoking 55
controls 14
convertDepth()
    QImage 175
convertSeparators()
    QDir 256
copy-and-paste
    clipboard 197
copyText()
    QMultiLineEdit 94, 200
count()
    QQueue 149
    QStack 149
create()
    QNPlugin 285

critical()
    QMessageBox 115
current()
    QCacheIterator 148
    QDictIterator 148
    QIntCacheIterator 148
    QIntDictIterator 148
    QListIterator 148
    QPtrDictIterator 148
currentChanged()
    QListView 109
currentDate()
    QDate 209
currentDateTime()
    QDateTime 209
currentItem()
    QComboBox 84
    QListBox 82
currentTime()
    QDate 209
cursorPosition()
    QMultiLineEdit 200
cursors
    overriding 177
custom widgets 211–236
    base classes 212
    browse box (example) 222
    coordinate selector (example) 213
    emitting signals 212
    event handlers 212
    subclassing from 213
cut()
    QMultiLineEdit 94, 200
cut-and-paste
    clipboard 197
cyan 158

D
darkBlue 158
darkCyan 158
darkGray 158
darkGreen 158
darkMagenta 158
darkRed 158
darkYellow 158
dataChanged()
    QClipboard 197
date values 209–210

debug() 190, 251, 256
debugging 251–252
    avoiding server grabs 252
    dumping object trees 252
    message handlers 251
    output 251
    synchronous X11 operations 252
    widget names 252
decode()
    QStoredDrag 206
    QTextDrag 206
defaultButtonPressed()
    QTabDialog 122
defineIOHandler()
    QImageIO 174
del()
    QMultiLineEdit 198
dequeue()
    QQueue 149
design see GUI design
desktop()
    QApplication 231
Developer Studio 301–303
dialogs
    custom 118–124
    file selection see file selection dialogs
    message boxes see message boxes
    predefined see predefined dialogs
    progress see progress dialogs
    tab see tab dialogs
directories 189–195
    filtering 192
    sorting 193
    traversing 191
disconnect()
    QObject 247
display()
    QLCDNumber 26, 97
documentation
    online see Qt, documentation, online
    printed see Qt, documentation, printed
double-buffering 168–173
doubleClicked()
    QListView 109
drag()
    QTextDrag 205
drag and drop 202–208
    accepting drops 206
    converting data 206

custom drag types 206
standards 203
starting drags 203
dragCopy()
    QTextDrag 205
dragEnterEvent()
    QDropSite 206
dragMove()
    QTextDrag 205
dragMoveEvent()
    QDropSite 206
drawArc()
    QPainter 162
drawChord()
    QPainter 163
drawContents()
    QFrame 91
drawContentsOffset()
    QScrollView 105
drawEllipse()
    QPainter 162
drawImage()
    QPainter 163
drawLine()
    QPainter 162
drawLineSegments()
    QPainter 163
drawPie()
    QPainter 163
drawPixmap()
    QPainter 163, 169, 170
drawPolygon()
    QPainter 155, 163
drawPolyline()
    QPainter 163
drawQuadBezier()
    QPainter 163
drawRect()
    QPainter 162
drawRotatedText() 164, 165
drawRoundRect()
    QPainter 162
drawText()
    QPainter 163
drawTiledPixmap()
    QPainter 162
dropEvent()
    QDropSite 206

dumpObjectInfo()
    QObject 252
dumpObjectTree()
    QObject 252

E
EBuilder (GUI builder) 268
elapsed()
    QStart 209
emit 25
end()
    QPainter 34
enqueue()
    QQueue 149
ensureVisible()
    QScrollView 88
enter_loop()
    QApplication 232
enterAllocContext()
    QColor 157
entryInfoList()
    QDir 193
error()
    QMessageBox 45
event filters 241–243
eventFilter()
    QObject 241
events 241–244
    filtering see event filters
    handling 29
    low-level 29
    semantic 30
    syntactic 30
    synthetic 243–244
exec()
    QApplication 15
    QDialog 118
    QPopupMenu 55, 63, 90
exists()
    QFile 190
exit_loop()
    QApplication 232
expand()
    QGridLayout 132
extensions 279–292
    OpenGL see OpenGL
    plugins see plugins

F
FALSE 72
fatal() 251, 256
    QMessageBox 45
file formats
    custom 173
file selection dialogs 63, 113
files 189–195
    getting information about 193
    handling 63
    reading from 190
    removing 190
    with binary data 191
    writing to 190
Filled
    QLCDNumber 97
find()
    QCache 147
    QDict 146
    QIntCache 147
    QIntDict 146
    QList 146
    QPtrDict 146
finished()
    QMovie 152
first()
    QList 147
firstChild()
    QListView 109
fixup()
    QValidator 184
Flat
    QLCDNumber 97
flicker, avoiding 168
flushX()
    QApplication 256
focus 237–239
    policies 237
    tab order 238
focusInEvent()
    QWidget 212
focusNextPrevChild()
    QWidget 238
focusOutEvent()
    QWidget 212

format()
   QGLWidget 280
frames 91
framework, application 2
freeze()
   QLayout 131

G
geometry management see layout management
geometry managers see layout management
getMIMEDescription()
   QNPlugin 285
getOpenFileName()
   QFileDialog 63, 64, 113
getPluginDescriptionString()
   QNPlugin 285
getPluginNameString()
   QNPlugin 285
getSaveFileName()
   QFileDialog 64, 113
Ghostscript 153
GIF (graphics file format) 151, 173
graphics 151–177
gray 158
green 158
group()
   QFileInfo 194
group boxes 91–92
GUI builders 263–268
GUI design 137–141
GUI emulation 4–5
GUI toolkits 1, 4–5
   emulating 5

H
handle()
   QCursor 256
   QFont 257
   QPaintDevice 257
   QPainter 257
hash tables 145
header files 13
help, getting 11
hide()
   QButtonGroup 249
highlighted()
   QComboBox 84

   QListBox 82
   QMenuBar 90
   QPopupMenu 90
homeDirPath()
   QDir 193
Hoover help see tool tips
Horizontal
   QScrollBar 88
HTTP 271

I
images
   file formats
      custom 173
   loading and saving 173
information()
   QMessageBox 45, 115
inheritance see C++, inheritance
initGM()
   QLayout 134
initializeGL()
   QGLWidget 280
input
   validating 179–184
insert()
   QButtonGroup 81, 92, 248
   QDict 146
   QIntDict 146
   QList 146
   QPtrDict 146
insertAt()
   QMultiLineEdit 94
insertItem()
   QComboBox 84
   QListBox 81
   QMenuBar 55
   QMenuData 43, 90
insertLine()
   QMultiLineEdit 94
insertSeparators()
   QDir 256
insertStrList()
   QComboBox 84
   QListBox 82
inSort()
   QListBox 82

installEventFilter()
    QObject 241
inter-application communication 197–208
internationalization 138
Internet Explorer 283
ISBNs 179
isChecked()
    QCheckBox 80
    QRadioButton 80
isDir()
    QFileInfo 194
isExecutable()
    QFileInfo 194
isFile()
    QFileInfo 194
isReadable()
    QFileInfo 194
isSymLink()
    QFileInfo 194
isWritable()
    QFileInfo 194
itemBelow()
    QListViewItem 109
iterators 148–149

J
JPEG (graphics file format) 173

K
KDE project 305
keyPressEvent()
    QWidget 212
    ScribbleWindow 36, 55

L
labels 14, 95–98
    alignment 95
    buddies 95
    for displaying graphics 96
    vs. read-only text entry fields 96
last()
    QList 147
lastModified()
    QFileInfo 194
lastRead()
    QFileInfo 194
layout management 125–135, 263
    box layout 128, 132

freezing layouts 132
    grid layout 132
    in group boxes 129
    layout policies 132
layout managers see layout management
LCD displays 97–98
    connecting with sliders 97
leaveAllocContext()
    QColor 157
lightGray 158
list boxes 81–82
    GUI design 140
    vs. combo boxes 84
list views 106–110
lists 145
QListView 106
load()
    QPixmap 72, 173, 174
    ScribbleWindow 64

M
magenta 158
main widget 15
main windows 98–99
mainHorizontalChain()
    QLayout 134
mainVerticalChain()
    QLayout 134
makeCurrent()
    QGLWidget 281
makefiles 257
mapFromGlobal()
    QWidget 231
mapToGlobal()
    QWidget 56, 231
match()
    QRegExp 186
maybeTip()
    QToolTip 102
menu bars 37
    in main windows 98
menuBar()
    QMainWindow 98
menus 37–47, 89–90
    context see context menus
    pop-up see context menus
message()
    QStatusBar 100

message boxes 45, 72, 115
metafiles 63
meta-object compiler
    moc 24
Microsoft Foundation Classes (MFC) 3, 22
MIME types 284
moc 24, 28–29
Motif 1, 4, 22, 203, 291
Motif style 77
mouseDoubleClickEvent()
    QWidget 36
mouseMoveEvent()
    QWidget 30
    ScribbleArea 54
    ScribbleWindow 30, 34, 44
mousePressEvent()
    QWidget 30, 212
    ScribbleArea 63
    ScribbleWindow 30
mouseReleaseEvent()
    QWidget 212
moveChild()
    QScrollView 105
moved()
    QHeader 111

N
name()
    QObject 252
Netscape Navigator 16, 283
network programming 271–278
newStreamCreated()
    QNPInstance 285
newWindow()
    QNPInstance 285
next()
    QList 147
nextLine()
    QScrollBar 88
nextPage()
    QScrollBar 88
number displays see LCD displays

O
office look 98
off-screen buffer 34
open()
    QFile 190, 257
OpenGL 279–281

operator overloading see C++ operator
    overloading
operator++()
    QCacheIterator 148
    QDictIterator 148
    QIntCacheIterator 148
    QIntDictIterator 148
    QListIterator 148
    QPtrDictIterator 148
option buttons 80
Orthovista 306–307
Outline
    QLCDNumber 97
overflow()
    QLCDNumber 97
overrideCursor()
    QApplication 177
owner()
    QFileInfo 194

P
paintCell()
    QKBrowseBox (example class) 232
    QTableView 223, 232
paintEvent()
    QWidget 30, 169, 212
    ScribbleWindow 30, 35
paintGL()
    QGLWidget 280
palettes see colors, palettes
parentWidget()
    QToolTip 102
paste()
    QMultiLineEdit 94, 200
pause()
    QMovie 152
paused()
    QMovie 152
pen 161
Perl 293–294
pixmap()
    QListBox 82
pixmaps 63
plugins 283–291
PNG (graphics file format) 173
PNM (graphics file format) 173
pointers
    as parameters of slots 54

pop()
  QStack 149
popup()
  QPopupMenu 55
pop-up menus see context menus
portability 3, 253–261
  benefits 253
  pitfalls in Qt 256
pos()
  QCursor 55
POSIX 255
postEvent()
  QApplication 243
PostScript 153
predefined dialogs 113–118
pressed()
  QButton 21, 79, 80
prev()
  QList 147
prevLine()
  QScrollBar 88
prevPage()
  QScrollBar 88
printer drivers 153
printing 153–157
  orientation 153
  print dialog 153
  setup 153
processEvents()
  QApplication 104, 155
progress bars 104
progress dialogs 116, 140
push()
  QStack 149
push-buttons 19, 79
  as toggle buttons 81
  auto-default 79
  connecting several to one slot 248
  default 79
  GUI design 141
  in tool bars 99

Q
Q_OBJECT macro 24
QAccel 90
qApp pointer 43
QApplication
  clipboard() 197
  desktop() 231
  enter_loop() 232

exec() 15
exit_loop() 232
flushX() 256
overrideCursor() 177
postEvent() 243
processEvents() 104, 155
quit() 21
restoreOverrideCursor() 177
sendEvent() 243
sendPostedEvents() 244
setColorSpec() 158, 256
setDoubleClickInterval() 256
setMainWidget() 256
setOverrideCursor() 177
setPalette() 161
setStyle() 78
syncX() 256
QApplication 14, 15, 19
qapplication.h, header file 14
QArray 143, 145
QBitArray 144, 145
qBlue() 175
QBoxLayout
  addStretch() 129
QBuffer 191, 202
QButton 19
  clicked() 20, 79, 80
  pressed() 21, 79, 80
  released() 79, 80
  setPixmap() 79
  setText() 79
  toggled() 80, 81
QButtonBox 91
QButtonGroup 91, 129, 248
  clicked() 248
  hide() 249
  insert() 81, 92, 248
  setExclusive() 92
QByteArray 143, 202
QCache 144, 147
  find() 147
  setMaxCost() 147
QCacheIterator 148
  current() 148
  operator++() 148
  toFirst() 148
  toLast() 148
QCheckBox
  isChecked() 80
  setChecked() 80

QClipboard 94, 197
  dataChanged() 197
  setPixmap() 197
  setText() 197, 198, 200
  text() 200
QColor 36, 157, 159, 191
  enterAllocContext() 157
  leaveAllocContext() 157
  setLazyAllocation() 157
QColorGroup 160
QComboBox
  activated() 84
  currentItem() 84
  highlighted() 84
  insertItem() 84
  insertStrList() 84
  setInsertionPolicy() 83
  setValidator() 179
QCursor
  handle() 256
  pos() 55
QDataStream 189, 191
QDate 209
  addDays() 209
  currentDate() 209
  currentTime() 209
  toString() 210
QDateTime 209
  addDays() 209
  addSecs() 209
  currentDateTime() 209
  toString() 210
QDialog 118, 119, 138
  accept() 118
  Accepted 118
  exec() 118
  reject() 118
  Rejected 118
  setCaption() 118
QDict 144, 145
  append() 146
  clear() 147
  find() 146
  insert() 146
  remove() 146
  setAutoDelete() 147
QDictIterator 148
  current() 148
  operator++() 148

  toFirst() 148
  toLast() 148
QDir 189, 191
  convertSeparators() 256
  entryInfoList() 193
  homeDirPath() 193
  insertSeparators() 256
  rootDirPath() 193
  separator() 193
  setFilter() 192, 256
  setFilterName() 193
  setMatchAllDirs() 193
  setSorting() 193
QDoubleValidator 179
QDragMoveEvent 207
qDrawPlainRect() 233
qDrawShadeLine() 233
qDrawShadePanel() 233
qDrawShadeRect() 233
qDrawWinButton() 233
qDrawWinPanel() 233
QDropSite 205
  accept() 206
  dragEnterEvent() 206
  dragMoveEvent() 206
  dropEvent() 206
QEvent 241
QFile 175, 189
  at() 190
  close() 190
  exists() 190
  open() 190, 257
  readBlock() 190
  remove() 190
  setName() 189
  writeBlock() 190
QFileDialog 113, 114, 134
  63
  getOpenFileName() 63, 64, 113
  getSaveFileName() 63, 64, 113
QFileInfo 189, 191, 193
  group() 194
  isDir() 194
  isExecutable() 194
  isFile() 194
  isReadable() 194
  isSymLink() 194
  isWritable() 194
  lastModified() 194

lastRead() 194
owner() 194
refresh() 195
setCaching() 195
QFileInfoList 191
QFont
  handle() 257
QFrame 19, 91, 129
  contentsRect() 91
  drawContents() 91
  setFrameStyle() 91
  setLineWidth() 91
  setMargin() 91
  setMidLineWidth() 91
QGLContext 280
QGLFormat 280
QGLWidget 280
  context() 280
  format() 280
  initializeGL() 280
  makeCurrent() 281
  paintGL() 280
  resizeGL() 280
  setContext() 280
  setFormat() 280
qGreen() 175
QGridLayout 132
  addColSpacing() 132
  addMultiCellWidget() 132
  addRowSpacing() 132
  addWidget() 132
  expand() 132
  setColStretch() 132
  setRowStretch() 132
QGroupBox 91, 129
  setAlignment() 91
  setTitle() 91
QHBoxLayout 128
  addStretch() 129
  addWidget() 128
QVBoxLayout
  addWidget() 128
QHeader 111
  addLabel() 111
  moved() 111
  sectionClicked() 111
  setClickEnabled() 111

setLabel() 111
setMovingEnabled() 111
setResizeEnabled() 111
setTracking() 111
sizeChanged() 111
QImage 175
  convertDepth() 175
QImageDrag 206
QImageFormatType 176
QImageIO 173
  defineIOHandler() 174
qInitImageIO() 173
qInitJpegIO() 173
qInitPngIO() 173
qInstallMsgHandler() 251
QIntCache 144, 147
  find() 147
  setMaxCost() 147
QIntCacheIterator 148
  current() 148
  operator++() 148
  toFirst() 148
  toLast() 148
QIntDict 144, 145
  append() 146
  clear() 147
  find() 146
  insert() 146
  remove() 146
  setAutoDelete() 147
QIntDictIterator 148
  current() 148
  operator++() 148
  toFirst() 148
  toLast() 148
QIntValidator 179
QIODevice 175, 189
QKBrowseBox (example class) 222, 230
  paintCell() 232
QKCoordSel (example class) 213, 215
  setFont() 220
  valueChanged() 214
QLabel 14, 17, 19, 20, 96, 138
  AlignLeft 95
  AlignVCenter 95
  setAlignment() 95
  setBuddy() 95

setMovie() 95, 152
setPixmap() 95
setText() 95
qlabel.h, header file 14
QLayout
   activate() 126
   addLayout() 126
   addWidget() 126
   freeze() 131
   initGM() 134
   mainHorizontalChain() 134
   mainVerticalChain() 134
QLCDNumber 26, 86, 95, 97
   checkOverFlow() 97
   display() 26, 97
   Filled 97
   Flat 97
   Outline 97
   overflow() 97
   setBinMode() 97
   setDecMode() 97
   setHexMode() 97
   setMode() 97
   setNumDigits() 97
   setOctMode() 97
   setSegmentStyle() 97
   setSmallDecimalPoint() 97
QLineEdit 94, 96, 140
   returnPressed() 95
   setText() 94
   setValidator() 179
   text() 94
   textChanged() 95
QList 144, 145
   append() 146
   clear() 147
   find() 146
   first() 147
   insert() 146
   last() 147
   next() 147
   prev() 147
   remove() 146
   setAutoDelete() 147
QListBox 84
   currentItem() 82
   highlighted() 82
   insertItem() 81

insertStrList() 82
inSort() 82
pixmap() 82
selected() 82
selectionChanged() 82
setMultiSelection() 82
text() 82
QListBoxItem 81
QListIterator 148
   current() 148
   operator++() 148
   toFirst() 148
   toLast() 148
QListView 105, 108, 109
   currentChanged() 109
   doubleClicked() 109
   firstChild() 109
   returnPressed() 109
   rightButtonClicked() 109
   rightButtonPressed() 109
   selectionChanged() 109
   setAllColumnsShowFocus() 109
   setColumnWidth() 109
   setColumnWidthMode() 109
   setCurrentItem() 109
   setMultiSelection() 109
   setSelected() 109
   setSorting() 109
   setTreeStepSize() 109
QListViewItem 106, 108, 110
   itemBelow() 109
   setOn() 108
   setOpen() 110
   setPixmap() 110
   setSelected() 110
   setup() 110
QMainWindow 43, 98
   addToolbar() 98
   menuBar() 98
   removeToolbar() 98
   setCentralWidget() 99
   setUsesBigPixmaps() 98
   statusBar() 98
QMenuBar 37, 43, 89, 98
   activated() 44
   highlighted() 90
   insertItem() 55

QMenuData 37, 89
  aboutQt() 45
  connectItem() 44
  insertItem() 43, 90
  removeItem() 90
  setAccel() 90
  setItemEnabled() 90
  updateItem() 90
QMessageBox 45, 72, 113, 115, 116
  critical() 115
  error() 45
  fatal() 45
  information() 45, 115
  setIcon() 116
  setIconPixmap() 116
  warning() 45, 115
QMouseEvent 36
QMovie 151
  connectResize() 152
  connectStatus() 152
  connectUpdate() 152
  finished() 152
  pause() 152
  paused() 152
  restart() 151, 152
  running() 152
  step() 152
  unpause() 152
QMultiLineEdit 96, 99, 140, 198
  copyText() 94, 200
  cursorPosition() 200
  cut() 94, 200
  del() 198
  insertAt() 94
  insertLine() 94
  paste() 94, 200
  removeLine() 94
  returnPressed() 95
  setReadOnly() 94
  text() 94
  textChanged() 95
QNPInstance 285
  newStreamCreated() 285
  newWindow() 285
  streamAsFile() 285
  write() 285
  writeReady() 285

QNPlugin 285
  create() 285
  getMIMEDescription() 285
  getPluginDescriptionString() 285
  getPluginNameString() 285
QNPStream 286
QNPWidget 285
QObject 23
  blockSignals() 247
  connect() 25, 27, 44, 54, 245, 246
  disconnect() 247
  dumpObjectInfo() 252
  dumpObjectTree() 252
  eventFilter() 241
  installEventFilter() 241
  name() 252
  startTimer() 257
QPaintDevice 34, 35
  handle() 257
  x11Display() 257
QPainter 29, 45, 47, 161, 163
  begin() 34
  drawArc() 162
  drawChord() 163
  drawEllipse() 162
  drawImage() 163
  drawLine() 162
  drawLineSegments() 163
  drawPie() 163
  drawPixmap() 163, 169, 170
  drawPolygon() 155, 163
  drawPolyline() 163
  drawQuadBezier() 163
  drawRect() 162
  drawRoundRect() 162
  drawText() 163
  drawTiledPixmap() 162
  end() 34
  handle() 257
  restore() 164, 165
  rotate() 164
  save() 164, 165
  scale() 165
  setBrush() 162
  setClipping() 168
  setClipRect() 168
  setFont() 162

setPen() 36, 161
setRasterOp() 170
setViewport() 166
setViewXForm() 167
setWorldMatrix() 165
setWorldXForm() 166
shear() 165
translate() 164
xForm() 166
xFormDev() 166
QPalette 160
  setActive() 160
  setDisabled() 160
  setNormal() 160
QPicture 34, 153
  save() 63
QPixmap 34, 47, 169
  load() 72, 173, 174
  save() 63, 72, 173, 174
  xForm() 170
QPoint 55
QPointArray 143
QPopupMenu 37, 43, 89
  activated() 44, 55, 90
  exec() 55, 63, 90
  highlighted() 90
  popup() 55
QPrinter 153, 155
  abort() 155
  aborted() 155
  setMinMax() 153
  setOrientation() 153
  setup() 153
QProgressBar 104, 140
  setProgress() 104
  setTotalSteps() 104
QProgressDialog 113, 117, 140, 156
  cancelled() 117
  setProgress() 117
  setTotalSteps() 117
QPtrDict 144, 145
  append() 146
  clear() 147
  find() 146
  insert() 146
  remove() 146
  setAutoDelete() 147
QPtrDictIterator 148
  current() 148

operator++() 148
toFirst() 148
toLast() 148
QPushButton 19, 20, 77, 79, 138
  setAutoDefault() 79
  setDefault() 79
  setToggleButton() 81
  toggled() 79
QQueue 144, 145, 149
  clear() 149
  count() 149
  dequeue() 149
  enqueue() 149
  remove() 149
QRadioButton 80
  isChecked() 80
  setChecked() 80
QRangeControl 213, 220
  setRange() 85, 87, 88
  setSteps() 85, 88
  setValue() 85, 88
  value() 85
qRed() 175
QRegExp 174, 184
  match() 186
  setCaseSensitive() 186
  setWildcard() 187
qRgb() 175
QScrollBar 87
  Horizontal 88
  nextLine() 88
  nextPage() 88
  prevLine() 88
  prevPage() 88
  setOrientation() 88
  setTracking() 88
  sliderMoved() 88
  sliderPressed() 88
  sliderReleased() 88
  valueChanged() 88
  Vertical 88
QScrollView 47, 87, 105
  addChild() 53, 88, 105
  center() 89, 105
  contentsMoving() 105
  drawContentsOffset() 105
  ensureVisible() 88
  moveChild() 105
  removeChild() 105

resizeContents() 105
scrollBy() 55, 105
setContentsPos() 105
setCornerWidget() 88
setHScrollBarMode() 55, 88, 105
setVScrollBarMode() 55, 105
showChild() 105
viewportMouseDoubleClickEvent() 105
viewportMouseMoveEvent() 105
viewportMousePressEvent() 105
viewportMouseReleaseEvent() 105
viewportPaintEvent() 105
QSemiModal 156
QSignalMapper 249
QSlider 26, 29, 85, 97
   setOrientation() 85
   setTickmarks() 85
   setTracking 85
   setValue() 85
   sliderMoved() 26, 85
   sliderPressed() 85
   sliderReleased() 85
   valueChanged() 85
QSocketNotifier 271
   activated() 271
QSpinBox
   setPrefix() 86
   setSpecialValueText() 86
   setSuffix() 86
   setValidator() 179
   setValue() 86
   stepDown() 87
   stepUp() 87
   value() 86
   valueChanged() 87
QSplitter 91, 92
   setOpaqueSize() 93
   setOrientation() 92
   setResizeMode() 93
   Vertical 92
QStack 144, 145, 149
   clear() 149
   count() 149
   pop() 149
   push() 149
   remove() 149
QStatusBar 98, 100
   addWidget() 101
   clear() 100

message() 100
   removeWidget() 101
QStoredDrag 206
   canDecode() 206
   decode() 206
   setEncodedData() 207
QString 143, 202
QStrList 82, 84
Qt
   acquiring 6
   advantages 3–4
   class tree 17
   compiling 8
   documentation
      online 16–19
      printed 19
   extensions 279
   future of 313
   header files see header files
   installing
      on Unix 7–9
      on Windows 9
QTabDialog 121, 124
   aboutToShow() 122
   addTab() 121
   applyButtonPressed() 122
   cancelButtonPressed() 122
   defaultButtonPressed() 122
   selected() 122
   setApplyButton() 122
   setCancelButton() 122
   setDefaultButton() 122
   setOKButton() 122
   setTabEnabled() 122
QTableView 111, 223
   paintCell() 223, 232
   setTableFlags() 230
QtArch (GUI builder) 264
QTDIR, environment variable 8, 9
QTextDrag 205
   canDecode() 206
   decode() 206
   drag() 205
   dragCopy() 205
   dragMove() 205
QTextStream 189, 190, 191, 277
   readLine() 189
QtEZ (GUI builder) 266

QTime 209
    addMSecs() 209
    addSecs() 209
    elapsed() 209
    start() 209
    toString() 210
qt-interest, mailing list 11
QToolBar 98, 99
    addSeparator() 100
    setStretchableWidget() 100
QToolBarButton 99
QToolButton 100
    setTextLabel() 100
    setUsesBigPixmap() 100
    setUsesTextLabel() 100
QToolTip
    add() 101
    maybeTip() 102
    parentWidget() 102
    remove() 102
QToolTipGroup 102
    clear() 102
    showTip() 102
queues 145, 149
quick help see tool tips
quit()
    QApplication 21
QValidator 84, 179
    fixup() 184
    validate() 184
QVBoxLayout
    addStretch() 129
QWhatsThis
    add() 103
    remove() 103
    whatsThisButton() 104
QWidget 14, 19, 24, 30, 34
    focusInEvent() 212
    focusNextPrevChild() 238
    focusOutEvent() 212
    keyPressEvent() 212
    mapFromGlobal() 231
    mapToGlobal() 56, 231
    mouseDoubleClickEvent() 36
    mouseMoveEvent() 30
    mousePressEvent() 30, 212
    mouseReleaseEvent() 212
    paintEvent() 30, 169, 212
    repaint() 168

resizeEvent() 30, 171
setBackgroundMode() 30, 35, 168
setCaption() 72
setEnabled() 77
setFocusPolicy() 237
setFont() 77, 171, 220
setGeometry() 20
setMaximumSize() 93, 127
setMinimumSize() 92, 127
setMouseTracking() 231
setPalette() 77, 161, 171
setSizeIncrement() 257
setStyle() 77
setTabOrder() 238
sizeHint() 127
winId() 257
QWidgetStack 91
    addWidget() 93
    raiseWidget() 94
    removeWidget() 93
QWMatrix 165, 166
    setMatrix() 166
QWMMatrix 165
QXtApplication 291, 292
QXtWidget 291, 292

R
radio buttons 80–81
    radio behaviour 80
raiseWidget()
    QWidgetStack 94
readBlock()
    QFile 190
readLine()
    QTextStream 189
red 158
refresh()
    QFileInfo 195
regular expressions (regexps) 184–187
    escape sequences 185
    metacharacters 184
reject()
    QDialog 118
Rejected
    QDialog 118
released() 85
    QButton 79, 80
remove()
    QDict 146

QFile 190
QIntDict 146
QList 146
QPtrDict 146
QQueue 149
QStack 149
QToolTip 102
QWhatsThis 103
removeChild()
   QScrollView 105
removeItem()
   QMenuData 90
removeLine()
   QMultiLineEdit 94
removeToolbar()
   QMainWindow 98
removeWidget()
   QStatusBar 101
   QWidgetStack 93
repaint()
   QWidget 168
resizeContents()
   QScrollView 105
resizeEvent()
   QWidget 30, 171
   ScribbleWindow 30, 35, 45
resizeGL()
   QGLWidget 280
restart()
   QMovie 151, 152
restore()
   QPainter 164, 165
restoreOverrideCursor()
   QApplication 177
returnPressed()
   QLineEdit 95
   QListView 109
   QMultiLineEdit 95
rightButtonClicked()
   QListView 109
rightButtonPressed()
   QListView 109
rootDirPath()
   QDir 193
rotate()
   QPainter 164
running()
   QMovie 152

S
save()
   QPainter 164, 165
   QPicture 63
   QPixmap 63, 72, 173, 174
   ScribbleWindow 64
scale()
   QPainter 165
ScribbleArea 53
   mouseMoveEvent() 54
   mousePressEvent() 63
   setColor() 54
   slotClearArea() 56
   slotLoad() 64, 72
   slotSave() 64
ScribbleWindow 53, 56, 64, 72
   colorChanged() 54
   keyPressEvent() 36, 55
   load() 64
   mouseMoveEvent() 30, 34, 44
   mousePressEvent() 30
   paintEvent 30
   paintEvent() 35
   resizeEvent() 30, 35, 45
   save() 64
   setGeometry() 35
   slotAbout() 37, 45, 53
   slotAboutQt() 37, 45, 53
   slotColorMenu() 45, 53
   slotColourMenu() 37, 44
scroll bars 47, 87–89
scrollBy()
   QScrollView 55, 105
scrolled views 47–55, 105–106
   scroll bar policies 105
sectionClicked()
   QHeader 111
selected()
   QListBox 82
   QTabDialog 122
selection widgets 81–84
selectionChanged()
   QListBox 82
   QListView 109
sendEvent()
   QApplication 243
sendPostedEvents()
   QApplication 244

separator()
    QDir 193
setAccel()
    QMenuData 90
setActive()
    QPalette 160
setAlignment()
    QGroupBox 91
    QLabel 95
setAllColumnsShowFocus()
    QListView 109
setApplyButton()
    QTabDialog 122
setAutoDefault()
    QPushButton 79
setAutoDelete()
    QDict 147
    QIntDict 147
    QList 147
    QPtrDict 147
setBackgroundMode()
    QWidget 30, 35, 168
setBinMode()
    QLCDNumber 97
setBrush()
    QPainter 162
setBuddy()
    QLabel 95
setCaching()
    QFileInfo 195
setCancelButton()
    QTabDialog 122
setCaption()
    QDialog 118
    QWidget 72
setCaseSensitive()
    QRegExp 186
setCentralWidget()
    QMainWindow 99
setChecked()
    QCheckBox 80
    QRadioButton 80
setClickEnabled()
    QHeader 111
setClipping()
    QPainter 168
setClipRect()
    QPainter 168

setColor()
    ScribbleArea 54
setColorSpec()
QApplication 158, 256
setColStretch()
    QGridLayout 132
setColumnWidth()
    QListView 109
setColumnWidthMode()
    QListView 109
setContentsPos()
    QScrollView 105
setContext()
    QGLWidget 280
setCornerWidget()
    QScrollView 88
setCurrentItem()
    QListView 109
setDecMode()
    QLCDNumber 97
setDefault
    QPushButton 79
setDefaultButton()
    QTabDialog 122
setDisabled()
    QPalette 160
setDoubleClickInterval()
    QApplication 256
setEnabled()
    QWidget 77
setEncodedData()
    QStoredDrag 207
setExclusive()
    QButtonGroup 92
setFilter()
    QDir 192, 256
setFilterName()
    QDir 193
setFocusPolicy()
    QWidget 237
setFont()
    QKCoordSel (example class) 220
    QPainter 162
    QWidget 77, 171, 220
setFormat()
    QGLWidget 280
setFrameStyle()
    QFrame 91

setGeometry()
  QWidget 20
  ScribbleWindow 35
setHexMode()
  QLCDNumber 97
setHScrollBarMode()
  QScrollView 55, 88, 105
setIcon()
  QMessageBox 116
setIconPixmap()
  QMessageBox 116
setInsertionPolicy()
  QComboBox 83
setItemEnabled()
  QMenuData 90
setLabel()
  QHeader 111
setLazyAllocation()
  QColor 157
setLineWidth()
  QFrame 91
setMainWidget()
  QApplication 256
setMargin()
  QFrame 91
setMatchAllDirs()
  QDir 193
setMatrix()
  QWMMatrix 166
setMaxCost()
  QCache 147
  QIntCache 147
setMaximumSize()
  QWidget 93, 127
setMidLineWidth()
  QFrame 91
setMinimumSize()
  QWidget 92, 127
setMinMax()
  QPrinter 153
setMode()
  QLCDNumber 97
setMouseTracking()
  QWidget 231
setMovie()
  QLabel 95, 152
setMovingEnabled()
  QHeader 111

setMultiSelection()
  QListBox 82
  QListView 109
setName()
  QFile 189
setNormal()
  QPalette 160
setNumDigits()
  QLCDNumber 97
setOctMode()
  QLCDNumber 97
setOKButton()
  QTabDialog 122
setOn()
  QListViewItem 108
setOpaqueSize()
  QSplitter 93
setOpen()
  QListViewItem 110
setOrientation()
  QPrinter 153
  QScrollBar 88
  QSlider 85
  QSplitter 92
setOverrideCursor()
  QApplication 177
setPalette()
  QApplication 161
  QWidget 77, 161, 171
setPen()
  QPainter 36, 161
setPixmvap()
  QButton 79
  QClipboard 197
  QLabel 95
  QListViewItem 110
setPrefix()
  QSpinBox 86
setProgress()
  QProgressBar 104
  QProgressDialog 117
setRange()
  QRangeControl 85, 87, 88
setRasterOp()
  QPainter 170
setReadOnly()
  setMultiLineEdit 94

setResizeEnabled()
  QHeader 111
setResizeMode()
  QSplitter 93
setRowStretch()
  QGridLayout 132
setSegmentStyle()
  QLCDNumber 97
setSelected()
  QListView 109
  QListViewItem 110
setSizeIncrement()
  QWidget 257
setSmallDecimalPoint()
  QLCDNumber 97
setSorting()
  QDir 193
  QListView 109
setSpecialValueText()
  QSpinBox 86
setSteps()
  QRangeControl 85, 88
setStretchableWidget()
  QToolBar 100
setStyle()
  QApplication 78
  QWidget 77
setSuffix()
  QSpinBox 86
setTabEnabled()
  QTabDialog 122
setTableFlags()
  QTableView 230
setTabOrder()
  QWidget 238
setText()
  QButton 79
  QClipboard 197, 198, 200
  QLabel 95
  QLineEdit 94
setTextLabel()
  QToolButton 100
setTickmarks()
  QSlider 85
setTitle()
  QGroupBox 91
setToggleButton()
  QPushButton 81

setTotalSteps()
  QProgressBar 104
  QProgressDialog 117
setTracking()
  QHeader 111
  QScrollBar 88
  QSlider 85
setTreeStepSize()
  QListView 109
setup()
  QListViewItem 110
  QPrinter 153
setUsesBigPixmap()
  QToolButton 100
setUsesBigPixmaps()
  QMainWindow 98
setUsesTextLabel()
  QToolButton 100
setValidator()
  QComboBox 179
  QLineEdit 179
  QSpinBox 179
setValue()
  QRangeControl 85, 88
  QSlider 85
  QSpinBox 86
setViewport()
  QPainter 166
setViewXForm()
  QPainter 167
setVScrollBarMode()
  QScrollView 55, 105
setWildcard()
  QRegExp 187
setWorldMatrix()
  QPainter 165
setWorldXForm()
  QPainter 166
shear()
  QPainter 165
showChild()
  QScrollView 105
showTip()
  QToolTipGroup 102
signal forwarding 54, 64
SIGNAL() macro 26
signals 21–29, 245–249
  advantages 23

connecting to slots 25
defining in Perl 294
in Qt 24
sizeChanged()
  QHeader 111
sizeHint()
  QWidget 127
sliderMoved()
  QScrollBar 88
  QSlider 26, 85
sliderPressed()
  QScrollBar 88
  QSlider 85
sliderReleased()
  QScrollBar 88
sliders 85–86
  connecting with LCD displays 97
SLOT() macro 26
slotAbout()
  ScribbleWindow 37, 45, 53
slotAboutQt()
  ScribbleWindow 37, 45, 53
slotClearArea()
  ScribbleArea 56
slotColorMenu()
  ScribbleWindow 45, 53
slotColourMenu()
  ScribbleWindow 37, 44
slotLoad()
  ScribbleArea 64, 72
slots 21–29, 245–249
  advantages 23
  connecting to signals 25
  defining in Perl 294
  in Qt 24
  parameters 25
slotSave()
  ScribbleArea 64
sockets 271
spin boxes 86–87
splitters 92
stacks 145, 149
start()
  QTime 209
startTimer()
  QObject 257
status bars 100–101
  connecting to tool tips 102
  in main windows 98

normal messages 101
permanent messages 101
temporary messages 100
statusBar()
  QMainWindow 98
step()
  QMovie 152
stepDown()
  QSpinBox 87
stepUp()
  QSpinBox 87
streamAsFile()
  QNPInstance 285
syncX()
  QApplication 256

T
tab dialogs 119
tab order 238
table views 111–112
templates see C++, templates
text()
  QClipboard 200
  QLineEdit 94
  QListBox 82
  QMultiLineEdit 94
text entry fields 94–95
  read-only, vs. labels 96
text processing 179–187
textChanged()
  QLineEdit 95
  QMultiLineEdit 95
TIFF (graphics file format) 173
time values 209–210
tmake 257–261, 303
toFirst()
  QCacheIterator 148
  QDictIterator 148
  QIntCacheIterator 148
  QIntDictIterator 148
  QListIterator 148
  QPtrDictIterator 148
toggled()
  QButton 80, 81
  QPushButton 79
toLast()
  QCacheIterator 148
  QDictIterator 148
  QIntCacheIterator 148

QIntDictIterator 148
QListIterator 148
QPtrDictIterator 148
tool bar buttons 99
tool bars 99–100
  in main windows 98
tool tips 101–104, 139
  connecting to status bars 102
  showing dynamically 102
toString()
  QDate 210
  QDateTime 210
  QTime 210
transformations
  two-dimensional 164–166
  view 166–167
translate()
  QPainter 164
TRUE 72

U
unpause()
  QMovie 152
updateItem()
  QMenuData 90

V
validate()
  QValidator 184
value()
  QRangeControl 85
  QSpinBox 86
valueChanged()
  QKCoordSel (example class) 214
  QScrollBar 88
  QSlider 85
  QSpinBox 87
Vertical
  QScrollBar 88
  QSplitter 92
viewportMouseDoubleClickEvent()
  QScrollView 105
viewportMouseMoveEvent()
  QScrollView 105
viewportMousePressEvent()
  QScrollView 105
viewportMouseReleaseEvent()
  QScrollView 105

viewportPaintEvent()
  QScrollView 105
virtual functions see C++, virtual functions
Visual C++ 301–303
  compiling 15

W
Wall, Larry 293
warning() 251, 256
  QMessageBox 45, 115
what's this windows 101
whatsThisButton()
  QWhatsThis 104
white 158
widget names 252
widget stacks 93–94
widgets 14
  arrangers see arrangers
  as containers for other widgets 19
  bounded range input see bounded range
    input widgets
  buttons see buttons
  check-boxes see check-boxes
  choosing 75–112
  combo boxes see combo boxes
  constructors 77
  custom see custom widgets
  disabling 77, 139
  enabling 77, 139
  fonts 77
  for creating tables 111
  frames see frames
  group boxes see group boxes
  labels see labels
  list boxes see list boxes
  list views see list views
  main see main widget
  menus see menus
  Motif
    integrating 291
  parameters
    general 77
  progress bars see progress bars
  push-buttons see push-buttons
  radio buttons see radio buttons
  repainting 34
  scroll bars see scroll bars
  scrolled views see scrolled views3

selection see selection widgets
showing 15
size 15
sliders see sliders
spin boxes see spin boxes
splitters see splitters
stacks see widget stacks
styles 77
table views see table views
text entry fields see text entry fields
Xt
    integrating 291
Windows API 1, 4
Windows style 77
winId()
    QWidget 257
write()
    QNPInstance 285
writeBlock()
    QFile 190
writeReady()
    QNPInstance 285
wxWindows 3, 4, 22

X
X Window System 1
x11Display()
    QPaintDevice 257
XBM (graphics file format) 173
XDND (drag and drop protocol) 203
xForm()
    QPainter 166
    QPixmap 170
xFormDev()
    QPainter 166
XPM (graphics file format) 173
Xt 291
Xt Intrinsics 1

Y
yellow 158

Z
Zinc 3

About the Author

Matthias Kalle Dalheimer (*kalle@dalheimer.de*) was born and grew up in Hamburg, Germany, where he also acquired his M.S. in computer science at the University of Hamburg. After working two and a half years for Star Division GmbH, where he was head of the Unix group and responsible for porting the company's office productivity suite StarOffice to Unix and Linux systems, he founded his own consulting company which specializes in designing and implementing cross-platform software solutions (often using Qt, of course!). Kalle also works as a technical editor for the German branch of O'Reilly & Associates, and has translated several American O'Reilly books to German (among these are *Advanced Perl Programming* and *Java Examples in a Nutshell*).

Kalle is a member of the board of directors of the KDE foundation, the legal entity behind the freely available desktop KDE (*http://www.kde.org*) for Unix and Linux systems which was developed with Qt, where he is responsible for the base libraries and several applications as well as public relations. In addition, he is a member of the board of directors of LiVe (Linux-Verband, *http://www.linux-verband.de*), a lobby group that advocates the use of Linux in commercial settings.

Kalle now lives in a tiny village in the North German countryside with his wife and his two-year-old son. In his spare time, he enjoys playing with his son, hiking in the forest and along the sea-side and traveling to Sweden as often as possible.

Colophon

Our look is the result of reader comments, our own experimentation and feedback from distribution channels. Distinctive covers complement our distinctive approach to technical topics, breathing personality and life into potentially dry subjects.

The bird featured on the cover of *Programming with Qt* is a toucan. Thirty-eight species of toucans are found in tropical America from southern Mexico to Bolivia and northern Argentina. The most obvious feature of a toucan is its bill. The biggest bill is that of the male toco toucan, reaching a size of nearly 10 inches, which is more than the body without the tail. In spite of its immense size, the bill is surprisingly light in weight. A thin horny sheath of hard keratin encloses a hollow that is crisscrossed by many thin supporting rods. However, the bill is so out-of-proportion that the bird seems to be handicapped during flight, leading to a quite awkward flight pattern with bursts of flapping followed by a glide. It is still unknown why toucans have such an exaggerated bill. It may be useful to reach berries or seeds from twigs too thin to bear the bird's weight, but a thinner and less vividly coloured bill would serve the same purpose. A function as a signal during courtship seems to be more likely. Hornbills, which can be found in Africa and Asia, have similar-looking bills, but they are not related to toucans. Toucans are related to woodpeckers, having a characteristic feature in common: Their feet are arranged in a pattern with two toes forward and two toes back. Toucans are primarily fruit eaters, but they also take insects, frogs, lizards, and eggs and nestlings of smaller birds. They are social birds and can often be seen in flocks of six or more individuals, making croaking noises similar to frogs. They live in rainforests and more open woodlands, where they nest in natural tree holes, often old woodpecker holes. Clutches are of two to four eggs which are incubated by both parents. The eggs hatch after two weeks. The young are quite ugly and very helpless. They have no feathers, and even in the age of more than three weeks, when they open their eyes for the first time, they show a lot of naked skin. Toucans have a lifespan of approximately 10 years. In captivity, they sometimes become quite tame. Native Indians used to keep toucans in their villages, but they also appreciated their feathers as ornaments.

Elke Hansel was the editor and production editor for *Programming with Qt*, and Claire Cloutier LeBlanc organized the copyediting with Mitzi and Debby. Margrit Müller was the production manager. Kalle Dalheimer wrote the index.

Edie Freedman designed the cover of this book, using an original illustration by Lorrie LeJeune. The cover layout was produced with Quark XPress 3.32 using the ITC Garamond font.

The inside layout out was designed by Margrit Müller and Nancy Priest, and implemented in FrameMaker 5.5 by Stefan Goebel. The text and heading fonts are ITC Garamond Light and Garamond Book. This colophon was written by Joachim Kurtz.

O'Reilly & Associates, Inc.
101 Morris Street
Sebastopol, CA 95472-9902
1-800-998-9938

Visit us online at:
http://www.ora.com/
orders@ora.com

O'REILLY WOULD LIKE TO HEAR FROM YOU

Which book did this card come from?

_____

Where did you buy this book?
- ❏ Bookstore
- ❏ Direct from O'Reilly
- ❏ Bundled with hardware/software
- ❏ Other _____

- ❏ Computer Store
- ❏ Class/seminar

What operating system do you use?
- ❏ UNIX
- ❏ Windows NT
- ❏ Other _____

- ❏ Macintosh
- ❏ PC(Windows/DOS)

What is your job description?
- ❏ System Administrator
- ❏ Network Administrator
- ❏ Web Developer
- ❏ Other _____

- ❏ Programmer
- ❏ Educator/Teacher

❏ Please send me O'Reilly's catalog, containing a complete listing of O'Reilly books and software.

Name _____ Company/Organization _____

Address _____

City _____ State _____ Zip/Postal Code _____ Country _____

Telephone _____ Internet or other email address (specify network) _____

Nineteenth century wood engraving
of a bear from the O'Reilly &
Associates Nutshell Handbook®
Using & Managing UUCP.

POST CARD

BUSINESS REPLY MAIL
FIRST CLASS MAIL   PERMIT NO. 80   SEBASTOPOL, CA

Postage will be paid by addressee

O'Reilly & Associates, Inc.
101 Morris Street
Sebastopol, CA 95472-9902